D1521347

GLOBAL TRENDS IN EDUCATIONAL POLICY

INTERNATIONAL PERSPECTIVES ON EDUCATION AND SOCIETY

Series Editor: Abraham Yogev

Volume 1: International Perspectives on Education and Society

Volume 2: Schooling and Status Attainment: Social Origins and Institutional Determinants

Volume 3: Education and Social Change

Volume 4: Educational Reform in International Perspective

Series Editor from Volume 5: David P. Baker

Volume 5: New Paradigms and Recurring Paradoxes in Education for Citizenship: An International Comparison

INTERNATIONAL PERSPECTIVES ON EDUCATION AND SOCIETY VOLUME 6

GLOBAL TRENDS IN EDUCATIONAL POLICY

EDITED BY

DAVID P. BAKER

Pennsylvania State University, USA

and

ALEXANDER W. WISEMAN

The University of Tulsa, USA

2005

ELSEVIER
JAI

Amsterdam – Boston – Heidelberg – London – New York – Oxford
Paris – San Diego – San Francisco – Singapore – Sydney – Tokyo

ELSEVIER B.V.	ELSEVIER Inc.	**ELSEVIER Ltd**	ELSEVIER Ltd
Radarweg 29	525 B Street, Suite 1900	**The Boulevard, Langford**	84 Theobalds Road
P.O. Box 211	San Diego	**Lane Kidlington**	London
1000 AE Amsterdam	CA 92101-4495	**Oxford OX5 1GB**	WC1X 8RR
The Netherlands	USA	**UK**	UK

First edition 2005

British Library Cataloguing in Publication Data
A catalogue record is available from the British Library.

ISBN: 0-7623-1175-4
ISSN: 1479-3679 (Series)

∞ The paper used in this publication meets the requirements of ANSI/NISO Z39.48-1992 (Permanence of Paper).
Printed in The Netherlands.

Working together to grow
libraries in developing countries

www.elsevier.com | www.bookaid.org | www.sabre.org

ELSEVIER   BOOK AID International   Sabre Foundation

CONTENTS

LIST OF CONTRIBUTORS   *vii*

PREFACE   *ix*

THE WORLDWIDE EXPLOSION OF
INTERNATIONALIZED EDUCATION POLICY
Alexander W. Wiseman and David P. Baker   *1*

THE HISTORY AND PROBLEMS IN THE MAKING
OF EDUCATION POLICY AT THE WORLD BANK,
1960–2000
Stephen P. Heyneman   *23*

IMPLEMENTING EDUCATIONAL
TRANSFORMATION POLICIES: INVESTIGATING
ISSUES OF IDEAL VERSUS REAL IN DEVELOPING
COUNTRIES
Diane Brook Napier   *59*

EDUCATION DECENTRALIZATION IN AFRICA:
GREAT EXPECTATIONS AND UNFULFILLED
PROMISES
Jordan Naidoo   *99*

FREE PRIMARY EDUCATION IN MALAWI:
THE PRACTICE OF GLOBAL POLICY IN
AID-DEPENDENT STATES
Nancy O'Gara Kendall   *125*

RE-POSITIONING FEMALES IN THE
INTERNATIONAL EDUCATIONAL CONTEXT:
THEORETICAL FRAMEWORKS, SHARED POLICIES,
AND FUTURE DIRECTIONS
Mary Ann Maslak   *145*

EDUCATION ON THE TRANSNATIONAL STAGE: A
SHARED SPOTLIGHT, A POCKET OF HOPE
Verónica R. Martini   *173*

GLOBALIZATION OF EDUCATION AND STIGMA: A
SENEGALESE CASE STUDY
Holger Daun   *197*

MAPPING PARADIGMS AND THEORIES IN
COMPARATIVE, INTERNATIONAL, AND
DEVELOPMENT EDUCATION (CIDE) RESEARCH
W. James Jacob and Sheng Yao Cheng   *221*

GLOBAL PERSPECTIVES FOR TEACHER
EDUCATION
Diane G. Gal   *259*

THE WORLD COUNCIL OF COMPARATIVE
EDUCATION SOCIETIES: A PRELIMINARY HISTORY
David N. Wilson   *289*

NOTES ON CONTRIBUTORS   *309*

AUTHOR INDEX   *315*

SUBJECT INDEX   *325*

LIST OF CONTRIBUTORS

David P. Baker	Pennsylvania State University, University Park, Pennsylvania, USA
Sheng Yao Cheng	National Chung Cheng University, Taiwan, Republic of China
Holger Daun	Stockholm University, Stockholm, Sweden
Diane G. Gal	Queens College CUNY, Flushing, New York, USA
Stephen P. Heyneman	Peabody College, Vanderbilt University Nashville, Tennessee, USA
W. James Jacob	University of California-Los Angeles, Los Angeles, California, USA
Nancy O'Gara Kendall	Florida State University, Tallahassee, Florida, USA
Verónica R. Martini	Harvard University, Cambridge, Massachusetts, USA
Mary Ann Maslak	St. John's University Queens, New York, USA
Jordan Naidoo	Save the Children, Washington DC, USA
Diane Brook Napier	University of Georgia, Athens, Georgia, USA
David N. Wilson	University of Toronto, Toronto, Ontario, Canada
Alexander W. Wiseman	The University of Tulsa, Tulsa, Oklahoma, USA

PREFACE

The role of policy in the development of education is crucial. So much rests on the decisions, support, and most of all resources that policymakers either give or withhold in any given situation. This volume of *International Perspectives on Education and Society* highlights the valuable role that educational policy plays in the development of education and society around the world.

Examining education and society by looking at global trends in educational policy allows for a holistic approach to understanding the impact that education has on society rather than trying to understand the relationship between education and society as a conglomeration of isolated local events. This is indeed no easy task. For one thing, educational policy is not centrally coordinated in many nations. For example, the United States' educational system is highly decentralized, and although new policies are frequently made at the federal, state, and even district levels, these policies are often diluted by school administrators or ignored by classroom teachers. By looking at the national impact of educational policies on society, the situations in which these policies are either diluted or ignored are balanced by other situations in which these policies are fully implemented.

Another benefit of looking at global trends in educational policy rather than at situation-specific policy implementation (i.e., as a collection of isolated activities) is that these global trends are not pushed and pulled by the variety of non-educational activities that are in some way derived from, or connected to, education and society as much as the individual schools and classrooms are. Rather than chasing each one of these non-educational activities by time, place, and subject, this volume's focus on global trends in educational policy gives the examination of education and society a framework upon which to rest.

The chapters in this volume share many common elements. As several of the chapter authors in this volume suggest, the defining rhetoric for both the public and educational experts alike in many countries has been one of national competition. There is a belief that each nation's social, political, and economic future in the world system is directly tied to their educational success at home. Right or wrong, decades of this rhetoric have pumped up the public's interest in information about how each nation's education system compares internationally. Since international comparisons often promise to shed light on processes influencing academic achievement, there is a sense that situating education in a global context will inform educational policymakers about what they should be doing with the schools.

Even after decades of extensive research, the social context of schooling is one of the most important, yet misunderstood influences on teaching and learning. The social context of schooling continues to be so important because the educational policymakers in most countries have borrowed school structures, curricula, or pedagogy from other nations' systems of education, as well as from images of education projected through world culture about society, individuals, and progress. Each of the chapter authors in this volume identifies what is unique and important about education for social development either through or with special reference to international or cross-national comparisons of educational policies and schooling. In so doing, the social context of educational policy decisions is emphasized.

Another benefit of reviewing international perspectives on education and society based on educational policy trends, is that it emphasizes the importance of schools as institutions both within and across national contexts of education. This means that there are commonly-shared beliefs about schools, and that the basic structure and organization of schools have become fairly uniform everywhere in the world. For example, all of the chapter authors in this volume define schooling as formal, public education – not informal apprenticeships or family-based teachings. These shared beliefs and structures of schools remain fairly stable even when the content and methods of instruction differ because of a school's unique context.

Our chapter in this volume, "The Worldwide Explosion of Internationalized Education Policy," sets the stage for the rest of this volume by discussing the important role that internationally comparative educational policy and research has played in shaping the educational systems of most nations around the world. We illustrate how the use of international comparisons of educational systems and achievement has quickly blossomed to the point where it is now virtually impossible for educational policymakers in any country to make and implement policies that affect schooling without first looking at what other nations do in similar situations. The importance of these international comparisons is not waning either. Instead, international comparisons of educational systems continue to grow at an explosive rate among educational policymakers, especially at the national and multinational policymaking level.

Multinational organizations play an important part in educational policymaking, as the second chapter in this volume extensively investigates.

This chapter by international educational policymaker and analyst, Stephen P. Heyneman, is titled "The History and Problems in the Making of Education Policy at the World Bank, 1960–2000." As Heyneman points out, "the Bank" is frequently and vehemently criticized for its educational influence even though it is the source of the largest "development capital in the field of international education." This chapter strikes a balance between those who criticize and those who praise the World Bank's educational influence. Heyneman not only describes and explains how the Bank makes decisions about loans and educational priorities, but he also outlines how the World Bank has become the dominant force behind the "global education agenda."

These first two chapters on internationalized education policy and the global education agenda of the World Bank lead nicely into the third chapter by Diane Brook Napier. Brook Napier's chapter, "Implementing Educational Transformation Policies: Investigating Issues of Ideal Versus Real in Developing Countries," focuses on the connections (or the disconnect) between the ideal impact of educational policies in developing countries versus the actual impact that these policies have. To illustrate this point, Brook Napier highlights the South African case. She concludes that while South Africa's experiences with democratization and deracialization are of interest to other developing nations that, multinational organizations and national educational policymakers must consider the educational transformation of South Africa within its proper historical and demographic context.

The fourth chapter by Jordan Naidoo looks at how the transformations in both schooling and society surrounding educational decentralization in several Sub-Saharan African nations have been a mixed bag of both success and failure. This chapter called "Education Decentralization in Africa: Great Expectations and Unfulfilled Promises" is an investigation of how the implementation of educational decentralization across much of Sub-Saharan Africa has not occurred as quickly or with as much impact on schooling conditions and student achievement as was initially expected. In particular, Naidoo asserts that top-down hierarchical management structures still dominate the decision-making processes regarding resource allocation, personnel hiring and placement, and other processes shown to have affected school performance. Overall, the implementation of decentralization policies across much of Sub-Saharan Africa has led to an increase in problems related to educational bureaucracy and resource shortages rather than an empowering move to strengthen local school systems and schools.

Nancy O'Gara Kendall's chapter titled, "Free Primary Education in Malawi: The Practice of Global Policy in Aid-Dependent States," places the arguments highlighting global trends in educational policy from the previous chapters within a specific social context. Kendall specifically explores the successes and failures of the installment of Free Primary Education in one African nation, Malawi. She begins her chapter with a discussion of the impact that globalized educational policies like Education for All have in developing nations that are also often experiencing recent political democratization. Unlike most of the other chapters in this volume, Kendall looks at the implementation of these global educational policies from the ground up – with particular attention to the social context of schooling in Malawi. She concludes that "the policy disconnect between Free Primary Education and democratization impedes the improvement of educational policy, investment, and practice." Kendall's chapter cements this idea of policy disconnect between globalized educational policies and school and classroom policy implementation as an integral theme of this volume.

The sixth chapter in this volume is by Mary Ann Maslak and is called "Re-Positioning Females in the International Educational Context: Theoretical Frameworks, Shared Policies and Future Directions." In this chapter, Maslak accomplishes three things. First, she positions female education within the leading frameworks in the field: women in development and gender and development. Second, she outlines how Education for All has influenced female education. And, third, she analyzes the policies derived from these global frameworks and policy declarations. While there are many results of this analysis one of the most topical is the role of family and social context in the development and provision of female education. Maslak points out that much of the existing educational policy regarding female education is written at the national level in response to multinational organizations' agendas for economic or political reform, but not often in response to or in conjunction with the local needs and aspirations of women in developing nations. This, Maslak points out, continues to be a concern in the development of equitable education for females.

The globalization of educational policies, as the previous chapters have alluded, can be both a benefit and a detriment in the development of local and national societies. In her chapter, "Education on the Transnational Stage: A Shared Spotlight, A Pocket of Hope," Verónica R. Martini discusses the impact that the globalization of educational policies and structures has had on the social transformation of communities and nations around the world. Martini takes a different approach to globalization than previous arguments have, however, because she suggests that globalization encourages educational opportunities through transnationalism. In other words, globalization allows the transnational stage to be experienced locally via schooling through experiences related to immigration, technology, and mass information. Martini also argues that the transnational stage exposes students in the developed world to global education through study abroad programs. Through transnational experiences in schooling, globalization's impact on society can be positive rather than merely the wreckage of a culture and identity-stealing monster that it is sometimes portrayed to be.

Of course, internationalized education policies and global frameworks for schooling can lead to the globalization of stigma as well. Holger Daun's chapter, "Globalization of Education and Stigma: A Senegalese Case Study," provides ample evidence of this. In the eighth chapter in this volume, Daun carefully explores the impact that educational classification systems designed and implemented by international organizations and national governments has had on students and schools in two Senegalese villages. In particular, the rapid expansion of primary and secondary education in Senegal has led to the classification of students based on efficient, but stigmatizing labels. These classification systems frequently require that a cutoff between passing and failing students be arbitrarily made and then opportunities and resources be allocated accordingly. As a result, Daun asserts that many students are not given the chance to become complete members of their communities and in some cases are marginalized as a result of their newly-expanded educational systems.

The first eight chapters in this volume rather directly explore the impact that global trends in educational policy have on social transformation or in specific social contexts. The last three chapters in this volume take a slightly different approach to the investigation of educational policy and society by looking at how comparative and international educational research and planning has impacted educational policymaking. The ninth chapter in this volume, titled "Metatheory Analysis of Comparative, International, and Development Education (CIDE) Research," provides an overview of some of the more prevalent theoretical paradigms for cross-nationally comparative educational policymaking and research. In this chapter, W. James Jacob and Sheng Yao Cheng provide a typology of the foundational theories and metatheories in the field and summarize various attempts to map CIDE theories in the past. Jacob and Cheng assert that the most relevant theoretical paradigms are the ones that are sensitive to social and cultural context, and present a Tai-Ji Model for the selection of appropriate theoretical frameworks and methodologies for comparative, international education research.

Diane G. Gal takes this volume in a different direction in the tenth chapter called "Global Perspectives for Teacher Education." Rather than look broadly at global education policies or frameworks, Gal turns her attention specifically to the incorporation of global perspectives into teacher education programs. Much like Martini's chapter on education on the transnational stage (Chapter 7 in this volume), Gal asserts that the globalization of education eliminates many social, economic, and political boundaries that separate the peoples of the world. Gal then focuses largely on how teachers are trained and educated in the United States as an example of how the theories and research in the field of comparative and international education can and are being incorporated into schools and classrooms around the world. Her focus throughout this chapter is on how the work of teachers can connect global social, economic, and political concerns to local schools, classrooms, and curricula.

Finally, there is a historical precedence for the use of educational policy to influence or develop the larger society. In his chapter titled "The World Council of Comparative Education Societies: A Preliminary History," David N. Wilson begins the process of rebuilding the history of the WCCES. Wilson's well-deserved reputation as a leading figure in the field of comparative and international education brings an added level of respectability to this chapter. As a starting point for a more in-depth history of the WCCES, Wilson provides an overview of the field of comparative and international education and how the WCCES fits into this field from the 1970s to the 2000s. Wilson concludes his chapter with a fitting commentary on the intersection of globalization and comparative and international education. He suggests that while there are negative and destructive effects of globalization resulting from internationalized educational policy and global education frameworks, there are also many positive results of international cooperation, borrowing, and exchange.

Taken together, the chapters in this volume in the *International Perspectives on Education and Society* series present persuasive arguments that the internationalization of educational policy has a wide and irreversible effect on schooling and society around the world.

David P. Baker
Pennsylvania State University

Alexander W. Wiseman
The University of Tulsa

THE WORLDWIDE EXPLOSION OF INTERNATIONALIZED EDUCATION POLICY

Alexander W. Wiseman and David P. Baker

The increasing availability of international and comparative educational information about how schools work and perform in many different nations has had a profound effect on educational policy around the world. It has intensified a policymaking environment already marked by extensive borrowing and copying from one nation to the next by raising the stakes for educational production and nation-state building (Ball, 1998). Further, international and comparative educational studies change the way that educational policy is organized and delivered in nations, as well as what it means to be educated and learned across societies. Much of this effect has to do with the fact that schools and their outcomes are increasingly quantified, measured, and compared on a global scale. These international comparisons of educational systems are then being fed back into individual nations' policymaking processes around the world. Using international information to assess the quality of a nation's schools is increasingly considered good governmental practice. All of this has led to widespread expansion of internationalized policymaking in individual nations.

The dimensions to which educational policymaking in many nations has become internationalized are well known. Over the past century nations have observed and actively studied schooling in other nations for their own

Global Trends in Educational Policy
International Perspectives on Education and Society, Volume 6, 1–21
Copyright © 2005 by Elsevier Ltd.
All rights of reproduction in any form reserved
ISSN: 1479-3679/doi:10.1016/S1479-3679(04)06001-3

benefit, but in the last several decades, the pace of production and breadth of scope of the most basic resource, namely comparable international information on education from a large number of nations, has hit unprecedented levels. Similarly, over the past 30 years observations of schooling across nations have shifted markedly from only comparing basic structures of schooling and enrollments to a laser-like focus on educational outcomes; primarily student achievement on assessments of academic subjects like language skills, mathematics, science, and social studies. This testing information, frequently packaged as a barometer of school quality, is often accompanied by in-depth information on processes and resources thought to relate to teaching and learning of academic subjects. Cross-national studies of achievement, curriculum, instruction, and school resources draw more nations into internationalizing their education policy, which in turn validates a greater deepening of interest among nations in international comparison.

What was once chiefly an erratic, exotic enterprise undertaken by small groups of pioneering academics from different nations has transformed itself into multi-lateral governmental undertakings of heavily funded, professionalized international studies of achievement. These studies produce huge amounts of information to judge one nation's performance against others and are now routine, regularly anticipated, and widely published.

For example, groups such as the International Association for the Evaluation of Educational Achievement (IEA) and the Organisation for Economic Co-operation and Development (OECD) have provided policy-makers with publicly-available and readily-digestible information on educational achievement and attainment since the 1960s. Some multinational organizations like the World Bank, International Monetary Fund (IMF), and the United Nations Educational, Scientific, and Cultural Organization (UNESCO) collect and disseminate their own internationally comparative data – sometimes publicly and sometimes not. In each case, the data reports made available to policymakers are largely descriptive and quantitative (LeTendre, Baker, Akiba, & Wiseman, 2001; Marginson & Mollis, 2001).

A cascade of high quality international information about education, that would have been unimaginable just a few decades ago, continues to expand into more academic topics, grade levels, and aspects of running schools and organizing instruction. Less and less of a nation's education system can be sacredly protected from the harsh light of cross-national comparisons. Curricular streaming, social class reproduction through private schooling, and other misapplications of well-institutionalized meritocratic principles in education have been exposed for national discussion because of cross-national studies whose results are openly reported, and in some cases, like the Third International Mathematics and Science Study (TIMSS) in the United States in the mid-1990s and the Programme for International Student Assessment (PISA) in Germany in the early 2000s, incessantly commented on in the national media.

In addition to the explosion of international information about education, on an ideological level internationalized education policymaking in nations results from an underlying assumption that public schooling is a powerful tool for creating individual productivity and citizenship within nations (Fuller & Rubinson, 1992). Whether it is or is not has become moot. The era of international comparison in education has arrived and has promised to shed light on current social, political, or economic concerns. And with this promise comes a sense that situating education in a global context will inform policymakers about nothing less than core tasks for making and maintaining an effective nation.

The general phenomenon of internationalized educational policymaking is examined here as a trend shaping the future of policy connecting formal education and society. In this chapter, possible causes and consequences of this trend are described and assessed. Additionally, recent political and technical critiques of the process are examined with an eye to what are likely future scenarios of this new influence on educational policy in many nations.

THE INSTITUTIONALIZATION OF INTERNATIONAL EDUCATION POLICY

Conventional wisdom has it that policymakers rationally approach an ongoing or potential problem, carefully consider the reasons for the problem, and then sensibly debate the information and research on this problem. The final stage of this ideal vision of the educational policymaking process is that the policymakers decide how to solve specific problems based on their consideration of all of the relevant data and possible options (Vickers, 1994). This is rarely, if ever, the case.

Like policymaking in all societal sectors, national educational policymaking is a limited rational process. It is rationalized to the degree that there are identified problems, solutions, and implementation strategies flowing around school systems, but the links between them are weaker and more randomly connected than often is assumed from a hyper-rational perspective (Weick, 1976). Instead, the entire educational policymaking process is porous – open to external influences to a varying degree. Observations of actual cases of educational policymaking are full of accounts of semi-rational actions penetrated by political and other external influences (Baker & LeTendre, 2005).

Further, once made, educational policies themselves do not necessarily drive local action or change in schools. Instead, educational policies are often in response to conflict and relationships at a variety of levels including local, national, and institutional levels (Deacon, Hulse, & Stubbs, 1997). There is even substantial evidence to suggest that at the world level there is a pervasive culture around schooling that can influence policy at the most local levels (Baker & LeTendre, 2005). And, at every level of educational policymaking reside deeply held beliefs about the ability of education to transform individuals and ameliorate social problems of a wide variety (Meyer, Ramirez, Rubinson, & Boli–Bennett, 1977). A porous political process aided by a moral imperative to use education to construct a 'good' society makes for a highly charged, highly volatile, and highly publicized environment within which international education policy is made.

Being open to external forces, like common worldwide understanding about how sectors like education should work in all nations, makes national policymaking ripe for internationalizing. As described above, both the increasing means to find and use more technically sophisticated information to compare school quality across nations, as well as a general homogenizing of how schools work in nations are responsible for the exploding use of international and cross-national comparisons in national politics and policymaking about formal schooling, including primary, secondary, tertiary, and continuing life-long education. In spite of the flaws in the policymaking process, international comparisons are thought to be a vital part of educational policymaking in most nations because of the perceived impact education has on national development.

Schools are indeed institutionalized organizations whose functions extend beyond the purely academic or economic. Most schools take on as one of their fundamental functions the creation and incorporation of students as citizens in largely democratic nations. Public schools are also venues for the translation of local culture and national education policy into the instruction and achievement of students.

So then, how does internationalized education policy become institutionalized in nations? Weiss (1977) suggests that there are slow moving ideas or concepts that start as responses to isolated or local problems, but that eventually spread throughout a nation and into multinational organizations as well as local policy. Weiss sees a bottom-up development of ideas around policymaking, starting for whatever reasons in a few nations and then slowly flowing out to others. As these ideas and concepts spread they gradually gain in shared popularity among educational policymakers across a broad spectrum of nations and multinational organizations. Eventually these ideas and concepts become a part of policymakers' fundamental understanding of educational systems and schooling, which changes the basic assumptions of both policymakers and educational practitioners (Vickers, 1994). As these ideas and concepts then re-enter the local schools and school boards, they become legitimate elements in global educational paradigms or models.

A contrasting model is one in which the ideas start, or at least are highly legitimated, at a larger institutional level. Ideas, or perhaps more accurately, ideologies flow down and outward through the world system (Meyer, 2000). This is not to say that specific national and local factors do not matter, they clearly do. But the expansion of internationalizing forces in nations' policymaking is a result of a world culture in education that continues to flow throughout the world system of nations (Baker & LeTendre, 2005).

The global legitimacy that accompanies international comparisons has contributed to the worldwide institutionalization of international comparative education policy. Regardless of its exact origins, educational policy models for nations that use international materials and concepts have become institutionalized in many nations' ministries of education as well as in multinational organizations' education sectors. There are several mechanisms that contribute to this institutionalization of internationalized education policy:

(1) International and comparative educational information (e.g. technical data) and research reports have become customary prerequisites for national and local policymaking.
(2) Training and decision-making models for policymakers have become standardized according to internationally legitimate norms.
(3) There are also models of legitimate international education policies at the multi-lateral level.
(4) Finally, the legitimate educational "wisdom" embodied by two dominant multinational economic organizations, in particular, the World Bank and the OECD; both of which have the international authority to disseminate ideas about education and some educational policy as well as enforce implementation of ideas within certain nations around the world.

In addition to explanations about internationalization of education policy based on ideas of institutionalized world culture, there are explanations based on ideas of dominance and power within the world system of nations. These explanations begin with the assumption that the hegemonic influence of Western institutions of higher education and U.S. universities, in particular, is overwhelming. In order to gain individual legitimacy, policymakers themselves must have attained legitimate credentials. For example, if Latin American economists want to become Latin American development experts, they must study development and Latin American issues in either U.S. or European universities (Max-Neef, Elizalde, & Hopenhayn, 1991). Without the legitimacy of U.S. or European higher education, it will be difficult for them to be respected at experts in Latin American development problems either at home or abroad.

The legitimacy of 'Western' credentials has become the accepted international norm for policymakers in every nation around the world. Yet, the policymakers themselves are not the only ingredients in the institutionalization of international education policy. The contribution of scientific studies of education is significant, too. Research-based educational policy is globally respected and sometimes required because basing educational policy in internationally comparative research imbues the resulting policies with a prestige that enhances overall state legitimacy (Eliason, Fagerlind, Merritt, & Weiler, 1987).

National production of research-based, scientific studies of education varies in volume across nations, with poorer and smaller nations producing less. This means that larger and wealthier nations tend to be forerunners in the production of international information. And further their governmental involvement leads to political investment in internationalizing policymaking processes. Larger and wealthier nations tend to be robust enough to keep their education policymaking relatively isolated from international comparison (Ramirez & Boli, 1987). These nations then become leading producers of international trends in all types of nations through investment and strong educational research communities within their borders.

While educational research is prestigious, respectable, and credible, it is also cheaper for a nation's policymakers to look at educational program use or policy implementation in other nations than to run full-scale experiments and evaluations on pilot educational programs or policies at home (Vickers, 1994). Thus, the legitimacy that the policymakers themselves and their data bring to international education policy is backed up by practical considerations. The reduced costs may not be the deciding factor in the creation of educational policies, but alongside the prestige and legitimacy that international comparative educational research brings these practical considerations ensure that the use of internationally comparative data will continue.

Finally, there is a high level of correspondence between a nation's perceived economic and political competitiveness, which contributes to the development of educational policy within an internationally comparative framework. Some educational policies at the national level, in particular, have become commodities themselves. This means that politicians, policymakers, and other decision-makers use certain educational policy models or adopt selected international educational models to communicate their abeyance to certain popular ideas about schools, youth, and the direction that a nation's economy and political organization is heading. Policymakers, in essence, make educational policies to engender public trust and further pre-existent political agendas (Taylor, Rizvi, Lingard, & Henry, 1997).

The use of international educational policies to garner prestige and legitimacy as well as support established agendas with recycled rationales resembles the cycle of decision making in complex organizational environments (March & Olsen, 1979). This cycle is often meaningless in terms of actual change in national educational achievement or attainment, but priceless in terms of the broader effects related to perceived economic and political competitiveness of a nation or community.

Although there may be certain elements of each nation, region, or culture that will influence local level schooling there is, for better or worse, a trend of isomorphism in educational policy and practice. This isomorphism is a product of national legitimacy-seeking efforts and leads national educational systems to develop, encourage, or require relatively similar models for local schooling and instruction, although the environments of schooling may vary considerably at the regional or local levels.

In other words, the organizational context of schooling is just as, if not more, influential on the outcomes of schooling than the technical processes of schooling are. At the cross-national level the institutional or organizational influences can often mask or override individual, micro-level influences through the strength of their relationship as much as their contextual influence because smaller level influences are nested within the larger ones. This means that internationalized education policy is oriented more toward systemic concerns than specific problems or regions, although extensive local knowledge cannot and should not be discounted. Therefore, internationalized education policy is not specific to particular problems of instruction and learning within individual schools.

INTERNATIONALIZED EDUCATION POLICY AS A TOOL FOR NATIONAL DEVELOPMENT

The worldwide explosion of the use of international educational information by governments is a product of a century-long process of nation-building as a manifest social project. Within this project in most nations, modern mass schooling is widely believed to be the main way to enhance the civil welfare, political status, and economy of a nation through the development of youth who become economically productive, socially and technically literate, and politically-active citizens (Benavot, 1992; Chabbott, 2003; Fuller & Rubinson, 1992; Meyer et al., 1977). The importance of education to nation-building is an article of civic faith in modern society (Ramirez & Boli, 1987). The strength of this belief enables it to penetrate many realms of political action related to schooling.

Within this context, the perceived benefit of international educational comparison for policymaking is two-fold: it creates an economically and politically productive citizenry which in turn either establishes or maintains a nation's international economic and political competitiveness. Educational policies often focus on schooling as a key to national economic security and competitiveness (Carnoy, 1985). Yet, the Western "myth of the individual," where the source of value and change in societies emphasizing school reform is the individual, provides the model framework for schooling around the world (Ramirez & Boli, 1987). Likewise, schooling contributes to the building of individuals as citizens in a nation-state (Anderson, 1996). Clearly the deeper institutional value of the "individual as moral social actor" is more influential than even the "individual as human capital producer," but both lead to the political justification of individual performance comparisons across nations, instead of old style comparison of schooling solely within nations.

The education of individuals can influence national economic growth and has contributed significantly to the economic development of nations (Benavot, 1992; Fuller & Rubinson, 1992; Hannum & Buchmann, 2003; McMahon & Boediono, 1992; McMahon, Jung, & Boediono, 1992). As such, international competition and economic interdependence create a community in which all nations have a stake in education (Carnoy, 1998; Deboer, 2000). As participation in the international community becomes increasingly important for individual nations, research-supported discussions about a standardized and consistently-skilled labor force become more frequent in the policy-relevant literature (Crowson, Wong, & Aypay, 2000;

Hughes, Bailey, & Karp, 2002). Around the world there are debates at all policymaking levels on educational priorities related to academic versus economic outcomes (Ashton, Green, Sung, & James, 2002; Taylor et al., 1997).

Intensification of market competition in the new global economic order enhances the importance among national policy makers of internationalizing education policy through adherence to an international model of education. Indeed, in most nations, education expenditures represent large state investments, usually ranking among health care and military spending. The political rationale behind this expenditure is the notion that investment in the human capital of a country's population is part of the state's commitment to the economic well-being of its populace (Altbach & Kelly, 1986). Central to human capital is educational attainment, and central to educational attainment is achievement. Following this rationale, therefore, educational agencies of the state become not only involved in providing access to schooling, but also in assessing educational quality and establishing policies aimed at increasing educational quality. This has been a marked trend in educational governance over the latter half of the 20th century opening a parallel interest in comparing educational quality across nations for use in domestic policymaking.

The integration of schooling, economics, and politics is a dominant factor throughout the policymaking process (Marginson & Mollis, 2001). The integration of these factors forms the globally legitimate educational model that internationalizes educational policy feeds (Carter & O'Neil, 1995). For example, school curricula are increasingly a reflection of perceived economic needs in terms of the employable skills and technical competencies that teachers are asked (or required) to teach (Ball, 1999). Research shows that the curriculum students receive in school does influence their future career choices (Te Riele & Crump, 2002). Many policymakers believe that in order to link education to labor market outcomes curricula should (a) focus on improving and providing basic employability skills, (b) inform students about opportunities in the labor market that relate to the curriculum learned in school, and (c) provide specific information about how to apply curriculum learned in school to future work situations (Lovejoy, 1998; Taylor, 2002).

An ideology about national economic purposes of schooling has become a commonly held and shared belief. When coupled with the strong beliefs about schooling for nation-building in general, a highly charged environment occurs in which local educational policies are driven and shaped by global comparisons.

THE IMPACT OF INTERNATIONALIZED
POLICYMAKING

The impact of international comparisons of national education systems and programs on domestic educational policy is direct rather than interpretive (Wiseman & Baker, 2002). Internationally comparative educational studies do impact policy through relatively direct transfer of models or ideas from one or several nations' educational systems to schools in other nations, rather than through critical evaluation of the most appropriate application of international models and ideas.

International comparative studies of education have been both praised and criticized, but consistently used by policymakers nonetheless. As momentum for international comparisons has increased worldwide, the frequency of international studies being used by national and multinational policy organizations has increased as well. As more policymakers become aware of these studies and are inundated with more recent and updated data from these studies, the relevance of frequent participation becomes a more pressing question (Wiseman & Baker, 2002).

Debates about the quantity and quality of impact of internationally comparative studies suggest that this impact warrants investigation (Baker, 1997). Participation in international comparative education studies is costly, both in terms of dollars and in terms of organization and planning effort. Since international comparative education studies are useful and extensive vehicles for comparing a nation's education system with those of other nations, the demand for these data are high among policymakers as well as the public. Knowing and estimating the impact of international comparative education studies on educational policy serves as a way to evaluate the effectiveness of participation in these studies as well as a proxy measure of a nation's global competitiveness.

Research reports and results emanating from international and comparative educational studies are and can be interpreted by interested parties ranging from educational policymakers at the national and state level to principals and teachers at the local level. Yet, international and comparative educational data and research can be overly simplified by political interests within nations (LeTendre et al., 2001).

Similarly and ironically some policy issues have become overly simplified through inclusion in international surveys that error toward homogenized measures and observation of phenomena to maximize comparability across nations, thus increasing the risk that important factors that vary across nations will be missed. For example, some have argued that the decentralized and localized nature of schooling disadvantages certain nations (e.g. the United States) in international, comparisons of performance because of increased variability in students opportunities to learn including individual student ability or curricular exposure (Bracey, 2004; Schmidt, McKnight, Valverde, Houang, & Wiley, 1997). In the past, the measurement of level of governance was very crude, and as a consequence the changing nature of governance was missed and led to oversimplified policy conclusions. Yet, in recent international studies, it has been observed that the decentralization of educational responsibility is often coupled with the centralization of educational authority, and this has made the issue of the effects of governance on school quality very complex (Astiz, Wiseman, & Baker, 2002).

International comparisons of national education systems and programs contribute to improved understanding of the basic nature of education systems. In particular, reference to specific elements of other nations' educational systems is frequent among educational policymakers. Unfortunately, most of the impact resulting from policies inspired by international comparative education studies is reactionary rather than proactive. This means that rather than using international comparative education studies as a tool for planning educational reform and improvement, they are often used as a way for educational policymakers to criticize schools and force accountability and standards reforms on them.

For example, policies related to educational equity are being reframed as "excellence" issues and vice versa. The mixed governance and policymaking model for education that is evident in most nations worldwide creates a form of policy legitimacy based on blame (Thrupp, 1998). Internationalized education policy is, in many cases, driven by "the general fearfulness about the political usefulness of 'crises' in international competitiveness" (Ball, 1999). This makes international education policy a powerful tool in the implementation of educational change. It is powerful because it is used as a way to target schooling through accountability programs and incentives that rely upon empirical performance indicators.

THE CRITICAL BACKLASH

As would be expected from its high degree of popularity, recently there has been a critical backlash against the internationalizing of educational policymaking. Most of this is aimed at technical and practical issues in generating the all important cross-national information. To date these focus on five concerns about international educational comparisons. The criticisms are as follows:

(1) Unstandardized methods of comparison lead to invalid and unreliable results from international comparative studies of education.
(2) The most discussed result of these studies, student achievement scores, are not valid, as these might not relate to economic growth and social improvement as much as is assumed.
(3) This explosion of international information means that cultural, contextual, and organizational variation among national systems of education, which may be incomparable, are being forced nonetheless into invalid comparisons.
(4) Unique national labor markets make comparisons among students' socioeconomic and other background factors impossible to compare.
(5) Within-nation variation and change is a more appropriate measure of educational impact than cross-national variation and change.

As these criticisms suggest, the value of cross-national comparisons of educational systems and outcomes is a long-standing point of debate. As a result, critics of national education systems and programs frequently ask if it is valid to compare national educational systems. In fact, the methodologies, rigor, and standards of cross-national comparative research are far from being standardized. As a result, there have been many claims that international comparisons of national educational systems are inappropriate (Atkin & Black, 1997; Bracey, 1999; Vickers, 1994). This critical argument flatly rejects the ability of cross-national comparisons of education to significantly predict or indicate anything about many nations' educational systems at all. There are several points that support this critical argument.

Some say that the instruments of assessment and evaluation themselves are invalid or unreliable measures of student achievement. In particular, there has been a substantial hue and cry that the large scale of cross-national assessments prevents the more technical elements of satisfactory validity and reliability with the data. Fletcher and Sabers (1995) make a good case for the manipulability of cross-national comparisons of student achievement. They suggest that although there are various cultural and contextual factors that influence educational systems and student achievement, it is just as important to consider the method of comparison and the interaction that certain factors may have with each other.

Another criticism of international comparative education studies and the resulting policies is that schools are often perceived as indicators of modernization and economic productivity, yet student achievement is not a consistent predictor of either. Inkeles (1969) made a rather convincing argument that schools are contexts for modernization, and this perspective seemed validated in the 1980s when the top ranking countries in student achievement were also many of the countries with the highest economic productivity or growth (Hanushek & Kimko, 2000). Yet other research has reduced the estimates of the relationship between achievement of students and the economics of a nation (Carnoy, 1998).

For example, Japan, typically one of the highest scorers in international assessments of math and science achievement, experienced severe economic setbacks throughout the 1990s. By contrast, the United States, which consistently ranked in the middle or below in international assessments of student achievement, had one of its most economically successful decades ever in the 1990s. Consequently, the popular logic that student performance indicates or predicts economic productivity and modernization crumbled with the Japanese and other high-scoring Asian nations' economies. Meanwhile, an alternative perspective on the cross-national comparison of student achievement was forming.

Scholars and policymakers began arguing that comparisons of student achievement guide policymakers to model their nations' or schools' policies on potentially incomparable systems of education in misguided efforts to attain systemic legitimization. This argument was based on the observation that little secondary or in-depth analysis of these data took place beyond the initial descriptions. Although descriptive statistics are usually the first results to appear from international comparisons, and often the most influential regarding policy, the contextual influence of national, regional, or local economic and curricular influence on both average educational performance as well as variation in educational performance has not often been empirically considered. Instead, relatively premature policy recommendations based on straightforward comparisons of national means of student achievement are often standard fare.

Even some educational comparativists began arguing that cross-national comparisons of educational systems and student achievement were ignoring important contextual factors. One such comparativist, Watson (1999), argued that the context of schooling is often as important or more important than the content:

> The research data upon which policies are based are too superficial to be really meaningful, as for example with the very broad International Association for the Evaluation of Educational Achievement (IEA) studies, which provide data from across, say, 30 or more countries. Unfortunately, this "scientific approach"...fails to take into account the local cultural and contextual issues.

Consequently, critics of international education policy assert that cultural, contextual, and organizational characteristics prevent straightforward cross-national comparison of educational systems and student achievement. Without a doubt, cultural contexts uniquely shape educational communities and learners. Cultural context is increasingly important in an era devoted to measuring trends in globalization and isomorphism.

Important to this cultural criticism of cross-national comparisons of student achievement are historical and traditional characteristics of educational systems. In particular, attention to local conditions and classroom pedagogy have been recent topics for consideration in studies estimating the effectiveness of schools. More than ever before studies that look at the national and local variation of schooling should be examined. In many cases, depending upon the questions that guide the research, studies may require the use of complementary methodologies (Greene, Caracelli, & Graham, 1989; Tashakkori & Teddlie, 1998).

Other critics of international education policy argue that family background and socioeconomic status are often insurmountable obstacles to appropriate cross-national comparison of schooling, including standardized outcomes such as student achievement. There is also a large body of literature that suggests that the background influences of students and education professionals are always such significant predictors of student achievement that cross-national variation in student achievement is moot. Therefore, cross-national studies should instead look at the variation in family background and other status indicators to predict the effectiveness or impact of schooling rather than its specific individual outcomes.

Finally, critics of international education studies and policy assert that alternative methods of cross-national comparison that focus more on between nation comparisons of within-nation change or variation in achievement are the most reasonable approaches to cross-national educational comparisons. In particular, critics suggest that specific content scores may seem to indicate where a nation's educational strengths and weaknesses are. But, it still may be contextually inappropriate to compare across nations, even with subscores for distinct topics. Thus, the crux of this criticism is that national development and productivity are often better represented by within-nation gains or variation than between-nation comparisons.

The critics of international education policy use a lot of ammunition, and while many of their accusations raise useful questions, much of the concerns are ultimately unfounded. Specific technical responses to each of these criticisms is beyond the scope of this chapter but there are some positive responses to criticisms aimed at internationalized education policymaking that are helpful.

POSITIVE RESPONSES TO THE CRITICS

Internationalized education policymaking has positively impacted national systems of education in several ways (Wiseman & Baker, 2002). In particular, internationalized education policymaking has,

(1) Built reform capacity within national systems of education,
(2) Contributed to an understanding of the basic nature of education systems both in and out of the policymaking community,
(3) Improved the quantity of national education research,
(4) Aided in the benchmarking of national education systems against international standards, and
(5) Increased the flow of ideas into national education systems.

Much educational policy relies upon available reports of international comparative research. The literature reporting this research extensively investigates math and science education, specifically, as well as many of the background factors that influence each. The breadth and depth of the research being conducted and reported both in primary as well as secondary sources is large and increasing.

There are many ways that the testing community is building capacity, although they are mostly small-scale rather than large-scale capacities. Through the information and testing structure that was put in place for the administration of many of the larger international comparative assessments backed by the IEA and OECD, there is an established venue for further large-scale (i.e. national level) testing. This is evidenced by the replication of both IEA and OECD-backed studies like TIMSS and PISA, respectively.

In addition, many regional and district-level educational administrative units are conducting large-scale assessments at their level as a result of either the structure or the pressure to assess provided by both internationally comparative results and the previous testing related to these international comparisons. Examples of this are the benchmarking studies that have been conducted in the United States as part of TIMSS replication in 1999 and 2003.

Dissemination is also a part of capacity building in national and international testing communities. Without the results of large-scale internationally comparative assessments being known, read, and studied by educational organizations and professionals, the capacity of the testing community is irrelevant. While dissemination data for key sources are limited due to insufficient records keeping or issues of confidentiality, the evidence suggests that early dissemination of printed material was not as

great as might be assumed from the volume of references to and awareness of key concepts from these reports and other key sources. But, in
spite of initial sluggishness, dissemination of international comparative
education reports and other literature to policymakers is steadily growing
and increasing in the speed at which they are produced once the data are
collected.

The same is true for the change in greater openness and access by independent analysts to the raw data. One reason for a certain amount of
persistent sluggishness is that the release of results from internationally
comparative studies of education is sometimes met with trepidation by policymakers and the educational community in various nations depending on
the topic. Since nations now "own" the process as a group, several nations
can block certain parts of the official reports, although not the use of data
by independent analysts (Baker, 1997). This is actually a good indication of
the growth in the potency of international information to have an impact on
domestic politics about schooling.

There is evidence of the penetration of internationalized information into
not only national level policy discussions, but to more local levels as well. It
is often inconsistencies in the dissemination of international comparative
education research that contribute to the critical backlash against policies
resulting from or relying on these data. For example, the ordinary U.S.
school administrator only knows TIMSS is part of a set of findings about
school performance in the United States, and overall American educational
administrators have limited knowledge of this (Boyd, 2002). The impact that
TIMSS has is much more on the "elite" or national level policy types. In
other words, the big picture is more informed than local issues.

In spite of these "irritations," international comparative education policy
has contributed to an understanding of the basic nature of education systems. In particular, reference to specific elements of other nations' educational systems is frequent from both policymakers and educational
practitioners such as principals and teachers. The frequency of these references tapers as the reference points approach the student. References to
foreign nations' educational systems at the state and district level outstrip
the references at the school or classroom level. For example, teachers and
administrators do not often make reference to education in other countries
when discussing their own schools and educational systems. This, however,
is not surprising. Teachers and school administrators are most concerned
with the day-to-day operation of their classrooms and students.

Policymakers and other decision makers at the state and district level are
both expected and pressured into international comparison or at the very

least basic benchmarking activity in order to maintain their legitimacy and viability within the national educational community. In fact, international comparative education data are a stimulus or catalyst to reform rather than a specific element upon which reform rests (Kimmelman, 2002). Although reference to international comparative education does not often come up in informal conversations among teacher educators, in reform-minded forums internationally comparative studies of education are important.

Contributions to understanding the basic nature of education systems are measured by the frequency with which specific elements of other nations' educational systems such as organizational, curricular, or pedagogical elements influence classroom practice, teacher education, state standards, and curriculum. The most frequent references to other nations' educational systems in the U.S. educational community come from the national, state, and sometimes district levels. At these levels of decision- and policymaking the frequency of reference to international comparative education or other nation's educational systems is often an indicator of the policy legitimacy of international comparative education or is required for continued support and funding from both government and non-governmental sources.

Increased reference to features of education systems in other nations by policymakers are measured by the amount of visits or references to the pedagogy or structure of foreign education systems by educational policy-makers and policy reports. Policy reports making reference to other nations' educational systems as either models to emulate or avoid have been a fixture for many years before the first large-scale internationally comparative studies of education conducted by the IEA in the late 1960s (LeTendre & Baker, 1999; Ramirez & Boli, 1987).

FUTURE POSSIBILITIES FOR INTERNATIONALIZED EDUCATION POLICY

Probably the easiest, and in our opinion the most likely, future scenario to imagine is that national policymakers and analysts will continue to recognize the advantages of international study and comparison. In the 1990s, Epstein (1994) explained the importance and necessity of international comparison and argued that educational comparativists explain "why educational systems and processes vary and how education relates to wider social factors and forces." Two decades earlier, Noah and Eckstein (1969) argued that an internationally comparative perspective allows researchers to explain phenomena not only within educational systems and institutions, but also phenomena surrounding education linking schooling to its social environment.

Obviously these ideas have been around for some time. The surge in technical capabilities of nations to compare their educational outputs has lent an additional force to internationalizing education policy as a common practice. Further, and perhaps most important, is that the very institutional character of schooling tempts many policymakers to compare systems in their work on domestic issues (Johnson, 1999; Meyer, 1980; Meyer & Baker, 1996).

Given these trends, will schooling in all nations look the same and perform the same with similar outcomes in a short time to come? Probably not. The national political process across countries is still robust and somewhat varied. Educational resources and their distribution will continue to be a nationally unique operation. And this can greatly influence what happens in one nation's school system versus another. What is more likely to happen is that the basic institutional understandings and values about schooling will become more homogeneous across nations; they already are in large part. These in a sense provide the rules of the game in education; exactly how nations play that game will continue to vary somewhat into the foreseeable future.

REFERENCES

Altbach, P. G., & Kelly, G. (Eds) (1986). *New approaches to comparative education.* Chicago: University of Chicago Press.
Anderson, B. (1996). *Imagined communities: Reflections on the origin and spread of nationalism.* New York: Verso.
Ashton, D., Green, F., Sung, J., & James, D. (2002). The evolution of education and training strategies in Singapore, Taiwan and S. Korea: A development model of skill formation. *Journal of Education and Work, 15*(1), 5–30.
Astiz, M. F., Wiseman, A. W., & Baker, D. P. (2002). Slouching towards decentralization: Consequences of globalization for curricular control in national education systems. *Comparative Education Review, 46*(1), 66–89.
Atkin, J. M., & Black, P. (1997). Policy perils of international comparisons: The TIMSS case. *Phi Delta Kappan* (September), 22–28.
Baker, D. P. (1997). Surviving TIMSS: Or, everything you blissfully forgot about international comparisons. *Phi Delta Kappan* (December), 295–300.
Baker, D. P., & LeTendre, G. K. (2005). *National differences, global similarities: Current and future world institutional trends in schooling.* Stanford: Stanford University Press.
Ball, S. J. (1998). Big policies/small world: An introduction to international perspectives in education policy. *Comparative Education, 34*(2), 119–130.

Ball, S. J. (1999). Labour, learning and the economy: A 'policy sociology' perspective. *Cambridge Journal of Education, 29*(2), 195–206.

Benavot, A. (1992). Curricular content, educational expansion, and economic growth. *Comparative Education Review, 36*(2), 150–174.

Boyd, W. L. (2002). Personal Communication. In: D. P. Baker (Ed.), *State College*, PA.

Bracey, G. W. (1999). The TIMSS "final year" study and report: A critique. *Educational Researcher, 29*(4), 4–10.

Bracey, G. W. (2004). International comparisons: Less than meets the eye? *Phi Delta Kappan, 85*(6), 477–478.

Carnoy, M. (1985). The political economy of education. *International Social Science Journal, 37*(2), 157–173.

Carnoy, M. (1998). The globalization of innovation, nationalist competition, and the internationalization of scientific training. *Competition & Change, 3*(1–2), 237–263.

Carter, D. S. G., & O'Neil, M. H. (1995). *International perspectives on educational reform and policy implementation*. London: Falmer Press.

Chabbott, C. (2003). *Constructing education for development*. New York: RoutledgeFalmer.

Crowson, R., Wong, K., & Aypay, A. (2000). The quiet reform in American education: Policy issues and conceptual challenges in the school-to-work transition. *Educational Policy, 14*(2), 241–258.

Deacon, B., Hulse, M., & Stubbs, P. (1997). *Global social policy: International organizations and the future of welfare*. London: Sage.

Deboer, G. E. (2000). Scientific literacy: Another look at its historical and contemporary meanings and its relationship to science education reform. *Journal of Research in Science Teaching, 20*(6), 582–601.

Eliason, L. C., Fagerlind, I., Merritt, R. L., & Weiler, H. (1987). Education, social science, and public policy: A critique of comparative research. In: M. Dierkes, H. N. Weiler & A. B. Antal (Eds), *Comparative policy research* (pp. 244–263). Aldershot: Gower.

Epstein, E. H. (1994). Comparative and international education: Overview and historical development. In: T. Husen & T. N. Postlethwaite (Eds), *International encyclopedia of education*. London: Elsevier.

Fletcher, T. V., & Sabers, D. L. (1995). Interaction effects in cross-national studies of achievement. *Comparative Education Review, 39*(4), 455–468.

Fuller, B., & Rubinson, R. (Eds) (1992). *The political construction of education: The state, economic change, and school expansion*. New York: Praeger.

Greene, J., Caracelli, V., & Graham, W. (1989). Toward a conceptual framework for mixed-method evaluation designs. *Educational Evaluation and Policy Analysis, 11*(3), 255–274.

Hannum, E., & Buchmann, C. (2003). *The consequences of global educational expansion*. Cambridge, MA: American Academy of Arts and Sciences.

Hanushek, E. A., & Kimko, D. (2000). Schooling, labor force quality, and the growth of nations. *American Economic Review, 90*(3), 1184–2008.

Hughes, K. L., Bailey, T. R., & Karp, M. M. (2002). School-to-work: Making a difference in education. *Phi Delta Kappan, 84*(4), 272–280.

Inkeles, A. (1969). Making Men modern: on the causes and consequences of individual change in six developing countries. *American Journal of Sociology, 75*(2), 208–225.

Johnson, S. (1999). International association for the evaluation of educational achievement science assessment in developing countries. *Assessment in Education, 6*(1), 57–73.

Kimmelman, P. (2002). D. P. Baker, Personal communication with, State college. PA.

LeTendre, G. K., & Baker, D. P. (1999). International comparisons and educational research policy. In: G. K. LeTendre (Ed.), *Competitor or ally? Japan's role in American educational debates*. New York: Falmer.

LeTendre, G. K., Baker, D. P., Akiba, M., & Wiseman, A. W. (2001). The policy trap: National educational policy and the third international math and science study. *International Journal of Educational Policy, Research and Practice, 2*(1), 45–64.

Lovejoy, B. (1998). Misleading America's youth. *Techniques: Making education & career connections*. p. 40.

March, J., & Olsen, J. (1979). *Ambiguity and choice in organizations*. Bergen: Universitetsforlaget.

Marginson, S., & Mollis, M. (2001). "The door opens and the tiger leaps": Theories and reflexivities of comparative education for a global millennium. *Comparative Education Review, 45*(4), 581–615.

Max-Neef, M., Elizalde, A., & Hopenhayn, M. (1991). *Human scale development: Conception, application, and further reflections*. New York: Apex.

McMahon, W. W., & Boediono (1992). Universal basic education: An overall strategy of investment priorities for economic growth. *Economics of Education Review, 11*(2), 137–151.

McMahon, W. W., Jung, J. H., & Boediono (1992). Vocational and technical education in development: Theoretical analysis of strategic effects on rates of return. *Economics of Education Review, 11*(3), 181–194.

Meyer, J. W. (1980). Levels of the educational system and schooling effects. In: C. E. Bidwell & D. M. Windham (Eds), *The analysis of educational productivity: Issues in macroanalysis*, Vol. 2 (pp. 15–63). Cambridge, MA: Ballinger.

Meyer, J. W. (2000). Reflections on education as transcendence. In: L. Cuban & D. Shipps (Eds), *Reconstructing the common good in education*. Stanford, CA: Stanford University Press.

Meyer, J. W., & Baker, D. P. (1996). Forming American educational policy with international data: Lessons from the sociology of education. *Sociology of Education* (Extra Issue), 123–130.

Meyer, J. W., Ramirez, F. O., Rubinson, R., & Boli-Bennett, J. (1977). The world educational revolution, 1950–1970. *Sociology of Education, 50*(4), 242–258.

Noah, H. J., & Eckstein, M. A. (1969). *Toward a science of comparative education*. New York: Macmillan.

Ramirez, F. O., & Boli, J. (1987). The political construction of mass schooling: European origins and worldwide institutionalization. *Sociology of Education, 60*(1), 2–17.

Schmidt, W. H., McKnight, C. C., Valverde, G. A., Houang, R. T., & Wiley, D. E. (1997). *Many visions, many aims: A cross-national investigation of curricular intentions in school mathematics*. Dordrecht: Kluwer.

Tashakkori, A., & Teddlie, C. (1998). *Mixed methodology: Combining qualitative and quantitative approaches*. Thousand Oaks, CA: Sage.

Taylor, A. (2002). Informing education policy. *Journal of Education Policy, 17*(1), 49–70.

Taylor, S., Rizvi, F., Lingard, B., & Henry, M. (1997). *Educational policy and the politics of change*. London: Routledge.

Te Riele, K., & Crump, S. (2002). Young people, education and hope: Bring vet in from the margins. *International Journal of Inclusive Education, 6*(3), 251–266.

Thrupp, M. (1998). Explaining the politics of blame. *Comparative Education, 34*(2), 193–202.

Vickers, M. (1994). Cross-national exchange, the OECD, and Australian education policy. *Knowledge & Policy, 7*(1), 25–47.

Watson, K. (1999). Comparative educational research: The need for reconceptualisation and fresh insights. *Compare, 29*(3), 233–248.

Weick, K. E. (1976). Educational organizations as loosely coupled systems. *Administrative Science Quarterly, 21*(1), 1–19.

Weiss, C. H. (Ed.) (1977). *Using social research in public policy making.* Lexington, MA: D.C. Heath.

Wiseman, A. W., & Baker, D. P. (2002). *A preliminary report on the impact of TIMSS-related activities on U.S. education, 1996–2001.* Washington, DC: Board on International Comparative Studies in Education, National Academy of Science/National Research Council.

THE HISTORY AND PROBLEMS IN THE MAKING OF EDUCATION POLICY AT THE WORLD BANK, 1960–2000

Stephen P. Heyneman

INTRODUCTION

The reports seem contradictory. With about three billion dollars per year in new loan commitments, the World Bank has become the single largest source of development capital in the field of international education. These resources help expand educational opportunities for young women in South Asia and rebuild primary schools following civil conflict in sub-Saharan Africa. They support textbooks, school meals, new curriculum, and teacher training in thousands, perhaps hundreds of thousands, of locations in over 100 countries in six regions.

But 'the Bank' as it is commonly referred to, is also the object of considerable criticism. Some argue that its loan covenants are too restrictive. Its policy reforms are based on narrow, neo-liberal assumptions about the role of the state. Local policymakers have become passive recipients of the Bank's agendas. To obtain loans, countries have agreed to raise education fees, which has exacerbated divisions between rich and poor.

Global Trends in Educational Policy
International Perspectives on Education and Society, Volume 6, 23–58
Copyright © 2005 by Elsevier Ltd.
All rights of reproduction in any form reserved
ISSN: 1479-3679/doi:10.1016/S1479-3679(04)06002-5

How is it that a multilateral U.N. lending institution, managed by its owners in proportion to shares of equity, has become involved in education? How are educational lending priorities and policies actually established and how have they changed over time? Is there validity to the many criticisms of the World Bank in the field of education, and how has the Bank responded? Finally, what changes and recommendations might be considered to ameliorate the long standing tension between the interests which generate lending and those which stand for more intelligence or effectiveness of that lending?

This chapter discusses how the Bank lending priorities are established and loans designed and approved. It attempts to illustrate how and why the Bank, as opposed to other international organizations, has increasingly influenced the global education agenda. It highlights why the Bank's policies on education have not been as effective as postulated, and in some cases have created significant educational distortions in a nation's education sector. This analysis is predicated on the Bank's tendency to become 'captured' by single methodologies beginning with manpower forecasting and later rate of return techniques. This tended to bias its views with respect to particular sub-sectors, educational functions, and purposes. Some of these distortions can be traced back to its entry into the sector in the 1960s. The article raises the question of who should be held accountable when over time the Bank policies prove to be dysfunctional. The article concludes that in spite of the importance of having intelligent education policies for social and economic development, there is no single international organization to effectively provide them. The article suggests three options for changing international organizations so as to deliver better analytic work, more intelligent policies and more effective programs of education assistance.

THE ENTRY OF HUMAN CAPITAL INTO THE WORLD BANK

It was the late 1950s that Schultz (1959, 1961, 1981), Becker (1964), Bowman et al. (1968), Anderson and Bowman (1967), and Bowman and Anderson (1968) had migrated to the University of Chicago, and began to investigate the contributions of human capital to national income growth. Frederick Harbison at Princeton (1964), Lewis (1969) with Blaug (1970) and Vaizey (1968) in London, and Hansen and Weisbrod (1969) in Madison and Berkeley were investigating similar avenues and drawing consistent conclusions. With India and Pakistan's independence in 1947, Ghana's independence in 1957, and the stirrings across Francophone and Anglophone Africa, the political landscape was shifting, and the demands on the International Bank for Reconstruction and Development were shifting in parallel fashion. The Bank's mandate for reconstruction, essential for war-torn Europe, was giving way to the priorities of the newly emerging developing countries.

Outside Europe though, the ingredients of development were different. It was clear to the Bank management that each nation would need to expand its trade and commerce and this would require an efficient infrastructure. In Europe this infrastructure had been destroyed and needed to be rebuilt. In Africa, Latin America, and Asia, for the most part, the infrastructure had to be created. The focus of attention had not changed: infrastructure was the purpose of the Bank lending and the central focus of its mandate. The question was how to create within developing countries of the 1960s an infrastructure where before there was none?

Human capital first entered the World Bank as a way to fix 'engineering problems'. Bridges, highways, ports, and railroads needed construction, traditionally with the assistance of external consultant firms. As the new countries become independent, the Bank was under increasing pressure to encourage local participation in the bidding and procurement process, and hence to use local as well as international providers of technical assistance.

The concept of infrastructure itself was changing too. The demand for borrowing was moving away from bridges and highways toward industry, agriculture, and manufacturing (Gavin & Rodrik, 1995). By nature, these new types of infrastructure investments were not 'turn key operations.' With bridges and highways, the Bank's role was to provide money for construction, but with industry, recurrent expenditures become important. The new types of infrastructure would require long-term management and technical skills to run efficiently, and whether these were in sufficient supply became the critical question. Would Bank investment in an agricultural industry be at risk because of the scarcity of agricultural engineers? Countries could borrow for foreign technical assistance to help manage the new industries, but foreign technical assistance is expensive and from the beginning there was political resistance. Why borrow for foreign management and technical talent when local talent could be developed? But how can one tell whether local skills are sufficient? And given the context of the new investments in a nation's infrastructure, how does one determine how much new technical skill to develop?

The Bank began to use human capital measurements in its analytic work in the early 1960s for reasons having little to do with the theory of economic development and more to do with the priority of human over physical capital goods.[1] The Bank began to use human capital measures because it had a specific problem: how could their investment in a new fertilizer manufacturing plant make any difference without a staff of agriculture engineers?

PROBLEMS, RESOLUTIONS, NEW PROBLEMS

Manpower Forecasting: Lending for Vocations

As Jones (1992) has pointed out, the first operational directives that allowed for a Bank investment in human capital limited the terms and involvement to those areas where the Bank's infrastructure investments might be at risk. The answer to the question of how to tell was the reason why the Bank began to utilize manpower forecasting models.[2] The question was not what human capital was necessary for development – an argument, full of dilemmas and debates,[3] – but how many engineers and technicians were required if an investment in a country's agricultural fertilizer is to be sustainable.

In October 1963, the Executive Directors approved the first of a series of operational directives governing the Bank's approach to education. The memo to the Board said that the Bank and IDA should Be prepared to consider financing a part of the capital requirements of priority education projects designed to produce trained manpower to forward economic development. In applying this criterion, the Bank and IDA should concentrate their attention on projects in the fields of (a) vocational and technical education and training at other levels, and (b) general secondary education (World Bank, 1963).

From 1962 to 1980 all education investments supported by the Bank required justifications on the basis of manpower demands. Hence all Bank education investments centered on the focus of manpower analytic techniques and the scarcities of technicians and engineers (Bartholomew, 1976). Understandable at the outset, this focus on one small part of the education sector became the first in a series of operational biases through which the Bank often sponsored, promoted, and financed with borrower resources projects with distorted content.

The drawbacks of manpower forecasting are relatively well-known (Anderson & Bowman, 1967; Jones, 1992; Foster, 1968; Heyneman, 1972, 1984 , 1995, 1999). Costs were not calculated to adjust for the fact that unit expenditures in engineering were higher than other higher education faculties did not figure in the internal debates. An investment in engineering was taken to be a necessary ingredient for the much larger investment in infrastructure. Much like a nail or a bolt, engineers were necessary to hold the much larger investment together.

The latent implication of this justification was the prohibition against assisting other parts of the education sector. These other parts were treated as consumption goods, and not a proper investment. The lending program prohibited any assistance to art, science and faculties of humanities, even libraries, all primary and academic (as opposed to diversified) secondary education, and post graduate education, none of which could be included in project appraisal reports.[4]

'Diversified' Secondary Education

By the late 1960s the Bank had created an Education Department to lead the analytic work underpinning its investments and to assess the results of those investments. The arrival of a new deputy director, however, helped pave the way for the Bank's expansion of educational responsibilities. The Permanent Secretary in the Swedish Ministry of Education helped popularize a new justification designed to convince the Bank's senior management to allow lending for secondary education.[5] If it could be demonstrated that secondary education would lead to 'practical employment' in areas necessary for technical efficiency, then the Bank could justify secondary education investments. The timing corresponded with new programs for comprehensive schools, a reform in Europe which combined academic with manual training in the same institutions (World Bank, 1970, 1972).

In 1971, the World Bank operational directive governing education underscored the reasons for diversified secondary education. It said:

> The education systems in developing countries are designed for an elite...usually a landed aristocracy, commercial upper class or cadre of civil servants: a substantial portion of the students in school are being miseducated; and the content of primary and secondary courses...is remote from the experience of today's student, especially the rural peasant child.
>
> (World Bank, 1971)

Similar assessments played a role in the 1974 Sector Policy Paper. In that paper it was argued that current educational content was 'dysfunctional' because it was 'more theoretical and abstract and less practical'. The education systems in developing countries were seen as being imbalanced. It was believed that there was a surplus of literary and general skills and an unmet demand of specific job-related skills. The recommended solution was a 're-orientation' of the curriculum from top to bottom so as to 'ensure that graduates can be employed. Improving the quality of education was assumed to be synonymous with making education 'more practical' and relevant by re-orienting the content away from academic and toward vocational purposes' (World Bank, 1974).[6]

By avoiding specialization and tracking, comprehensive diversified schools were thought to encourage social mobility, and hence be more 'democratic'. Most nations in Africa and Asia, as well as Latin America, were interested in expanding educational opportunities, wished to borrow for that purpose. However, the Bank allowed them to borrow only if their secondary education investments included diversified curricula. From Somalia to Indonesia, each project for which the Bank assisted secondary education, included metal shop and woodshop for boys, and domestic science for girls. These subjects were thought to be more 'practical' and would avoid the dangers of educated unemployment and political alienation.

In Somalia for instance, these workshops included 'electric cookers' for girls who had never before seen an electric stove. Where only metal or cement was used in construction, woodshop facilities were required in all secondary schools receiving assistance by the World Bank, and since wood was not locally available, it had to be imported from Europe (Heyneman, 1987).[7]

These two early examples serve to illustrate a pattern. Human capital theories were used to justify investments in those areas where the Bank's education sector could argue for more lending to those who allocate resources within the Bank, i.e. the country economists. The education sector acted rationally in the competition for 'slots' reserved for projects within the country's lending program (Jones, 1992, 1997; Mundy, 1998). However, before continuing with the story on educational policy toward lending, the reader might benefit from a brief synopsis of how lending priorities, in fact, are established and how loans are approved.

THE LENDING PROCESS

Rationales for educational investment must fit within the overall context of national allocations. The incentives for staff to create new loans can outweigh incentives for making current loans implement more effectively. A high degree of competition exists among staff to be responsible for new loans – across regions, country departments, between and within sectors (transport, health, education, banking etc.) and those responsible for macro-economic lending. In spite of the periodic worry about 'moral hazard'[8] (Wapenhans, 1992), the pressure and prestige of new lending is a permanent feature of Bank culture.

Ideas for what shall be funded are generated by each country department within each region. There are six regions, and between four and six country departments in each region.[9] Each country director sets priorities to which the sectors respond. Priorities may include public sector efficiency, export promotion, and tax reform. Sectors respond accordingly.

For instance, in response to a priority on tax reform set by a country director, the education sector staff might recommend a loan to improve an institute for tax officer training; the staff in the social protection sector might recommend assisting the shift in social security tax. In both cases, the object would to ameliorate a problem in the tax policy using the resources of the sector to which one had been assigned. This accountability structure for lending explains how the Bank regularly lends for purposes which are at a tangent from its own stated sector priorities.[10]

Staff in the education sector respond to administrative incentives derived from macro-economic priorities. They determine the tendency for the Education Sector to collect certain kinds of data and not others, conduct certain analyses and not others, and sponsor certain lending and not others. If the Bank has been imbalanced in education lending, or mistaken in the education covenants required from countries, it is partly due to the internal incentives to which the Education Sector must respond. It is important to remember that the Education Sector does not establish operational priorities. It may seek to influence priorities, but the allocation of internal resources and the establishment of operational priorities are solely in the hands of country economists.[11]

The education sector staff might give a hearing to new human capital rationales providing these rationales did not threaten loans already in the 'pipeline' or the justifications for further loans. New rationales, however, would require that the education staff have the training and skills to incorporate the new techniques. Until 1980, Bank education staff fell into three broad categories (Heyneman, 1999). For the most part, economists in fact were educational planners with expertise in manpower forecasting. Educators, the second group, helped decide the content of a practical curriculum. The function of the last group, project architects, was to calculate the costs of construction for the proposed new facilities. The focus of operational staff was not on educational issues as known in the wider world, but rather on issues of relevance to the internal requirements of bank lending.

The focus was on the techniques to justify engineering education, the content of vocational curriculum, and the alternative choices for construction. Rewards derived from successfully answering the 'how to implement' question, not the 'why to invest' question.

Consequently, within the regions there was little incentive to question the reasoning on which the lending depended. Since the mechanisms of manpower forecasting were pervasive, the countries rapidly responded to the incentives, by confining requests those areas they knew to be of interest to the Bank, vocational and technical education, and technician training.[12]

McNAMARA'S BALANCE OF POWER

Robert McNamara left the U.S. Department of Defense to become President of the World Bank in 1968. He remained the President for the next decade, and was responsible for increasing lending for four or five fold during his tenure, and for pushing the Bank into population and family planning, public health, and education. One of his primary concerns was how to structure the proper balance between generating quick and effective loans and yet at the same time, assuring the technical quality of those loans. The natural tension between speedy response to demand and technical standards might have analogies in any production process. After careful study, the Bank was re-configured into three major sections, each with a Vice President: one based on research in development economics, one based on policy and lending strategy, and the last (with six vice presidents) based on regional responsibilities (Fig. 1).

The key to McNamara's plan was to give the research staff significant visibility, but little operational authority, and the two other sections virtual veto power over both lending and policy. No policy could be called 'official' without mutual agreement between the Central Projects Staff and the Regional Staff. Similarly no loan could be cleared for the Board approval without consensus across the two sections. This 'balance of power' was designed to protect the institution from two important hazards: loans based the whims of local officials and policies based on models and paradigms of little or no relevance 'on the ground'. As the story continues, the reader will notice that this design changed radically in the 1980s, and disappeared altogether in the 1990s with significant effects on the quality of both lending and policy.

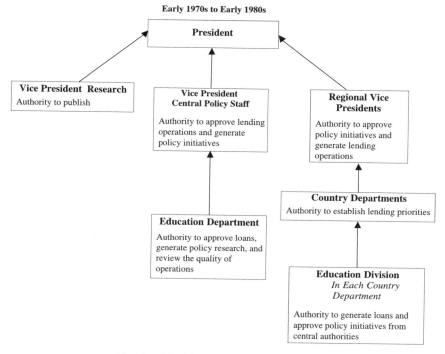

Early 1970s to Early 1980s

Fig. 1. World Bank Internal Processes.

CHALLENGES TO MANPOWER FORECASTING

Change first came with the assignment within the Education Department of the Bank's first science educator and educational sociologist in 1974. The functions of these new staff included the analysis of curriculum theories and the promotion of 'tracer studies' of graduates, to reinforce the practical nature of the curricula.[13] Countries were encouraged to borrow for the implementation of tracer studies and analyze their results. In April 1976, the second education sociologist entered the World Bank, and quickly found two problems.

Although the 'vocational school fallacy' argument (Foster, 1965, 1968) had been published a decade earlier, most World Bank staff were unaware that there was an alternative to the 'practical' education assumptions under

which lending was justified.[14] It was taken as axiomatic that 'practical subjects' and technical skill training were more useful in the labor market. That
the opposite might be the case, that academic skills might be more useful,
was heresy because it threatened the philosophic underpinnings for the
lending program (Heyneman, 1985a, 1985b; Habte, Psacharopoulos, &
Heyneman, 1983; Psacharopoulos & Loxley, 1985).[15]

The second problem was that manpower forecasting distorted the lending
program toward specific vocations against other priorities. Loans could not
be justified on the basis that they could improve academic skills because
academic skills were thought to be economically 'impractical' (Balogh &
Streeten, 1968–1969). On the other hand, there was an alternative economic
methodology for calculating an economic rate of return to educational investments (Levin, 1983; Windham, 1975; Psacharopoulos, 1973;
Psacharopoulos & Woodhall, 1985), known in the more renowned universities, which could test the theory of skill practicality. With a long tradition
of publishing manpower figures and forecasts, however, the Chief Education
Economist at the time argued that this 'rate of return methodology' had
serious shortcomings. Earnings and educational cost data on which the
methodology depends were scarce and unreliable. The methodology might
be of interest to academics but impractical for World Bank operations
where specific decisions on investment decisions had to be made and quickly. It was an 'experimental' methodology, and not feasible for the real world
of operations.

The relative autonomy of the Education Department within the Central
Project Staff allowed for some experimentation with earnings and cost and
earnings data. Some of these data came from secondary sources; others were
derived from the tracer studies put into place a few years earlier. The appearance of the first reports to use rate of return analyses on India and
Malawi (Heyneman, 1980a, b), laid the groundwork for inviting more rate
of return expertise into the Bank.

This divided the education economics profession in half, one in which
manpower forecasting was considered the dominant mechanism; the other
which promoted the use of rate of return studies. For the most part, regional
operations sided with the former because it was the mechanism of economic
discourse most familiar, and necessary to protect projects in the pipeline.
The Research Unit in the Education Department and the Human Resources
Division within Development Economics (research) Department, however,
tended to side with the rate of return methodologies. It was pointed out that
similar methodologies were used in other Bank sectors, the rate of return
formulae included costs and benefits two sacrosanct elements within the

economics profession, and hence the reasoning for using the 'rate of return' methodologies in education were considered to be within the precedent set by other sectors and more compelling. The differing economic rationales for educational lending were not the only source of operational distortions stemming from the era of World Bank 'infrastructure'. Also important were the definitions at the time of 'recurrent' and 'capital' costs as applied to education. A brief word about this issue follows.

RECURRENT EXPENDITURES AND THE PROHIBITION AGAINST LENDING FOR TEXTBOOKS

A common principle from the beginning of the World Bank has been the notion that lending was analogous to start up capital. If an economy could not generate sufficient resources to maintain a paved road, then an investment should be limited to dirt roads. Key to a project's justification was its sustainability. One method of determining a project's affordability (i.e. the ability to pay for sustainability) was to declare the country responsible for recurrent costs and the Bank responsible for capital costs. If a country could not maintain the capital investment, then it was assumed that it could not afford it.

The bulk of expenses in infrastructure consist of the cost of capital construction. But education is labor intensive. The bulk of the educational expenditures are for salaries and other expenses that regularly reoccur. Since identical economic principles were applied across sectors, the definition of recurrent expenditure had the effect of prohibiting the Bank from lending for essential reading materials. To educators experienced in developing countries, however, the provision of reading materials was among the most essential ingredients for a system to function, and the absence of those materials called into question whether institutions should continue to operate at all.

The definition of 'recurrent expenditure' shifted for several reasons. It was clear from the research evidence that textbooks were important (Heyneman, Farrell, & Sepulveda-Stuardo, 1978), but it was also clear that textbooks themselves were a 'bankable item' (Jones, 1992). The debate over whether the bank should loan for textbooks was characteristic: the definition of recurrent costs had been set in an era that focused on the reconstruction of Europe when national economic expectations and the investment role of the Bank were quite different. The definition shifted not because the economics profession has changed its view, or because the professional education community was united in recognizing that reading materials were important for students who were trying to learn to read. It shifted because it became clear that reading materials were a viable avenue for lending. One could think of reading materials as an investment rather than consumption. If textbooks were not consumption items, then they did not need to be categorized as a 'recurrent expenditure'. And if they were not a recurrent expenditure, then the bank could loan for them. In spite of the circular logic, the effect was constructive.[16]

All these issues lay behind the *1980 Education Sector Policy Paper* (World Bank, 1980), and may help explain to the non-specialist,[17] why knowing what was not in the paper was as important as knowing what the paper contained. The bank would no longer be limited to lending for vocational and technical education or to diversified secondary education. Educational quality was a legitimate object for lending, as was education research. And all parts of the education system, from elementary to higher education were legitimate objects of Bank assistance. Most importantly, the economic tools used to answer the question of how much to invest, were not limited to manpower forecasting. Rarely are Bank policy papers recognized as revolutionary (Williams, 1975), but with reflection on the significant distortions from which the Bank Education Sector had to operate heretofore, the policies for the 1980s were radical indeed. This was indeed progress. But would this progress lead to better lending and to more justified objectives for that lending?

NEW METHODOLOGIES, INTERNAL PROCEDURES, AND PROBLEMS

In the 1980s the Bank began to suffer from increasing, and relentless criticism from environmentalists, human rights activists, and spokespersons for indigenous peoples, women, and the poor. In response, Barber Conable, as the new President, made the decision to 'study the problem' and commissioned a high power group which interviewed a large number of academics, business personalities, and internal staff. The report recommended a complete re-organization in 1986, which was put into effect in 1987.

Structures and procedures changed dramatically. The previous method of mutual consensus between policy and operational staff was thought to slow down decisions. The new Bank of the 1980s required speed. Policy issues were elevated. With the shift toward policy-based lending, policies required more technical sophistication, visibility, and leverage. The structures and procedures were changed to make that possible (Fig. 2).

For the first time, regional leadership was given authority to send loans to the Board without clearance from the central policy authorities. The latter could object to specific loan objectives and these objections would precipitate a formal meeting to discuss them. The purpose of the meetings would be to air differences in view and to give 'direction' for future loans. But formal clearance was not required.

The opposite was also true. Policies required comment from regional authorities, but policy itself was thought to be within the purview of 'the center' (World Bank, 1987). Adding to the new equation was the fact that the center was endowed with a new Senior Vice President for Operations. In

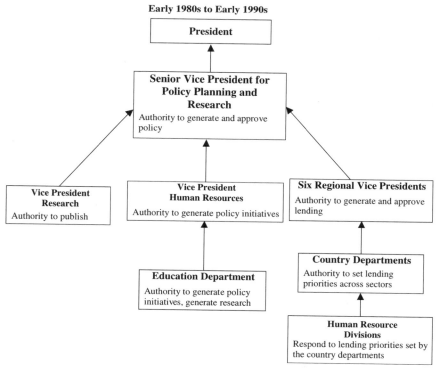

Fig. 2. World Bank Processes, Early 1980s to Early 1990s.

some ways, this new structure 'trumped' the role of the Regional Vice Presidents. Officially, Regional Vice Presidents were equivalent to a sector Vice President. However, a sector Vice President could refer a matter to a supra-authority, the Senior Vice President, and structure affected the outcome of the debates over education policy in the 1980s.

Following the publication of the Education Sector Policy Paper of 1980, Bank staff were encouraged to use the rate of return methodologies in its analytic work. This led to greater and clearer justification for primary and academic secondary education. However, the interpretation of the rate of return methods heavily influenced the content of the lending in new ways, and nowhere was this truer than in the Latin America region during the era of economic adjustment.

The crisis of Latin America came precipitously, apparently taking the industrialized countries by surprise. The 'Baker Plan' for rapid economic adjustment named after the U.S. Secretary of the Treasury was perhaps the most important event of that era. The bank's internal crisis was precipitated by a comment of James Baker noting that with its traditional emphasis on 5 year implementation cycle of development projects the World Bank was all but 'invisible', in the environment of fiscal crisis. This comment caused the Bank's management to search for a way to be a part of the solution.

The Bank's mandate required it to loan for long-term development. The mandate of the International Monetary Fund called for it to respond to fiscal crisis with rapidly disbursement (over several months for instance instead of the bank's 5 years). Since being 'invisible' was not an acceptable option, and the bank's management responded with a new category, called an Adjustment Loan, in which the Bank would advance resources in exchange for rapid changes in policy. That this category of lending might overlap with the mandate of the International Monetary Fund was worrisome, but considered of secondary importance by comparison to the scale of the fiscal crisis which adjustment operations were designed to fix.

Latin America was well-known for both poverty and inequality, and there was concern that a decline in public resources would exacerbate both. When called upon by fiscal authorities in the countries themselves, the Bank became involved in attempts, some more manifest than others, to protect public expenditures that directly benefited the poor.[18] Leaders of the health, environment, and education sectors among others, were asked which public expenditures should be included.

The education message suggested by Bank in the era of adjustment was based on the economic rate of return methodology. These results averaged across countries have been consistent from the outset (Psacharopoulos,

1973, 1980, 1985, 1990) In general the returns were higher for completing primary education than for completing secondary, and higher for completing secondary than tertiary education. Returns were higher on average for completing academic as opposed to vocational education. And returns tended to be higher in the poorer countries.

Using these findings to determine lending priorities has been more problematic than generating the research findings themselves. Nevertheless, the rate of return studies led to three common recommendations: (i) to shift public expenditures away from vocational and higher education toward academic and basic education, (ii) to increase the private cost for attending universities, and (iii) to install loan schemes to off set the financial burden on individuals who now must face high tuition fees for higher education. These three recommendations become typical of the 'short education policy menu', which emerged from the educational rate of return analyses.

The 'short education policy menu' (Patrinos & Ariasingam, 1996; Patrinos, 2000; Psacharopoulos, 1980; World Bank, 1986, 1988, November, 1991) was sometimes nested within a larger list of changes in fiscal, trade, taxation and industrial policy, and within a longer list of regulations designed to protect the poor – subsidies for food, public health, unemployment benefits, and child welfare (Stewart, 1995; Nelson, 1995; Fox & Brown, 1998; Brown & Hunter, 2000; Wood, 1986; Kardam, 1993; Ascher, 1983). Sometimes education issues were a minor ingredient of the overall macro-economic adjustment program. For this reason, the 'short education policy menu' was sometimes negotiated over the heads of the education authorities, through the Ministry of Finance instead of the Ministry of Education.

As others have observed, the effect of the adjustment era was problematic for the Bank and for the Education Sector (Samoff, 1994). With the short education policy menu the Bank acquired a reputation in some academic and NGO circles for abrogating the rights to a 'free education', and the desire to be self sufficient in higher education. Some criticisms may have served personal or narrow institutional agendas but their appearance had an important impact on how well the Bank could portray its education adjustment policies as serving the interests of the poor (Heilleiner, 1986, 1992; Biersteker, 1992; Colclough & Manor, 1991; Colclough, 1996; Hinchliffe, 1993; Ilon, 1996; International Labour Organization, 1996; Carnoy, 1995; Barnett & Finnemore, 1999).

The other side too had compelling rationales. The budgets of many countries were distorted in favor of higher and vocational education and were often determined by vested interests. These distortions created a considerable amount of inequality, where privileged families were able to garner

excessive shares of public education subsidies. The Bank had every justification to question these distortions in Latin America, Africa, and elsewhere. It is also the case that the methods for calculating the economic rates
of return are among the best for highlighting distortions in public finance.
But while the 'short education policy menu' contained considerable truth, it
did not contain all the truth.

In Asia, the Middle East, and North Africa, adjustment operations were
rare, hence the 'short education policy menu' had less impact.[19] In sub-
Saharan Africa, however, the appearance of adjustment operations and the
same short education policy menu were more common[20] and hence the
controversy more pronounced (Bennell, 1996; Chung, 1989; Mazrui, 1997;
Welch, 2000; Colclough, 1990; Buchert & King, 1995; Reimers, 1994;
Samoff, 1996, 1999; Stevenson, 1991; Berman, 1992; Craig, 1990; Woodhall,
1994; World Bank, 1994b, 1994c; 1998; Altbach, 1989).[21]

By creating a Senior Vice President for Policy, Planning, and Research,
the old system of checks and balances, so carefully constructed under
Robert McNamara, had broken down. And by coincidence placing the most
articulate proponent of the short education policy menu within the Senior
Vice President office, led to consistent objections to higher and vocational
education lending. The reaction of regional operational authorities was to
protest the constraint on their lending. Even the education staff within the
same central vice presidency often joined the views of the regional operational staff. In one instance it was suggested that no loan should be made
for higher education unless a country canceled legislation against tuition. In
a protest note, a director also within the central vice presidency objected on
grounds that many countries which borrow from the Bank have such legislation which is often derived from constitutional provisions adopted by
democratically elected governments (internal note, January, 1995).[22]

Because of the changes in structure and personnel, the higher education
policy paper was the subject of more debate than earlier papers. Since investments in higher education had lower social rates of return than investments in primary education, the executive summary of the higher education
paper included a statement that:

> Primary and secondary education will continue to be the highest priority sub-sectors in
> the Bank's education lending to countries that have not yet achieved universal literacy
> and adequate access, equity, and quality at the primary and secondary levels. In these
> countries, our involvement in higher education will continue to be mainly to make its
> financing more equitable and cost-effective, so that primary and secondary education
> can receive increased attention at the margin.
>
> (World Bank, 1994a, p. 12)[23]

Justifications for higher education lending were thus confined to efficiency and equity rationales. Quality improvement and national capacity were not included. This statement created considerable consternation particularly in sub-Saharan Africa where it was felt that the bank was artificially constraining the development objectives of the most impoverished countries.

Within the Bank, this statement raised concerns among the operations staff that the short education policy menu might be forced on the countries around the world regardless of the consequences. It raised the specter of having arbitrary authority within the Bank's structure which might work against the interests of Education Sector. Staff suspicions laid the groundwork for the confrontation over the next policy paper.

Strategies and Priorities for Education

Clearly the central education department had a daunting task. It had to summarize the experiences of all the sub-sectors, operations, and regions simultaneously. It had to accommodate for the fact that much of the developing world had changed. Latin America was rapidly democratizing. Economies in East Asia were rapidly expanding, often with private sources of development finance. Twenty-seven new borrowers from the former Soviet Union and Eastern and Central Europe were making their development needs known, and they were quite different from other the traditional 'developing' countries. These represented a very different set of circumstances from that which the Bank had faced in the 1970s and 1980s.

The task of writing the new policy paper was sometimes contradictory with the experience of many staff that had only worked on low-income countries in sub-Saharan Africa and South Asia. In the eyes of the managers from the other regions, demands had shifted. From the middle-income regions, demands were no confined to altruistic objectives such as how to create more access for girls in primary education. Many countries had over 30 years of experience since independence; others were nuclear powers and major trading partners of the industrialized nations. They were led by new generations of educational leadership concerned with new problems and questions.

In many instances their questions concerned the kinds of innovations sweeping the OECD countries – voucher systems, merit pay, site-based management, performance standards. The professional experience of many Bank education staff did not include educational debates in their own countries (Heyneman, 1997). Hence, the Bank's education sector was the object of 'adjustment' of a kind not unlike the client countries.

In spite of the storm warnings, the confrontation between the central and the regional education staff continued. One version of the sector policy paper for instance called for all higher education to be funded privately. A note from one regional spokesperson to the authors stated the case simply: take it out. It was, but in a later version regional authorities were confronted with policy recommendations, which they believed would endanger the relations with their borrowers. In a note recommending changes, one region said:

> The paper draws upon the same rate of return evidence to guide policy and future investment priorities, and that leads to catastrophe. The evidence is faulty; drawn from a few traditional borrowers; only provides a backward explanation of trends and only refers to the most simple of educational categories –primary, secondary, and higher. Because the paper relies exclusively on rates of return, it excludes other possible justifications for allocations of public finance: national interest, market failure, and equity. ...Though over one half of World Bank lending is devoted to post secondary education the paper is silent on the role of higher education. It is also silent on graduate education, adult education, pre-school education, and educational research, educational technology, and education for the handicapped. All professional education is ignored, including medical education, engineering education, law education, public administration, and the social sciences. Every single country makes public investments in these areas and it would be irresponsible to treat them in cavalier fashion. One division chief characterized the problem by saying that the paper takes us racing into the future with our face pressed firmly against the rear view mirror (internal note: November 18, 1994).

In spite of the dissent from within the Bank, the text of the paper changed very little between drafts. In the end spokespersons for four of the six regions agreed to meet privately.[24] They agreed that the publication of the new Sector Policy Paper Priorities and Strategies was likely to place regional operations at risk. They agreed that previous comments and objections had been ignored. They also agreed to draft a new set of objections to the paper's publication and to send these objections directly to their Regional Vice Presidents. In December 1994 spokespersons for East Asia, South Asia, sub-Saharan Africa, Europe and Central Asia, and the Middle East and North Africa signed parallel memoranda.[25] The problem was the short education policy menu. The Bank's Education Sector was in revolt.

The paper was eventually recast, but the result was unaltered. Even after unprecedented internal protest, the publication of the Priorities and Strategies paper led to objections and replies which had been predicted (Burnett, 1996; Burnett & Patrinos, 1996; Jones, 2000; Lauglo, 1996; Samoff, 1996, 1999; Watson, 1996).

The experience illustrates several principles. Institutions, as well as countries, are at risk of becoming distorted. If attached to unbalanced seniority, a single message can be propagated over the best professional efforts to counter it. In this instance, a single point of view, placed in a central position, propagated the Bank's short policy menu, and in so doing, led the Bank into a chorus of criticism and calls for the end of the education sector altogether.

Another principle of note is that at the time, there were no external institutions able to counter the Bank's educational position. If there had been institutions to which the Bank deferred in sector policy, the risk of distortion might have been lessened. But UNESCO was no longer in a position to command the same professional credibility as it had a decade earlier.[26] UNESCO's Cooperative Program for instance was 75% financed by the Bank hence often placing UNESCO in a position of compromise.[27] The Bank virtually had the field of education policy to itself.

Following the publication of Priorities and Strategies for Education, the Bank became engaged in a substantive internal debate over the weaknesses of the methodologies (Hammer, 1996; Heyneman, 1995, 1997), which was matched by a number of external criticisms (Colclough, 1996; Carnoy, 1995; Alexander, 1998; Bennell, 1996a, 1996b; Curtin, 1995, 1996). Like manpower forecasting 20 years earlier, the assumptions and distortions were recognized and the rate of return methodology *ex post facto* placed in its proper context. Since credibility had been lost, however, the 'final word' with respect to the short policy menu had to be expressed by a bank-sponsored, but independent, task force. Its conclusions:

The Task Force believes that traditional economic arguments are based on a limited understanding of what higher education institutions contribute. Rate of return studies treat educated people as valuable only through their higher earnings and greater tax revenues extracted by society. But educated people clearly have many other effects on society: educated people are well positioned to be economic and social entrepreneurs, having a far-reaching impact on economic and social well-being of their communities. They are also vital to creating an environment in which economic development is possible. Good governance, strong institutions, and a developed infrastructure are all needed if business is to thrive – and none of these is possible without highly educated people. Finally, rate of return analyses entirely misses the impact of university based research on the economy – a far reaching social benefit that is at the heart of any argument for developing strong higher education systems (Task Force on Higher Education and Society, 2000, p. 39)

NEW RATIONALES: ABSENT A NEW METHODOLOGY

In building consensus and motivating the education profession toward its policy messages, the costs of developing *Priorities and Strategies* outweighed the benefits. Critics suggested that the Bank had little in the way of a new message or vision, and instead was summarizing what it had been doing for decades. Policy messages were said to be inapplicable to middle-income countries.[28] However, it some thought the Bank was overly focused on the poorest countries, the paper could hardly be said to have been welcomed by the academics claiming to represent the interests of those countries.[29]

Drawing from the experience of large corporations, the Bank began to emphasize Knowledge Management (KM) (Samoff & Stromquist, 2000; Khanna, 2000; Denning, 1998; Department for Trade and Industry, 1998; Feinberg, 1986; Haas, 1990) over policy analysis. Education Knowledge Management has become integral to a general strategy of public relations. Since it can be safely nested within larger initiatives and, therefore, is less vulnerable to criticism. KM consists largely of dissemination and links to external websites, and can gain support as a public service at comparatively low cost.

But new rationales for education lending have been developing at the same time. For over 50 years there has been a steady demand to better understand what education a country should invest in, and why (McMahon, 1999). One response has been to avoid setting *ex ante* content and allocation choices; and instead to lay out a short list of policies designed to 'enable' an Education Sector to respond to public demands in the many new democracies. These enabling policies have been very creatively designed. These enabling policies include an emphasis on local and international performance standards, effective contribution to social cohesion, universal access and completion of basic education, improvements and open access to educational statistics, public debate over objectives, transparent development of policy choices and trade offs (World Bank, 1999a–d), consistent with the philosophy suggested by Gutmann (1987). These developments illustrate the fact that while there have been problems; at the same time there has been progress.

The new *ex ante* agnosticism of the Bank's current education policy frameworks is more comfortable for the country as well for the Bank's education sector. It continues, as it should, to utilize studies of external efficiency using economic rates of return analytic methods. But these studies now tend to be used to highlight problems rather than determine priorities for lending. The difference is important. No method, however, is able to adequately answer the age-old question of how much a country should invest in education and why. Until the 1990s, the standard response to this question concentrated on human capital rationales – measured by changes in productivity and differences in income.

The embarrassment over the Priorities and Strategies policy paper may help explain why the policy arm of the Bank may have retreated so far away in terms of policy substance. The quickly generated and released Education Sector Strategy paper in 1999 (World Bank, 1999a, b; World Bank, 2000), resembled a laundry list of altruistic platitudes – reasons why girls should have access to elementary education for instance. As difficult as problems are and as painful as many of the decisions to be made may be, no one is well served by avoiding the natural dilemmas associated with education and development. And as important as the new priorities may be, such as better female access to primary education, such issues can hardly be said to adequately represent the problems of education and development in an increasingly heterogeneous world where many developing countries achieved universal access long ago (Heyneman, 1995, 1997, 1999; de Siqueira, 2000).

In terms of the Bank's use of the human capital model for quantifying educational impact on development, the experience in Russia and the former Soviet Union more generally, precipitated a rethinking about its utility.[30] Due to the danger of ethnic strife, and the link between ethnic strife and civil war, the role of the school began to be seen differently (World Bank, 1995; Picciotto, 1996; Salmi, 2000; Heyneman, 1998, 2000). Though non-monetary benefits had been part of human capital reasoning from the beginning, little progress has been evident on its measurement. Today, however, a great deal of focus is on the degree to which education may contribute to social cohesion objectives of society (Heyneman, 2000).

Parliaments, the press, divergent political parties, as well as the defense and foreign policy communities have become focused on the issue of social cohesion. Concern over social cohesion issues have been raised as a priority in Latin America, Asia, and Africa (Heyneman & Todoric-Bebic, 2000). While it is true that skills and productivity matter; it is also true that the public debate has not always centered on them. Public debate often raises more important issues, even if economics has little by which to measure them. If there is a next stage in the Bank's analytic work, it will likely focus on the degree to which one might distinguish between a school or a school system which is doing a 'good job' of contributing to social cohesion from others which are not. The next stage of the bank's analytic work will place a metric on schools and school systems in performing their non-monetary functions.

CONCLUSIONS

Professionally Sound Loan Covenants

The mandate of the World Bank includes the notion that the financing is only part of its purpose; that the leveraging value of policy change is at least as important. Much of the leveraging is conducted through covenants and conditionality attached to the loans. The executive directors – the representatives of the Bank's owners – frequently take Bank staff to task if the covenants in a proposed loan are insufficient in number or severity.[31] Covenants, therefore, are a permanent part of Bank lending.

This is acceptable so long as the covenants are intelligent and professionally correct. If a loan for a power plant is required to include health, safety, and environmental regulations considered necessary and normal practice elsewhere, one can say that covenants appear intelligent and professionally correct. But what if the covenants require a country to vocationalize its curriculum? What if the covenants are based on faulty analytic techniques or unsound professional practice? What if the policy requirements recommended by the Bank and agreed to by a country are dead wrong? Who is accountable for the adverse results? Who is responsible for institutional and political controversies which poor policies inevitably generate? Who is responsible for repaying the financial resources which bad policies waste?

The first lesson of this educational history is that the Bank has been recommending faulty education policies since the beginning of the sector in 1962. This is not to suggest that all Bank education policy recommendations have been faulty; nor is it to suggest that the benefits of the lending have not been substantial. It is only to point out that poor education recommendations have a long tradition in the Bank, and thus far, no one has been able to answer the question of who is accountable.

Regaining the Balance of Power

McNamara's original concern continues. How can an organization respond rapidly to on ground demand and, at the same time, be technically and professionally sound? The balance of power between policy and operations that existed in the 1980s. In the place of quality control is a system of informal peer reviews. Each region, sometimes each country department, may create a system of review. There are guidelines but no common standards. Except for votes at the Board itself, there is no formal external review process in place. Without a strong balance of power within the Bank, and absent of a balance of power from external sources, education lending and policy are at risk of new distortions.

Avoiding Monopoly by Single Professional Interests

From the beginning, the Bank Education policy machinery has been influenced by important and powerful agendas. These endogenous pressures on the Bank are to be expected. What matters most is how they get managed. Under the MacNamara 'balance of power' organizational structure, the research, policy, and operations could challenge each other's assumptions. Such challenges were not encouraged by the later structure of the 1980s and early 1990s (Fig. 2). In this stage central policy could 'trump' all other challenges. It was in the context of this structure that the Bank could become captive of one narrow agenda, the short education policy menu. Without the necessary internal checks and balances, internal debate was stifled. Publications were released only if they reinforced *ex ante* assumptions. Even when protest emerged from a majority of the sector's operational division chiefs, objections could be bypassed.

What made the experience of the short policy menu pernicious was the fact that the agenda suddenly included all aspects of education by virtue of the claim that the Bank could speak for all public expenditures. It was inevitable therefore that the Bank would speak for expenditures in areas of education over which it had no professional experience.[32] Ministers of Education have to manage programs and priorities of which the Bank has little knowledge or experience – special education for the handicapped, new pedagogies, curricular innovations. In the 1970s, when the Bank limited its assistance to vocational education, it admitted that it had little competence in the other educational areas. Though it led to artificial biases in favor of vocational education, its institutional candor was a sign of honesty. But once the Bank began to speak for all public educational expenditures, *ipso facto*, it acquired obligations over areas of education in which it was ill prepared to understand or accept responsibility.

Every policy has a counter effects and costs. These have sometimes been under-estimated in economic models. This may hold true for policy implementation in taxation, transportation, health, and other areas. But is it also true of education. When there is a vibrant system of internal checks and balances within the system, these counter effects can be monitored and corrected; a breakdown of that system, however, may lead to extreme reactions outside the institution to which the bank will be held accountable. The key question is how to re-install a system of professional checks and balances in the making of international educational policy?

OPTIONS

Is there a way in which the Education role of the Bank can be managed so that it might continue its assistance but with a balanced sense of sector priorities?[33] Three suggestions:

Countries might decide what to analyze and who should perform the analyses

One option might be to place analytic capacity in the hands of the countries themselves. The Asian Development Bank, for instance, makes grants for the technical assistance that underpins lending.[34] The World Bank might grant monies for analytic work. Countries would request proposals just as they do for other forms of technical assistance. Bids would emerge from universities, private companies, and perhaps other public agencies, both local and international.

The World Bank might continue to sponsor analyses, but regional banks would be responsible for education lending

One recommendation of the Meltzer Commission (Meltzer Commission Report, 2000) has been to take the word 'bank' out of the World Bank. The newly renamed World Development Organization would analyze development problems and make recommendations, but the lending would be the responsibility of the regional development banks. Were the Meltzer Commission recommendations to be adopted for the Bank as a whole, it would de-link the analytic work from the lending program, and thus allow a natural set of checks and balances to occur within the countries themselves.

Education policy could be jointly decided within the U.N. system

A third suggestion would be to re-invest in the policymaking responsibility of UNESCO (Mundy, 1998, 1999). The virtue of this option would be to avoid the problems from having a monopoly over education policy. This would place professional responsibility for education policy within the institution whose terms of reference covers the full gamut of educational activities, not just the activities related to internal and external efficiency.[35] Clearly, the lesson is that efficiency is an essential element in a country's education policy. But just as clearly, no work on efficiency has been able to adequately capture the range of professional responsibilities that are a normal part of education. This is also true to for health, agriculture, industry and today, even power and telecommunications.

SUMMARY

Problems in education operations have been evident from the first activities in the early 1960s. These have been costly to developing countries. At the Bank's insistence countries over-invested in vocational and technical education. Due to the narrow definition of recurrent costs, countries ignored investments in reading materials and in maintaining teacher salaries. Later at the Bank's insistence, countries invested in thousands of workshops and laboratories that, for the most part, became useless 'white elephants'. And later, countries were forced to shift public expenditures away from higher education without any prior professional experience with the consequences to sector cohesion. That there has been wastage of significant resources is not the most important lesson for us to draw. That the Bank was negligent in these areas is not the most important lesson. One important lesson is that the world is faced with a significant new upsurge in demand for educational analysis and professional trade in ideas for education reform, and there is no single international institution with the capability to track, much less ameliorate, educational problems.

NOTES

1. The Bank generally separates analytic work into different functions: project appraisal, sector work, country economic work, regional economic work, evaluation, research on sector policy, and research on development economies. Differences concern which part of the Bank sponsors the work more than it does the content of the work, hence no distinction will be made in this paper among them.

2. Manpower forecasting was not only the preferred technique of the Bank; it was the dominant analytic rationale in UNESCO, OECD, ILO, and many other international organizations. It acted as the common analytic currency across institutions and national governments in the field of education.

3. Lewis (1969) for instance was concerned about educated employment, suggesting that a country could over invest in education. Baloch and Streeton (1963) were concerned that education that was not sufficiently 'practical' would lead to unemployment, and social protest on the part of 'school leavers.'

4. What is mentioned as part of an appraisal report and what is actually in a project, differed. University libraries were assisted in the context of engineering programs for instance. A library building could be used for purposes other than for engineering materials. But this could not be highlighted in the Project Appraisal Report in a manifest way.

5. At that time, lending for primary education was considered out of the question. In 1979 for instance, the Chief Economist for sub-Saharan Africa argued that because of the problem of 'educated unemployment,' lending for primary education was not economically justified nor did the Bank have a comparative advantage in lending for primary education. How could the Bank oversee the construction in so many different isolated locations?

6. None of the education staff in the Bank were aware that this 'practical' curriculum argument had been the subject of long and contentious debate in colonial policy (Foster, 1965; Heyneman, 1971). Had staff understood history better the Bank might have had a more 'balanced' approach to diversified curriculum and been less dogmatic in its approaches.

7. Diversified secondary education was 30–50% more expensive to construct and manage. This was not a trivial issue in countries where less than two percent of the age cohort had an opportunity to enter secondary education. Diversified secondary schools added complexities to project implementation. Between 1962 and 1980, 22% of all Bank education lending was devoted to diversified secondary education. No project had reported an underutilization of academic facilities; in reality many academic facilities were over-subscribed. No project had reported a scarcity of teachers for mathematics or science. But of the 90 education loans approved during that period, the rate of workshop utilization was only 58%. Forty percent of the loans had instituted new diversified curriculum which for some reason was found to be 'unavailable' (never implemented) at the time of completion. In 75% of the loans equipment was reported to have maintenance problems. Fifty percent had experienced problems of teacher availability, and one out of three reported a lack of materials and supplies (Heyneman, 1985a,b). In spite of these problems, metal shop, woodshop, agriculture, and domestic science for girls were considered essential

elements for developing countries across different regions and levels of absorptive capacity, and considered justified on the basis of a theory popular at that time: that the curriculum was 'practical' and socially more democratic.

8. Moral hazard is a policy of assistance to those in need which raises the risk that recipients may engage in irresponsible behavior because they know they can receive assistance if they get into trouble. Some bankruptcy laws for instance are said to raise the risk of moral hazard.

9. The number of country departments shift over time along with the responsibilities of the country manager. In general the number of regions has remained stable for 30 years. The only major change has been to combine East and West Africa into a single region and to add Europe and Central Asia as a new region.

10. Often underestimated too is the influence of the Ministry of Finance on lending priorities. Lending in all sectors must be cleared with fiscal authorities.

11. Within the Bank, county economics acts as a monopoly. Staff who allocate resources, also allocate resources to their own 'sector', that of macro-economic and adjustment lending operations. This helps explain the long-standing incongruence between the colorful and compelling Bank literature on the importance of education in economic development and the fact that education remains at only 4% of the lending portfolio.

12. This behavior of countries is not unusual. Most developing countries know very well which agency to approach for what kind of foreign assistance. They know too that in any sector, agency interests are governed by internal beliefs and priorities.

13. These appointments helped generate Staff Working papers, which questioned the necessity of laboratories to teach secondary school science and the assumptions behind small class sizes as an indicator of quality. They also generated manuals on tracer studies and school location planning, considered essential ingredients in education planning at the time.

14. This lack of awareness of alternative theories was not uniform. In general, those trained at Columbia Teachers College in History, and at Harvard in educational planning were aware of them; those trained at other universities in North America, or at universities in Europe, Latin America, or Asia, were not.

15. Popular demand for access to academic education instead of terminal vocational training was interpreted as economically dysfunctional. Those who sought academic training were thought to be seeking 'white collar' instead of 'practical' employment. Seeking more schooling was thought to be a sign of 'credentialism', seeking a credential for its own sake rather than for enhancement of one's skill and earnings. During the 1970s it was common for Bank loans to contain legal covenants, which required that a country restrict access to academic training, and instead develop terminal vocational training as an alternative. In most instances, however, Bank restrictive covenants were quickly overwhelmed by the strength of the popular demand for access to general academic skills and occupational mobility, which 20 years later, the Bank would applaud.

16. Allowing lending for reading materials illustrates the continuing history of dilemmas in another way. Once allowed in, Bank staff discovered that the textbook sector was more complex than originally anticipated; that textbook lending raised new issues of local vs. international bidding procedures, local vs. centralized control, and public vs. private provision. Where the Bank has continued to lend for gov-

ernment textbook monopolies, it has created new policy distortions that it would not have created were the Bank not allowed to loan for textbooks at all. In the end, the question is whether the benefits of having more textbooks outweigh the costs of handicapping the competitiveness of the local private publishing industry.

17. Reading education policy the World Bank has sometimes been compared to 'Kremlinology'.

18. By the end of the decade external pressure from the NGO community as well as from other development assistance agencies, forced the Bank into being more proactive with respect to protecting the poor from fiscal austerity (Cornia, Jolly, & Stewart, 1987; Jolly, 1991; George and Sabelli, 1994; Feinburg, 1961).

19. The 'short education policy menu' might have remained primarily a problem confined to Latin America and Africa if the menu's principal proponent had remained within regional operations. But the Central Vice President for Policy and Planning invited the menu's principal proponent into his office to maintain 'quality control' over lending and operations policy, and following that all lending proposals for higher and vocational education precipitated objections and all policy papers had to have a rate of return rationale. This was regarded as akin to placing the 'fox in charge of the henhouse'.

20. Policy papers were not criticized uniformly. Those on primary education (World Bank, 1990; Lockheed & Verspoor, 1991) and vocational education (World Bank, 1991), finished beforehand, received considerable praise from many of the organizations which would soon become intense critics.

21. Adjustment operations were not by any means the sole source of objections to Bank education policies. Bank papers on Higher Education and education finance were also sources of controversy in Africa.

22. The Universal Declaration of Human Rights (1948) in its Article 26 proclaims that 'elementary education shall be free'. This provision has since been included in most international legal conventions related to education. The legal conventions of course did not imply that basic education was free in fact. Fees in public elementary schools were common in the People's Republic of China, and throughout much of sub-Saharan Africa and South Asia. However, the legal issue has recently become a source of tension between the Bank and other parts of the U.N. system and particularly in those instances in which the Bank has recommended private fees in elementary education (Tomaseveski, 2000).

23. What the outside world did not know was that this statement itself had been inserted within the Office of the Senior Vice President after the final draft without approval of the regional division chiefs. Even the authors of the paper did not see the statement until after the paper had been published (personal communication, 1994).

24. Tensions over the short education policy menu were high, and to be inconspicuous, the meeting was conducted on a night walk through a park.

25. Of 26 division chiefs responsible for education, 20 signed memoranda on February 2, 1995 asking that the paper not be sent to the Board. Two others agreed with the memoranda in principle but did not wish to sign, one objected to the memoranda, and three others could not be reached.

26. UNESCO objected to the Bank's involvement in education policy from the beginning in the 1970s.

27. The World Bank actively maintained 'cooperative programs' in ILO, WHO, and UNESCO. These consisted of a department of technical staff situated in those institutions at the ready to support World Bank lending or sector work operations. These technical staff were justified on grounds their specialized skills were necessary to maintain technical quality. But being specialized the staff was more easily justified if situated within the technical U.N. agency responsible for the sector. However, tension existed from the beginning over whether their loyalties were more to the Bank than to the U.N. agency of 'their home', but these tensions appeared to be significantly more serious in the case of UNESCO than either ILO or WHO. From the Bank's side in the field of education, continual worry existed over the degree to which Cooperative Program staff at UNESCO was technically justified.

28. The paper could not be widely distributed in the Europe and Central Asia region because it appeared to suggest that their problems were the same as those in Africa and South Asia. Experience in vocational education in Eastern Europe was added to the text when findings on vocational education's low demand were consistent with ex ante assumptions; but regional evidence showing vocational education to be in high demand in ECA was not included, and in the end had to be published outside the Bank (Castro, Feonova, & Litman, 1997).

29. See, for instance, the special issue of the *International Journal for Education Development, 16*(3), 1996.

30. Much of this social cohesion theory was drawn from the earlier work in institutional economics (Olson, 1971).

31. In one instance a proposed loan to education in the education sector in Uganda following the departure of Idi Amin was rejected by the country department because there were no recommended covenants. When informed that the education system had the right management but lacked resources, the education sector was informed that poverty was an insufficient justification for lending (personal communication, 1979).

32. Due to the much reorganization, by the late 1990s most staff that worked on education had been reassigned from other sectors. Of the 400 staff assigned to Human Resources, 250 worked on education; of those only 20% (less than 50) had received any academic training in education, and only about a dozen had ever published in the field. Using staff of which only 20% had academic exposure to the field, was expected to underpin a lending program of about 2–3 billion dollars/year. This absence of professional training placed the education sector at risk of 'crowd mentality' when choosing options and priorities which had not already been approved ex ante by country economists.

33. There are a number of important recommendations in the public realm about how to restructure the World Bank. Among the most significant: (International Financial Institution Advisory Commission, 2000; Cavanagh, Wysham, & Arruda, 1994; Danaher, 1994; Williams & Young, 1994; French, 1994; Gilbert & Vines, 2000; Bergesen & Lunde 1999; Gibbon, 1993; Gore, 2000; Collier, 2000; Woods, 2000a, 2000b; Sanford, 1996).

34. The quality of donor-led technical assistance cannot be guaranteed. Since the borrower chooses the analytic work to be implemented is no guarantee that the choice will be the right one.

35. The argument against this is that UNESCO is governed by the Ministries of Education and can set its policy agenda independent of fiscal constraints. The solution may be a joint authority so that both institutions would have to agree to policy proposals which had fiscal implications.

REFERENCES

Alexander, N. (December 1998). *Paying for education: The influence of the World Bank and the IMF on education in developing countries.* Report prepared for Oxfam America. (Mimeo).

Altbach, P. (Ed.). (1989). Symposium: World Bank report on education in sub-Saharan Africa. *Comparative Education Review, 33,* 93–134.

Anderson, C. A., & Bowman, M. J. (1967). Theoretical considerations in educational planning. In: M. Blaug (Ed.), *Economics of education,* (Vol. I, pp. 351–381). Oxford: Pergamon Press.

Ascher, W. (1983). New development approaches and the adaptability of international agencies: The case of the World Bank. *International Organization, 37,* 415–439.

Balogh, T., & Streeten, P. (1968–1969). The planning of education in poor countries. In: M. Blaug (Ed.), *Economics of education,* (Vol. I, pp. 383–395). Oxford, Harmondsworth: Penguin.

Barnett, M., & Finnemore, M. (1999). The politics, power, and pathologies of international organizations. *International Organization, 53,* 699–732.

Bartholomew, D. J. (Ed.) (1976). *Manpower planning.* London: Penguin Publishers.

Becker, G. S. (1964). *Human capital: A theoretical and empirical analysis, with special reference to education.* New York: Columbia University Press.

Bennell, P. (1996a). Using and abusing rates of return: A critique of the World Bank's 1995 education sector review. *International Journal of Educational Development, 16,* 235–248.

Bennell, P. (January 1996b). Rates of return to education: Does the conventional pattern prevail in sub-Saharan Africa? *World Development, 24,* 183–199.

Bennell, P. (1996). Privatization choice and competition: The World Bank's reform agenda for vocational education in sub-Saharan Africa. *Journal of International Development, 8,* 467–487.

Bergsen, H., & Lunde, L. (1999). *Dinosaurs or dynamos? The United Nations and the World Bank at the turn of the century.* London: Earthscan.

Berman, E. (1992) Donor agencies and Third World educational development, 1945–1985. In: R. F. Arnove, P. G. Altbach, & G. P. Kelly (Eds), *Emergent issues in education: comparative perspectives.* Buffalo, NY: State University of New York Press.

Biersteker, T. (1992). The triumph of neoclassical economics in the developing world: Policy Convergence and basis of governance in the international economic order. In: J. Rosenau & E. O. Czempiel (Eds), *Governance without government* (pp. 102–131). New York: Cambridge University Press.

Blaug, M. (1970). *Economics of education: A selected annotated bibliography* (2nd ed.). Oxford, New York: Pergamon Press.

Bowman, M. J., Debeauvais, M., Komarov, V. E., & Vaizey, J. (1968). *Readings in the economics of education: A selection of articles, essays and texts from the works of economists, past and present, on the relationships between economics and education.* Paris: UNESCO.

Bowman, M. J., & Anderson, C. A. (1968). Concerning the role of education in development. In: M. J. Bowman (Ed.), *Readings in the economics of education: A selection of articles, essays and texts from the works of economists, past and present, on the relationships between economics and education* (pp. 113–134). Paris: UNESCO.

Brown, D., & Hunter, W. (February 2000). World Bank directives, domestic interests and the politics of human capital investments in Latin America. *Comparative Political Studies, 33*, 113–143.

Buchert, L., & King, K. (Eds) (1995). *Learning from experience: Policy and practice in aid to higher education.* Paris: UNESCO.

Burnett, N. (1996). Priorities and strategies for education a World Bank review: The process and the key messages. *International Journal of Educational Development, 16*, 215–220.

Burnett, N., & Patrinos, H. (1996). Response to critiques of priorities and strategies for education: A World Bank review. *International Journal of Educational Development, 16*, 273–276.

Carnoy, M. (1995). Structural adjustment and the changing face of education. *International Labour Review, 134*, 653–673.

Castro, C., de Moura, Feonova, M., & Litman, A. (1997). *Education and production in the Russian Federation.* Paris: UNESCO, International Institute of Educational Planning.

Cavanagh, J., Wysham, D., & Arruda, M. (Eds) (1994). *Beyond Bretton Woods: Alternatives to the global economic order.* London: Pluto Press.

Chung, F. C. (1989). Policies for primary and secondary education in Zimbabwe: Alternatives to the World Bank perspective. *Zimbabwe Journal of Education Research, 1*, 22–42.

Colclough, C. (1996). Education and the market: Which parts of the neo-liberal solution are correct? *World Development, 24*, 589–610.

Colclough, C. (1990). Raising additional resources for education in developing countries: Are graduate payroll taxes superior to student loans? *International Journal of Educational Development, 10*, 169–180.

Colclough, C., & Manor, J. (1991). *States of markets? neo-liberalism and the development policy debate.* Oxford: Clarendon Press.

Collier, P. (2000). Conditionality, dependence and coordination: Three current debates in aid policy. In: G. Gilbert & D. Vines (Eds), *The World Bank: Politics and structure.* Cambridge: Cambridge University Press.

Cornia, G., Jolly, R., & Stewart, F. (1987). *Adjustment with a human face.* Oxford: Clarendon Press.

Craig, J. (1990). *Comparative African experiences in implementing educational policies.* Discussion Paper 83. Washington, DC: World Bank.

Curtin, T. R. C. (June 1996). Project appraisal and human capital theory. *Social Investment, 11*, 66–78.

Curtin, T. R. C. (1995). Fallacy and fraud in human capital theory. *Papua New Guinea Journal of Education, 31*, 73–88.

Danaher, K. (Ed.) (1994). *50 Years is enough: The case against the World Bank and the International Monetary Fund.* Boston: South End Press.

De Sigueira, A. C. (2000) The World Bank: New discourses and the 1999 education sector strategy paper. Paper presented at the *Annual meeting of the comparative and international education society*, San Antonia, Texas, March 7–12, 2000.

Denning, S. (1998). *What is knowledge management?* Washington DC: World Bank.

Department for Trade and Industry. (1998). *Our competitive future: Building the knowledge-driven economy*. London: Cm 4176.

Feinberg, R. (Ed.) (1986). *Between two worlds: The World Bank's next decade*. New Brunswick, NJ: Transaction Books.

Foster, P. J. (1965). *Education and social change in Ghana*. Chicago: University of Chicago Press.

Foster, P. J. (1968). The vocational school fallacy in development planning. In: M. Blaug (Ed.), *Economics of education*, (Vol. I, pp. 396–423). Oxford: Pergamon Press.

Fox, J., & Brown, L. D. (1998). *The struggle for accountability: The World Bank, NGOs and grassroots movements*. Cambridge: MIT Press.

French, H. (1994). Chapter nine: Rebuilding the World Bank. In: L. Starke (Ed.), *State of the world*. New York: W. W. Norton and Company.

Gavin, M., & Rodrik, D. (1995). The World Bank in historical perspective. *American Economic Review, Papers and Proceedings, 85*, 329–334.

George, S., & Sabelli, F. (1994). *Faith and credit: The World Bank's secular empire*. Westview Press.

Gibbon, P. (1993). The World Bank and the new politics of aid. *European Journal of Development Research, 5*, 35–62.

Gilbert, C., & Vines, D. (2000). *The World Bank: Structures and policies*. Cambridge, Boulder: Westview Press.

Gore, C. (2000). The Rise and fall of the Washington consensus as a paradigm for developing countries. *World Development, 28*, 789–804.

Gutmann, A. (1987). *Democratic education*. Princeton: Princeton University Press.

Haas, E. B. (1990). *When knowledge is power: Three models of change in international organizations*. Berkeley: University of California Press.

Habte, A., Psacharopoulos, G., & Heyneman, S. (1983). *Education and development: Views from the World Bank*. Washington, DC: World Bank.

Hammer, J. (1996). *The public economics of education*. Mimeo: Public Economics Division, Policy Research Department, and The World Bank.

Hansen, W. L., & Weisbrod, B. A. (1969). *Benefits, costs and finance of public higher education*. Chicago: Markham Publishing Company.

Heilleiner, G. (1986). Policy-based program lending: A look at the Bank's new role. In R. Feinberg (Ed), *Between two worlds: The World Bank's next decade*. New Brunswick, NJ: Transaction Books.

Helleiner, G. (1992). The IMF, the World Bank and Africa's adjustment and external debt problems: An unofficial view. *World Development, 20*, 779–792.

Heyneman, S. P. (1987). Curricular economics in secondary education: An emerging crisis in developing countries. *Prospects XVII*, 63–74.

Heyneman, S. P. (1985a). Diversifying secondary school curriculum in developing countries: An implementation history and some policy options. *International Journal of Educational Development, 5*, 283–288.

Heyneman, S. P. (1984). Educational investment and economic productivity: The evidence from Malawi. *International Journal of Educational Development, 4*, 9–15.

Heyneman, S. P. (1985b). Investing in education: A quarter century of bank experience. *Economic Development Institute Seminar* Paper 30. Washington DC: The World Bank.

Heyneman, S. P. (1972). Platitudes in educational economics: A short list of heresies relevant to African planning. *Manpower and Unemployment Research in Africa, 5*, 31–37.

Heyneman, S. P. (1980a). *The evaluation of human capital in Malawi*. Washington DC: World Bank, Staff Working Paper, No. 420.

Heyneman, S. P. (1980b). Investment in Indian education: Uneconomic? Washington DC: World Bank, Staff Working Paper No. 327. Also appears with the same title in *World Development, 4*, 145–163.

Heyneman, S. P. (1999). Development aid in education: A personal view. *International Journal of Educational Development, 19*, 183–190.

Heyneman, S. P. (1995). Economics of education: Disappointments and potential. *Prospects (Paris), XXV*, 559–583.

Heyneman, S. P. (1997). Economic growth and the international trade in education reform. *Prospects (Paris), XXVII*, 501–530.

Heyneman, S. P. (2000). From the party/state to multiethnic democracy: Education and social cohesion in Europe and Central Asia. *Educational Evaluation and Policy Analysis, 22*, 173–191.

Heyneman, S. P., Farrell, J. P., & Sepulveda–Stuardo, M. (1978). *Textbooks and achievement: What we know.* Washington, DC: World Bank.

Heyneman, S. P., & Todoric–Bebic, S. (2000). A renewed sense for the purposes of schooling: The challenges of education and social cohesion in Asia, Africa, Latin America, Europe and Central Asia. *Prospects (Paris), XXX*, 1–23.

Hinchcliffe, K. (1993). Neo-liberal prescriptions for education finance: Unfortunately necessary or inherently desirable? *International Journal of Educational Development, 13*, 183–187.

Ilon, L. (1996). The changing role of the World Bank: Education policy as global welfare. *Policy and Politics, 24*, 413–424.

International Financial Institution Advisory Commission. (April, 2000). *The Meltzer Commission Report.* Washington DC: U.S. Government Printing Office.

International Labor Organization. (1996). Impact of structural adjustment on the employment and training of teacher. Report for discussion at the *Joint meeting on the impact of structural adjustment on educational personnel.* Geneva: ILO.

Jolly, R. (1991). Adjustment with a human face: A UNICEF record and perspective on the 1980s. *World Development, 19*, 1807–1821.

Jones, E. (2000). Increasing aid effectiveness in Africa? The World Bank and sector investment programs. In: C. Bilbert & D. Vines (Eds), *The World Bank: Structures and policies.* Cambridge: Cambridge University Press.

Jones, P. (1992). *World Bank financing of education: Lending, learning and development.* London: Routledge.

Jones, P. (1997). Review article: On World Bank education financing. *Comparative Education, 33*, 117–129.

Kardam, N. (1993). Development approaches and the role of policy advocacy: The case of the World Bank. *World Development, 21*, 1773–1786.

Khanna, A. (2000). *Knowledge creation and management in global enterprises.* Washington, DC: World Bank.

Lauglo, J. (1996). Banking on education and the uses of research a critique of World Bank priorities and strategies for education. *International Journal of Educational Development, 16*, 221–233.

Levin, H. (1983). *Cost effectiveness: A primer.* Beverly Hills: California: Sage.

Lewis, W. A. (1969). Education and economic development. In: M. J. Bowman (Ed.), *Readings in the economics of education: A selection of articles essays and texts from the works of economists, past and present, on the relationships between economics and education* (pp. 135–147). Paris: UNESCO.

Lockheed, M., & Verspoor, A. (1991). *Improving primary education in developing countries.* Washington DC: Oxford University Press for the World Bank.

Mazrui, A. (1997). World Bank: The language question and the future of African education. *Race and Class, 38*(3), 35–48.

McMahon, W. (1999). *Education and development: Measuring the social benefits.* New York and Oxford, England: Oxford University Press.

Meltzer Commission. (2000, March). *International financial institution advisory commission.* Report to Congress.

Mundy, K. (1998). Educational multilateralism and world (dis)order. *Comparative Education Review, 42*, 448–478.

Mundy, K. (1999). Educational multilateralism in a changing world order: UNESCO and the limits of the possible. *International Journal of Educational Development, 19*, 27–52.

Nelson, P. (1995). *The World Bank and NGOs: The limits of a political development.* New York: St. Martin's.

Olson, M., Jr. (1971). *The logic of collective action: Public goods and the theory of groups* (Revised ed.). New York: Schocken Books.

Patrinos, J., & Ariasingam, D. L. (1996). *Decentralization of education: Demand side financing.* Washington, DC: The World Bank.

Patrinos, H. (2000). Market forces in education. *European Journal of Education, 35*, 61–80.

Picciotto, R. (November, 1996). *What is education worth? from production function to institutional capital.* Washington, DC: HCO Working Paper World Bank.

Psacharopoulos, G. (1990). *Why educational policies can fail: An overview of selected African experiences.* Discussion Paper 82. Washington, DC: World Bank.

Psacharopoulos, G. (1973). *Returns to education: An international comparison.* Amsterdam: Elsevier Scientific Publishing.

Psacharopoulos, G. (1980). *Higher education in developing countries: A cost-benefit analysis.* World Bank staff working paper No. 440. Washington, DC: World Bank.

Psacharopoulos, G. (1985). Returns to education: A further international update and implications. *The Journal of Human Resources, 20*, 583–604.

Psacharapoulos, G., & Loxley, W. (1985). *Diversified secondary education and development: Evidence from Columbia and Tanzania.* Baltimore: Johns Hopkins University Press for the World Bank.

Psacharopoulos, G., & Woodhall, M. (1985). *Education for development: An analysis of investment choices.* New York: Oxford University Press.

Reimers, F. (1994). Education and structural adjustment in Latin America and subSaharan Africa. *International Journal of Educational Development, 14*, 119–129.

Salmi, J. (2000). *Violence, democracy and education: An analytical framework.* LCSHD Paper Series, Department of Human Development, Latin America and Caribbean Regional Office. Washington DC: The World Bank.

Samoff, J. (Ed). (1994). *Coping with crisis: Austerity adjustment and human resources.* London.

Samoff, J. (1996). Which priorities and strategies for education? *International Journal of Educational Development, 16*, 1–27.

Samoff, J. (1999). Institutionalizing international influence. In: R. Arnove & C. Torres (Eds), *Comparative education: The dialectic of the global and the local.* Lanham: Rowman and Littlefield.

Samoff, J., & Stromquist, N. P. (2000). Knowledge banks: Promises and problems. Paper presented at the *Comparative and International Education Society*, San Antonio.

Sanford, J. (1996). Alternative ways to fund the international development association (IDA). *World Development, 25,* 297–310.

Schultz, T. (1961). Investment in human capital. *American Economic Review, 51,* 1–17.

Schultz, T. (1981). *Investing in people: The economics of population quality.* Berkeley: University of California Press.

Schultz, T. (1959). Investing in man: An economist's view. *The Social Service Review, 33,* 109–117.

Stewart, F. (1995). *Adjustment and poverty.* New York: Routledge.

Task Force on Higher Education and Society. (2000). *Higher education in developing countries: Perils and promise.* Washington, DC: The World Bank.

Tomasevski, K. (August 2000). *Annual report of the special rapporteur on the right to education.* U.N. Commission on Human Rights Resolution 2000/9.

Vaizey, J. (1968). What some economists said about education. In: M. J. Bowman (Ed.), *Reading in the economics of education: A selection of articles, essays and texts from the works of economists, past and present, on the relationships between economics and education* (pp. 50–58). Paris: UNESCO.

Wapenhans, W. (1992). *Report on the task force on portfolio management.* Washington, DC: World Bank.

Watson, K. (1996). Banking on key reforms for educational development: A critique of the World Bank review. *Mediterranean Journal of Educational Studies, 1,* 41–61.

Welch, A. (2000). *Third world education: Quality and equality.* New York: Garland.

Williams, P. (1975). Education in developing countries: The view from mount olympus. In: P. Williams (Ed.), *Prescription for progress? A commentary on the education policy of the World Bank* (pp. 20–40). Windsor, Berks: The NFER Publishing Company.

Williams, D., & Young, T. (1994). Governance, the World Bank and liberal theory. *Political Studies, 42,* 84–100.

Windham, D. (May, 1975). The macro planning of education: Why it fails why it survives the alternatives. *Comparative Education Review, 19,* 187–201.

Woodhall, M. (1994). The effects of austerity on adjustment in the allocation and use of resources. In: J. Samoff (Ed.), *Coping with crisis austerity, adjustment and human resources* (pp. 173–202). Paris: UNESCO/ILO.

Woods, N. (2000a). The Challenge of Good Governance for the IMF and the World Bank Themselves. *World Development, 28,* 823–841.

Woods, N. (2000b). The challenges of multilateralism and development. In: G. Gilbert & D. Vines (Eds), *The World Bank: Politics and structure.* Cambridge: Cambridge University Press.

Wood, R. (1986). *From Marshall plan to debt crisis: Foreign aid and development choices in the world economy.* Berkeley, CA: University of California Press.

World Bank (1963). *Proposed bank/IDA policies in the field of education.* Washington, DC: World Bank.

World Bank (1970). *Lending in education.* Washington, DC: World Bank.

World Bank (1971). *Education sector working paper.* Washington, DC: World Bank.

World Bank (1972). *World Bank operations: Sectoral programs and policies.* Baltimore: Johns Hopkins University Press.

World Bank (1974). *Education sector working paper.* Washington, DC: World Bank.

World Bank (1980). *Education sector policy paper.* Washington, DC: World Bank.

World Bank (1986). *Financing education in developing countries: An exploration of policy options.* Washington, DC: World Bank.

World Bank (1987). *A guide to institutional changes: The World Bank reorganization 1987.* Washington, DC: World Bank.

World Bank (1988). *Education in sub-Saharan Africa: Policies for adjustment, revitalization and expansion.* Washington, DC: World Bank.

World Bank (1990). *Primary education: A World Bank policy paper.* Washington, DC: World Bank.

World Bank (November 1991). *Adjustment lending and the education sector.* Washington: World Bank.

World Bank (1991). *Vocational and technical education and training: A World Bank policy paper.* Washington, DC: The World Bank.

World Bank (1994a). *Adjustment in Africa: Reforms, results and the road ahead.* Washington, DC: The World Bank.

World Bank (1994b). *Higher education: The lessons of experience.* Washington, DC: World Bank.

World Bank (1994c). *The World Bank's role in human resource development in sub-Saharan Africa: Education, training and technical assistance.* Operations Evaluation Department, Sector Study. No. 13449, 06/01/94. Washington, DC: World Bank.

World Bank (1995). *Priorities and strategies for education.* Washington, DC: World Bank.

World Bank (1998). *Assessing aid: What works, what doesn't, and why.* Washington, DC: World Bank.

World Bank (1999a). *Education and training in East Asia and Pacific Region.* Washington, DC: World Bank, Human Development Network East Asia and Pacific.

World Bank (1999b). *Education in the Middle East and North Africa: A strategy towards learning for development.* Washington, DC: World Bank Group, Human Development Middle East and North Africa.

World Bank (1999c). *Education sector strategy.* Washington, DC: World Bank.

World Bank (1999d). *Educational change in Latin America and the Caribbean.* Washington, DC: The World Bank.

World Bank (2000). *Hidden challenges to education systems in transition economies.* Washington, DC: World Bank, Europe and Central Asia Region, Human Development Sector. A

World Bank/OED (1999a). *Annual review of development effectiveness.* Operations Evaluation Department Report 19905. Washington, DC: The World Bank.

World Bank/OED (1999b). *sub-Saharan Africa: Lessons from four sectors.* Precis Number 182, Operations Evaluation Department, 05/01/99. Washington, DC: The World Bank.

IMPLEMENTING EDUCATIONAL TRANSFORMATION POLICIES: INVESTIGATING ISSUES OF IDEAL VERSUS REAL IN DEVELOPING COUNTRIES ✩

Diane Brook Napier

INTRODUCTION

Most comparative education research has included investigation of dimensions of educational reform but not all research in the field has focused
concertedly on reform in relation to the realities in practice. In the latter half
of the 20th century comparativists underscored the need to investigate implementation issues, not just reform policies, as had often been the case in
earlier comparative research, since time had shown that political processes
did not always equate with educational outcomes. Reforms can be thwarted

✩ The author wishes to acknowledge the contributions of Dr. John van der Vyver to many of
the training and research projects in South Africa referred to herein. John van der Vyver was
Senior Lecturer at Soweto College of Education, then served as a Senior Administrator in the
Gauteng Department of Education until his death in 2002. He devoted most of his career to the
design and implementation of democratization programs in schools and teacher training colleges.

Global Trends in Educational Policy
International Perspectives on Education and Society, Volume 6, 59–98
Copyright © 2005 by Elsevier Ltd.
ISSN: 1479-3679/doi:10.1016/S1479-3679(04)06003-7

altogether, significantly modified or mediated in practice, embraced with qualification, or differentially implemented across regions or levels within a given country. Reform implementation might produce intended and unintended change (for better or for worse); or no change at all might be the outcome; or change might occur ahead of reform. Some of the most fascinating findings in comparative research are dichotomous considerations of change such as policy versus practice, ideal versus real, de facto change versus de jure change, intended and unintended outcomes of reform, grassroots (bottom–up) versus centralized (top–down) reforms, and de facto change legitimized-after-the-fact through reform or new policy.

Consequently, there is reason to consider actualities as well as what is intended in reform but also to examine dilemmas of why education is so hard to change, why reforms are often so hard to implement, whether one can seriously consider reforms outright successes or failures, whether educational change is reformist or revolutionary (or if it can be both), and what factors facilitate or obstruct reform implementation. Several leading comparativists such as Ginsburg (1991) and Reimers and McGinn (1997) have argued thus. The world's disadvantaged countries face particularly acute and complex challenges in enacting educational change because they suffer from complicating factors of context and history. In turn, this makes for special research challenges if one sincerely wishes to understand if and how reform works in reality to produce beneficial change.

The purpose of this chapter is twofold: first, focusing on key aspects of the study of reform implementation by comparative educationists to date, *to review where we have been and what we have done, with special reference to research on reform implementation in developing countries*; and second, *to contemplate what is needed and what we should reconsider in future research* as we proceed into the new millennium in which contemporary issues and needs may be different to those in past decades.

Within this general purpose, the overriding theme of the chapter is to investigate the connections between the ideal and the real educational transformation policies in developing countries, and to reflect on the range of facilitating and blocking factors that shape the course of policy implementation, as documented in research. Following an overview of ways in which policy is generally implemented in developing countries, the theoretical framework for the arguments and illustrations in the remainder of the chapter is offered in a brief overview of several comparative education models most useful for understanding the special considerations of reform implementation in developing countries. A selection of cases in point illustrate how reform results in developing countries have been viewed variously as being failures, as being successes, or as having mixed results. The case of South African educational transformation is highlighted as it epitomizes the complexities of reform implementation and it illustrates vividly how the global – local continuum exists with processes such as lending and borrowing (of foreign reform ingredients) and creolization shaping the connections between ideal and real transformation. After considering what the field contains in abundance with regard to reform implementation in developing countries, the discussion returns to the question of viewing reform implementation as success, failure, or otherwise. The chapter concludes with a challenge to scholars based on recommendations by leaders in the field and on the author's own experiences as a researcher focusing on reform implementation issues in developing countries.

PROCESSES OF IMPLEMENTING EDUCATIONAL REFORM IN DEVELOPING COUNTRIES

Educational reform in developing countries has generally been fashioned with broad considerations of development in mind. These became the focus of much comparativist research investigating the relationships between education and national development; reforms for improving the quality of education in any country; the institutionalization of global education policies such as the building of mass education systems and addressing the goal of "education for all" or EFA (see, for example, Chabbott & Ramirez, 2000; Chowdhury, 1984; Dorsey, 1989; Haddad, 1990; Kafula, 2001; UNESCO, 1978, 1979) and the provision of basic education or "universal primary education" or UPE (Johanson, 1987; World Bank, 1995). Periodically there was a call for scholars to return to a general "common purpose," to study how educational reforms address pressing needs regardless of the particular settings or issues under study. For instance Thompson, Shaw, and Bane (2000) urged comparativists to examine social exclusion, education for citizenship, and lifelong learning needs. Arnove (1992), Kelly and Altbach (1986), and Paulston (1975, 1976) were among those who noted the variety of methodologies, theoretical perspectives, and ideological orientations in comparative research investigating reform policies, implementation processes, and the issues associated with these.

In general terms, all countries undertaking reform encounter suites of facilitating factors as well as blocking factors or obstacles that influence the reform implementation process, as well as sets of contradictions and dilemmas inherent in education and the wider society. However, in developing countries dilemmas in and obstacles to reform are among the variables that demand scrutiny of the special circumstances of educational reform implementation. It has become evident from the past record that research on reform implementation in developing countries and post-colonial states presents a problematic. One needs to consider *first* the reform source, since reforms or programs are often imported from or imposed by dominant countries, and *then* one needs to consider the implementation issues relative to needs and realities on the ground that are often complicated by factors such as poverty, disadvantage, corruption, neocolonial domination, foreign debt, and rapidly growing populations.

The discussion in this chapter is framed with an eclectic theoretical perspective since the research given overview encompasses a variety of orientations and perspectives from traditional structural functionalist to post-structuralist and critical. In general, because the overwhelming majority of developing countries had centralized educational systems imposed by colonial powers, with many centralized structures retained even after independence, it is necessary to consider how reform policies are implemented in largely top–down fashion even in the face of decentralization initiatives, at the same time as considering the specific features of the reform. Several theoretical models, explanations of reform processes, and general ways of thinking about educational transformation inform the arguments presented here. They illustrate how facilitating and blocking factors, and processes such as creolization, operate in reform implementation in developing countries, producing a complex array of mixed results and relatively rare cases of unequivocal "success" or "failure". In the following overview, eight explanations of reform processes are presented as most useful for understanding the often-torturous path of converting policymaking into practice, as illustrated by the cases in this chapter.

Some schools of thought about development and educational endeavors have been prevalent in educational policymaking and practice. First, the human capital approach to development (Shultz, 1966) has been widely employed in educational and other development policies, in structural adjustment, and aid programs funded by the World Bank and other organizations. Second, the linear input–output "factory model" of educational production (Johnson, 1967) that still today dogs the debate over what is needed to improve education in any country, also became a prevalent way of thinking about education in developing countries. Thinking about education along these lines remains an important underlying stratum in developing countries.

Several step-wise models have proven most helpful in illustrating how reform implementation works in any country; and they pertain to the arguments and cases in this chapter. Goodlad's (1984) cascading model of educational processes and the manner in which top–down reforms move from the ideological or policy level down to the formal-, perceived-, experiential-, and operational levels are useful in understanding frustrated reform efforts in developing countries. The model demonstrates how critical components such as teacher training and support (that are chronically inadequate in reform programs) can scuttle a reform initiative and the manner in which reforms can be blocked at lower structural levels in predominantly centralized systems. In similar vein, Reimers and McGinn (1997) offered a multiple-stage process model designed to inform reform policy using research and to demonstrate where reform can go wrong and Lindahl (1998) explained an eight-step process of implementing reforms in Cuba.

Ginsburg, Cooper, Raghu, and Zegarra (1990) synthesized various scholars' explanations of reform in a four-part model of national- and global level equilibrium approaches contrasted with national- and global level conflict approaches. This scheme of thinking is helpful in viewing the spread of reform efforts in developing countries as collective explanations of how reforms are precipitated and how the implementation process unfolds whether one views these from an equilibrium or a conflict perspective. The model contains elements that shed light on a host of ideal – real connections in developing countries mentioned in this chapter and on the complexities of educational change that can be both reformist and revolutionary (in different aspects) within the same country.

The sources of reform ideas in developing countries are important to consider if one is concerned with the connections between ideal and real reform. Hence, the arguments in this chapter are informed by comparativists' accounts of how education systems around the world became standardized with uniform features largely based on the Napoleonic model, how Western style democracy came to influence many education systems, and how countries engaged in processes of lending and borrowing of educational ideas and practices (Kelly & Altbach, 1982; McGinn & Cummings, 1997; Ramirez & Boli-Bennett, 1982).

Pressures for reform in developing countries also need to be viewed against the late 20th century popularity of cross-national comparisons of educational achievement measured on standardized tests such as in the IEA Civic Education and TIMSS studies (Torney-Purta, Lehmann, Oswald, & Schulz, 2001). The phenomenon exerts pressure on developing countries to participate, lest they be left behind. Developing countries have also been impacted by the urge to identify what "works" in high performing countries, to adopt the ingredients of a "world class school system" (for instance Chalker & Haynes, 1994) that can be used to "fix" educational problems elsewhere. Theissen, Achola, and Boakari (1986) were among several scholars who argued against cross-national comparisons because of the underlying problems of comparing "apples to oranges" particularly if comparing developed with developing countries and because of the inability of standardized tests to reflect contextual factors within countries. However, reform ingredients remain significantly colored by this version of comparative thinking and by tendencies to borrow or import ideas from abroad.

Given these patterns of global educational standardization, convergence, and wholesale lending and borrowing of reform ingredients, a family of universal reform targets appears in the reform agendas of countries worldwide, whatever their level of development. They exist in contextually shaped local forms and in different combinations within countries as threads and themes in educational policy and practice. They include considerations of content; method; technology development and use; teacher issues, numbers, and statistics in many forms; teacher–administrator relations; funding and budget issues; community–school relations; societal/national needs in relation to education; the role of government in education in terms of centralization; and decentralization processes. As illustrated in the cases in this chapter, these reform targets in developing countries amount to ambitious sets of feasible, and sometimes idealistic, plans.

A final theoretical consideration that underlies and informs the substance of this chapter is that of world culture theory and the global – local continuum. These ideas have assumed an important place in comparative scholarship as global priorities for school reform were translated into programs within countries, and as they became "creolized" and hybridized into a variety of recognizable and unrecognizable forms at the intermediate and local levels. Consideration of reform implementation from this standpoint in any country, but perhaps particularly in developing countries, provides a powerful vehicle for understanding the contortions of implementation, as illustrated in the studies compiled by Arnove and Torres (2003) and Anderson-Levitt (2003). Further, Astiz, Wiseman, and Baker (2002) offered commentary on the issues associated with the global push for decentralization and the varieties of national adoption that variously impact educators at the local level. The case of South Africa, highlighted later in this chapter, provides a clear-cut illustration of the global – local continuum and of creolization processes at work. Taken in combination, the preceding theories and explanations of how reform policies are conceived and implemented provide useful perspective for the discussion to follow, in which the varied story of reform implementation in developing countries is considered in light of facilitating and blocking factors that lead to a rich mix of outcomes.

SPECIAL CONSIDERATIONS OF EDUCATIONAL REFORM IN DEVELOPING COUNTRIES

Developing countries are variously called lesser developed countries (LDCs), pre-industrial states, industrializing countries, post-colonial states, third/fourth/fifth world countries, or semi-peripheral and peripheral states (Gomes, 1996). Although post-Communist states in eastern European share many problems with developing countries despite the fact that they are considered relatively developed, "Second World" industrialized countries, these countries are not included in this discussion.

Although all countries face similar sets of issues in educational reform as noted previously, these reform targets or challenges manifest themselves in quite different ways in developing countries in large part due to the paucity of facilitating factors and the plethora of inhibiting or blocking factors. Facilitating factors, often noted as elements of "success" of educational reforms, include but are not limited to supply and availability of funding, resources, public support, and training programs; homogeneous target populations or communities; single language populations; infrastructure; enabling administrative structures; consultation mechanisms; availability of current data; and mechanisms for organizational learning (see, for example, Abdel Halim & Shaker, 1979; Brook, 1996a; Reimers & McGinn, 1997).

Obstacles to reform are a prominent theme in reform research worldwide but developing countries face *aggravated* challenges and constraints such as resistance by teachers, communities, stakeholders; inadequate resources; uneven or inequitable distribution of funding and resources, uneven regional and subregional development levels; urban–rural differentials in needs and capacity; heterogeneity in language, ethnicity, and disadvantaged groups/ populations; rapidly expanding populations; geographic isolation; conflicting stakeholder groups; corruption; internal or regional ethnic conflict, even genocide; competing human resource development needs in housing, education, water supply, and healthcare sectors; lack of capacity; undeveloped or ill-maintained infrastructure; cultural context factors that are overlooked or ignored; financing dilemmas linked to external debt and control by donor agencies; lack of comparative advantage in trade; and dependence on and exploitation by multinational corporations, more powerful states, or former colonial powers. These constraints hamper the wherewithal of developing countries to enact reform and development projects as highlighted in reports by Brook (1996a), Haddad (1980), Jansen (1990), Johanson (1987), Johnson (1995), and Marais (1995) in African countries; Spalding (1990) in Mongolia and Laos; Karagozoglu (1991) in Turkey; and Miller (1987) on general issues. Other research highlighting the common issues but the different contexts for reform in developed- and developing countries, includes that by Attah-Safoh (1982), Blaug (1977), Canales, Gomez, and Villenueva (1995), Gill and Alvarez de Testa (1995), and UNESCO (1978, 1997).

Very small countries, island states, and archipelago states have their own special problems by virtue of factors such as geographic isolation or fragmentation, small populations or physical size, paucity of resources, neocolonial dependence, and poverty levels, as portrayed in the work by Bray (1996) in Bhutan, Palmer (1979) on the Solomon Islands, Fergus (1991) on the reform challenges facing "microstates" in the Caribbean, London (2003) on reform issues in Trinidad and Tobago, Schmitz and Pono (1995) on Micronesia, and Tavana (1997) on Western Samoa. Conversely, very large countries like China face their own problems of distance and regional differences exacerbated by inadequate infrastructure (Bhola, 1994; Hannum, 2003).

Developing countries face particularly acute contradictions and dilemmas as they enact reforms to improve, modernize, and democratize education. These include tensions between seemingly contradictory goals including *quality* (standards, performance levels) *and quantity* (delivery levels, accessibility); *centralization* (top–down administration and control) *and decentralization* (devolution of some authority and control to regional or local levels, local choice); *local needs* (micro-level, in communities, schools) *versus national* goals (for the nation, overall); *internal needs* (specific to local and regional factors and capacity levels) *versus imported ideas* (global trends such as in technology and outcomes based systems); *teacher problems* (untrained teachers, dependence on expatriate teachers, surplus/shortage) *versus high teacher/pupil ratios; neocolonialism* (sustained dependence) *versus independence* (that requires capacity); *equity* (such as in resource allocation and use) *versus local autonomy* (that can lead to sustained inequity); and *continuity* (selective traditional cultural revival, stability) *versus change* (modernization, progress). Economic and political realities often dictate which forces prevail, and hence disadvantage in a developing country makes for vulnerability to a variety of forces such as financing, external aid and influences, corruption, and compromised outcomes of reforms. Whole programs or policies can exist in a seemingly contradictory relationship, such as in reforms for centralization and for decentralization that operate within the same country but that impact different levels or different spheres, as illustrated in research in South Africa by Brook Napier (2003a) and Brook Napier, Lepata, and Zungu (2000), and elsewhere by Cummings (1992), Evans (1977), Hanson (1989), and Johanson (1987).

Riddell (1998) summarized the themes prevalent in educational reform research in developing countries during the late 20th century as planning/ management and efficiency reforms, quality reforms, and curricular reforms. The goal of "education for all" or EFA for universal compulsory education emerged as a prominent focus for reform and research in post-colonial and other developing countries (Chabbott & Ramirez, 2000; Chowdhury, 1984; Paulston & Rippberger, 1990; UNESCO 1977, 1978). The 1991 World Conference on "Education for All" held in Zambia established principles for relevant, practical, basic education, becoming the basis of entire new reform programs in countries such as Zambia to replace academically focused reforms that had failed previously (Kafula, 2001). Similarly, the use of educational reform as a national development strategy was the focus for many scholars including Arnove (1992), Cheng (1999), Franke and Chasin (1994), Lee and Kim (1991), Paulston (1975), and Saif (1987). Research on the uses of educational reform to further the goals of socialism or democracy, therefore to effect sociopolitical and ideological transformation (linked to economic development) has also been prevalent for example in work by Cummings and Altbach (1997), Fass et al. (1991), Ginsburg (1991), Kazi (1991), Mtonga (1993), and Paulston (1975).

Education programs specifically tailored to basic needs and development of village-level practical skills, particularly in rural areas, have taken several forms including "education with production" or EWP (Haddad, 1990; World Bank, 1995); "education for self reliance or ESR (Saunders & Vulliamy, 1983), and "education for copeability" (Attah-Safoh, 1982). Some research has focused specifically on the address of human rights and the development of identity or self actualization in reform programs, for example in education for human rights in Sri Lanka (Asian-South Pacific Bureau of Adult Education, 1993; Adams & Chen, 1981); "popular education" in several Latin American countries (van Dam, 1992); and ethno-national questions and political socialization programs in Pakistan (Kazi, 1991).

The workings of bureaucracy and the issues associated with particular educational delivery systems (public, private, NGOs; formal, informal) are

other dimensions with special significance in developing countries (see, for
examples, Arnove, 1992; Cummings, 1992, Altbach, 1993; and Fuentes &
Elizandro Y Carr, 1993) as are alternative forms of education such as distance education in varying forms across countries (Sharma, 1997) and
community colleges (Attah-Safoh, 1982). Teacher education issues are very
common in research in developing countries for example in work by
Chapman (1991), Dzvimbo (1989) on Zimbabwe, Bryson (1978) on Cameroon, and Saif (1987) on Bahrain. Stromquist (1994) provided an overview
of educational issues in urban areas and how these differ across countries.
Girls' versus boys' education, girls' education issues, diversity issues in
general, and notions such as popular education linked to identity and self
actualization have also appeared increasingly in recent decades as critical
perspectives became more prevalent, such as in the work of Bryson (1978) in
Cameroon; Mehran (2003) in the Islamic Republic of Iran, and Hannum
(2003) in China, Lloyd, El Tawila, Clark, and Mensch (2003) in Egypt, and
in an overview by the World Bank (1995).

In developing countries one cannot undertake study of educational transformation and development in isolation from the precolonial-, colonial-,
and post-colonial legacies. Similarly, one could not sensibly examine post-
communist states without considering the communist and pre-communist
historical legacies in these countries. Nor is it reasonable to ignore notions
of core-periphery in terms of the country's indebtedness to-, influence by-,
and dependence on core industrial and post-industrial powers and former
mother countries.

Reforms and their implementation in post-colonial states are obviously
significantly colored by contextual factors related to colonialism including
sustained dependence on the former mother country or on other dominant
states, neocolonialism, and inadequate capacity to become fully independent
and self-sustaining. In many post-colonial states, there has been selective
retention of colonial institutional structures, and reformed or modernized
educational delivery systems might be seen as perpetuating the system of
standardized mass education inherited from the colonial era. At the same
time there might be the emergence of a new or reshaped educational system
linked to the creation of a new post-colonial nation state or other political
entity.

Colonial roots and influences can be at odds with indigenous needs in
reform programs, as occurred in the Philippines (Doronila, 1997), Zambia
(Lulat & Clarke, 1982; Muyebaa, 2001), Micronesia (Schmitz & Pono,
1995), and Western Samoa (Tavana, 1997). Centuries-old non-formal educational traditions are sometimes ignored in the course of new reforms being

implemented, as reported by Lynch (1992) in Sudan's reforms that ignored Muslim traditions while seeking to modernize education beyond the British colonial system. Milligan (2003) offered the example of tensions between Islamic and Christian religious traditions and their educational implications in the Southern Philippines. Thus, the mix of retained colonial system elements and new elements (themselves often borrowed from elsewhere) in many developing countries makes for challenging investigations of transformative education processes in which one has to sort out what is borrowed, what is truly new and homegrown or indigenized, or what is held over from the past.

Since so many of the world's colonial states inherited centralized systems of education that were installed by the colonizers, issues of decentralization linked to democratization and modernization are very common. Comparative research in developing countries frequently focuses on the broad processes of *democratization or modernization* that do not appear on the list of reform targets in most developed and western countries. Educational "transformation" and "national development" tend to be the terms applied to huge reform undertakings in developing countries or in new democracies. The range of issues pertaining to decentralization in various countries is illustrated in the work of Astiz et al. (2002) considering centralization–decentralization interrelationships in a score of countries, Cummings (1988) on the Basic Research and Implementation in Developing Educational Systems (BRIDGES) projects in Sri Lanka and elsewhere, Bjork (2003) on local responses to decentralization policy in Indonesia, and the work of Brook Napier (2003a) on decentralization policies and centralized thinking in South Africa.

American- and other dominant country influences are a related major consideration in developing countries, particularly given the historical colonial legacy and the global convergence of ideas and reform strategies. For instance, the dilemmas associated with promoting Western, or American-style development, while preserving traditional indigenous culture and identity, were examined in Taiwan by Lee and Kim (1991). Neocolonialism and American influences in Micronesia were documented by Schmitz and Pono (1995); Attah-Safoh (1982); and Plank and Adams (1989) offered additional illustrations and Thomas (1997) argued why American consultants need to observe participants' needs when conducting evaluation or research projects.

Contemporary societal issues and needs compound the problems associated with the historical context. These might include new forms of status quo and corruption and cross-sector development dilemmas that create severe competition for resources. Globalization processes add still other pressures on developing countries, for instance in the drive to keep pace with global developments in technology and information-age priorities. Indigenization or localization of curriculum and programs, as well as of the workforce (such as in reducing dependence on expatriate teachers) and creation of post-colonial national identity and to individual/group identities are other distinguishing features of reform in post-colonial states. Some illustrations of these aspects can be found in the work of Tsodzo (1997) in Zimbabwe, Basabas-Ikegucchi (1991) on the issue of "relevant education" in the Philippines; Merryfield and Tlou (1995) on indigenizing social studies in several African states and Brook and Brook (1993) in Somalia; and Brook (1991) on multicultural education in South Africa. Teacher education issues in general feature prominently in research in developing countries because of the added complications of context and capacity that manifest themselves in reforms targeting this sub-sector. Obstacles to improving education often feature as teacher-related issues as discussed by Brook (1996a, b), Brook Napier et al., 2000, Chapman (1991), and Samoff (1998, 1999).

Many educational reform and modernization programs in developing countries were modeled on what were perceived to be important global trends and innovations in developed countries, or in other developing countries. Here, the global – local continuum of reform and implementation takes on special meaning. For instance, outcomes based education (OBE) innovations introduced in Zambia were heavily influenced by similar programs introduced in the neighboring post-colonial states of Malawi, Botswana, and Uganda that had been fashioned on principles of OBE adopted in England, Finland, and the Netherlands (Kafula, 2001). Similarly, in South Africa, OBE reforms were based on ideas adopted from programs in the United States, New Zealand, Canada, and the United Kingdom, many of which had become outmoded and criticized in their countries of origin and their wholesale adoption in the South African context created implementation difficulties in abundance, as described by Brook Napier (2003a). Additional illustrations were compiled by Anderson-Levitt (2003).

Questions of financing are ubiquitous in educational reform, but in developing countries these are frequently linked to complex relationships with donor agencies and dominant countries whose money plays an integral role in financing reform of delivery systems in education and other human resource development sectors such as health (Albrecht & Ziderman 1992; Heath, 1998; Kent, 1995; World Bank, 1998). Financing of higher education reform has received much attention in research in developing countries, for instance in Indian higher education reform and the question of context validity (Tilak, 1997), in African higher education financing (Saint, 1992), and in questions of cross-sector development programs attacking poverty and education in Uganda and other African countries (World Bank, 1996). Aid and development programs contain special implications for developing countries wherein strings are attached to donor funds and priorities are often externally determined, out of line with real needs on the ground. As many countries adopt fiscal decentralization policies, local community resource issues play an important role in educational provision and in possibly perpetuating stratification or inequity, as argued by Hannum (2003) in the case of rural China.

The viability of alternative forms of education such as distance education, vocational-technical education, agricultural/vocational programs and community colleges also finds a key place in the literature, illustrating dominant country influences and the global convergence of ideas, as well as indigenous needs as developing countries seek to address internal demands for relevant education as illustrated by Attah-Safoh (1982), Hu (1996), Palmer (1979), and Sharma (1997). Alternative delivery systems such as distance education and NGO programs are often also underdeveloped, or they might be the only viable means of access to education in remote areas of developing countries.

Reforms and realities associated with particular levels of education are yet another common thread in research, in higher education, basic education, and primary education. Underdeveloped secondary and higher education levels are a chronic problem. The goal of universal primary education has yet to be attained in many developing countries. These huge areas of underdevelopment demand careful formulation of notions of "success" or "failure" of reform programs when capacity is lacking and when goals are overly ambitious in the face of stark realities.

The thorny questions of neocolonialism and continued exploitation have to be considered in countries where post-colonial development and relative prosperity in terms of resources do not always translate into real democratization or educational development if corruption or other forces prevail. Hence another question for consideration is "who benefits?" The beneficiaries of reform might well not be students and communities, or even the deliverers of educational programs. Other parties might be the beneficiaries; it might be in the interests of a regime or dominant group to ensure that no change occurs. Yet another thorny question for comparativists interested in reform implementation in developing countries is whether they can set aside prejudices against fairly examining the record of reform in states with "pariah" status. For instance, can scholars ideologically opposed to the

Castro regime still acknowledge Cuba's successes in education and health programs, as advocated by Lutjens (2004) and Hickling-Hudson (2004)?

In summary, in developing countries a disproportionate presence of blocking factors, constraints, and contradictions compromise reform efforts. Many universal issues are exacerbated by the colonial legacy and by other contextual variables. In the ensuing discussion, a sampling of research in developing countries illustrates these issues and their implications for implementing education and national development reforms. What emerges is a complicated picture with relatively few cases of complete success or outright failure of educational reforms. Instead, most research has documented a mix of constraints, unmet needs, success factors, goals yet to be achieved, and variations of change, no change, inertia, or paralysis. If the need for research on the complex realities of implementation became evident in previous years as Spalding (1990) and others pointed out, it remains even more so today.

IMPLEMENTATION ISSUES IN DEVELOPING COUNTRIES: CASES OF SUCCESS AND FAILURE?

Given the complexity of the challenges facing developing countries, it is not surprising that the record contains a rather mixed bag of reform results. The overarching question of "who benefits from reform implementation?" is a reasonable preliminary consideration. For example, Lungu (1985) reported on the seeming success of educational reforms in the post-colonial state of Zambia but argued that the real beneficiaries of the reforms were the elite, not the masses. Alternatively, Carnoy (1981) reported on the success of Cuban educational development programs in furthering the goals of develop a socialist state, and the fact that educational reforms were successful because they were linked to economic development programs. Clearly, the notion of "success", therefore, depends on one's ideological perspective, as well as one's perception of who should benefit and what the desirable outcomes should be. Success or failure might also be akin to perceptions that educational reform glass is half full or half empty.

CASES OF CHANGE OR NO CHANGE:

Some reform results are expressed in permutations of change, no change or inertia, or of continuity. For instance, implementation reports about a new educational policy enacted in Mali in 1976 – independence was won in 1962

– consisted largely of "unmet needs" in key sub-sectors of education, rather than any significant change (National Ministry of Education, 1977) but it is not surprising to see little change at that early stage in a long-term endeavor. In Egypt, Hanson (1988, 1990) and Reimers and McGinn (1997) described the bureaucratic inertia in the Ministry of Education that compromised reform efforts. Lulat and Clarke (1982) and Muyebaa (2001) described how the far-reaching "Education for Development" reform plan in Zambia in 1976–1977 never left the drawing board due to an array of seemingly insoluble implementation problems, and because it was too academically focused on priority subjects rather than on real societal needs. In neighboring Zimbabwe, Jansen (1990) described how curriculum reforms designed for post-colonial indigenization failed to materialize. Instead, curriculum continuity or "lack of change" was the outcome resulting from various factors including continued dependence, failure to legitimate policies of the new state, and conflicting notions of relevance between local culture and imported curriculum. Brook (1992) also described the absence of real change resulting from Zambia's and Zimbabwe's post-independence curriculum reform programs while in Botswana reforms yielded real change in new development studies programs.

Altbach (1993) provided another example, described as "bureaucratic inertia," in an examination of higher education in India in comparison with this sub-sector in other countries. In fact, the issue of timing and pacing of reform emerges as a universal significant factor related to change and lack of change through reform. Rushed reform became a contentious issue in South Africa, as is discussed later in this chapter.

On a positive note regarding educational change, Paulston (1975) described Cuban reform efforts since 1959 as "important strides" made because they were linked to social, economic, and political changes in the larger society under policies for creation of a "new socialist man" upon whose efforts Castro's Marxist society could rest. Complementarity between educational reform, work opportunities and national development goals was shown to be responsible for individual and social change in Cuba, a case that points to the need to consider reform and change in a cross-sector context rather than only in education.

CASES OF "FAILURE"?

Some writers elect to focus on the problems and constraints in developing countries' reform implementation efforts, but relatively few report outright "failure." Lillis (1985) reported on reasons for the "failure" of efforts to Africanize the literature curriculum in Kenya shortly after independence and offered an explanation for continued dependence on Western curricular forms. Youngman and Ishengoma (1999) contemplated the "imperiled promise of reform" in Tanzania owing to historical context factors and controversial reforms endorsed by extra-national organizations. Musonda (1999) described donor influenced education reforms in Zambia as a "square peg in a round hole" amounting to a misfit with the local context and needs, because teachers were caught in a new paradigm that was at cross purposes with, and was destabilizing, the professional beliefs of the practice and culture of teacher education institutions. Successive rounds of reform in Zambia since independence in 1964 (1964–1975, 1975–1989, 1990–2001) each encountered severe obstacles and funding inadequacies, despite their well-intentioned nature (Muyebaa, 2001). In another well-intentioned effort Brook and Brook (1993) described the ill-fated Somali Nomad Education Program whose developers in the Ministry of Education underestimated the strength of clan loyalties among nomads and their suspicion of directives coming from the capital Mogadishu. Despite its good intentions to educate nomads in basic first aid, animal husbandry, and social studies (for cultivating Somali national identity), the program fell victim to resistance, lack of funding, and the advent of civil war in the 1980s.

Focusing on aspects of failure, Taylor and Vlaardingerbroek (2000) reported on an evaluation project addressing science education "deficiencies" in 12 Pacific Island countries. Brook Napier et al. (2000) and Brook Napier (2003a) reported on the overwhelming feelings of failure among remote area teachers in South Africa when they were confronted with outcomes based reform initiatives and inadequate training and support. Only in some of these cases that focus on problems or on "failure" per se, do the writers add recommendations for improvement or rectification (Arrieta et al., 1990; Taylor & Vlaardingerbroek, 2000; Brook Napier et al., 2000).

CASES OF "SUCCESS"?

It is somewhat more common research to see reports on "success," or an enumerating of success factors with some qualifications added. There is generally caution in reporting outright "success." Many authors elect to articulate positive reform outcomes in terms such as "what can be accomplished...when conditions are favorable" as articulated by Bray (1996) reporting on positive reform results in the small state of Bhutan under the

New Approach to Primary Education (NAPE) program. Carnoy (1981) described the educational developments in Cuba that were reportedly linked to economic development under the Castro regime and Lutjens (2004) pointed out the benefits of Cuban centralized bureaucracy that made possible mass mobilization and success in the literacy campaign. Zachariah (1989) offered a positive report of "growth" and "involvement" (of more than just the elite) in the Kerala Sastra Sahitya Parishad (KSSP, Kerala Science Literature Society) in India, suggesting that KSSP could serve as an innovative, indigenous model for mass education reform in other countries. However, he too added qualification in the form of "dilemmas" and problems. Similarly, Franke and Chasin (1994) reported on the radical reform in Kerala as a development strategy whose successful ingredients could be seen in levels of health, education, and social justice that were some of the highest in the developing world. However, these authors also commented on the limitations of the reform, as in creating employment or raising per capita income.

Many authors provide a general account of reform implementation in terms of a range of "success factors" that emerged in the findings of research or evaluations. For instance, under U.S. AID projects to improve girls' education in Guatemala, the Basic Education Strengthening (BEST) project and the Girls Education Program (GEP), yielded an array of positive interventions, but outcomes were also articulated in terms of "synergies unrealized" and in terms of U.S. AID's comparative advantage. The overall success report however focused on the "lessons learned" regarding the need for broader and deeper participation and for concentrating on system-wide sustainable impacts (IDCA, 1991). Verspoor (1989) provided an overview of 21 programs supported by 42 World Bank-assisted projects designed to improve the quality of education in developing countries. Profiles of "successful programs" were juxtaposed with profiles of "less successful programs," and three "success factors" were identified as being particularly crucial for implementation: administrative development/institutional development; significant in-service teacher training; and strategies for commitment among key groups.

Cummings (1986) offered another rendition of "success factors" in a series of reports on Instructional Management by Parents, Community, and Teachers (IMPACT) projects in the Philippines, Malaysia, Indonesia, Bangladesh, Jamaica, and Liberia. Cummings reported some 26 "lessons learned" from these projects. Dharmadasa (1996) reported on the success of teacher development reforms in Sri Lanka, in that 71% of Sri Lankan teachers had received or completed professional training by 1989, and that literacy rates of 90% had been achieved. However, the authors acknowledged that this success was accompanied by teacher-related issues still to be tackled, including quality of training, financing, and need for new strategies and expanded curricula. Reimers and McGinn (1997) described the value of consultation and stakeholder input as success factors in educational development programs in Namibia and El Salvador. Heneveld and Craig (1995) reported on the implementation process in a Madagascan study of in-school factors that most influenced student learning and academic persistence. Hickling-Hudson (2004) described successful Cuban scholarship programs providing study opportunities in Cuba to students from many other developing countries including Jamaica and South Africa, in "south–south" collaborations.

Finally, on the question of unequivocal "success" in reform, scholarly debate over South African educational transformation to date has focused minimally on the success in (at least officially) dismantling that country's four racially segregated education systems in the first years of democracy. Successful components within an overall transformation plan can be overlooked in the face of critique and high profile problems.

IMPLEMENTATION: MIXED RESULTS?

Rather than provide an articulation of outcomes in overtly negative or positive terms, many reform implementation studies yield reports of a mixed bag of results that include improvements or gains, obstacles to reform and suggestions on how to overcome these, and other general insights in a spectrum of implementation realities. These studies point to the importance of examining the complex variety of reform outcomes and impinging factors within and across developing countries.

Several writers highlighted the obstacles to reform, adding suggestions for ways to overcome these. For instance Gill, Fluitman, and Dar (2000) reported on 19 studies of vocational education and training programs mostly in developing countries, describing the different countries' experiences, obstacles to implementation, and innovative approaches to overcome these obstacles. Reilly (1992) juxtaposed variables associated with successful and unsuccessful educational change programs in Kenya, Japan, Malaysia, the Soviet Union, and the United States in which they identified seven influences affecting the character of national systems of education, and the interplay of social, political, and economic activities (SPEA) was highlighted in relation to successful and unsuccessful reform efforts.

In Latin America, projects in the Dominican Republic, El Salvador, Jamaica, and Paraguay in the 1990s provided additional illustrations of the double-edged sword of educational reform implementation, as reported by Alvarez (1998) who also pointed out the similarities in reform origins and components in these countries, despite the differences in contexts and exact reform paths across the countries. Cisneros-Cohernour, Merchant, and Moreno (1999) documented the tensions between national standards and local needs in an evaluation of the implementation of a new secondary curriculum in Mexico, arguing that homogeneously implemented national standards deny the needs and rights of indigenous populations, leaving children of indigenous-ancestry particularly at risk. Fuentes and Elizandro Y Carr (1993) pointed out that Mexican reforms resulted in modernization and increased educational opportunities, but that they were also plagued by problems including excessive bureaucracy and desertion by students and teachers. In a survey of four decades of reform in Latin American countries, Aguerrondo (1992) identified structural deficiencies that blocked equitable access to education. Here, while many quantitative goals were achieved, as in expansion of educational participation, cumulative partial innovations were reportedly more successful than were whole large reform undertakings.

There is a similar record of mixed results from reform in Asian countries. Parkay, Potisook, Chantharaskul, and Chunsakorn (1999) enumerated an array of "problems" in the teaching profession in Thailand and outlined reform recommendations for addressing these. Giacchino-Baker (1995) listed the problems of educational systems in the Lao People's Democratic Republic (including inadequate facilities and equipment, teacher shortages, high dropout rates, unequal access for minorities, and unstable financing) but contrasted these with charities and international organizations that offered "promising alternatives" for educational improvement. Bhola (1990) described the problems that emerged in China's literacy effort – among the world's largest and most promising experiments at the time. He listed "lessons" to be learned from the Chinese experience, ways to overcome the problems inherent in such large-scale endeavors at reform and modernization. Tsang (1996) reported on the success of decentralized funding reforms in Chinese basic education, and on the glaring inequities and inefficiencies that remained to be resolved. Similarly, Attah-Safoh (1982) and Yang (1991) reported on Chinese curriculum reforms implemented in the 1980s in that the problems were actually a function of the rapidly expanding system, itself a positive achievement. More recently, Hannum's (2003) work in rural communities in China underscored the need to examine variations in community resources and their implications for educational stratification in the context of fiscal decentralization.

Other implementation studies in Asia highlighted enabling factors or aspects of success and negative factors as constraints. Wheeler (1989) and Cummings (1992) described these for BRIDGES projects in Thailand and in Sri Lanka and elsewhere, respectively. Chen and Chung (2000) reported on Taiwanese school-based curriculum development and school improvement programs in a study of practitioners' views of reform implementation that highlighted both the promises and the problems underlying the school-based curriculum development movement. Huang (1999) underscored another issue in Taiwanese educational reform (common in post-colonial states), that of the tension between "Americanization" and the "Taiwanization" thrusts, the latter being the post 1994 effort to refocus from Chinese nationalism to indigenous understanding. Sloper and Le (1995) described general reform implementation issues in Vietnamese higher education, further illustrations of the mixed results of reform.

In Africa, there is likewise a record of mixed results. Capper, Nderitu, and Ogala (1997) described the School Improvement Programme (SIP) in Kismayu, Kenya in similar vein, admitting that the long-term sustainability of that program was doubtful due to an array of inhibiting or blocking factors and offering recommendations for the program, training, and policy. In Botswana, Vlaardingerbroek (1998) reported on the differential success of junior secondary science education programs, with good results in developing environmental awareness and in HIV/AIDS education, but mediocre results in preparing students for self-employment. In Ghana, after independence, female educational participation expanded but as Yeboah (1997) reported, school quality and a girl's performance became the basis for decisions for girls to discontinue their schooling. Lynch (1992) revealed the irony in Sudenese top–down reforms to indigenize the curriculum that ignored the ancient Khalawi, Muslim institutions that had been operating successfully at the local level for hundreds of years. Dorsey (1989) summarized the complex post-colonial reforms in Zimbabwe and some achievements, but she highlighted the dilemmas of quantity versus quality in Zimbabwe and raised the question of whether the change to mass education indeed furthered the revolution's goal of a more egalitarian society. Subsequent developments in Zimbabwe lend credence to Dorsey's contentions, as the long-term outcome of post-independence reforms has been anything but the emergence of a more egalitarian society.

SOUTH AFRICA: A CLASSIC CASE OF COMPLEX REFORM IMPLEMENTATION, AND OF IDEAL VERSUS REAL

South Africa attracted much attention by comparativists when the apartheid era ended with installation of a new multiracial democratic government in 1994. The radical, multi-sector transformation policies enacted under the new dispensation were a prime opportunity to observe the dilemmas involved in implementing sweeping educational reforms designed to transform and democratize a colonial, rigidly segregated and centralized system, to obtain insights into universal dilemmas as well as into needs peculiar to all developing. South Africa is a microcosm of nearly all of the issues discussed previously, with the added dimension that the country is at once a first world country and a third world country in terms of its schizophrenic development legacy. Its story contains vivid examples of facilitating factors as well as a woeful list of constraints and dilemmas. South Africa also exemplifies the need to consider real successes juxtaposed with persistent backlogs and difficulties in consistently implementing contradictory reforms in a climate of inadequate training and support. Finally, South Africa's educational transformation record to date also illustrates the need to consider just who is benefiting from transformation, and whose ideological position equates with assessments of "success" or "failure."

In South Africa, the legacy of colonial domination and apartheid had created a landscape of unparalleled inequality. By the 1990s the problems in education (for non-whites, not for whites) added up to an overwhelming set of constraints or backlogs including a chronic shortage of qualified teachers and textbooks, inadequate facilities, widespread indiscipline among teachers and pupils, low performance rates, lack of capacity in traditionally disadvantaged higher education institutions compared to the privileged white universities, corruption, and poor management of a bloated bureaucracy. A "lost generation" of students existed in thousands of township pupils whose schooling had been sacrificed in the height of the struggle during the 1980s and early 1990s under the philosophy of "liberation first, education second." During the struggle, "culture of learning" was lost in African schools in particular, generating issues within these schools that mitigated against change, even as educational transformation and deracialization reforms began (Mandela, 1994).

The backlogs in black schools represented perhaps the most daunting challenge to reform. Hartshorne (1992) offered a detailed account of apartheid-era black education and predicted the challenges ahead for transforming education in all respects. Other scholars added insight into the many challenges ahead, including Brook (1996a, 1996b), Johnson (1995), and Samoff (1998). Mission schools did provide quality education to a very small number of Africans but as Brook (1996a) noted, they served a small slice of the black population and they suffered from geographic isolation, shortages of teachers qualified to teach English, and dependence on foreign volunteers.

Even before the official end of apartheid in 1994, de facto educational change occurred. Beginning as early as 1976 some progressive private schools began admitting pupils of all races, spawning an "open" schools movement that paved the way for a new non-racial public system years ahead of official policy change. These pioneering efforts in deracialization came to be legitimized under the new dispensation in 1994 and in subsequent legislation. Open schools experimented with multicultural curriculum development, they tackled the realities of coping with multiracial and multilingual classes; and they offered leadership and training workshops to other schools before and after official transformation began. Teachers in these pioneering schools experienced enormous pressures, lacking training but enjoying courageous administrator and parent/community support. Here, the micro-level research conducted on school realities was crucial in shedding light on educational change both in advance of- and during official transformation (see Bigelow, 1987; Brook, 1991, 1996a, b; Brook Napier, 2003a; Christie, 1990; Freer, 1991; McGurk, 1990).

In the wake of pressure from international sanctions and escalating mass actions at home, the liberation struggle undermined the status quo and prompted the drafting of official plans to dismantle apartheid education in the period 1987–1994 (DNE, 1991). Education was one of the priority areas for transformation under the Reconstruction and Development Programme along with job creation, housing, land redistribution, water supply, and health care (ANC, 1994). The new Constitution provided for non-racialism in all aspects of life, and recognized 11 national languages with the right to instruction in one's own language (Constitution, 1996). The overall transformation agenda promoted multiracialism in a new "rainbow nation" and the spirit of pan-Africanism (Mbeki, 1998; Mandela, 1994).

The first reforms of education were primarily quantitative, to restructure four racially segregated systems into a single non-racial system, to "rationalize" the system by eliminating duplication of facilities, and to expand accessibility. Subsequent educational reforms were also qualitative, focusing on substance and encased in the controversial Curriculum 2005/21 outcomes based reform program (based on British and American ideas) that was designed to transform and indigenize the curriculum at all levels, linked to a National Qualifications Framework whose major tenets were imported from Canada, New Zealand, and Britain. In education and language planning, the Constitutional provisions and subsequent legislation were remarkably detailed, yet they provided no clear guidelines for implementation, and this resulted in a swarm of legal, logistical, and emotional outcomes.

The focus of transformation in education and other sectors followed a two-stage process in South Africa. In the 1994–1999 transition period policy formulation was dominant. Thereafter, the focus switched to policy implementation and modification. Heated debate ensued among policy makers, stakeholders, and scholars. For examples of commentary on the policy context and implementation issues see Brook (1996a, 1997), Brook Napier et al. (2000), Cross, Mkwanazi-Twala, and Klein (1998), Jansen and Christie (1999), Marais (1995), and Smith (1993) and Smith (1996). The agonizing dilemmas for teachers were enumerated by Brook (1996a), Howard and Herman (1998) and Samoff (1998). The legacy of apartheid persisted in the segregated landscape of former-townships and rural area schools noted by Brook (1996b), and by Geldt (1996) who predicted poor prospects for real change in these schools even in a transformed system.

Even by the end of the transition period, results of the educational reforms were plentiful, amounting to unprecedented success in some respects. The four racially segregated and unequal education systems were collapsed into a single non-racial democratic system. Vast numbers of disadvantaged African and other non-white children gained access to schooling, and in schools of their parents' choice, for the first time. Racial integration pioneered in the open schools extended to all government schools, but it occurred overwhelmingly in former white schools as non-white pupils enrolled in the well-resourced suburban and urban schools. Non-white schools in the townships and rural areas remained racially unchanged. Massive teacher training programs were initiated. An outcome-based curriculum plan and qualifications framework were installed. The entire system underwent a degree of decentralization with devolution of some authority to provinces and to local levels. The National Literacy Initiative and a bevy of adult education and non-formal education programs extended educational opportunities to vast numbers of people previously denied it. The multiple languages policy and instructional medium rights spawned the beginnings of a new language hierarchy. In short, despite the enormous problems that were to be addressed, there was quite remarkable change in early post-apartheid South African education in which the old rigid system was toppled, and the long transformation process began.

One of the most difficult to measure changes was widely reported, that now there was hope for a better future. For examples of the hopes and frustrations voiced by teachers in remote area schools see Brook (1996a) and Pitsoe and Nieuwenhuis (2001). While white South Africans had enjoyed quality education, and performance and literacy levels on a par with other western countries, the changes associated with transformation really occurred in the non-white population, narrowing the gap between the first- and the third-world in the same country.

A host of unintended outcomes accompanied the intended changes. Under the policy of "rationalization", or the restructuring of teacher education and higher education, thousands of experienced teachers were retrenched. Many who stayed in the profession were un- or under-qualified teachers, and the number of teacher training institutions was cut by 75%. Many former white schools were simply closed. Thousands of educators became preoccupied with the prospects for retaining their positions, rather than with tackling new methodologies and approaches. Inertia and anxiety were the result. Former white schools retained their resources and quality of programs since demand for these schools enabled them to charge high fees. Township schools became progressively more impoverished as they lost pupils to the former white schools. Violence, high failure rates, and absenteeism continued to plague township schools. The number of private schools more than trebled in the years 1995–2000 as parents of all races sought a more secure education for their children rather than risk the radically changed circumstances in government schools. With white flight, some former white schools became predominantly African in enrollment. Brook (1996a, b), Jansen and Christie (1999), Maseko (2001), and Pitsoe and Nieuwenhuis (2001) were among the South African scholars who documented these painful changes.

Among the most hotly debated reforms was Curriculum 2003, modified to be Curriculum 2005, and again postponed and renamed as Curriculum 21 in 2000. This plan was attacked for being ill-conceived and overly influenced by foreign ideas, impractical for meeting real needs, and haphazardly rushed into implementation without adequate teacher training and support (Chisholm, 2000; Cross et al., 1998; DNE, 2000; Jansen & Christie, 1999; and Potenza, 2000). Many critics declared the reform to be an outright failure. Teachers resisted and feared adopting the new "paradigm". OBE became a hated word. Repeated changes, lack of proper communication, and sporadic and inadequate training elevated teachers' anxieties.

In general, educators grappled with the host of new issues: white teachers in predominantly African schools, multilingual and multiracial classes, inadequate training and support to deal with curriculum development as well as diverse students' needs, discipline and morale problems, and a persistent anxiety and insecurity as mandates continued to be delivered in predominantly top–down fashion. A legacy of centralized thinking pervaded the system at all levels, obstructing initiative and creating inertia. The matriculation rates declined for several years, casting a pall over the much-touted reforms, but these statistics were also a reflection of a larger pool of candidates now in the more democratic system. The familiar dilemma of quality versus quantity was evident. Language and instructional medium questions proliferated on the use of vernacular, dual medium instruction, and demands for English-medium instruction. South Africa joined other post-colonial states in wrestling with issues of implementing a multiple language policy without marginalizing minority or disadvantaged populations or perpetuating linguistic and cultural domination (Brook Napier, 2003b; Hobson & Nyathi, 2001; Matsaso, 2001; and Smith, 1993).

In response to the array of implementation problems, Minister of Education Asmal acknowledged a "crisis" in education in 2000. The curriculum plan was redesigned and implementation strategies were re-drafted. A five-year revised plan based on the slogan "tirisano" (Sotho for "working together") included new strategies for training and support, making teachers and schools accountable for poor performance, improving coordination between national and provincial departments of education, and revitalizing schools as community centers with multiple functions (DNE, 2001; Review of Curriculum 2005, 2000; http://education.pwv.gov.za).

The debate over policy implementation and reformulation in South Africa highlighted some universal reform dilemmas including too-rapid change with inadequate training and support, lack of capacity and institutional memory in many institutions, and inadequate information on micro-level realities. Ironically, the policies for rapid change resulted in inertia and also in haphazard, unintended outcomes. For instance, many vacant posts at intermediate levels of administration in the Gauteng Department of Education crippled implementation of some initiatives. Affirmative action bursary schemes, providing bus fares, and books for disadvantaged students, failed to be implemented at some local teachers training colleges because administrators deemed them impractical. While thousands of South African teachers were laid off in the cities, Cuban and Libyan teachers were recruited to fill posts in remote, hardship area schools where South African teachers refused to work (Tejane, L., June 6, 1999, personal communication; van der Vyver, J., June–July 2001, personal communications).

National and provincial reforms resulted in inconsistent intended change at the micro-level. A modest amount of research on implementation issues in South African schools provided compelling evidence of the need to study micro-level realities and the emerging mosaic of differential change across urban/suburban, former township, and rural settings. For instance, Soudien (2001) described youth identity formation and conflict in Western Cape schools. Brook Napier (2003a) documented some cases of reforms implemented true to the original intent, and others creolized into some mediated version or subverted altogether. Odav and Ndandane (1998) revealed how some local schools subverted racial integration and language policy. Pitsoe and Nieuwenhuis (2001) described teachers' frustrations and feelings of uncertainty associated with OBE implementation in the Lichtenburg area, and Luneta (2001) reported likewise in Northern Province. The complexities of transformation in South Africa exemplify the global – local continuum concept and the processes whereby global reforms are translated into national reform plans and successively "creolized" at various levels in the system as they are either implemented in original form, creolized into new forms, or even subverted altogether. Lack of coordination between national, provincial, and local levels has emerged as another chronic problem as reforms are implemented in South Africa.

As South Africa moved into the post-transitional phases of its educational transformation process, implementation issues loomed large. The need to understand the complexities of implementation processes became increasingly evident. South Africa exhibits examples of nearly all of the constraints, contradictions and dilemmas mentioned earlier in this chapter. Despite the country's wealth by African standards, facilitating factors are few and resources available for transformation are stretched to the limit. The daunting problems in wider society include an outflow of skilled workers, a massive influx of refugees and illegal residents, demands in housing and other human resource development sectors that are straining government funds, reduced foreign investment, and high crime rates.

While transformation in schools is well under way, real success is patchy and uneven, still predominantly in progressive private schools and in the former white schools. The higher education sector is seriously embattled by lack of skilled workers and capacity at all levels, problems of redeployment of large numbers of workers (from closed institutions), declining enrollments and correspondingly lowered subsidies, and mismanagement (SAIRR, 2001b). Most daunting is the HIV/AIDs problem in South Africa that has demanded changed thinking in terms of the toll on skilled workers, and the costs to be borne in dealing with the impacted populations. AIDS-related issues have penetrated all sectors including education, and the costs and implications are feared to be so large that they will threaten long-term implementation of transformation reforms (SAIRR, 2001a).

The degree of change toward a more democratic, inclusive system of education has been quite revolutionary, without the bloodbath that many predicted, and with the involvement of people at the grass-roots level in what was called a "silent revolution" (Kane Berman, 1991). What has been achieved in education to date deserves to be credited as a success story. But the swarm of constraints and backlogs still jeopardize hopes for achieving rapid progress.

Uncertainty remains rampant in all spheres of education. In 2003, the government released its ten-year review, the official verdict on the first decade of transformation and programs to achieve RDP aims. The report noted significant achievements in education and other sectors, such as in adult literacy increases from 83% in 1996 to 89% in 2001 and for 15–24 year-olds from 83% to 96%, and the matric pass rate increase from 54% in 1996 to 69% in 2002. Early-stage progress was reported in "addressing social exclusion" in that "plans are under way to fully implement the constitutional recognition of 11 languages in South Africa as official languages."

The challenges for the second decade of transformation are many, with education needs jostling for position alongside pressing needs in other sectors and with a heavy focus on consolidating the "two economies" in the country, as well as a leadership role for South Africa in the African development agenda NEPAD (New Plan for Economic Development) and an expanded role for the country in global affairs (www.10years.gov.za/review/documents.htm). The government report and other reports (see, for example, Sunday Times, 19 April, 2004, "10 years of Democracy", www.sundaytimes.co.za/specialreports/10years) celebrate the successes to date but underscore the challenges ahead in affording educational transformation a place in the crowded development agenda, in a prime example of the mixed results of reform implementation.

The third democratic elections in April 2004 provided a resounding victory for the democratic government and endorsement of its policies (www.sundaytimes.co.za/2004/04/18). There are disaffected views too. White Afrikaners now see themselves as a dispossessed group at risk of losing their language and identity (Gilliomee, 2003; Schlemmer, 2001). Some scholars question the transformation process as a vehicle for production of a democratic, egalitarian society (Weber, 2002). South Africa remains a country with two faces: one poor and black, or third world in level of development; and one rich and white, or first world in level of development, as President Mbeki argued (Mbeki, 1998). In South Africa as elsewhere, the verdict on the success or failure of educational transformation depends on whom one asks and on one's ideological perspective. South Africa's experience also underscores the need to consider educational reform in a cross-sector perspective.

It is crucial to consider change in a country like South Africa in light of similar processes in other countries (Weber, 2002), particularly when its deracialization experience is of interest to many countries such as the United States. However, attempts to draw parallels with democratization and deracialization elsewhere can be flawed if South African educational transformation is not considered in proper historical and demographic context (Brook Napier et al., 2000).

REFLECTING ON THE FIELD AT THE TURN OF THE CENTURY; WHAT IS NEEDED IN THE FUTURE?

By the close of the 20th century the field of comparative education provided a plethora of descriptive and quantitative studies and a complex variety of models and approaches to studying educational reform and implementation. There is a wealth of insight into different forms of educational reform around the world, but many studies have a somewhat narrow academic focus that is of limited practical use to educational policy makers and implementers. There is perhaps a predominance of macro-level studies, fewer macro–micro-level studies and rather few "bottom–up" micro-level studies of complex realities in different settings.

What is needed in the coming decades? For enhanced understanding and documentation of educational reform implementation as *real change*, still more studies of substance, process, and contextual realities will benefit the field. Research questions that are framed in terms with practical benefit for policy makers and educationists could enable more successful implementation by informing policy makers, as recommended by Reimers and McGinn (1997). More studies of macro-level policies versus micro-level realities; investigations of the complexities of educational innovation and the importance of planning, the end products of implementation processes, and the levels at which implementation is obstructed, terminated, or successfully completed are also needed, as suggested by researchers some time ago (Adams & Chen, 1981; Ketudat, 1984). New models and approaches are likely to emerge, as scholars continue to attempt to understand and explain the complexities of implementation in developing countries, in light of current and future issues.

There is an increasingly acknowledged need for cross-sector research examining education in relation to other human resources development sectors (health, housing, labor/jobs, environment) and for practical, reality-based examinations of process as noted by many scholars cited in this chapter. Longitudinal studies are needed to investigate how micro-level issues in schools evolve over time as seen in South Africa where some issues were persistent, while others intensified or abated (Brook, 1996a, 1996b) and in Zambia long-term study of the reform history is needed to understand successive rounds of reform designed to rectify past mistakes (Muyebaa, 2001). Schwille and Wheeler (1992) and Hannum (2003) were among those who pointed out the need to consider implementation strategies within the realities of cost constraints, fiscal decentralization, and local community inputs.

CONTEMPLATING REFORM IMPLEMENTATION AS "SUCCESS" OR "FAILURE": DIRECTIONS FOR THE FUTURE

Comparative education researchers have documented a wealth of complex reform results in different countries, pointing out success factors and lessons learned in the process of implementing reforms, and also enumerating obstacles, backlogs, blocking factors, or other hindrances that cripple reform efforts. There exists a wealth of insights into reform efforts in countries large and small, relatively developed, and severely impoverished. Overall, a family of universal issues and dilemmas appears repeatedly, but the mix of contextual factors and permutations of school realities is endless. The moral is that caution is urged in citing unequivocal reasons for "success" or "failure" of educational reform implementation in developing countries. As new contradictions and dilemmas emerge in response to efforts to implement educational reform policies that are a function of internal and external influences, global trends and pressures, and new dynamics of context and circumstance, these too need to be documented to add to the store of information and insight into the complex variety of realities.

The Challenges to Scholars

In advocating needed future directions of comparative education research focusing on developing country settings, the considerations voiced by

McGinn (1999), offer a worthy challenge, as follows. There is a need to investigate reform as complex processes of learning through errors as well as successes, also to heed what plans were rejected. This is the most relevant point, that we remove blinders and western perspectives on what actual "success" or "failure" constitutes in developing country experiences of reform (in contrast to those in developed countries, but also in ways that enhance understanding of universal issues and processes); that we accept the mixed bag of outcomes rather than seek either unequivocal success or abject failure. Still more research is needed on education sector realities and dilemmas of dealing with multiple sets of stakeholders, the importance of political skills rather than technical skills in successfully implementing reforms, and the need for institutional and organizational learning.

Building on McGinn's recommendations, this author offers some additional thoughts based on her own research and experience and on the research cited in this chapter. There is clearly a need for still more implementation-focused research documenting how policy works in practice (macro–meso–micro-level studies) and how realities on the ground impinge on or are manifestations of reform. There is also need for additional empirical studies within and across countries to add to the store of insight into local, regional, national, and supranational contextual factors that color and shape reform implementation. As the case of South Africa shows, a paucity of micro-level research risks leaving policy critique as little more than armchair academic argument instead of providing real insight to inform policy implementation.

Ideally, research-addressing questions directly relevant to policymakers and educationists working for real change is needed so that the findings of research can provide feedback to enable policy adjustments sensitive to realities on the ground in a variety of settings. The issues of timing and pacing of reform, and financing mechanisms have also emerged as crucial in many countries. New success stories in particular settings should be given exposure with clear and valid documentation, so that they can serve as models or beacons of hope for others, particularly in highly stressed reform implementation settings such as currently exist in South Africa. New configurations of reform and development to watch include the continental-scale New Plan for African Development that incorporates education and economic development; successful models (such as Cuba's literacy campaign) potentially adoptable elsewhere where contextual factors are similar; and what Hickling-Hudson (2004) called "South–South Collaboration" among developing countries.

Realistically, new priorities need to be acknowledged when education might not be at the forefront of reform priorities in a crowded reform agenda when cross-sector needs competing for resources. Finally, as the experiences in most developing countries show, there is a continuing need to scrutinize change in its many different dimensions: change ahead of reform; de facto change; no change; inertia or paralysis, slow versus rapid change, and change independent of reform; macro–meso–micro-level interrelationships; and so on.

It is apparent that the heightened attention given to implementation issues in current comparative education research is likely to persist and even increase in the coming decades, as will the value of exposing differences between real change and ideal change as argued by many, including Ginsburg and Gorostiaga (2001) and Zimba and Kasanda (2001). The recommendations by McGinn (1999) and many others in the field point to the desirability of understanding what is happening in as many different contexts on the ground as possible, and to the need for comparative education scholars to investigate and document the issues that have direct relevance both for policymakers and for educators.

REFERENCES

Abdel Halim, A. E., & Shaker, P. (1979). A strategy for promoting educational reform in developing countries. Paper presented at the *Annual meeting of the American Educational Research Association*. San Francisco, CA, April.

Adams, R. S., & Chen, D. (1981). *The process of educational innovation: An international perspective*. Paris: International Institute for Educational Planning.

African National Congress (ANC). (1994). *The reconstruction and development programme: A policy framework*. Johannesburg: African National Congress.

Aguerrondo, I. (1992). Educational reform in Latin America: A survey of four decades. *Prospects, 22*(3), 353–365.

Albrecht, D., & Ziderman, A. (1992). *Funding mechanisms for higher education: Financing for stability, efficiency, and responsiveness*. World Bank discussion papers. Washington, DC: World Bank. ED344518.

Altbach, P. G. (1993). The dilemma of change in Indian higher education. *Higher Education, 26*(1), 3–20.

Altbach, P. G., & Kelly, G. P. (1986). Introduction: Perspectives on comparative education. In: P. G. Altbach & G. P. Kelly (Eds), *New approaches to comparative education*. Chicago: University of Chicago Press.

Alvarez, B. (1998). Life cycle and legacy of the educational reforms in Latin America and the Caribbean. *International Journal of Educational Reform, 7*(1), 34–45.

Arnove, R. F. (Ed.). (1992). Emergent issues in education: Comparative perspectives. *SUNY Series: Frontiers in education*. Albany, NY: SUNY Press.

Arnove, R. F., & Torres, C. A. (Eds) (2003). *Comparative education: The dialectic of the global and the local.* Oxford: Rowman and Littlefield.

Asian-South Pacific Bureau of Adult Education. (December, 1993). Learning to live in harmony and diversity: Focus on human rights education. *ASPBAE Courier, 57,* 1–62.

Astiz, M. F., Wiseman, A. W., & Baker, D. P. (2002). Slouching toward decentralization: Consequences of globalization for curricular control in national education systems. *Comparative Education Review, 46*(1), 66–88.

Attah-Safoh, A. (1982). *Education for copeability: Perspective on developing countries.* Report (43 pp.). Washington, DC: World Bank.

Basabas-Ikegucchi, C. (1991). *The Issue of relevant education: Theories and reality.* Report (16pp.). ED360125.

Bhola, H.S. (1990). Adult literacy and adult education in the socialist modernization of china: Policy, performance, lessons. Paper presented at the *International literacy year colloquium: Literacy – foundation for development.* Washington, DC, Center for Applied Linguistics, October.

Bigelow, W. (1987). Challenging "Gutter Education". *Social Education, 51*(2), 120–123.

Bjork, C. (2003). Local responses to decentralization policy in Indonesia. *Comparative Education Review, 47*(2), 184–216.

Blaug, M. (1977). *Economics of education in developing countries: Current trends and new priorities.* Report (18 pp.). Berlin: Max Planck Institut fur Bildungsforschung.

Bray, M. (1996). Educational reform in a small state: Bhutan's new approach to primary education. *International Journal of Educational Reform, 5*(1), 15–25.

Brook, D. L. (1991). Social studies for multicultural education: A case study of a racially integrated school in South Africa. *Georgia Social Science Journal, 22*(1), 1–10.

Brook, D. L. (1992). *Social studies and national development in Botswana, Zambia, and Zimbabwe.* Unpublished Ed.D. dissertation. Athens: University of Georgia.

Brook, D. L. (1996a). From exclusion to inclusion: Racial politics and educational reform in South Africa. *Anthropology & Education Quarterly, 27*(2), 204–231.

Brook, D. L. (1996b). Racism, violence, and the liberation struggle: The impact on South African education. In: C. Wulf, & B. Diekman (Eds). *Violence: racism, nationalism, xenophobia,* Chapter 20 (pp. 315–328). *European studies in education.* New York/Munster: Waxmann.

Brook, D. L. (1997). South Africa after Apartheid: Recent events and future prospects. *Social Education, Special Issue on Sub-Saharan Africa, 61*(7), 395–403.

Brook, D. L., & Brook, G. A. (1993). Social studies for Somali Nomads. *The Social Studies, 84*(1), 5–13.

Brook Napier, D. (2003a). Transformations in South Africa: Policies and practices from ministry to classroom. In: K. A. Anderson-Levitt (Ed.), *Local meanings, global schooling: Anthropology and world culture theory* (pp. 51–74). Palgrave: Macmillan.

Brook Napier, D. (2003b). Language issues in South Africa: Education, identity, and democratization. In: P. Ryan & R. Terborg (Eds), *Language: Issues of inequality* (pp. 41–75). Mexico City: Universidad Nacional Autonoma de Mexico.

Brook Napier, D., Lebeta, V., & Zungu, B. (2000). Race, history, and education: South African perspectives on the struggle for democracy. *Theory and Research in Social Education, 28*(3), 445–451.

Bryson, J. C. (1978). *Women and economic development in Cameroon.* Report (155 pp.). Washington, DC: Agency for International Development ED214694.

Canales, J., Gomez., L. C., & Villenueva, N. (1995). *The educational systems of Mexico and the United States: Prospects for reform and collaboration.* A working paper series on higher education in Mexico and the United States. Boulder, CO.: Western Interstate Commission for Higher Education. ED410827.

Capper, J., Nderitu, S., & Ogala, P. (1997). *The school improvement programme of the Aga Khan education service, Kenya at Kismayu, Western Kenya: Evaluation report.* Geneva: Aga Khan Foundation.

Carnoy, M. (1981). Educational reform and economic development in Cuba: Recent developments. Paper presented at the *Annual meeting of the American Educational Research Association.* Los Angeles, CA, April.

Chabbott, C., & Ramirez, F. O. (2000). Development and Education. In: M. T. Hallinan (Ed.), *Handbook of the sociology of education.* New York: Kluver Academic/Plenum.

Chalker, D. M., & Haynes, R. M. (1994). *World class schools: New standards for education.* Lancaster: Tecnomic.

Chapman, D. W. (1991). *Teacher incentives in the third World.* Research Reports. Tallahassee, FL: Learning systems institute; improving the efficiency of educational systems consortium. ED354621.

Chen, H. S., & Chung, J. (2000). The implementation of school-based curriculum development. School improvement in Taiwan: Problems and possibilities. Paper presented at the *International Congress for school effectiveness and improvement.* Hong Kong, China. ED443159.

Cheng, Y. C. (1999). Recent education developments in South East Asia: An introduction. *School Effectiveness and School Improvement, 10*(1), 3–9.

Chisholm, L. (2000). Report on curriculum 2005. Pretoria, Department of National Education.

Chowdhury, K. P. (1984). *Efforts in universalization of primary education: The case of Bangladesh.* Occasional papers series: *Vol. 12.* SUNY Buffalo: Comparative Education Center.

Christie, P. (1990). *Open schools: Racially mixed catholic schools in South Africa, 1976–1986.* Johannesburg: Ravan Press.

Cisneros-Cohernour, E. J., Merchant, B. M., & Moreno, R. P. (1999). Evaluating curriculum reform in Mexico: Challenges addressing a diverse population. Paper presented at the *Annual meeting of the American Educational Research Association,* Montreal, Canada, April.

Constitution of the Republic of South Africa (1996). Act 108. Pretoria: Government Printer.

Cross, M., Mkwanazi-Twala, Z., & Klein, G. (Eds) (1998). *Dealing with diversity in South African education: A debate on the politics of a national curriculum.* Johannesburg: Juta, Kenwyn.

Cummings, W. K. (1986). *Low-cost primary education: Implementing an innovation in six nations.* Report (137 pp.). Ottawa: International Development Research Center ED312084.

Cummings, W. K. (1988). *The decentralization of education.* Project BRIDGES. Report (48 pp.). ED300897.

Cummings, W. K. (1992). The implementation of management reforms: The case of Sri Lanka. *BRIDGES research report series: Vol. 11.* Cambridge, MA: Harvard Institute for International Development. (55 pp.).

Cummings, W. K., & Altbach, P. G. (Eds). (1997). *The challenge of eastern Asian education: Implications for America.* SUNY series, Frontiers in education. Albany: SUNY Press.

92   DIANE BROOK NAPIER

Department of National Education (DNE). (1991). *Education renewal strategy: Discussion document*. Pretoria, South Africa: Committee of Heads of Education Departments.

Department of National Education (DNE). (2000). Report of C2005 review committee: Executive summary (6pp.). Pretoria: Government Printer.

Department of National Education (DNE). (2001). *National Curriculum Statement*. Pretoria, Government Printer. Available: http://education.pwv.gov.za/DoE.

Dharmadasa, K. H. (1996). *SriLankan teachers' development*. Paper presented at the *Annual meeting of the Mid-South Educational Research Association*. Tuscaloosa, Alabama, November.

Doronila, M. L. C. (1997). A research and development approach to the delivery of comprehensive functional education and literacy in the Philippines. Paper presented at the *Asian Literacy Regional Forum*. Manila, Philippines, May.

Dorsey, B. J. (1989). Educational development and reform in Zimbabwe. *Comparative Education Review, 33*(1), 40–58.

Dzvimbo, K. P. (1989). The dilemmas of teacher education reform in Zimbabwe. *Interchange, 20*(4), 16–31.

Evans, D. (1977). *Responsive educational planning: Myth or reality?* Report (51 pp.). Paris: UNESCO International Institute for Educational Planning.

Fass, S. M., and others (1991). *The political economy of education in the Sahel efficiency indicators activity*. IEES Project Monograph. Tallahassee, FL: Learning Systems Institute; Improving the Efficiency of Educational Systems Consortium. ED353648.

Fergus, H. A. (1991). The challenge of educational reform in microstates: A case study of the organization of eastern Caribbean states. *Prospects, 21*(4), 561–571.

Franke, R. W., & Chasin, B. H. (1994). *Kerala: Radical reform as development in an Indian state*. Monroe, OR: Food First Books.

Freer, D. (Ed.) (1991). *Towards open schools: Possibilities and realities for non-racial education in South Africa*. Manzini: McMillan Boleswa.

Fuentes, B. O., & Elizandro Y Carr, S. (1993). Educational reform in Mexico. *International journal of educational reform, 2*(1), 12–18.

Geldt, J. (1996). Distance education into group areas won't go? *Open Learning, 11*(1), 12–21.

Giacchino-Baker, R. (1995). A tale of two bridges: Educational reform in the Lao people's democratic republic. *International Journal of Educational Reform, 3*(4), 376–383.

Gill, I. S., Fluitman, F., & Dar, A. (Eds) (2000). *Vocational education and training reform: Matching skills to markets and budgets*. Washington, DC: World Bank.

Gill, J. I., & Alvarez de Testa, L. (1995). Understanding the differences: An essay on higher education in Mexico and the United States. Comparative report. *A working paper series on higher education in Mexico and the United States*. Boulder, CO.: Western Interstate Commission for Higher Education. ED410830.

Gilliomee, H. (2003). *The Afrikaners*. Charlottesville: University of Virginia Press.

Ginsburg, M. (Ed.) (1991). *Understanding educational reform in global context: Economy, ideology, and the state*. New York: Garland.

Ginsburg, M. B., Cooper, S., Raghu, R., & Zegarra, H. (1990). National and World-system explanations of educational reform. *Comparative Education Review, 34*(4), 474–499.

Ginsburg, M. B., & Gorostioga, J. M. (2001). Relationships between theorists/researchers and policy makers/practitioners: Rethinking the two-cultures thesis and the possibility of dialogue. *Comparative Education Review, 45*(2), 173–196.

Gomes, R. (1996). The reform of mass schooling in Portugal (1974–1991). *Mediterranean Journal of Educational Studies, 1*(1), 29–42.

Goodlad, J. I. (1984). *A place called school.* New York: McGraw-Hill.

Haddad, W. D. (1990). Education for all: The role of international aid. *Prospects, 20*(4), 525–536.

Hannum, E. (2003). Poverty and basic education in rural China: Villages, households, and girls' and boys' enrollment. *Comparative Education Review, 47*(2), 141–159.

Hanson, E. M. (1988). *Administrative reform and the Egyptian ministry of education.* Report (35 pp.). ED 310483.

Hanson, E. M. (1989). *Decentralization and regionalization in educational administration: Comparisons of Venezuela, Colombia and Spain.* Report (37pp.). ED302873.

Hanson, E. M. (1990). Administrative reform and the Egyptian ministry of education. *Journal of Educational Administration, 28*(4), 46–62.

Hartshorne, K. (1992). *Crisis and challenge: Black education 1910–1990.* Cape Town: Oxford University Press.

Heath, J. (1998). The financing and provisioning of education and health services in developing countries. Review article. *Economics of Education Review,, 17*(3), 359–362.

Heneveld, W., & Craig, H. (1995). A framework for using qualitative research to inform policymakers and empower practitioners: Lessons from Madagascar. Paper presented at the *Annual meeting of the International Congress for school effectiveness and improvement.* Leeuwarden, Netherlands, January.

Hickling-Hudson, A. (2004). Cuba's policy of internationalism in education: Forging an approach to South-South collaboration. Paper presented at the *48th Annual conference of the comparative and International Education Society.* Salt Lake City, March.

Hobson, R. K., & Nyathi, F. S. (2001). Countering intellectual genocide and underdevelopment: Language research in Africa for sustainable development and democracy. Paper presented at the *9th BOLESWA International Educational Research Symposium.* Gaborone, Botswana, July–August.

Howard, S., & Herman, H. (Eds). (1998). Coping with rapid Change: Special focus on South Africa's teachers. *Democracy and Education, 12*(2), 1–49.

Hu, N. B. (1996). Planning and developing community colleges in China. Paper presented at the *Conference "Toward the 21st century: The trends in world education development and China's education reform".* Washington, DC, August.

Huang, H. S. (1999). Educational reform in Taiwan: A brighter American moon? *International Journal of Educational Reform, 8*(2), 145–153.

IDCA Agency for International Development (1999). Improving girls' education in Guatemala. *Impact evaluation.* Washington, DC: Center for Development Information and Evaluation. ED433313.

Jansen, J. (1990). The State and curriculum in transition societies: The Zimbabwean experience. Paper presented at the *Annual meeting of the comparative and International Education Society.* Anaheim, CA, March.

Jansen, J., & Christie, P. (Eds) (1999). *Changing curriculum: Studies on OBE in South Africa.* Johannesburg: Juta, Kenwyn.

Johanson, R. K. (Ed.). (1987). Africa's agenda for action: Reform policies, renew progress. *World Bank Education News, 2*(1), 1–6.

Johnson, D. (1995). Introduction: The challenges of educational reconstruction and transformation in South Africa. *Comparative Education, 31*(2), 131–140.

Johnson, M. (1967). Definitions and models in curriculum theory. *Educational Theory, 17*, 127.

Kafula, H. (2001). Curriculum for sustainable development in Zambia. Paper presented at the *9th BOLESWA international educational research symposium.* Gaborone, Botswana, July–August.

Kane Berman, J. (1991). *South Africa's silent revolution.* Johannesburg: South African Institute of Race Relations.

Karagozoglu, G. (1991). Teacher education reform in Turkey. *Action in Teacher Education, 13*(3), 26–29.

Kazi, A. A. (1991). Ethnonational questions, educational reform, and political socialization in the Post-Cold War Era: Case of Pakistan. Paper presented at the *Oxford conference on educational reform and local and national needs.* Oxford, September.

Kelly, G. P., & Altbach, P. G. (1982). Introduction: Approaches and perspectives. In: P. G. Altbach, R. F. Arnove & G. P. Kelly (Eds), *Comparative education.* New York: McMillan.

Kent, R. (1995). Two Positions on the international debate about higher education: The World Bank and UNESCO. Paper presented at the *Annual meeting of the Latin American Studies Association.* Washington, DC, September.

Lee, M. & Kim, H. (1991). *The educational reform in Korea and People's Republic of Chine within a transnational context.* Report (32 pp.). ED341318.

Lillis, K. M. (1985). Processes of secondary curriculum innovation in Kenya. *Comparative Education Review, 29*(1), 80–96.

Lindahl, R. A. (1998). Reflections on educational reform in Cuba. *International Journal of Educational Reform, 7*(4), 300–308.

Lloyd, C. B., El Tawila, S., Clark, W. H., & Mensch, B. S. (2003). The impact of educational quality on school exit in Egypt. *Comparative Education Review, 47*(4), 444–467.

London, N. A. (2003). Ideology and politics in English-language education in Trinidad and Tobago: The colonial experience and a postcolonial critique. *Comparative Education Review, 47*(3), 287–320.

Lulat, Y. G. M., & Clarke, R. (1982). Political constraints on educational reform for development: Lessons from an African experience. *Comparative Education Review, 26*(2), 235–253.

Luneta, K. (2001). Teaching practicum: A triangulation of college lecturers', co-operating teachers' and students' perspectives: a case of ndebele college of education, South Africa. Paper presented at the *9th BOLESWA international educational research symposium.* Gaborone, Botswana, July–August, 2001.

Lungu, G. F. (1985). Elites, incrementalism and educational policy-making in post-independence Zambia. *Comparative Education, 21*(3), 287–296.

Lutjens, S. (2004). (Re)reading reforms: Cuban education in the 2000s. Paper presented at the *48th annual conference of the comparative and international education society.* Salt Lake City, March.

Lynch, P. D. (1992). Educational change and the "Khalwa" in the Sudan: Reform reformed. *Journal of Educational Administration, 30*(4), 53–62.

Mali National Ministry of Education (1977). *The educational development in Mali since 1975.* Report (18 pp.). Bamako: Mali National Ministry of Education.

Mandela, N. (1994). *Long walk to freedom.* Boston: Little Brown.

Marais, M. A. (1995). The distribution of resources in education in South Africa. *Economics of Education Review, 14*(1), 47–52.

Maseko, J. (2001). Why teachers need reskilling on African culture to sustain the culture of learning in township secondary schools. Paper presented at the *9th BOLESWA international educational research symposium.* Gaborone, Botswana, July–August.

Matsaso, L. M. (2001). Observance of human rights and accessibility of basic education in national language policies: Lesotho's language policy in the voices of minority group citizens. Paper presented at the *9th BOLESWA international educational research symposium.* Gaborone, Botswana, July–August.

Mbeki, T. (1998). *Africa: The time has come. Selected speeches.* Cape Town: Tafelberg.

McGinn, N. F., & Cummings, W. K. (1997). Introduction. In: W. K. Cummings & N. F. McGinn (Eds), *International handbook of education and development: Preparing schools, students, and nations for the twenty-first century.* New York: Elsevier/Pergamon.

McGurk, N. J. (1990). *I speak as a white: Education, culture, nation.* Marshalltown: Heinemann Southern Africa.

Mehran, G. (2003). The paradox of tradition and modernity in female education in the Islamic Republic of Iran. *Comparative Education Review, 47*(3), 269–286.

Merryfield, M., & Tlou, J. (1995). The process of Africanizing the social studies. *Social Studies, 86*(6), 260–269.

Miller, R. M. (1987). The fading future. *Comparative Education Review, 31*(2), 218–240.

Milligan, J. A. (2003). Teaching between the cross and the crescent moon: Islamic identity, postcoloniality, and public education in the Southern Philippines. *Comparative Education Review, 47*(4), 468–492.

Mtonga, H. L. (1993). Comparing the role of education in serving socioeconomic and political development in Tanzania and Cuba. *Journal of Black Studies, 23*(3), 382–402.

Musonda, L. W. (1999). Teacher education reform in Zambia...Is it a case of a square peg in a round hole? *Teaching and Teacher Education, 15*(2), 157–168.

Muyebaa, K. C. (2001). In search of a curriculum for sustainable development in Zambia. Paper presented at the *9th BOLESWA international educational research symposium.* Gaborone, Botswana, July–August, 2001.

Odav, K., & Ndandane, M. (1998). Between school policy and practice: Comparing the Potgietersrus and Vryburg crises in the light of the South African schools act 2996. Paper presented at the *10th world congress of comparative education societies.* Cape Town, August.

Palmer, B. S. (1979). The school type as an instrument of educational reform: The Solomon Islands example. *CORE, 3*(2), f11–f12.

Parkay, F. W., Potisook, P., Chantharaskul, A., & Chunsakorn, P. (1999). Transforming the profession of teaching in Thailand. *International Journal of Educational Reform, 6*(1), 60–73.

Paulston, R. G. (1975). Revolutionary educational reform efforts in Latin America. *Pitt Magazine, 30*(2), 16–20.

Paulston, R. G. (1976). *Evaluating educational reform: An international casebook.* Report (449 pp.). ED133243.

Pitsoe, V. J. & Nieuwenhuis, F. J. (2001). The views of teachers on the impact of OBE on classroom management: A study of schools in the Lichtenburg District. Paper presented at the *9th BOLESWA international educational research symposium.* Gaborone, Botswana, July–August.

Plank, D. N., & Adams, D. (1989). Death taxes, and school reform: Educational policy change in comparative perspective. *Administrator's Notebook, 33*(1), 1–4.

Potenza, E. (2000). No name change for C2005. *The Teacher September 19, 2000 (3 pp.)*. Johannesburg: Daily Mail & Guardian.

Ramirez, F. O., & Boli-Bennett, J. (1982). World trends in education. In: P. G. Altbach, R. F. Arnove & G. P. Kelly (Eds), *Comparative education*. New York: McMillan.

Reilly, D. (1992). *Social, political, and economic variables associated with successful and unsuccessful educational change efforts: Kenya, Japan, Malaysia, the Soviet Union, and the United States*. Report (108 pp.). ED 350256.

Reimers, F., & McGinn, N. F. (1997). *Informed dialogue: Using research to shape education policy around the world*. London/Westport: Praeger.

Review of Curriculum 2005 (2000). *The Review of Curriculum 2005*. The Teacher/Daily Mail & Guardian, July 24, 2000. Available: http://teacher.co.za/200007/curriculum_resource.html.

Riddell, A. (1998). Reforms of educational efficiency and quality in developing countries: An overview. *Compare, 28*(3), 277–291.

Saif, P. S. (1987). Current reform in higher education in Bahrain. Paper presented at the *Annual meeting of the American Educational Research Association*. Washington, DC, April.

Saint, W. S. (1992). Universities in Africa: Strategies for stabilization and revitalization. World Bank technical paper No. 194. *Africa technical department series*. Washington, DC: World Bank.

Samoff, J. (1998). Institutionalizing international influence: The context for education reform in Africa. Paper presented at the *Conference on international trends in teacher education*. Durban, South Africa, July. ED443767.

Samoff, J. (1999). No teachers guide, no textbooks, no chairs: Contending with crisis in African education. In: R. E. Arnove & C. A. Torres (Eds), *Comparative education: The dialectic of the global and the local*. Oxford: Rowman and Littlefield.

Saunders, M., & Vulliamy, G. (1983). The implementation of curricular reform: Tanzania and Papua New Guinea. *Comparative Education Review, 27*(3), 351–373.

Schlemmer, L. (2001). Race relations and racism in everyday life. *Fast Facts 9/2001*, 2–12. Johannesburg: South African Institute of Race Relations.

Schmitz, S., & Pono, M. O. (1995). We are the Neocolonialists of Micronesia. Paper presented at the *annual Pacific education conference*. Koror, Palau, August.

Schwille, J., & Wheeler, C.W. (Eds). (1992). Primary education in Thailand: An integrated approach to policy research. *International Journal of Educational Research, 17*(2), 123–226.

Sharma, M. (1997). Revitalizing teacher education through distance education. Paper presented at the *regional workshop on teachers training through distance education*. Phuket, Thailand, October.

Sloper, D., & Le, T. C. (Eds) (1995). *Higher education in Vietnam: Change and response*. Singapore: Institute of Southeast Asian Studies ED388205.

Smith, F. (1993). *Whose language? What power?: A universal conflict in a South African setting*. New York: Teachers College Press.

Smith, W. L. (1996). Education reform in South Africa: Preparing for higher education beyond apartheid. Paper presented at the *Meeting "Investing in South Africa"*. Costa Mesa, CA: Coast Community College, March.

Soudien, C. (2001). Certainty and ambiguity in youth identities in South Africa: Discourses in Transition. Paper presented at the *9th BOLESWA international educational research symposium*. Gaborone, Botswana, July–August.

South African Institute of Race Relations (SAIRR) (2001a). South Africa survey: 2000–2001. *Population, education, policy sections.* Johannesburg: South African Institute of Race Relations.

South African Institute of Race Relations (2001b). Hold your applause for education. *Fast Facts, 2. 2–8.* Johannesburg: South African Institute of Race Relations.

Spalding, S. (1990). Educational development and reform in the soviet periphery: Mongolian People's Republic and Lao people's democratic republic. *Journal of Asian and African Affairs, 2*(1), 109–124.

Stromquist, N. (Ed.) (1994). *Education in urban areas: Cross-national perspectives.* Westport, CT: Greenwood Publishing.

Tavana, G. V. (1997). Cultural values and education in Western Samoa: Tensions between colonial roots and influences and contemporary indigenous needs. *International Journal of Educational Reform, 6*(1), 11–19.

Taylor, N., & Vlaardingerbroek, B. (2000). Pacific elementary science: A case study of educational planning for small developing nations. *International Journal of Educational Reform, 9*(2), 155–162.

Theissen, G. T., Achola, P. P. W., & Boakari, F. M. (1986). The underachievement of cross-national studies of education. In: P. G. Altbach & G. P. Kelly (Eds), *New approaches to comparative education.* Chicago: University of Chicago Press.

Thomas, H. (1997). Confessions of an International Education Consultant. *International Journal of Educational Reform, 6*(1), 4–10.

Thompson, J., Shaw, M., & Bane, L. (Eds). (2000). Reclaiming common purpose. *Special millennium issue.* Leicester: National Institute of Adult Continuing Education.

Tilak, J. B. G. (1997). The dilemma of reforms in financing higher education in India. *Higher Education Policy, 10*(1), 7–21.

Torney-Purta, J., Lehmann, Oswald, H., & Schulz, W. (2001). *Citizenship and education in twenty-eight countries: civic knowledge and engagement at age fourteen.* Executive Summary, (16 pp.); Full Report, (237 pp.). Amsterdam: International Association for the Evaluation of Educational Achievement.

Tsodzo, T. K. (1997). In our own eyes: A new look at African history. *International Journal of Educational Reform, 6*(4), 434–440.

Tsang, M. C. (1996). Financial reform of basic education in China. *Economics of Education Review, 15*(4), 323–344.

UNESCO (1977). Education in Africa in Light of the Lagos Conference (1976). Report, (53 pp.). Paris: UNESCO.

UNESCO (1978). Educational reforms and innovations in Africa. *Experiments and innovations in education, Number 34,* Paris: UNESCO.

Van Dam, A. (Ed.). (1992). Popular education in Latin America. Synthesis of the discussion themes. *Verhandelingen, No. 50.* The Hague: Centre for the Study of Education in Developing Countries.

Verspoor, A. (1989). Pathways to change: Improving the quality of education in developing countries. *World Bank Discussion Papers 53.* Washington, DC: World Bank.

Vlaardingerbroek, B. (1998). Challenges to reform: Botswana junior secondary school science teachers' perceptions of the development functions of science education. *International Journal of Educational Reform, 7*(3), 264–270.

Weber, E. (2002). Shifting to the right: The evolution of equity in the South African govern-
    ment's developmental and education policies. *Comparative Education Review, 46*(3),
    261–290.
Wheeler, C. W. (1989). Policy initiatives to improve primary school quality in Thailand: An
    essay on implementation, constraints, and opportunities for educational improvement.
    BRIDGES Research report series: Vol. 5. Cambridge, MA: Harvard Institute for Inter-
    national Development.
World Bank (1995). Priorities and strategies for education: A World Bank review. *Development
    in practice series*. Washington, DC: World Bank ED391671.
World Bank. (1996). *Uganda: The challenge of growth and poverty reduction: A World Bank
    country study*. Washington, DC: World Bank ED396874.
Yang, A. (1991). China's school curriculum reforms in the 1980s: Achievements and problems.
    Paper presented at the *Meeting of the New England Educational Research Association*.
    Portsmith, NH, April.
Yeboah, A. (1997). Precious beads multiply: Family decision making and girls' access to pri-
    mary schooling in Ghana. *International Journal of Educational Reform, 6*(4), 412–418.
Youngman, D. J., & Ishengoma, J. M. (1999). Educational equity in Tanzania: The imperiled
    promise of reform. *Journal of Education, 181*(1), 59–73.
Zachariah, M. (1989). Dilemmas of a successful people's education movement in India. Paper
    presented at the *Annual meeting of the comparative and international education society*.
    Cambridge, MA, March.
Zimba, R. F., & Kasanda, C. D. (2001). The role of educational research in educational change
    and reform: The case of Namibia. Paper presented at the *9th BOLESWA international
    educational research symposium*. Gaborone, Botswana, July–August.

EDUCATION DECENTRALIZATION IN AFRICA: GREAT EXPECTATIONS AND UNFULFILLED PROMISES ☆

Jordan Naidoo

INTRODUCTION

Over the past decade most central governments across sub-Saharan Africa (SSA) have begun to decentralize some fiscal, political, and administrative responsibilities to lower-levels of government, local institutions, and the private sector in pursuit of greater accountability and more efficient service delivery, often in an attempt to solve broader political, social, or economic problems (SARA, 1997). Education, in particular, has been fertile ground for such decentralization efforts. From Ethiopia to South Africa, SSA countries have engaged in some form of education decentralization, though the pace has been quite uneven. Ethiopia, Uganda, Senegal, and South Africa, for example, are proceeding fast, while Ghana, Mali, Tanzania, and Zimbabwe are under way more slowly. Guinea, Niger, Zambia, and Nigeria are at the other end of the continuum. Decentralization of social services, including

☆ I would like to acknowledge the Association for the Development of Education (ADEA) as major parts of this review draw from work that was undertaken for the ADEA project, "The Challenge of Learning: Improving the Quality of Basic Education in Sub Saharan Africa".

Global Trends in Educational Policy
International Perspectives on Education and Society, Volume 6, 99–124
ISSN: 1479-3679/doi:10.1016/S1479-3679(04)06004-9

education appears to be embedded in the political changes occurring in the region. In almost all SSA countries the introduction of decentralized systems are accompanied by popular elections for local councils as part of the general trend of the introduction of or return to democratization.

Almost all SSA education systems have, until recently, been managed through highly centralized bureaucracies. Most functions are carried out directly by the central Ministry of Education (MOE) or by officials posted at the regional, district or school level acting on detailed instructions issued by ministry officials at the national level. Changes in the relationship among economy (with calls to reduce public investment and increase privatization), politics (with support for deregulation and limiting the welfare role of the state), and education (with a push for local accountability and standardization) have begun to challenge previous notions about the role and structure of education (Torres (2000)). As a result many countries have begun to implement changes in the way education is managed by decentralizing functions and resources, diversifying service delivery modes, and transforming roles and responsibilities within the central MOE.

Despite the considerable support for and the near universality of decentralization policies, there are on-going debates about their impact. With little real evidence for the clear superiority of centralization or decentralization, justification for either is often based largely on ideological preferences. Many who opt for centralized reform are indifferent to possible obstacles to change. Advocates of decentralization, on the other hand, promote decentralized management and local governance as an end in itself. There is also ambivalence about which way to go, resulting in flip-flops or swings from top-down to bottom-up emphases. Both strategies are often pursued simultaneously, but in a completely disconnected manner. As a result the relative roles and relationships of centralized and decentralized strategies for educational reform is a morass, badly in need of conceptual and strategic clarification (Fullan, 1994). To better understand the process of decentralization in SSA, we need to examine the rationales and assumptions, how the programs are carried out (mechanisms and processes) and outcomes. Thus, this chapter reviews the evidence on the experience with these changes in a selection of SSA countries.

OVERVIEW OF EDUCATION DECENTRALIZATION IN SSA

In the education sector, there is slow (but sure) progress toward decentralization of the provision, decision-making (powers), and control of education services in the SSA region (ADEA, 1999). Although many of the countries have very specific management cultures linked to their particular colonial heritage, the context that shapes education decentralization management reforms in SSA is quite similar, with limited resources, fragile political systems and inefficient education systems and low capacity. Furthermore, despite considerable emphasis on decentralization of education in the past decade, central governments of SSA countries continue to play a major role in the allocation of educational resources. Even when authority is delegated to sub-national levels such as provinces or municipalities, individual school administrators, and parents play only a limited role. In many instances implementation of decentralization plans has been much slower than expected and the evidence of a positive impact on the conditions of schooling and student learning achievement remains unclear.

BACKGROUND

Compared to other regions of the world, Africa has the weakest formal local government structures, judged by size of expenditures and employees, yet decentralization is not new to the region. Since 1917 there have been four waves of decentralization in Francophone West Africa – after the World Wars, after independence in the 1960s, and in the current decade. Some Francophone African countries also decentralized just before independence. The Anglophone and Lusophone African countries have also seen multiple pre- and post-colonial decentralizations (Ribot, 2002). The changing and complex role of the state was crucially linked to many of these decentralization initiatives. Initially, decentralization proceeded by deconcentration,[1] but some Francophone West African governments decentralized after independence with the express purpose of introducing "participatory local governments". However, where democratic local government was legally mandated, for example in Senegal, Ghana, and Nigeria, the reforms did not alter central government control and administrative oversight that strangled local autonomy (Ribot, 2002). After the 1960's many decentralization initiatives were designed to bring "government closer to people", to tap the contributions and resources of communities, and to allow them to participate in national development (Crook & Manor, 1998). The economic crisis of the 1970s, followed by structural adjustment and political reforms in the 1980s and 1990s led to initiatives designed to improve state systems that were regarded to have failed or collapsed (Olowu, 2001). Thus the decentralization in SSA, which often involved a transfer of power, resources, and responsibilities to sub-national governments and/or to other actors, encompassed different institutional solutions to internal and external political pressures (Brosio, 2000).

In many ways current efforts reflect a move towards an idealized model of decentralization, in which the national MOE is seen as a proactive agent for change (Winkler & Gershberg, 2003).[2] In intent, if not in practice, decentralization policies and programs that most SSA countries have embarked upon in the past decade are different from previous efforts in two main respects. First, their primary objective is to empower the people as a part of efforts aimed at democratizing state institutions and initiate/support local self-governing structures, and not merely the extension of state control. Second, there is a growing appreciation of the need to develop not local government as such but local governance, focusing on processes rather than structures alone. This implies not only the vertical transfer of responsibilities and resources from central to local governments (the conventional conception of devolutionary decentralization) but also the development of horizontal networks between local governments and local non-state actors such as the private sector, civil society, and international organizations (Olowu, 2001).

BASIC TRENDS AFFECTING EDUCATION DECENTRALIZATION IN SSA

Basic trends that continue to affect education decentralization management across the SSA region:

1. The management of education across Africa has improved over the last 10 years, but remains a weak link in the quest for quality and efficiency of schooling. Educational systems are still not very efficient, and do not take sufficient account of popular needs and expectations. In almost all SSA countries there is still a fairly limited pool of people with the necessary management skills. With decentralization, pre-existing shortages of human resources may be exacerbated as demand at lower levels increases. The quality of personnel willing to work in the regions and local levels often leaves much to be desired. The situation is exacerbated when there are no resources for transport to visit schools, organize training workshops, or disseminate newsletters.

2. Groups like women, the rural population, and ethnic and linguistic minorities are still marginalized or relatively excluded from education

systems. Parents and families, many of whom face extreme poverty, still bear substantial costs of education (Niane, 2003a).

3. Many of the most serious problems facing education managers across SSA are not in and of themselves education problems, but are linked to the larger socio-political situation and severely constrained economic context. Serious threats posed are by wars and internal strife, HIV/AIDS, persisting poverty, and expanding population (especially school age).

4. Education decentralization is often embedded in larger state reforms, and in the context of elected local governments with few important responsibilities and smaller revenues (Winkler & Gershberg, 2003).

Despite major management reforms, education management in most SSA countries still follows a pyramid model, in which national policy, programs, and logistics are formulated by a central MOE organized into a set of divisions, bureaus, and units. This central ministry works through a network of provincial, regional, and district education offices that largely duplicate the structure of the central MOE and are responsible for ensuring that central policies are communicated and implemented in the schools. Individual schools are managed by head teachers whose authority and responsibilities may differ by country to country, but usually involve some combination of school management, school–ministry communications, school–community relations, and instructional supervision. The reforms introduced in the last ten years, include:

- Decentralizing functions and resources from the central level to the lower levels of the administration and to the schools.
- Strengthening the autonomy and decision-making power of the schools.
- Introducing more effective methods for community participation in the school system and in ensuring the quality of the services delivered and the results.
- Consolidating and reforming school inspection and support programs.
- Introducing systems to monitor and assess performance so that political decisions are taken with full knowledge of the facts and in a way that empowers those involved.
- Changes in funding and financial management in education and in schools.

Problems that have slowed this process include limited resources, bureaucratic resistance, low capacity of local government, and lack of consultation and coordination between different levels of government. In several countries sub-regional or district offices have failed to fulfil their mandates owing to lack of adequately trained personnel, essential resources, and the absence of administrative systems and controls, overwhelming multiple demands, and lack of clear definition of roles. A lack of willingness to delegate authority and reliance on complex, but often, irrelevant administrative texts present serious problems. There is an overemphasis on routine tasks by top managers, leaving them overworked and with little time to devote their efforts to the strategic management and external relations and other critical management tasks. The lack of commitment to flexibility, delegation, and decentralization of authority in general seriously compromises their effectiveness at the local, municipal, and regional levels (Vengroff, 2000). Moreover the effect on equity has been mixed. In some cases the distribution of funds between regions has become more equitable and additional resources have been targeted towards marginalized groups. However, differences in learner expenditure between well off and disadvantaged remain or have widened.

TYPOLOGY OF EDUCATION DECENTRALIZATION IN SSA

Education decentralization is a complex process that can result in major changes in the way education systems are organized, make policy, generate revenues and spend funds, manage schools, and develop and deliver the curriculum (Fiske, 1996). While there is wide variation in decentralization designs, in general, education decentralization reforms in SSA have revolved around attempts to restructure centralized education bureaucracies and create devolved systems with different administrative levels, varying degrees of institutional autonomy. At the school level it varies from giving school councils or governing bodies limited authority to allocate non-personnel budgets to allowing autonomy under strict performance contracts to almost complete management autonomy. Using the interaction between level of decision-making and degree of decision-making power one may use the following *typology to describe decentralization of education management* reforms in sub-Saharan Africa[3]: as Table 1 shows the process has also involved the transfer of some form (and degree) of authority from central governments to: (i) provincial, state, or regional entities; (ii) municipal, county, or district governments, and (iii) schools.

(1) From central government (or central ministries of education) to provincial, state or regional entities:
    Primarily *deconcentration* – the transfer of some decision-making from the central government MOE to the regional/local offices of the MOE or

Table 1. Typology of Education Decentralization in SSA.

Level	Form	Functions
Central government (MOE) to provincial, state regional or district offices	*Deconcentration*	Regional/district offices are in charge of personnel and financial management functions. Central government retains control of fiscal allocations and appointments
Central government (MOE) to municipal, county, or district governments	*Delegation and/or Devolution*	Management decisions-staff appointments and allocation of local education budgets. Central governments retain accountability – control financial transfers from national treasuries
From Central government (MOE) and regional/ district offices or local governments to schools	*Devolution*	Schools responsible for routine administrative decisions or more substantial powers. May include: maintenance, appointment of staff, school policy, development plans, curriculum choices, fund-raising, and financial management

of the central government. Regional offices may take charge of personnel and financial management functions personnel and in terms of allocating and reallocating budgets. Central government retains control over fiscal allocations and teacher appointments.

(2) From central government (central ministries of education) to municipal, county or district governments:

Primarily *devolution* – transfer of decision-making from the central government to elected regional or local governments. Management decisions, including appointment of school principals/head teachers and allocation of regional or local education budgets are the responsibility of regional or local authorities. While central governments retain accountability by controlling financial transfers from national treasuries to regions, regional and local authorities enjoy substantial independent decision-making authority.

(3) From central government (central ministries of education) and regional offices or local governments to schools:

Primarily *delegation or devolution*[4] – transfer of management or governance decision-making authority from central or regional government to principals or school governing bodies. The functions or powers may span routine administrative decisions to substantial school-wide policy;

and, range from maintenance of buildings to appointment of staff, setting school policy, school development plans, curriculum choices, and fund raising and financial management. This category includes what Winkler and Gershberg (2003) call implicit devolution where grassroots initiatives (as in community schools) ensure that school or community based structures hold decision-making power.

Devolution, and the distribution of authority to make decisions and to take action by local governments or local communities independently of central administrative oversight, appears to occur less frequently than deconcentration, where local entities act largely as the local agents of central governments. There is greater deconcentration in Ghana, Nigeria, Niger, Tanzania, and Zimbabwe and more devolution in South Africa, Uganda, Senegal, and Mali for example.

Different management functions that are being distributed, to varying degrees, among the levels of the education management system include functions such as: organization of instruction (textbooks, teaching methods, curricula, schedule); personnel management (hiring/firing, pay, assigning teaching responsibilities, pre- and in-service training); planning and structures (school openings/closings, course content, school improvement plans); resource management (expenditures, budget allocations); and, monitoring and evaluation (inspections and supervision, examinations). In most cases, however, ultimate curriculum authority, personnel management and financing responsibilities remain firmly located at the center. The partial transfer of responsibility often reflects a desire to ensure that national educational development goals, and equity objectives remain under the purview of the central authority.

In particular, in cases where it is acknowledged that the primary mode of decentralization is administrative and the devolution of power is largely rhetorical, the center continues to play a significant role both in policy setting and in carrying out routine functions. In most, if not all SSA, countries strong central regulation of education remains. Key responsibilities in governance, management, finance, and curriculum at regional, community, and school levels continue to be defined by national ministries of education. Sometimes this is done in partnership with local authorities but more than not often it unilateral. National guidelines continue to be an important mechanism in translating state policy into local reality and defining how schools are run.

Much of the transfer of responsibilities in the context of education decentralization to local government units or to local communities appears to be limited to how they can generate more revenues to support schools. The reality is that the center often still retains power over how revenues at the local level are managed and spent. This is necessary for a number of reasons. There is not much of a tax base at the local level; and even if there were, financing education with locally generated revenue (the U.S. model) inevitably leads to "savage inequalities". Most of the African models involve transfers of resources from the national government to local governments, administrations or to schools. Much of these transfers are in kind (teachers and instructional materials) but increasingly decentralization involves transferring financial resources to local administrations or schools for them to decide on the allocation within certain guidelines.

MOTIVES FOR EDUCATION DECENTRALIZATION IN SSA

It is necessary to pay attention to these stated rationales as well as the unstated motives. While the motives for decentralization are numerous, disparate, and often, contradictory, most education decentralization efforts in SSA, have been motivated by a mix of political, administrative, and fiscal considerations. In many cases it involved a challenge to the prevailing model of the national welfare state by the neoliberal model promoting withdrawal, privatization, and localization (Astiz, Wiseman, & David, 2002).

Although improvement in teaching/learning processes is always desirable, it is not generally the sole or even primary objective of many educational management changes in the selected countries. Political and economic objectives such as: transferring costs from the national to regional budgets, bringing stability to divided regions, agreeing to pressures from external organizations, and addressing demands for local autonomy may drive the reform rather than educational considerations per se. Yet there is always the hopeful expectation of clear and conclusive information about the positive impact of educational decentralization at the classroom level.

Motives in general include: increasing efficiency, accountability, democratization, and community participation; becoming more responsive to local needs; mobilizing resources; and devolving financial responsibility (Welsh & McGinn, 1999). The CEF Program in Tanzania[5], for example, demonstrates the multiple motivations in practice – it involves communities in school management and attempts to mobilize resources. The distinction between economic (administrative) and political (governance) aims is helpful in making sense of the disparate aims associated with decentralization of

education in SSA. Where economic/administrative aims are central (e.g. in
Burkina Faso, Niger, and Tanzania) deconcentration with little relinquish-
ing of central authority is apparent. Where the political motive is primary, a
common goal for decentralization (e.g. in Senegal, South Africa, Ghana,
and Uganda) there tends to be a break from a strong, "central" location of
power, and greater devolution of power and resources to sub-national levels
of government and local communities.

While improvement in teaching/learning processes is always desirable, it is
not generally the sole or even primary objective of many educational management changes in the selected countries. The primary reasons for decentralization are often both political, a means to attain greater political
legitimacy, and economic, a response to financial constraints that these
states face. Political and economic objectives such as: transferring costs from
the national to regional budgets, bringing stability to divided regions,
agreeing to pressures from external organizations, and addressing demands
for local autonomy may drive the reform rather than educational considerations per se. Yet there is always the hopeful expectation of clear and
conclusive information about the positive impact of educational decentralization at the classroom level.

It is clear from this review and others (Azfar, Kahkonen, Lanyi, Meagher,
& Rutherford, 1999; Brosio, 2000; Manor, 1997; SARA, 1997) that certain
central assumptions behind the economic/administrative and political/
governance motives for decentralization, are often quite problematic and do
not take into account contextual realities. There is often a blind faith and
belief in a causal link between decentralization and better economic performance and democratization. Similarly, when participation and accountability are asserted in decentralization policies and programs, one must
question whose participation the architects of the program had in mind and
for whose benefit is the accountability. In Ghana, for example, the main
objective of increasing participation was to strengthen the hand of national
and local political and bureaucratic elites, and to improve central administration (Ayee, 1994). Often, then decentralization advanced for its instrumental administrative value may actually be for political consolidation at
the center. In such cases it serves as a rhetorical mechanism to manage
conflict and provide "compensatory legitimization". The center is able to
purchase state legitimacy and maintain power through participation at the
expense of reform and change (Weiler, 1983).

Efficiency is often provided as the underlying rationale for decentralized
provision of public services, including education. However, it is not always
justifiable because significant diseconomies of scale may result in higher unit

costs for public services under decentralized arrangements; and spillover costs or benefits may mean that locally derived outcomes are not efficient from a broader, national perspective. Furthermore, in the quest for efficiency, the other goals of equity and democratization may be overlooked. However, there is little reason to believe that changes in education management *alone* necessarily improve the situation.

REVIEW OF SELECTED SSA COUNTRY EXPERIENCES WITH DECENTRALIZATION

Country experiences include: Ethiopia, Ghana, Nigeria, South Africa, Tanzania, Uganda, and Zambia (Anglophone), and Burkina Faso, Guinea, Niger, Mali, and Senegal (Francophone). The countries were selected based on two criteria: countries currently carrying out educational reforms and access to information on education decentralization[6]. While there are significant variations in population size, geographical expanse, economic level, and education attainment among the countries, there are also commonalities in terms of similar colonial legacies, relationships with external donor organizations, and economic status. All are extremely poor and have suffered varying degrees of economic and political turmoil since independence; and, poverty and external pressures shape the reforms that occurring across the region. Rationales for decentralization include increasing quality education, bringing schools closer to the community, and reducing financial responsibility of the central government. Table 2 lists the selected countries reviewed in terms of a typology of the management functions decentralized.

Each country has relocated different management functions that range from financial responsibility to the monitoring and evaluation of school progress. The main shifts in management functions appear to be administrative, mainly the deconcentration of responsibilities from the central government to intermediate levels. The types of responsibilities that have been transferred include implementation of decisions made by the central government and some responsibility for financial generation of school funding.

While most SSA education systems appear to be somewhat resistant to change, current initiatives do represent important steps in shifting educational decision-making closer to the locus of action. Deconcentration and/or devolution reforms of the last 10 years have: strengthened the autonomy and decision-making power of many schools, encouraged the development of local leadership and administrative competence, introduced effective methods for community participation; improved capacity, and systems to

Table 2. Typology of Management Decentralization in Selected
Countries.

	Deconcentration to Region	Devolution to Localities/Regions	Devolution/ Delegation to Schools
Burkina Faso	x		
Ethiopia	x	X	x
Ghana		X	x
Guinea	x		
Mali		X	x
Niger		x	
Nigeria	x	x	
Senegal	x		x
South Africa	x		x
Tanzania	x		x
Uganda	x		x
Zambia	x	x	x

monitor and assess performance; and, in some cases, has changed funding
and financial management. It should be noted, however, that no system is
either totally centralized or totally decentralized; efficient systems will always have a combination of centrally and locally managed responsibilities;
and the local context will largely determine what the most efficient combination is in a given situation.

FORMS OF EDUCATION DECENTRALIZATION IN SSA

Forms of education decentralization evident in SSA include: *School-based
Management, Community-based Initiatives, Community Schools, Private
Provision, Outsourcing, Program Contracts, and De-concentrated Teacher
Management*:

• *School-based management*: In SSA, School-based management (SBM) includes a variety of initiatives that enable school and/or community-based
structures to assume powers related to school and educational decisions
more broadly. Schools are expected to become increasingly self-managed,
and make decisions regarding curriculum, budget and resource allocation, and staff and students (Abu-Duhou, 1999). For example education
decentralization initiatives in Uganda, South Africa, and Senegal have

focused more directly on management reforms at the school level. SBM is
expected to improve the quality of teaching and learning by locating decisions closer to the school providing for sensitivity to local conditions
and allowing teachers to design education programs to meet local needs.

• *Community-based initiatives*: Community participation ranges from familiar forms of support – such as community involvement in construction
– to more active involvement in management, planning, and learning.
Community participation in SSA is not only many faceted, and the ability
of communities to participate in and support education varies widely, its
impact is often uneven. Some well resourced, highly motivated, and co-
hesive communities are single-handedly financing and managing education on an ongoing basis. Other communities lack the resources to make
anything more than a minor contribution to the costs of education, or are
unable or unwilling to work together (Watt, 2001). Parents/Students' Associations (PAs/APEs), nevertheless, constitute one of the most striking
features of the community's participation in basic education schooling. In
Mali, NGOs are supporting the operation of the Centers of Education for
Development (CED), while the community, which sets up a management
committee, pays teachers. In Guinea, a seven-person management committee, designated by the community, oversees the NAFA centers, or
second-chance schools for 10–16 year olds not in regular schools. The
management committee ensures the provision of premises and the
enrollment of 60–90 children, and is responsible for payment of the
organizers (Niane, 2003b). In Senegal as part of the *"Faire Faire"* strategy, community schools are playing an important role in providing
greater access to education for at risk youth.

• *Community schools*: Community schools often functioning as an alternate
system are an important part of the educational landscape in SSA. While
the types of community schools and government relationships to community schools vary from country to country, one can identify two main
community school models in SSA[7]: (1) new community (often with NGO
involvement) established and managed schools and (2) take over or
strengthening community management in existing public schools. In
Zambia there are over 700 community schools that are the result of the
population's desire to send their children to nearby schools, which are
less expensive and less rigid than traditional schools. These schools are
open to under-privileged children and place emphasis on the acquisition
of the basic principals of reading, writing, arithmetic, and relevant life-
skills. In Mali, 10% of primary children are enrolled in community
schools, many of which resemble public primary schools. Transforming

community schools into those administered by local communes (local government offices) and receiving communal funding is part of the educational decentralization process in Mali. Community schools or *écoles d'initiative locale* (EDIL) in Togo, make up about 20% of all primary schools. Although the *écoles communautaires de base* (ECB) in Senegal are part of non-formal education, students who graduate from ECBs can move into the public system. Many community schools exist in Ethiopia and local officials are increasingly involved in community school programs. *Ecoles spontanées* in Chad are created and financed by village communities where there are no public schools (Miller-Grandvaux & Yoder, 2002). However, many of the schools are often under-funded, of low quality and a poor substitute even for under-performing government schools.

- *Private provision*: Private schools are expanding in most SSA countries given the state's difficulty in ensuring adequate provision. For example, Côte d'Ivoire now put 60% of its secondary schools in private hands, a trend the government actively supports through the provision of financial incentives. In a number of countries the demand for private provision is growing as more and more "clients" (parents) perceive those schools to have better quality and accountability. SSA experience with private schools is of some importance a broader strategy to diversify sources of funding and service provision and enhance school autonomy. Some see it as a form of *"stakeholding"* – of building loyalty among partners who receive a targeted service (Niane, 2003b). Experiences with private provision can suggest how gains in public school efficiency and effectiveness may be achieved by adopting successful management practices employed in private schools (Republic of Gambia/ DOSE, 2003). However, in SSA private school quality varies and often they are no better than public schools and sometimes the quality may be worse.

- *Outsourcing*: Outsourcing, i.e. contracting external providers is another way to involve the private sector. It is usually done through a bidding process, where the winning group enters into a contract with the responsible government agency to set up and implement a subproject within a larger program. In education, outsourcing has been used to implement services such as school transport, canteen, cleaning, and maintenance, and to set up infrastructure and support programs (Nordtveit, 2003). Many argue that outsourcing services is preferable to government-implemented programs not only because specialized providers are more efficient, but also because the services provided are user-friendlier, since the providers are often community based and provide services that are based on actual demand and need. An example of this approach is the *Faire Faire* strategy used in Senegal.

- *Program contracts* (PC): Program contracts have been tried out in Madagascar (and are based on local traditions of agreement and commitment)[8] in order to increase community involvement in the life of the school. Each contract involves five parties: the village community, the teachers, the principal, the school district, and the support project. The Madagascan experience indicates that successful scale up of the *Program Contract* approach requires: mobilization of communities; adapting *Program Contracts* to the realities of the local and/or regional context; defining the roles and responsibilities; drawing on existing local structures to ensure contracts are met; setting up inclusive monitoring systems; and, a participatory approach to support community skills and motivate contracting parties at community level.
- *Deconcentrated teacher management*: Several countries have begun to decentralize certain administrative responsibilities relating to teachers. Changes include: the "uniformization" of databases and processes of data collection on teachers, and computerization of information systems for personnel management. Decision-making powers have been devolved, particularly to the intermediate – i.e. district (Uganda) and/or regional (Ethiopia, South Africa, Botswana, and Malawi) – level. School heads, and in some cases school boards (South Africa) and local councils (Uganda), have been given an important say on teacher deployment and recruitment (Guinea – the prefectures are to be responsible for recruiting new teachers).

Ultimate curriculum authority, personnel management and financing responsibility remain firmly located at the center in most countries, whereas the responsibility for providing the service is actually moving down into the system. This is expected since the transfer of responsibility will always be partial – certain areas will always remain the purview of the central authority given national development goals, equity concerns, and so on. But current initiatives do represent important steps in shifting educational decision-making closer to the locus of action. In a few countries, South Africa, Ethiopia, and Uganda, school governing bodies appear to be established. However, due to lack of documentation, the actual authority and implementation at the school-level is unknown.

CHANGING ROLE OF CENTRAL EDUCATION
MINISTRIES IN THE MANAGEMENT OF
EDUCATION SYSTEMS

Despite major management reforms, education management across SSA still follows a pyramid model, in which national policy, programs, and logistics are formulated by a central MOE organized into a set of divisions, bureaus, and units. Central ministries usually work through a network of provincial, regional, and district education offices that largely duplicate the structure of the central MOE and are responsible for ensuring that central policies are communicated and implemented in the schools. Individual schools are managed by head teachers whose authority and responsibilities may differ by country to country, but usually involve some combination of school management, school–ministry communications, school–community relations, and instructional supervision. Recently, however, as many SSA countries move from an emphasis on access alone to quality improvement, there is a growing recognition of the need for viable and appropriate management systems, in which the day-to-day work of education managers at all levels is different from that in the traditional bureaucratic systems of these countries. New laws, policies, and strategies have been formulated from Mauritania to Madagascar in attempts at transforming their education systems.

Many still face a central challenge in decentralization, namely, how to balance increased diversity, flexibility, and local control with the responsibility of the national authorities for ensuring that an orderly provision of education occurs across a nation, and that it is equitable across regions and socio-economic and ethnic divisions (Abu-Duhou, 1999, p. 20). As a result, a paradigm shift is occurring in education management suggesting a changed role for central education ministries in Africa. The responsibilities of the different government levels and actors are being redefined and reallocated. In centralized systems, national ministry "functions" usually covered the gamut of planning, program implementation, coordination, personnel supervision, monitoring, and evaluation. But as they begin to decentralize, the central ministries' roles are changing from implementer to technical consultant and coordinator responsible for policy formulation, and overall quality assurance, monitoring, and evaluation. New steering instruments and practices have been proposed in a number of countries. In Uganda for example, District Education Officers (DEOs) are responsible, in conjunction with communities, for the delivery of primary education, while the MOE focuses on policy-making, investment management, and quality assurance. In practice, DEOs are responsible for monitoring and supporting all primary schools in their districts. Through the District Service Commission, each district recruits and assigns primary school teachers, while payment of teachers' salaries remains a central responsibility (Moulton, 2000). In Tanzania, the Ministry of Regional Administration and Local Government is responsible for delivering basic education through its district administration.

While the role of the central ministry as implementer is decreasing, it still has a significant role to play in management, financing, and oversight of the system. The central ministry and sub-national and school actors may share the responsibility for ensuring minimum educational standards necessary to safeguard equity of access and outcomes. The central ministries generally plan the national curriculum (e.g. South Africa) and are responsible for national-level examinations. In heterogeneous societies such as Nigeria or Ethiopia, local governments are given some latitude to localize curriculum, by introducing indigenous languages. While textbook approval and procurement is usually centralized for efficiency reasons, distribution is often outsourced. Uganda and Kenya, for example have decentralized the choice of textbooks to the school level. More central ministries are also taking responsibility for overall accountability, making the systematic collection, analysis, and reporting of information critical elements. The development of an Educational Management Information System (EMIS) system in Namibia, for example is meeting the information needs of users at all levels of the system (Voigts, 1999).

In reflecting on the changing role of central ministries of education it is important to draw a distinction between provision of education services and financing. The first deals with delivering and managing the education services, while the latter relates to the source of funding. Since local governments in Africa have little effective taxation power or revenue generation capacity, financing will have to remain a national responsibility. However, it does not follow that provision and management of education should be a sole national responsibility. To address the challenge of achieving efficiency, equity, and quality, responsibility for provision and management is increasingly being shared among different levels of government, schools, and communities (e.g. in Mali, Tanzania, and South Africa).

SOME PROMISING DEVELOPMENTS IN DECENTRALIZATION AND QUALITY IMPROVEMENT IN SSA

Few decentralization reforms have in the past connected directly to educational quality expectations mainly because the implementation experience in SSA is relatively recent and often has been uneven, weak, and focused more on resource mobilization than on improvements in instructional quality. More recently, there have been some positive developments with decentralization experiences now seemingly deeper and more significant than just 5 years ago. Several recent initiatives related to decentralization and management are changing the way schools are organizing and directly affect the learning and teaching process:

- *Local curriculum adaptation*: Some countries have created space for local curriculum adaptation. Experiences in Lesotho, Nigeria, Niger, and Zambia highlight the role that teachers, school management, and communities can play in curriculum development.
- *Involving school management committees:* In responsibilities beyond resource mobilization and classroom construction. In Guinea they play a prominent role in the management of the textbook program. In Madagascar the contribution of different stakeholders are formalized in a program-contract.
- *Managing school resources*: In South Africa, Kenya Tanzania, and Uganda, school management committees or governing bodies are responsible for the utilization of funds disbursed to schools by the national or state Ministries of Education. Funds are used for instructional materials and operating cost like support staff salaries and maintenance.
- *Adapting school calendar*: Autonomy of schools to adapt the school calendar to local conditions. Community schools in Mali and Senegal enjoy strong community support in which the school becomes a "village project". The community school model is in a number of countries, accompanied by interesting innovations in adapting the school calendar, integrating local languages and developing practical community-based activities.
- *Monitoring and evaluation*: Programs in Mali, Benin, and Guinea implement community managed monitoring systems through which parents collect, analyze and use information to improve the schools in their communities.
- *Moving responsibility for personnel management to lower levels*: In some Francophone countries some attempts are being made to move the responsibility for personnel management to lower levels. In Guinea and Senegal alternate policies and practices have been adopted in recent years and a partnership has been developed with local education authorities, which are encouraged to hire and pay teachers in exchange for government assistance and support. In Senegal, the government opted for a policy of hiring teachers as "Education volunteers" outside civil service regulations and salaries.

- *Decentralized delivery of in-service teacher training programs*: A system of regular in-service workshops organized regionally or locally (for example, Uganda, Ethiopia, and Tanzania) to ensure regular participation by teachers and opportunities for practice and follow up. Successful decentralization of in-service activities includes leadership development and the establishment of local resource centers, local teacher groups, and school cluster networks (Guinea, Namibia, South Africa, Senegal, Zambia, and Zimbabwe).
- *Involving teachers in quality improvement*: In Guinea and several other Francophone countries small grants programs enable teachers to become partners in the improvement of teaching and learning by initiating and carrying out their own professional development projects. With ministry personnel as facilitators, teams of teachers design projects and compete for small grants to carry them out.

Despite these promising examples, the decentralization of education management as implemented has not yet had a major impact on instructional practice. The little evidence that is available, provides some indications that the absence of a "clear connection between education management reforms and improved education quality" is due in some cases to problems of implementation (interventions have not been fully operationalized) and yet others to a failure of design logic (lack of connection between decentralization and quality improvements). Establishing this connection in SSA is difficult since the experience is relatively recent and uneven, and often focused more on resource mobilization than on improvements in quality. Moreover, there is little reason to believe that changes in education management alone will improve teaching practice and student learning. Decentralization and management reforms can contribute to improvements in service delivery and efficiency of resource utilization but successful implementation will require improvement in the other intervening variables such as leadership, teacher training, parent support, availability of resources, student and teacher motivation, and peer group pressure (Hanson, 2000).

LESSONS AND REFLECTIONS ON EDUCATION DECENTRALIZATION IN SSA

Given the complexity of factors that contribute to effective schooling and quality education, it is extremely difficult to assess the impact of education decentralization on quality. In the context of SSA, this issue is exacerbated by the lack of detailed empirical work on educational quality outcomes more generally. Nevertheless from this review it is apparent that whatever the assumed benefits, a number of unintended consequences are contributing to the unfulfilled promise of decentralization in SSA. A connection between high quality learning and education management reforms has not been clearly substantiated in the countries reviewed. However, this may be due in part to lack of information on actual outcomes. There are few, if any, large-scale longitudinal studies that have examined the impact of education decentralization and management across the region. The comments on progress are based on limited empirical evidence and need to be viewed in that light.

Across SSA problems that have slowed the actual devolution of power include a lack of resources, bureaucratic resistance, low capacity of local government, and the lack of consultation and coordination between different levels of government. Yet, it arguable whether extreme forms of education decentralization or devolution is actually practical or desirable in SSA owing to equity concerns. Ensuring equality of educational opportunity, as measured by equality in educational spending, requires that a high degree of centralized financing is the norm in sub-Saharan Africa where income inequality is extremely high.

Education decentralization has not yet necessarily led to better quality education, improved governance, or greater efficiency in resource allocation or service delivery. This is not unexpected given that improving education quality while maintaining the integrity of the national education system and ensuring equity is a much greater challenge than administering expansion of enrollments (Adams & Chapman, 2002). The challenge is greater still in SSA because most education management changes as initially conceived within the context of decentralization, hardly touched key management issues relating to the organization of instruction, planning of programs, course content, financial management of funds, and personnel management.

Nevertheless, there are signs of the reforms making some difference to overall management improvements, and in some cases improvements in teaching and learning. Successes include better financial management, more involvement, and interest in schools at the community and school level, and increasing administrative capability at the local level. Furthermore many of the decentralization and management reforms have stimulated discussion and created greater recognition of the need to focus on changes that impact learning and teaching more directly.

Top–down hierarchical management structures still dominate institutional arrangement in ostensibly decentralized systems. Hierarchy is maintained in decision-making processes over resource allocation, the recruitment and deployment of personnel, and procurement of inputs, all of which impact school performance. Hierarchical control inhibits communication between authorities and communities. Grassroots communities and local players are still on the margins of the education management system, which remains relatively dominated by the central bodies or by certain local actors. For example, while new models of democratic management and governance are being introduced at school level in many countries, the central influence of the principal or headmaster in school leadership should not be underestimated. Official reports and policy statements exhibit contradictions between a predilection for strong and effective school leaders and a commitment to consultation and participation in decision-making.

A large number of countries have embarked on education decentralization, often within a context of a broader national policy. The process is mainly being implemented in three ways: administrative deconcentration, diversification of providers and differentiation of programs. It almost always includes administrative decentralization but the evidence suggests that this is an important but far from sufficient element in improving the quality and efficiency of service delivery. The deconcentration process requires deliberate efforts to involve communities in the process of schooling and the provision of direct support to schools. Such support is particularly important as decentralization in SSA may actually be increasing the unit costs of providing education, and may not be contributing to efficiency or quality gains as expected. In addition to the greater capacity and resources needed by the center to manage a decentralized system, increasing parents' voice raises the inputs of private time and effort. Such private costs are often not included in public sector accounting of the costs and benefits of decentralization, whereas they should be. These costs may be considerable and may limit the participation of parents, thus undermining quality improvement efforts that depend on greater community participation. This was clear for example in efforts in Tanzania and South Africa to encourage greater parent and community contribution.

There is some evidence of localities' innovative efforts to manage their own affairs, the growing involvement of community groups, and a remarkable degree of public awareness and understanding of the decentralization program. Community members are able and willing to raise significant resources for the improvement of their schools. It has enabled hard-pressed schools to access alternate sources of support, including informal contributions from pupils and families, and mobilized local support. However, resource mobilization benefits have limited application especially since in most cases there are extremely poor communities, and decentralization and cost recovery have very serious equity implications. There has been some improvement towards a more equitable distribution of funds between regions, and for marginalized groups. However, differences in learner expenditure between well off and traditionally disadvantaged remain and in some cases may have widened as a result of decentralization.

In SSA, as elsewhere, schooling investments are determined by a number of factors, including school characteristics. For example, schools with higher quality or are the first to introduce decentralization may tend to be in areas in which expected rates of returns from education are greater. If so, the impact of school quality and decentralization on investments may be overestimated. To identify the impact of schooling induced by decentralization, on quality outcomes, it is important in the SSA context where there is such wide variation to control for individual, family, and community characteristics.

The restructuring of education management has important implications for lower levels of the hierarchy as well as for the central services. Effective restructuring will require sustained capacity development, including clear definition of roles and responsibilities, incentives for performance, continuous training, and technical support at all levels of the system. Capacity development programs should: be flexible enough to accommodate contextual variations across the country; focus on both short and long-term objectives; and, go beyond technocratic aspects and attend to power relationships, and political processes as well.

CONCLUSION

In general the adoption of decentralization policies across SSA represents confused attempts to devolve responsibility to individual schools, leaving them without the collective support structures they need and, ironically, leading to an increase rather than a decrease in bureaucracy (as each institution has to deal with administrative matters formerly handled centrally) (Humes, 2000). The idealized model on which such attempts are based suggests a tacit assumption made by most central policy-makers involved in formulating and implementing large scale educational reforms, including education decentralization reforms: a universally applied remedy is received by local schools in uniform ways; and, by lifting the heavy hand of central regulation and bureaucratic control, a thousand (organizational) flowers will bloom and school actors will assume wise leadership and work towards improving school quality (Fuller & Rivarola, 1998). In many cases, this, of course, does not transpire – internal dynamics and institutionalized features of environments condition the evolution and impact of reforms. Therefore, putting one's faith in education decentralization as a solution to problems of school improvement is quite problematic. A more prudent approach involvers a mix of political will (policy-makers working together with stakeholders), technical inputs (competent policies and personnel in education), and economic factors (adequate resources). There has to be congruency between "bottom-up" and "top-down" principles, emphasizing expertise, rights, and power of local communities while taking into account central responsibilities, contexts, and constraints.

NOTES

1. Based on Rondinelli's conceptualization of decentralization, deconcentration, delegation, and devolution have been applied to the form or functional dimension where: deconcentration refers to the transfer of planning, decision-making or administrative authority from the central government to its field organizations and local units, local government or to non-governmental organizations; delegation refers to the transfer of some powers of decision-making and management authority for specific functions to units or organizations that are not under direct control of central government ministries; and devolution refers to the transfer of authority for decision-making, finance, and management to quasi-autonomous units of local government such as municipalities that elect their own mayors and councils, raise their own revenues, and have independent authority to make investment decisions (Cheema & Rondinelli, 1983; Rondinelli, 1981, 1999). See Table 1 for a typology of education decentralization in SSA.
2. The review by Winkler and Gersberg (2003) is a draft, and is used by permission of Donald Winkler.
3. Similarly, Winkler and Gershberg apply Rondinelli's general deconcentration–devolution–delegation typology to education decentralization in the African context, but add a fourth category, implicit devolution. Since this typology is particularly helpful in understanding the mechanics of education decentralization in SSA it used substantially in the typology presented here. It used by permission of one of the authors, Donald Winkler.
4. Whether one refers to it as delegation or devolution may depend largely on the degree of autonomy that is granted to local actors, that is principals, teachers, support staff, parents and community members, and in some cases students.
5. The Community Education Fund (CEF), a component of the Human Resources Development Project (HRDP) operating in 1642 schools in 16 districts, matches funds mobilized at the community level with a government grant, to support implementation of a school plan developed by the community, in collaboration with the school staff.

6. Other SSA countries that are decentralizing their system were also examined; however, due to a lack of specific information about implementation, their experiences are only reflected in the general lessons.

7. The kinds of community schools that this chapter focuses on in the context of community involvement and decentralization are community schools that have a connection to the public primary education system to distinguish them from those community "schools" that form part of non-formal education.

8. In Madagascar, the "dina" is an oral or written agreement made between community members (fokonolona) and is accepted by all the contracting parties as having the force of law, with sanctions (social or financial) for any breach.

REFERENCES

Abu-Duhou, I. (1999). *School based management.* Paris: IIEP/UNECO.

Adams, D. W., & Chapman, D. W. (2002). *The quality of education: Dimensions and strategies.* Manila, Philippines: Asian Development Bank.

Association for the Development of Education in Africa (ADEA) (1999). *Prospective, stock-taking review of education in Africa: Draft synthesis document for the 1999 biennial meeting.* Available: http://www.adeanet.org/programs/biennial99/en_synthesis.pdf

Astiz, M. F., Wiseman, A. W., & Baker, D. P. (2002). Slouching towards decentralization: consequences of globalization for curricular control in national education systems. *Comparative Education Review, 46*(1), 66–88.

Ayee, J. R. A. (1994). *An anatomy of public policy implementation: The case of decentralization policies in Ghana.* Aldershot, England: Avebury.

Azfar, O., Kahkonen, S., Lanyi, A., Meagher, P., & Rutherford, D. (1999). *Decentralization, governance and public services the impact of institutional arrangements: A review of the literature.* IRIS Center, University of Maryland.

Brosio, G. (October 2000). Decentralization in Africa. Available: http://www.imf.org/external/pubs/ft/seminar/2000/fiscal/brosio.pdf

Cheema, G. S., & Rondinelli, D. (Eds). (1983). *Decentralization and development: Policy implementation in developing countries.* Beverly Hills: Sage.

Crook, R. C., & Manor, J. (1998). *Democracy and decentralization in South Asia and West Africa: Participation, accountability and performance.* Cambridge, UK: Cambridge University Press.

Fiske, E. B. (1996). *Decentralization of education: Politics and consensus.* Washington, DC: The World Bank.

Fullan M. G. (September 1994). Coordinating top-down and bottom-up strategies for educational reform. Systemic reform: Perspectives on personalizing education. Available: http://www.ed.gov/pubs/EdReformStudies/SysReforms/fullan1.html

Fuller, B., & Rivarola, M. (1998). *Nicaragua's experiment to decentralize schools: Views of parents, teachers, and directors.* Working paper series on impact evaluation of education reforms, paper no. 5. Washington DC: The World Bank.

Hanson, M. (2000). Educational decentralization around the Pacific Rim. Available: http://www1.worldbank.org/education/globaleducationreform/pdf/Hanson%20Editorial.pdf

Humes, W. (2000). The discourses of educational management. *Journal of Educational Enquiry, 1*(1), 35–53.

Miller-Grandvaux, Y., & Yoder, K. (February 2002). A literature review of community schools in Africa. Support for analysis and research in Africa (SARA) *Project, Academy for Educational Development.* Available: http://www.dec.org/pdf_docs/PNACP215.pdf

Moulton, J. (December 2000). *Support to Uganda primary education reform final report – The basic education and policy support (BEPS) activity.* Washington, DC: The Global Bureau, Human Capacity Development Center, U.S. Agency for International Development. Available: http://www.usaid.gov/regions/afr/country_info/uganda.html

Niane, B. (2003a). *Improving education management systems in Africa: Analytical elements concerning the French speaking countries – Burkina Faso, Guinea, Mali, Niger, and Senegal. Background paper for ADEA study: The challenge of learning – improving the quality of basic education in sub-Saharan Africa.* Paris: ADEA.

Niane, B. (2003b). *Synthesis – Theme 2: Decentralization and diversification of delivery systems.* ADEA study: The challenge of learning – improving the quality of basic education in SSA. Paris: ADEA.

Nordtveit, B. H. (June 2003). *Partnership through outsourcing: The case of non-formal literacy education in Senegal.* A study prepared for The World Bank. (Draft)

Olowu, D. (2001). Local political and institutional structures and processes. A summary report prepared for the *UNCDF Symposium on decentralization local governance in Africa.* Cape town, 26–30 March, 2001.

Republic of The Gambia, Department of State for Education (DOSE). (2003). Study to investigate quality factors in private schools – For ADEA study: *the challenge of learning – improving the quality of basic education in Sub-Saharan Africa – May 2003.* Paris: ADEA (unpublished).

Ribot, J. (2002). *Democratic decentralization of natural resources: Institutionalizing popular participation.* Washington, DC: World Resources Institute.

Rondinelli, D. (1981). Government decentralization in comparative perspective: Theory and practice in developing countries. *International Review of Administrative Sciences, 47,* 133–145.

Rondinelli, D. A. (1999). *What is decentralization?* In J. Litvack & J. Seddon (Eds), *Decentralization briefing notes.* World Bank Institute working papers. Washington, DC: The World Bank. Available: http://www.worldbank.org/html/fpd/urban/cds/mf/decentralization_briefing_notes.pdf

Support for Research and Analysis in Africa (SARA). (1997). *Education decentralization in Africa: As viewed through the literature and USAID Projects.* Washington, DC: Academy for Educational Development.

Torres, R. M. (2000). *A decade of education for all: The challenge ahead.* Buenos Aires: IIPE UNESCO.

Vengroff, R. (2000). Decentralization, democratization and development in Senegal Paper prepared for delivery at the *Yale Colloquium on decentralization and development* January 21, 2000. Available: http://www.yale.edu/ycias/events/decentralization/papers/vengroff.pdf

Voigts, F. G. G. (1999). Development of an education management information system (EMIS) in Namibia. 1999 Prospective, *Stock-Taking Review of Education* in Africa (ADEA) Available: http://www.adeanet.org/programs/pstr99/en_pstr99.html

Watt, P. (2001). *Community support for basic education in Sub-Saharan Africa.* Africa region human development working paper series. Washington, DC: The World Bank.

Weiler, H. (1983). Legalization, expertise, and participation: Strategies of compensatory legit-
    imation in educational policy. *Comparative Education Review, 27*(2), 259–277.
Welsh, T., & McGinn, N. F. (1999). *Decentralization of education: What and how?* Paris: IIEP/
    UNESCO.
Winkler, D. R., & Gershberg, A.I. (February, 2003). *Education decentralization in Africa: A
    review of recent policy and practice.* Draft (used by permission of the author).

FREE PRIMARY EDUCATION IN MALAWI: THE PRACTICE OF GLOBAL POLICY IN AID-DEPENDENT STATES

Nancy O'Gara Kendall

The "success" or "failure" of Free Primary Education (FPE) in daily practice in Malawi differs significantly from that envisioned in national and international education policy discourse. This difference has great significance for the efficacy, efficiency, and practical outcomes of globalized policies such as Education for All (EFA) and political democratization.

Africa is often presented as having transitioned from a period of "African Independence" in the 1960s to "African Crisis" in the 1970s to "African Tragedy" in the 1990s (Arriaghi, 2002). Social indicators have declined significantly over the past two decades, to the point that many people are living shorter, less healthy lives than they were 20 years ago. Malawi, a small country in Central Eastern Africa, is part of this general trend; it is one of the 15 poorest countries in the world and has experienced dropping GDP/capita and life expectancy rates over the past 20 years.

Over the past two decades, international development efforts have focused growing resources on formulating and implementing global policies that aim to align the economic, political, and social institutions and conditions of developing states such as Malawi with those considered either

Global Trends in Educational Policy
International Perspectives on Education and Society, Volume 6, 125–143
Copyright © 2005 by Elsevier Ltd.
ISSN: 1479-3679/doi:10.1016/S1479-3679(04)06005-0

universal (for example, certain standards of human rights) or developed (for example, certain levels of industrialization).

Global policies have roots in institutions, individuals, and discourses that are inter- or transnational (such as various U.N. declarations), receive international support (technical and financial), and are implemented and evaluated in light of supra-national guidelines or mandates. The global nature of these policies is in large part responsible for the similarities in their official[1] formulation, implementation, and evaluation across states, as well as for their initial shape and scope.[2]

Malawi has been at the center of some of the most important global policy trends to shape states, markets, and societies in Africa and the world over the past two decades. In 1981, Malawi became one of the first countries in Africa to adopt a Structural Adjustment Program (SAP) with the support of the International Monetary Fund (IMF). In 1994, Malawi joined the "Third Wave" of political democratization that swept Africa in the late 1980s and early 1990s.[3] In 1990 and again in 1994, the Malawian government implemented policies directed at fulfilling the World Conference on Education For All (WCEFA) declaration.

In 1990, Dr. H.K. Banda's 26-year dictatorial regime moved toward the provision of FPE following Malawi's involvement in the WCEFA and increased donor pressure for the government to improve its human rights record. In 1994, the first multiparty elections in 30 years brought in a new government led by Dr. Bakili Muluzi. One of Muluzi's first acts as President, and the one 87% of Malawians identified as the single most evident change since democracy, was to declare immediate FPE.[4]

The FPE declaration consisted of a number of sub-policies, all designed to increase access to schools. They included fee-free primary education, banning corporal punishment, restating that school uniforms were not required, a language policy designed to institutionalize the use of the mother tongue in the first four grades, and so forth.

The public's response to the FPE declaration was tremendous; primary school enrollment increased from 1.8 to 2.8 million children within 6 months. By 2000, the Government of Malawi (GOM) was committing almost one-third of the national budget to education (one half of which was spent on FPE), and international donors were providing extensive technical and financial resources to support the education sector. By 2002, international donors provided 91% of the education development budget and almost one-quarter of the entire education sector budget (Ministry of Education, Science, and Technology (MOEST), 2002).

EXAMINING FPE IN CONTEXT

Malawi's FPE policy is grounded in the history of governance, education, Christianity, and international aid in Malawi. It also is centered in and draws from the global EFA movement.

Official linkages of education with poverty, development, and democracy are relatively recent in Malawi.[5] Until recently educational expansion was viewed as a dangerous response to local demand for increased educational access. Concerns about cost recovery, educational quality, the balance of education and other social provisions, and the intended output of the educational system led to very different sorts of arguments about educational expansion. It also led to very different realities concerning the role of public education in the formation of political and economic elites. For example, as late as 1984, Tan, Lee, and Mingat (1984) in a World Bank report argued that:

> Ideally both social demands and the noble goal of democratization should be met. In the real world, however, education must compete for limited public financial resources with a host of other economic activities of the government, such as programs for poverty alleviation, health and housing. This competition has been keener in recent years because the slow-down in international economic activity has affected growth rates in many LDCs. In this setting, substantial increases in public financing for education is unlikely, not least because investments in the sector typically require longer gestation than in other sectors.

Education was conceived as being in competition with funding for health and poverty alleviation efforts, and social demands for education were viewed as a threat to the state and its limited resources. Donors encouraged newly independent African governments to disinvest in education throughout this period.

Education was repositioned as a near cure-all for underdevelopment, poor health, and women's inequality in the late 1980s development discourses. At the same time, it was centered in the growing international universal human rights discourses and activities. Although African states had been discussing the importance of and moving toward EFA since independence in the 1960s, the WCEFA, held in 1990, brought new pressure on states and donors to support basic education for all as a human right. New funding streams were established and donors in countries like Malawi began to call for increased educational opportunity as part of their broader efforts to pressure undemocratic governments to improve their human rights record.

Today the global movement (led by the legal codification of international rights-based frameworks in 1990) to provide EFA in all states and the Third

Wave of political democratization serve as a bifocal lens for examining education in Malawi. Multi-level, multi-site, historical research methods are exceptionally useful for examining relationships between "global" phenomena and international, state, and local policy practices in education. This chapter is based on an ethnographic examination of these interrelations between 1996 and 2002. Extended fieldwork was conducted in three areas consisting of a full primary school and the multiple villages it served (hereafter referred to as "school complexes"), one in each administrative region[6] of Malawi, between 2001 and 2002.[7] Research was also conducted at the district and national levels with government and university officials, nongovernmental organization personnel, and international donors.

An examination of the interrelations between FPE, EFA, and democratization at the community level of the education system in Malawi is crucial to better conceptualizing and analyzing the effects of democratizing (political and educational) reforms and various government- and internationally led efforts to consolidate democratic and educational gains in Malawi.

The interrelationship of EFA and political democratization is of growing relevance, particularly for those examining educational processes in third and fourth world states. Many of these states are pressured concurrently to transition toward political democratization and to expand educational access, even while their educational, financial, and political systems are increasingly dependent on foreign funding for their regular functioning.[8] As in many other countries, the official literatures on education and democratization in Malawi seldom link the two phenomena, despite the relationship that exists in many African countries between efforts to democratize politically and efforts to expand (particularly primary) educational opportunity.

In a poor state where such a large percentage of resources are being invested in FPE, the judgments of success or failure of this policy effort take on added importance.[9] And despite people's early and widespread support and excitement, in the decade following its declaration FPE and the education sector more generally began to be described in official literatures as failures. Declining enrollment and retention rates were interpreted as proof that the general populace shared this view as well. It is important to examine the actual and perceived effects of FPE across these levels, not only because FPE receives such a large percentage of state, international donors', and often communities', resources, but also because it affects – both practically and symbolically – people's conception of their place in the world and the institutions to which they can turn for assistance, support, and inclusion.

THE OFFICIAL FRAMING OF THE FPE POLICY

The official FPE policy – as overtly democratic and liberating as it appeared – embodies a top-down or impact model, in which is embedded a series of assumptions about development, policy cycles, implementation practices, analysis and evaluation methods and purposes, state-social relations, and the shape and scope of potential policy "success" and "failure".

The official discourse and policy process begins and ends with state and international declarations and policymakers, or to use Mitchell's (2002) term, techno-experts. They determine what the policy will look like and how it will be implemented; based on their initial goals and expectations for the policy, they judge its "success" or "failure" and begin the cycle again (LeTendre, Baker, Akiba, & Wiseman, 2001). This results in a unilinear model of policy implementation, evaluation, and judgment. The practice of policy in schools and communities, and actors' experiences and judgments of the policy's success and failure, generally disappear in this unilinear model (Fig. 1 for a visual representation of a unilinear model).

Current official international donor and Malawian government discourses present EFA policies and policy processes within the framework of a top-down, impact model grounded in official discourses on development, globalization, and neo-liberalism. Official discourses and the models of policy processes embedded in them are powerful, and the consequences of errors or incomplete construction are significant. Official policies are backed by resources and have real effects on the shape and scope of policy practices at every level of a society.

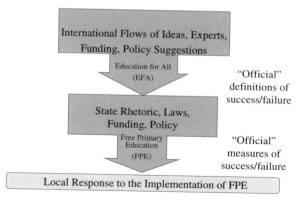

Fig. 1. Impact Model of Global Policy Processes.

Extended ethnographic research on the implementation of FPE in the
three school complexes examined in Malawi reveals a very different set of
dynamics surrounding FPE, the role of official policy in shaping local and
national relations of power and authority, and the measures and experiences
of "success" and "failure" used to judge policy effects. In each community a
distinct constellation of forces, events, social relations, local contingencies,
geographies, histories, and material realities shaped the practice of FPE.
FPE was interrelated with political democratization within a single symbolic
system that articulates the relations of power and authority at the local,
state, and international levels. Since the constellation of forces was different
in the three sites studied, the articulation of these forces was also different.

The diversity of practical effects and articulation provides some guidelines
for anticipating the effects – intended and unintended – of global policies
such as EFA. Policy in practice at the community level is not accurately or
effectively measured by the unilinear yardstick of "success" and "failure"
used to officially judge policy effects. The constellations of forces in each
school complex result, in effect, in FPE "policies in practice" that differ
significantly from official models. In practice, there is no one FPE policy
and, therefore, no one measure of success or failure that accurately or effectively captures the practical success and failures of the various policies.
Instead of a unilinear model, this research indicates that in practice policy is
best modeled as non-linear or as a "bush" of practical variation (Gould,
1996; Ferguson, 2001).

Ethnographic and comparative research in communities also shows that
in practice, FPE is inextricably entwined with other global policies (for
example, political democratization and economic structural adjustment),
and sweeping contextual events identified with other sectors (for example,
famine and HIV/AIDS). FPE cannot be understood – or well managed – in
isolation from these interrelated policies and events.

BACKGROUND

Malawi is described in official literatures as a small, resource-poor, indebted, underdeveloped country in Central Eastern Africa. Landlocked, with
few natural resources, it has a population of about 11.9 million, about one-
half of whom are under the age of 15. Eighty-five percent of the population
is rural; most survive on subsistence agricultural activities. The population is
in generally poor health; poverty rates are high; HIV infection rates stand at
15% and are increasing, and the life expectancy rate is 38 years and

decreasing. The state is heavily indebted to international donors (Overseas Development Assistance accounts for 22% of the Gross National Income and 23% of export earnings are spent on debt servicing), and the industrial production growth rate is negative.

Six percent of the GOM's budget is allocated to health; 23% is allocated to education. A full 20% of the education budget is provided by international donors. Seventy five percent of adult males and 47% of adult females are literate. Net primary enrollment rates stand at 100%, but Gross Primary Enrollment rates stand at 138%, indicating a high level of inefficiency in the education sector. Only 49% of pupils reach Grade 5, another indicator of inefficiency.[10]

The health, nutrition, education, and infrastructure statistics provided in the official narratives highlight the many areas in which poverty and underdevelopment are presented as threatening the daily existence of Malawi's citizens. This general overview is repeated in different forms, but generally to the same effect, in official document after official document. It serves to create a particular characterization of the country and the life of its populace.

The unremitting focus on these indicators of poverty and dependence creates opportunities for parceling problems and creating space for the insertion of external techno-expertise – it makes the country accessible to the culture of development (Escobar, 1994). Such accounts describe a country and a populace in desperate need be acted upon; they present a country that cannot support itself internally, does not have the human resources to "make it", and is on the edge of collapse.

These narratives position developing states as attractive recipients for donors' particular brand of techno-expertise and for their need to craft programs that result in outcomes valued by their home constituents. It positions developing states and societies in particular ways that create new spaces for international donors and other non-governmental organizations.[11]

Ferguson (1994) provides a detailed account of the construction of Lesotho in donor reports and the extent to which this framing reflects the "culture" of donor organizations, which in turn fundamentally shapes the types of development "problems" and "solutions" that donors can envision in Lesotho. In some cases, the construction is factually incorrect; in others, it is simply one perspective among what could be many different ways of determining what is worth saying or acting upon.

The construction both mirrors and continuously (re)makes the donor perspective. In the case of countries such as Lesotho and Malawi, where it becomes the "official" story, it is important to consider what other stories could be told and what those stories would do to conceptions of "problems" and "solutions", and policy "successes" and "failures" in the area. This problematization in official presentations of Malawi provides the environment in which the practices of FPE develop in all three villages/schools.

FPE: "SUCCESS" OR "FAILURE"?

Comparisons of policy practice across schools and communities call into question a number of assumptions embedded in the policy impact model. This model shapes the role of policies such as FPE as tools for development and governance and the methodologies and scope of current policy analyses. There is almost no discussion in the literature, however, of the political or relational effects of FPE on the educational arena itself. Although the threat posed by FPE is never stated clearly, the sense of threat visible in the official literatures likely arises from the large percentage of state resources channeled into the education system (which results in greater pressure on the state for education to succeed since other legitimizing social services are receiving less funding) and the heavy dependence on foreign aid required to fund the initiative. This dependence has practical effects. For example, the educational policymaking and planning arena now have donors and donor-selected "civil society" actors playing much greater roles in educational policy planning than was the case during the Banda regime (Mundy, Murphy, Kendall, & Martin-Beltrans, 2004).

Comparisons of the *practice* of FPE in each community emphasize that there is no one "civil society" and no one FPE policy in Malawi. In the three school complexes examined in this study, at least three distinct policies in practice are well documented (Kendall, 2004). In practice, there is no "education sector policy" that can be analyzed as separate from the ebb and flow of daily life, and there is, therefore, no one definition of the success or failure of FPE.

Anthropologists of education argue that the study of educational policy is best undertaken as a study of policy practices, defined by Sutton and Levinson as a way of analyzing policy "…in terms of how people appropriate its meanings" (Sutton & Levinson, 2000, p. 3) Sutton and Levinson use this term to "…draw attention to how previously excluded actors lay claim to the right to create policy." This lens focuses on how actors at all levels of the system create policy within the framework of their own lived experiences and their own cultural logics.

A "policy in practice" approach to educational policy analysis is particularly useful in examining and (re)interpreting the discourse and analysis of "success" and "failure" of various educational policies such as FPE. Given that a growing number of highly indebted countries are spending upwards of 25% of their annual national budgets on educational provision, and often increasing their dependence on external aid to fund these efforts (which are generally judged to be "failures"), attending carefully to the ramifications of educational policy on states and communities must be given priority.

Examining the multiple practices of FPE across sites reveals the importance of capturing this notion of a multiplicity of non-linear policy practices in policy analyses. Top-down models and measures of success and failure do not capture or address the most powerful impacts of global policy efforts on people's daily lives. These relate not only to technical measures of the policy's success or failure (for example, enrollment, retention, and repetition rates), but also to the symbolic effects of these policies.

In all three villages studied, the practice of FPE is intimately related to the practice of another important global policy – political democratization – that was, as noted earlier, adopted in Malawi at the same time as FPE. The official literatures on FPE note the political and economic changes occurring during the implementation of FPE only as a passing contextual reference, and then analyze FPE in relation to specific, (apparently) easily measured criteria (generally termed measures of quality, or, sometimes, efficiency) such as enrollment, repetition, and dropout rates; teacher:pupil, classroom:pupil, textbook:pupil, and desk:pupil ratios; pass rates on the Primary School Leaving Exam, statistics on teacher qualification, and so forth.[12]

By many of these measures, FPE is deemed a failure threatening the stability of the state. For example, the *Joint Review of the Malawi Education Sector: Review Report*, authored by the Ministry of Education, Science and Culture (2000), frames the introduction and effects of FPE as follows:

It has been nearly six years since Government launched its Free Primary Education. Since then we have seen unprecedented expansion of access to education…As we take stock of our past, the balance sheet presents a mixed picture. On the one hand, for the first time in the history of this country, we have the majority of school-going children in school at the primary level, nearly half of whom are girls…On the other hand, this rosy picture is marred by the inevitable spin-offs of rapid expansion…A dysfunctional management system which cannot provide adequate oversight to all key sections of the sector…Inadequately trained and poorly motivated teachers…Substandard and ageing infrastructure… Insufficient learning and teaching materials…Declining student performance indicators characterized by poor examination results and inability of graduates at the secondary and tertiary level to satisfy basic employer expectations…Deteriorating teacher/student ratio in most primary schools…And worse still, falling real monetary investment per child…The net result is that although we have more pupils and students enrolled, no effective teaching/learning is taking place in many of our schools. This in turn means that the return on investment in the sector as measured by student achievement and performance is much lower than it should be. Drop out and repetition rates do not look particularly good either. *Clearly this poses and major threat to our survival as a nation* (p. 15–16) (emphasis mine).

Contrast this official characterization of FPE failure with a very different profile of failure and the reasons for failure derived from observations and interviews at a primary school in the Southern Region that same year (2000). Pupils at this school arrived late, then ran around the outstretched arms of the head teacher to either enter their classroom or simply leave school altogether for the day. The head teacher yelled at those students he could catch, but otherwise let them go. A teacher, who was standing nearby and observing these interactions, said:

> You see, this is because of democracy. We cannot punish pupils anymore, they say 'It is a democracy, I can do whatever and you cannot tell me no'. This one [points at another teacher] was actually abused by parents who came to yell at him because he punished a pupil for tardiness. [He shakes his head] This could not have been with Kamuzu [the previous president]. Teachers are losing too much respect.

The head teacher, who by this time had given up, chimed in:

> We keep telling them [parents] that democracy does not mean you should keep your child from school, but they say they can do anything. They think because it is free then they don't have to care [if their child attends] if it is free, it is not worth. They do not police their child like before, so these children skip school, or come just a few days.

The local Minister of Parliament refused to return to the school to oversee the School Committee elections, and so forth:

> In our days, if you arrived late you were punished, and the punishments were very harsh. Maybe you could be forced to dig a deep hole for tardiness. We did not behave like pupils these days.

Likewise, teachers and parents at this school regularly identified the perceived post-FPE surge in girls' pregnancies and students' absences from school with changes in families' survival strategies. People reported that some mothers would force their daughters out of the house, or force them into relationships with teachers, telling them not to return until they had some sugar or tea to contribute to the family's larder – goods girls could usually only gain through exchanges of sex for goods.

This change in parental behavior was viewed as relatively new – if not in its nature at least in its scope – and due to the new government's deregulation of prices, a concomitant increase in the prices of basic goods, changes in local marketing patterns, a period of relative drought, and an overall lowering of family food security. With the exception of the drought, these various changes were considered direct outcomes of "demokarasi" – and in fact, in most cases these outcomes can be linked to economic policy reforms implemented by the new government under the direction of international donors.

People's narratives and practices indicated that education was perceived as being complexly interwoven with various aspects of everyday life – some natural, some social – and with various forces, institutions, ideas, and actions emanating from multiple levels of analysis (e.g. local, national, international). That is, education and the changes occurring in the school were impacted by and had an impact on a whole range of social, political, and economic activities occurring outside of the "education sector", and sometimes outside of Malawi (policy reforms in the economic arena, changes in health service provision, changes in the price of fertilizer, the central government push for the decentralization of social services, changing migration patterns of Malawian workers, and so forth).

Since these interrelations varied by community (depending, for example, on local resources, geography, politics, and economies), people's understandings and judgments of FPE differed significantly across communities and between levels of analysis. The Southern quote above can be contrasted with a vignette from the field notes recorded at the school visited in the Northern region, which responded to one of the FPE policies (the ban on corporal punishment) as follows:

When the Head Teacher, Mr. Kalonga, heard about the newest policy change through a circular he picked up during a trip to the Boma [district capital], he knew that something had to be done. The Ministry of Education (MOE) was ordering all schools to immediately halt the use of corporal punishment in schools. This was, from Mr. Kalonga's perspective, a ludicrous, misplaced call from the government that would undermine not only the teachers and the education system more generally, but also Malawi itself. Schools, he says, are places where we teach our children how to live properly; how to be respectful, educated, and modern. Above all else, this requires discipline—discipline to do well on (what are in point of fact) foreign exams, discipline to behave properly in society, discipline to survive in whatever bureaucracy or company you are employed. To make school a place where discipline is neither taught nor enforceable would be to fundamentally destroy children's opportunities to succeed, and more broadly, Malawi's opportunity to succeed. This was, in other words, a direct attack against the school, the surrounding communities, and the country itself by the government. As he explained: "Child rights are preached on the radio these days. We hear about these rights. The right to speak rudely, and misbehave, and absent themselves from school. It is giving them the right to do as they want. We poor Malawians, to believe this...This government just wants these schools to fall. They want teachers to be nothing."...Mr. Kalonga decided he could not let this policy change stand. He said it fundamentally threatened the ability of the school to fulfill its duties and it threatened teachers' ability to hold authority over children. He called a meeting with the School Committee to discuss the matter. They agreed with him and his proposed response to the policy directive, and gave him permission to call a PTA meeting to jointly address the community about this issue. He, the Village Head, and the School Committee presented a united front: the policy would be discarded in favor of the previous policy, which allowed corporal punishment in school. Any parent who had a complaint with this policy was free to withdraw their child and enroll them in another school (this was, he said wryly, one of their new democratic rights), but no parent could file a complaint or abuse teachers over the use of continued corporal punishment in a situation that during the Banda regime would have led to the use of corporal punishment. The parents, he reported (and parent interviews supported) overwhelmingly approved of this decision, and praised it as one designed to uphold the quality of education and of local norms of socialization.

By official standards, the Northern school was a much greater technical success (as measured, for example, but enrollment and retention rates) than the Southern school. At the Northern school, however, increased technical success came at a heavy cost. Not only did parents and teachers unite to reject key aspects of the official FPE policy, but they also said they perceived the policy as an attack by the government on their community and on Malawi. They viewed the new government as a threat, and consistently compared it unfavorably to the Banda regime.

In the Central region school, FPE and the perceived concomitant loosening of government oversight and accountability in the schools (because of overstretched resources and changes in teachers' behaviors that were associated with democracy) led people to view FPE as an act of desertion by the state. Teachers farmed during school time instead of teaching; district education officials did not visit the area; the local Minister of Parliament, who was called back to oversee the School Committee elections, did not come to visit them, and so forth.

The school, as one of the last state institutions operating at the village level, became a central site in which people narrated what they discussed as the state's broader desertion. People regularly compared teachers leaving the classroom with the central government refusing to provide fertilizer or food subsidies during the famine that struck in 2001. FPE was reframed as a government effort to place responsibility for the school on people's shoulders while the state itself withdrew from the area, leaving behind an abjected community.[13]

In the Southern region, where FPE was a much greater failure by official measures, few children enrolled or attended school regularly, but the FPE policy was generally discussed as a benign and caring effort on the new government's part to fulfill the promises it had made about what democracy would bring to people. Parents and pupils alike displayed lower levels of interest in the school itself (and there is much less of a history of community involvement in Western schools in the area), but FPE played an important symbolic role in people's discourse about the new democratic state.

Despite FPE's positive reception in the area, people did not feel that FPE offered them real opportunities for survival and many interviews focused on people's concerns over food security and the government's lack of action in that arena. The most expensive social service provided by the state was, therefore, viewed as a benign but useless gesture of goodwill, while people's primary concerns went unaddressed.

While FPE is a technical failure (that is, has negatively affected the quality of education in Malawi) according to the official literature, comparative research in villages indicates that FPE is "successful" at transforming relations of power and authority across villages, the state, and the international community. At the national level, FPE succeeds at creating particular relations of dependence between the state and international donor organizations as the government takes on increasing debt to finance FPE. At the local level, FPE is generally judged a technical failure; more importantly, it fails to legitimize the state as a caring, accountable, sovereign body to its citizens and in some cases fuels opposition to the new government and the democratic state.

FPE AND DEMOCRATIZATION: BOUNDARIES IN CONCEPT, NOT PRACTICE

In contrast to community analyses of FPE and its effects, national and international policy analyses seldom link FPE with democratization. The official literature presents education as standing apart from both material realities – most strikingly visible when education memoranda do not, for example, discuss the severity of the 2000/2001 famine that led many families to pull their children from school – and other socially constructed "sectors" such as health, agriculture, and transportation.[14] This separation of sectors leads to blind spots concerning the effects of policies such as FPE on people's daily lives and relations of power and authority.

In the Northern and Central villages examined in this study, the perceived lack of concern on the part of the government for people's suffering during the famine was viewed as mirroring the government's lack of concern about the decline of local school quality. These perceptions fed on one another, increasing people's sense that the new democratic government was less legitimate than the previous dictatorship. In the Northern region, the community began "jumping scales" in their approach to assuring educational quality. For example, they drew directly on international connections through retired civil servants from the area to gather funds from various international sources to support the construction of a school library, and regularly discussed the new state's inability to support the school in a similar manner.

Official government and donor literatures isolate the FPE reform and the education sector from other sectors, but communities do not. Community members link FPE and democracy in their discussions of what happens in schools, in society, and in their daily lives. In rural communities, the reality of people's experiences with and feelings about their local schools and the FPE policy contrast sharply with the literatures about FPE and its success or failure in Malawi. Community members in Malawi frequently attribute changes in the schools to democracy. The AfroBarometer (1999) survey's finding that 87% of Malawians identified FPE as the most evident change since democratization provides just a hint of the symbolism with which FPE was invested in most people's discourse.

In important ways, the implementation of democracy and EFA policies in Malawi reflects a top-down impact model of policymaking. Official plans, discourses, and literatures reflect the notion that international ideas impact the state through economic and technical support, and the state in turn impacts communities through the creation and implementation of political and educational policy reforms. On the ground, the interrelations between FPE and democracy show clearly that varied constellations of forces shape the practice of policy.

The complexity of policy in practice at the community level differs in shape and scope from the defined boundaries of top-down models discussed in national and international policy arenas. Community discourses link these complex national and international policy relationships in their understanding of policy in practice; in fact, communities link them more explicitly than do national and international policy literatures. Discussions and observations with people about FPE reveal that complex interrelations give FPE its meaning and effects in daily life. People's judgments of the success or failure of FPE are part and parcel of their judgments about the success and failure of political democracy and associated economic liberalization.

Conversations about FPE shed new light on the symbolic role that FPE plays in people's conceptions of democratization and vice versa. People are aware that classes are larger and that teachers are less well-trained than before, and these are important considerations in judging the success or failure of FPE. However, people are much more concerned about the social changes that they felt accompanied the "democratization" of schools and society. It mattered less to most interviewees how much training teachers had received, for example, than that many teachers were leaving classrooms unstaffed during school hours, impregnating schoolgirls at an increasing rate, or sending pupils to work in their gardens.

The rise and fall of enrollment rates may reflect the rise and fall of people's hopes about the new democracy and new economic prospects more than it does technical failures that can be addressed by improving the quality of school infrastructure or classroom teaching. People's fundamental sense that much of what happens in schools is a mirror of broader social transformations (and, therefore, cannot be measured solely by school-based indicators) is largely missing from the national and international literatures. For example, teachers and parents agree with official concerns about corruption in school exams, which they agree is a growing problem, but they feel that this corruption is both a reflection and result of the "democratization" of corruption among politicians in the new government. The calculus of success and failure developed in communities and in national and international literatures map only unevenly onto one another.

In communities, policies in practice do not respect sectoral boundaries (education, governance, health, etc.) and levels of analysis (local, national, international). Community realities rearrange notions of policy cycles and stakeholders, and challenge current models of policy analysis and judgments of success and failure.

POLICY AS PRACTICE: ADDRESSING THE "SUCCESSFUL FAILURE" OF CURRENT POLICY

The differences between government and donor discourse compared to community conclusions about the successes and failures of FPE are central to understanding how educational and political practices are developing in Malawi. Moreover, the policy disconnect between FPE and democratization impedes improvement of educational policy, investment and practice.

It threatens the success of international and national top–down policy initiatives both in the education sector and in the arena of governance. Due to the symbolic link between FPE and political democratization, people in Malawi say that as schools collapse, so too does the promise of democracy.

A large and growing literature aims to determine the best policies for consolidating democracy in countries like Malawi (see, for example, Diamond & Plattner, 1996; Kondowe, 1996). An equally large and growing literature discusses how to achieve EFA in countries like Malawi (see, for example, UNESCO, 2001 and Ministry of Education (MOE) and the Malawi National Commission for UNESCO, 2001). These literatures do not generally overlap, and in this gap lies much of the symbolic weight attributed to both EFA and democratization in countries like Malawi. Using comparative analysis to lay out this disjoint in the conceptualization of the relations between EFA and broader political, economic, and social forces (in this case, democratization), highlights some of the important directions in which future research on education and educational policy analysis might take.

Future research could define spaces for reconceptualizing and reconciling multiple perspectives on the goals and scope of EFA, international policy construction, national policy design, community ideation of policy in practice, judgments of the success and failure of the FPE policy, and the interrelations and effects of multiple policy efforts such as FPE and political democratization. Should such approaches evolve, new opportunities could be created to re-imagine the role of global policies in shaping relations of power and authority in developing states, markets, and societies. Perhaps in the future models of multi-linear or non-linear policy practices and processes could interact. Decentralized, multi-level policy construction – that gives significant weight to policy in practice – might more accurately predict the outcomes of international and national policy initiatives and investments, and thus more effectively improve people's daily lives.

NOTES

1. The term "official" is used here to demarcate written or verbal materials that originate from governmental or international organizations, are stated as representing the views of these organizations, and are made part of the public record.

2. I am not arguing here that global policies are shaped internationally and simply introduced to developing states, as I hope the rest of this chapter reveals. Aid recipient states play an integral role in shaping when, why, and how such policies are introduced, as well as shaping many of the symbolic uses to which such policies are put. The states work, however, within a framework of possibilities that is largely

constrained by international and transnational organizations, discourses, and flows of information and resources.

3. The "Third Wave" of democratization is a term coined by Samuel Huntington; he defines a wave of democratization as "a group of [democratic] transitions...that occur within a specified period of time and that significantly outnumber transitions in the opposite direction during that period" (quoted in Diamond, 1999, p. 2). The Third Wave of democratization began in the 1970s with Portugal's transition, then spread to Eastern Europe and Africa in the late 1980s and 1990s.

4. Similar moves towards EFA linked to election cycles or in the wake of political transitions have occurred in a number of states in the region, including Kenya, Mozambique, South Africa, and Uganda.

5. In the missionary and colonial eras, there already was a great deal of debate about the costs and benefits of expanding educational opportunities for Malawians. Histories that touch on these subjects include Banda (1982), Kuster (1999), and Kendall (2004).

6. The three regions have significantly different historical relationships with the state and with Western education, which allows for fruitful comparison of responses to political and educational change efforts. A more comprehensive comparison of the policy practices across the three sites may be found in Kendall (2004).

7. This 12-month ethnographic study was supported by a Fulbright–Hays dissertation research grant. Research was also conducted in 17 other school complexes and three urban areas between 1996 and 2001. Much of this research was funded by U.S. Department of Education Foreign Language and Area Studies fellowships. To protect the identity of schools and interviewees, references to school complexes by region are made in the singular but refer to data collected from all schools examined in the region over the course of the research.

8. The implication is not that these same issues do not arise for those studying so-called first or second world states; in fact, just the opposite. However, it is true that these issues are more readily evident in third and fourth world states, and thus make themselves more indispensably central to such analyses.

9. See, for example, Riddell's (1999) argument about the particular importance of "efficient" policy spending in developing countries.

10. Most data from: UNICEF (2004). *The State of the World's Children: Annual Report.* New York, NY: UNICEF. Data on agriculture from: CIA (2003). *World Factbook.* At http://www.cia.gov/cia/publications/factbook/geos/mi.html UNESCO collects these data from secondary sources, primarily other U.N. organizations and the World Bank. These organizations in turn collect most data from the host government. Many of these data differ from organization to organization and report to report, although there is general agreement within about 10% of most measures in these sources. Moreover, data collection and presentation efforts of the host countries reflect particular host country politics and conditions, and may reflect on-the-ground realities to greater or lesser extents. The data should, therefore, be reviewed with caution.

11. See Ferguson and Gupta (2002) for a discussion of the re-spatialization of governance in relation to developing states.

12. These are the primary areas of data collection during 1999–2004 Ministry of Education Annual Education Reports. Additional areas that are of less interest to us

in this study, but are closely related to the government efforts to influence policy processes include data on special education and language of instruction/students' mother tongue.

13. See Ferguson (2002) for a similar discussion of abjection following the implementation of structural adjustment programs in Zambia.

14. Parallel arguments about local versus national and international "constructions" of democracy in Malawi appear in Kendall (2004).

REFERENCES

AfroBarometer. (1999). *Round one survey: Malawi.* Available: http://www.afrobarometer.org/ surveys.html

Arriaghi, G. (2002). The African crisis. *New Left Review, 15.* Available: http://www. newleftreview.net/PDFarticles/NLR24901.pdf

Banda, K. (1982). *A brief history of education in Malawi.* Blantyre: Dzuka Publishing Company.

Diamond, L., & Plattner, M. (Eds) (1996). *The global resurgence of democracy,* (2nd ed.). Baltimore, MD and London: John Hopkins University Press.

Escobar, A. (1994). *Encountering development: The making and unmaking of the third world.* Princeton, NJ: Princeton University Press.

Ferguson, J. (1994). *The anti-politics machine: Development depoliticization, and bureaucratic power in Lesotho.* Minneapolis: University of Minnesota Press.

Ferguson, J. (2001). Global disconnect: Abjection and the aftermath of modernism. In: Inda & Rosaldo (Eds), *The anthropology of globalization.* Malden, MA: Blackwell.

Ferguson, J., & Gupta, A. (2002). Spatializing states: Toward and ethnography of neoliberal governmentality. *American Ethnologist, 29,* 4.

Kendall, N. (2004). *Global policy in practice: The successful failure of free primary education in Malawi.* Dissertation thesis, Stanford University.

Kondowe, S. (1996). *Report on the workshop: Malawi: The way forward.* Held at Boadzulu Holiday Resort, Mangochi, October 13–15, 1996. Blantyre: Malawi Institute for Democratic and Economic Affairs.

Kuster, S. (1999). *African education in colonial Zimbabwe, Zambia, and Malawi: Government control, settler antagonism and African agency, 1890–1964.* Studien zur Afrikanischen Geschichte Bd. 23. New Jersey: Transaction Publishers.

LeTendre, G. K., Baker, D. P., Akiba, M., & Wiseman, A. W. (2001). The policy trap: National educational policy and the third international math and science study. *International Journal of Educational Policy Research and Practice, 2,* 1.

Ministry of Education (MOE) and the Malawi National Commission for UNESCO. (2001). *The development of education in Malawi: 1996–2001. Report for the 46th session of the International Conference on Education,* September 5–8, Lilongwe: MOE.

Ministry of Education, Science, and Culture (MOESC). (2000). *Joint review of the Malawi education sector: Review report.* Held at the Malawi Institute of Management, Lilongwe, Malawi, October 2–10, 2000.

Ministry of Education, Science, and Technology (MOEST). (2002). *The main education challenges facing Malawi.* Lilongwe: MOEST. Available: http://www.malawi.gov.mw/educ/ educchalle.htm

Mitchell, T. (2002). *Rule of experts: Egypt, techno-politics, modernity.* Berkeley, CA; London: University of California Press.

Mundy, K., Murphy, L., Kendall, N. O., & Martin-Beltrans, M. (2004). Transnational advocacy in education: Examining the effects on global/local education policy arenas – Uganda, Malawi, and Brazil. Presented at the *Annual meeting of the Comparative and International Education Society meeting.* Held in Salt Lake City, UT, March 9–12.

Riddell, A. (1999). Evaluations of educational reform programmes in developing countries: Whose life is this anyway? *International Journal of Educational Development, 19.*

Sutton, M., & Levinson, B. (Eds) (2000). *Policy as practice: Toward a comparative sociocultural analysis of educational policy.* Stamford, CT: Ablex Publishing.

Tan, J., Lee, K., & Mingat, A. (1984). *User charges for education: The ability and willingness to pay in Malawi.* World Bank Staff Working Papers No. 661. Washington, DC: World Bank.

UNESCO. (2001). *Monitoring report on education for all.* Paris: UNESCO Publishing.

RE-POSITIONING FEMALES IN THE INTERNATIONAL EDUCATIONAL CONTEXT: THEORETICAL FRAMEWORKS, SHARED POLICIES, AND FUTURE DIRECTIONS

Mary Ann Maslak

This volume asks pertinent and important questions about current trends in the field: Where is the comparative and international study of education heading in the 21st century? What are the current theoretical issues, problems, and practices that need to be reviewed, discussed, and debated? How have specific sub-fields fared over the past decade? Accordingly, in terms of offering some answers, the purposes of this chapter are: to position the topic of female education in terms of women in development (WID) and gender and development (GAD) frameworks that typically structure current development initiatives; to provide an overview of the ways in which education for all (EFA) – one of the most widely recognized educational policies in the world – has addressed female education; to analyze the policy in terms of those development frameworks; and to suggest some future directions for the field based on existing knowledge and its perceived efficacy and inadequacy.

Global Trends in Educational Policy
International Perspectives on Education and Society, Volume 6, 145–171
Copyright © 2005 by Elsevier Ltd.
ISSN: 1479-3679/doi:10.1016/S1479-3679(04)06006-2

This chapter begins by examining the two leading frameworks, WID and GAD, that have guided the development field. The overview of WID and GAD will be followed by a survey of the EFA documents for references to female education in the 1990, 1996 and 2000 conferences, using content analysis. The ways in which the EFA texts reflect the theoretical premises and epistemological origins of WID and GAD frameworks will be revealed. Lastly, the chapter proffers some new directions for the field, suggesting that educational policy can benefit from the same rigorous and critical consideration of current development thought concerning females. In particular, it argues for the need for research on girls in order to enrich and complement future EFA policies.

WID APPROACH

WID emerged in reaction to the failure of the modernization development policy based on the notion that every individual has equal access to opportunities for achieving goals and objectives deemed reasonable by society. It sought to provide a more comprehensive framework within which the goals of better living conditions, wages, and education could be achieved by *all* individuals.[1] Specifically, given the fact that females in emerging countries lag behind males in terms of economic prosperity and education, WID addressed their advancement through development projects and programs.

WID's origins can be traced to the growth of both liberal feminist theories of modernization and socialization theory of sex roles. Liberal feminists argued that women's exclusion from the public sector occurred because a socially sanctioned sexual division of labor contributed to their inferior status and low social position. Hence, liberal feminists sought to subvert and redefine the social norms that conditioned and affected the traditional roles thereby re-structuring economic opportunities for women and men. In their early works, WID theories optimistically increased availability of diverse occupations for women.[2] In terms of educational policy research, the liberal feminist perspective attributed the lower enrollment and attainment of girls to negative socialization messages in both the family and the school, which the state has not been able to correct. But, as Stromquist (2001) reminds us, it does not explain the underlying causes of the different processes of socialization of men and women.

Another cornerstone of WID was Marxist feminist theories.[3] Classic Marxism, which identifies capitalism as a source of class inequity, explains women's oppression in terms of an economic order that supports males in superior positions, and women in inferior positions.[4] Women's confinement to domestic labor, whose jobs offer little financial gains and limit their ability to engage in economic endeavors that generate power, is a commonly used example of the cause of women's oppression.[5] Transposed to the domain of educational policy, the Marxist–feminist view asserts that inequitable economic demands on females' time prohibit or at best drastically impede their educational obtainment.

Related to the Marxist feminist theory is the Socialist feminist perspective. While this stream of Marxist theory emphasizes the relationship between women and the proletariat, a fundamental facet of modernization theory, Socialist feminism recognizes the distinction between wage or non-wage earners, especially when men assume the role as wage earner (Donovan, 1988; Hartmann, 1981). By simply using (or spending), a husband's earnings without access to individual earning potential neither provide women with power nor access to it (Donovan, 1988). In addition, "family wage," paid to the male, is often viewed as money that is earned by *either* the husband or the wife, but that is shared and used by both. Failing to recognize women's monetary contributions to the family perpetuates the myth that males are the providers for the family. In both cases this differentiation of roles and income by sex sets up both a figurative and literal hierarchy where women rank lower than men. Thus, in educational terms, the socialist feminist perspective focuses on the ideological messages of economic roles and rules in order to explain the inferior educational participation and attainment of females. A gendered (and hence ideologically driven) division of labor that prohibits or discourages females from wage-earning positions consigns them to an economic order that exploits their work and limits their educational opportunities.

Yet another stream of feminist thought that has guided WID is dependency feminism, which is based on sex role. Dependency feminists attribute the perpetuation of women's oppression to patriarchal domination, which is both the cause and result of the economic order that deprives women of power. Patriarchy here refers to the social values and practices in a hierarchically ordered world where females have far fewer social and economic opportunities than males. The application of dependency feminism in educational policy helps explain the social system that supports males in dominant positions in the household where educational decisions are made.

The pragmatic application of these academic feminist theories have yielded a number of policy approaches to designing and implementing development programs and initiatives to raise the status of women in society, usefully re-shaping the traditional practices of development agencies.[6] Caroline Moser (1993), a leading figure in the development literature who extended Buvinic's work (1983), classified development initiatives during the WID era in terms of five approaches – the welfare approach (1950–1970), the equity approach (1975–1985), the anti-poverty approach (1970s and beyond), the efficiency approach, and the empowerment approach (1975 onwards). The welfare approach strove to include WID initiatives consistent with their roles as wife and mother through participation in food aid and family planning programs. The equity approach, based on the early work of Ester Boserup (1970; 1986), identified women as equal partners in the development process and supported an affirmative action-type policy whereby political and economic autonomy for women heightened their status. The anti-poverty approach, which emerged as a result of the backlash from the equity approach, cited poverty as the main cause of women's oppression, and thus addressed it by supporting women's participation in small-scale income-generating projects. The efficiency approach focused on women as equal contributors to the world economy and emphasized increased economic efficiency and effectiveness as a result of women's contributions. The empowerment approach strove to promote women's self-reliance with the help of grassroots organizations. Self-reliance was based on the realization that women experience oppression differently according to their race, class, and colonial history. The goal of empowerment begins with the examination of women's lives in the context of the social parameters that define them.

In sum, WID explained women's oppression in terms of both economic inequity in the market place and social inequity in the household.[7] It held that entry into the public sphere would reduce and perhaps even eliminate women's artificially induced inferiority. It depicted women as oppressed individuals whose situation was defined by the universally accepted notions of hierarchy, based on sex, in the socio-economic systems that determine status. Efforts to battle women's oppression were attempted on several fronts by different entities: large international non-government interest groups such as the World Bank and IMF; national governing bodies within country systems; and non-governmental organizations (NGOs) from local communities. These agencies offered pragmatic solutions. Feminist scholars in academic circles contributed theoretical perspectives and analytic insights. Their combined efforts led to educational programs that aimed to engage women in learning so as to increase their skills in the work place, thereby enhancing their economic status and correspondingly social status. Given the justifiable criticism of the realistic causation of female oppression offered in the WID framework, and the questionable long-term success rate of programs that sought to accomplish its goals, a shift in development thinking occurred.

GENDER AND DEVELOPMENT (GAD)

Whereas the WID movement utilized a microscopic perspective, narrowly defining universal sexual inequity in terms of economic and social status, and specifically developing targeted programs for women to counteract it, the GAD era employed a macroscopic perspective to understand female oppression. GAD broadly positioned gender inequality in the wide-ranging historical, political, economic, social, and cultural contexts in which women and men live.[8]

Two schools of feminist theory in particular offer the philosophic underpinning of GAD – radical and socialist feminism. Radical feminism asserts that the social system legitimizes patriarchal hierarchy, the source of women's oppression. Drawn from the earlier works of MacKinnon (1987) and Jagger and Rothenberg (1984), radical feminists claim that male domination over women – especially in efforts to control women's reproductive capabilities – accounts for their reduced role and status in society. When used in educational research, the radical feminist perspective usually underscores how women's reproductive capacities and associated responsibilities constrain the opportunities for their education. Moreover, patriarchal control of women's sexuality and the definition of women primarily as mothers and wives affect parental decisions concerning their daughters' schooling (Stromquist, 1998). The radical feminist perspective sees the state as a key agent in the perpetuation of women's subordination because of its strong defense of women as mothers and the family as the fundamental unit of society. The state presumes the family functions according to traditional roles performed by both men and women. Men serve as the breadwinners of the family; women provide childrearing and childcare.[9] The appropriateness of women's role is repeatedly reinforced by the society's informal and formal systems of education.

Socialist feminism explains women's oppression by coupling patriarchy with class oppression in the forms of production, reproduction, socialization, and sexuality. For example, Hartman (1981) shows how capitalist economics creates gendered divisions of labor within a patriarchal system. Socialist feminism offers a comprehensive perspective of female oppression by positioning the individual in broad social systems that define a strict set of rules for social, economic, and political participation. Its application in educational research ferrets out the ways activities and responsibilities associated with traditional gender roles for women and men contribute to the unequal levels of participation in school.

In sum, the GAD ideology consists of several key propositions. First, GAD endorses a holistic conceptualization and analysis of the problems women face in order to explain their unequal status.[10] By examining gender relations embedded in prevailing organizational, institutional, political, economic, and social norms, GAD casts a wide net in its quest for the causes of women's oppression. Another key GAD proposition holds the state and local communities equally responsible for promoting women's emancipation. GAD points to the dual role of the state as employer of labor and distributor of economic capital. It also emphasizes the duty of the state to provide social capital, in other words, the social expenditures for education, health, and training for the care and maintenance of the future generation. Thus, GAD stresses foremost the need for enhancing women's education, but specifies neither particular programs nor curricula that targets gender inequality. Overall, GAD is more interested in a fundamental re-examination of social structures and institutions that are perforced gendered, than in offering pragmatic solutions that seemed to characterize the traditional approaches of the WID era.

Whatever their merits or demerits are, WID and GAD have been the most influential theoretical frameworks and arguments dedicated to the advancement for women in the emerging world, of which education is part and parcel.[11] What follows is a content analysis of the Education for All conferences, focusing on *Preamble* and *Framework for Action* from the 1990 Jomtien conference, the *Preamble* and *Affirmation* from the 1996 meeting in Amman, and the *Introduction and Commentary*, and *Regional Frameworks* from the 2003 conference in Dakar. The content analysis positions these texts within the WID and GAD premises so as to reveal the extent to which paradigmatic thinking in the global issue of development has informed practical educational policy.

SOME CONSIDERATIONS OF CONTENT ANALYSIS

Content analysis was selected for this work because it allows us to examine text in a logical and informative way. Moreover, it is a very helpful tool to investigate and probe the meanings of the language of policy. Four steps were followed in the analysis of the contents of the EFA policies of 1990, 1996, and 2000. First, all the documents were perused in an effort to develop a general understanding of their structural, narrative, and rhetorical form.[12] Second, the selected documents were read again specifically for the purpose of establishing familiarity with their contents. Third, key words central to the notions of both WID and GAD were pinpointed and counted for frequency, not merely existence, since only three sets of documents were used. Words were coded exactly as they appeared in the texts, but derivations (e.g. child, child's children) were clustered with each root word.[13] Fourth, a series of charts were developed to summarize the frequency with which each item appeared.

The following words and terms, selected because they capture the fundamental concepts of the WID and GAD frameworks, were counted in the documents' content analysis: children (child); boy(s); girl(s); youth; adolescent(s); adult(s); men; and women. In addition, the terms social(ly) and political were counted for frequency. In the category of economics, the terms economic; poverty; finance; financial; budgeting; and expenditures were counted. The terms culture(al), as well as the terms value(s); moral(s); spiritual, and religion (religious) in the religion category were also tallied. I did not differentiate the frequency of the terms used in the categories of economics and religion because of the infrequency of their appearance. In addition, I also counted the frequency of the terms: gender and gender gap; gender stereotyping; gender discrimination; gender disparity(ies); gender equity; gender issues; gender-sensitive; gender awareness; gender bias; gender parity; and gender responsiveness.[14]

There are commonly known and interrelated limitations in this and other content analyses. It is restricted to quantitative examinations, which yield only some insights while disguising others. Most notably, it lacks the ability to test causal relationships between variables. The information generated from such analyses is only useful for indicating the frequency of terms and comparing those responses between and amongst documents over time.

CONFERENCES AS THE CONTEXT: INTERNATIONAL POLICIES ON EDUCATION FOR FEMALES

In spite of the achievements since the Universal Declaration of Human Rights in 1948, countries around the world still struggle with the issues of providing access to and obtainment of schooling for children, and functional literacy and marketable skills for adults. Hence, the converging

of international educational conferences, which furnish the appropriate
venue in which representatives from state and national governments,
international and national non-government organizations gather to discuss
the current state of affairs and future challenges in the education field, have
become regularly established meetings. The World Declaration on Education for All and Framework for Action, held in Jomtien Thailand in 1990,
was the first large-scale conference to address educational access and
achievement for both children and adults. The purposes of the conference,
as listed in the Articles of the *Framework*, include: "meeting basic learning
needs;" "shaping the vision" (for education for all); "universalizing access
and promoting equity"; "focusing on learning"; "broadening the means and
scope of basic education"; "enhancing the environment for learning";
"strengthening partnerships"; "developing a supportive policy context";
"mobilizing resources"; and "strengthening international solidarity." Four
years later, the Mid-Decade Meeting in Amman Jordan (June 16–19, 1996)
reviewed progress made since the Jomtien conference, and addressed
persistent problems and new challenges. The most recent conference, The
World Education Forum in Dakar, Senegal (April 26–29, 2000) was
"convened to assess progress toward EFA since Jomtien, to analyze where
and why the goal has remained elusive, and to renew commitments to turn
this vision into a reality" (World Education Forum, 2000, p. 7). These
Conferences generated a series of documents that provide a guide to
improving education worldwide. They were selected because they are the
most widely recognized educational policy for girls and women worldwide,
and offer the possibility for the most consistent comparison of documents
produced during EFA's 10-year history.

   Here, I specifically examine how the policy documents generated at those
conferences deal with female education by way of a content analysis of the
Preamble and *Framework* from the Jomtien conference, the *Preamble* and
Affirmation from the Amman Mid-Decade meeting, and the *Introduction*
and *Regional Frameworks* from the Dakar conference. The first part of the
analysis shows the frequency of individual descriptors (the terms children,
boys, girls, youth, adolescent(s), adults, women, and men); the second part
reveals the frequency of gender- and structure-related terms.[15]

Individuals' Descriptors

I begin the content analysis by recording the number of times individual
descriptors (children/child; boy(s); girl(s); youth; adolescent(s); adult(s);

men; women) appear in the documents. These terms are typically associated with the WID literature.

Jomtien, 1990

The seven-page *Preamble* and 17-page Jomtien *Framework for Action* mention the term children 26 times. The term girls is mentioned six times. Boys are not indicated. Youth are cited eight times and adults 19 times. Men are noted twice and the term women is used 12 times. The term adults is noted 12 times.

Amman, 1996

The two-page *Preamble* and the four-page *Affirmation* for the meeting includes similar terms found in the Jomtien *Preamble*, but with different frequency. The document references children 18 times, compared to zero times for boys and two times for girls. The term adolescent appears in this document five times. Adults, men and women are mentioned eight, one, and seven times, respectively. Similar to the Jomtien *Preamble*, reference to adults occurs more frequently than reference to either men or women, although women are mentioned seven times as many times as men, who are referenced once in the policy.

Dakar, 2000

The Dakar meeting's *Introduction* also refers to the same words found in the earlier documents. The content analysis of its *Introduction* reveals the use of the term children 46 times. The term girl(s) appear more frequently than the term boy(s), 22 and six times, respectively. The term youth is used 17 times. The terms adults and women are mentioned 22 and 12 times, respectively. The term men is used four times (Fig. 1).

The Dakar conference also includes a component not included in the proceedings of the previous meetings. This conference generated a *Regional Framework for Action, Education for All: Meeting our Collective Commitments* statement. The *Regional Framework's* portion of the document is divided into six geographic regional sections: Africa; the Americas; the Arab States; Asia and the Pacific; Europe and North American, and the E9 countries.[16] The following graph shows the frequency of the terms children, boys, girls, youth, adolescents, adults, men, and women (Fig. 2).

The terms children (child/child's), boys, girls, youth, adults, men, and women occur at different frequencies for each region's *Framework*. The term children is mentioned most often in the Arab States, Asia and the Pacific, Europe and North America, and African regional reports. The E9 countries'

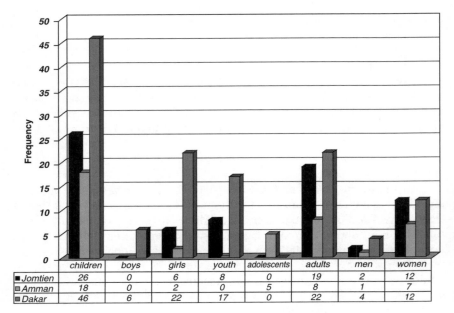

	children	boys	girls	youth	adolescents	adults	men	women
■ Jomtien	26	0	6	8	0	19	2	12
▣ Amman	18	0	2	0	5	8	1	7
▣ Dakar	46	6	22	17	0	22	4	12

Fig. 1.   EFA Introduction statements.

document mentions the term twice.[17] The term girls outnumbers the term boys in all documents. The Africa and the Arab States' reports mention girls 19 and 10 times, respectively. In addition, five of the six reports show that the term girl(s) is used twice as often as the term boy(s). The term youth appears most frequently in the report on the Americas (12 times), but also in all the other reports except the E9 document.[18] The term adults exists most frequently in the Africa and Arab States reports, with each mentioning the term 12 times. The term women occurs more frequently in most reports. Men are only mentioned in the Europe and North American report.

GENDER- AND STRUCTURE-RELATED TERMS IN THE EFA POLICIES

The next part of the content analysis includes the gender- and the structure-related terms frequently associated with the GAD literature. These gender-related terms include: gender; gender gap; gender stereotyping; gender

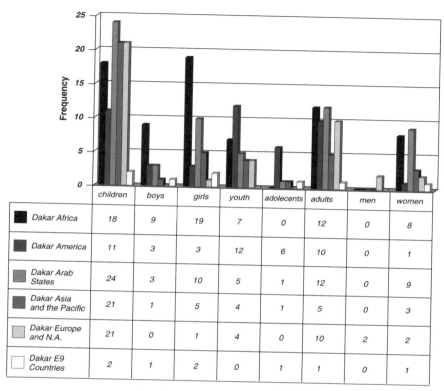

Fig. 2. Regional Framework I.

	children	boys	girls	youth	adolecents	adults	men	women
■ Dakar Africa	18	9	19	7	0	12	0	8
■ Dakar America	11	3	3	12	6	10	0	1
■ Dakar Arab States	24	3	10	5	1	12	0	9
■ Dakar Asia and the Pacific	21	1	5	4	1	5	0	3
▨ Dakar Europe and N.A.	21	0	1	4	0	10	2	2
☐ Dakar E9 Countries	2	1	2	0	1	1	0	1

discrimination; gender disparity(ies); gender equity; gender issues; gender-sensitive; gender awareness; gender bias; gender parity; and gender responsiveness. In addition, I counted the structure-related terms: social(ly); political; and terms in the economic category, including economic; poverty; finance; financial; budgeting; expenditures. I also noted the frequency of the terms culture(al), and the terms religion(ous); value(s); moral(s), and spiritual in the religion category.

Jomtien, 1990

The Jomtien's *Preamble* and *Framework for Action* documents in the Introduction mention the term gender-sensitive once. The term gender

occurs two times in the EFA documents. The term gender-stereotype occurs
once. No other gender-related terms appear (Fig. 1). The documents utilize
the term social 13 times. Political appears five times. The category of
economy has 21 references; culture appears 20 times. The term religion is
noted six times (Fig. 4).

Amman, 1996
The *Preamble* and *Affirmation* from the Amman Introduction document
contain the term gender gap three times. All other gender-related terms are
not found in the two documents. References to the terms economic and
cultural appear once and twice, respectively.

Dakar, 2000
The gender-related and structural terms appear more frequently in the
Introduction statement of the Dakar conference than in the earlier EFA
documents. For example, the terms gender, gender discrimination, and
gender disparities are noted one, three, and four times, respectively. Gender
equity is mentioned six times and gender issues noted once. Gender sensitive
appears two times; gender awareness is noted once and gender bias is stated
two times. Gender sensitive, gender awareness, and gender bias occur twice,
once, and twice, respectively. The *Introduction* also includes structural
terms. Social and political occur six and three times, respectively. Nineteen
references to terms in the economic category are noted. Culture appears
seven times and religion appears twice in the document's *Introduction* (Figs.
3 and 4).

The *Regional Frameworks* part of the Dakar document also
mentions gender-related terms. The term gender is used twice in the
EFA policies of the African, Americans, and the Arab States. Gender gap
is mentioned in the Arab States and Asia and the Pacific documents twice
and once, respectively. Gender discrimination is noted in the Americas
report once, and in the Arab States document twice. It is not mentioned
in the other countries' *Regional Framework* report. Africa, the Arab States,
and Asia and the Pacific country documents mentions the term gender
disparity. The African document mention it twice; the other cases note it
once. Gender equality is mentioned twice in the African document, and
once in the E9 document. The term gender sensitive appears twice in the
Africa and once in the Europe and North America documents.
Gender awareness is used once in the Africa *Regional Framework*.
The Arab States Framework uses the term gender bias once. Gender parity
appears in the Africa and Arab documents once and thrice, respectively.

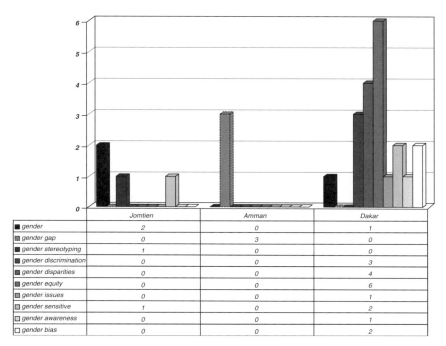

	Jomtien	Amman	Dakar
■ gender	2	0	1
▦ gender gap	0	3	0
■ gender stereotyping	1	0	0
■ gender discrimination	0	0	3
■ gender disparities	0	0	4
■ gender equity	0	0	6
▨ gender issues	0	0	1
☐ gender sensitive	1	0	2
☐ gender awareness	0	0	1
☐ gender bias	0	0	2

Fig. 3. Introductions' gender-related terms.

Gender responsiveness is mentioned three times in the Africa document. The terms gender stereotype and gender issues found in the earlier documents are not cited here (Fig. 5).

If we tally the total number of times the gender-related terms are found in each region's documents, we note that Africa and the Arab States reports mention these words most frequently, 50 and 38 times, respectively. The Americans, Asian and European reports use the terms 24, 15, and 12 times, respectively.[19] While we cannot establish causation, we can speculate that gender-related issues regarding female education are more pertinent to these countries, thus their relative frequency in the documents. However, it must be noted that the E9 countries do maintain unequal participation rates for males and females, and this is a widely recognized fact. Yet attention to this situation in terms of gender-related language is not evident in this document.

The structure-related terms also appears in each region's document, with the exception of the E9 piece. The term social appeared ten times in the

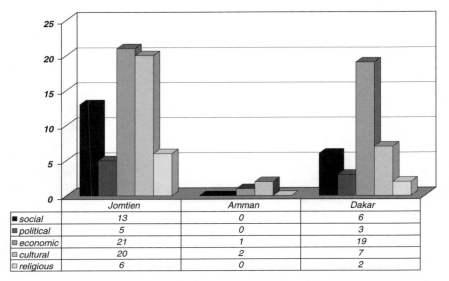

	Jomtien	Amman	Dakar
■ social	13	0	6
■ political	5	0	3
■ economic	21	1	19
▢ cultural	20	2	7
▢ religious	6	0	2

Fig. 4.   Introductions' structure-related terms.

Africa and Arab documents, seven times in the Americas document, and
five and four times, respectively, in the Asia and Europe documents.
The term political appears one time in the Africa document, two times in
the Asia document, and one time in the Europe document. It does
not appear in any of the other documents. The term economy (and
its related terms) appears most often in the Arab document (11 times).
Economy-related terms appear ten times in the Africa report, five times
in the Americas report, and one time in both the Asia and Europe
reports. They does not appear the E9 report. The term culture
(and its related terms) appears most often in the Africa report (12 times),
half that number in the Americans report (6), and a third that number
in both the Arab and Asia reports (4). The terms are noted in the
Europe document three times. Religion (and its related terms) is the
least frequently cited structural terms, appearing in Africa's document
four times, the E9 countries three times, Arab States twice, and in
the Americas, Asia and Europe documents one time. Fig. 6 provides
this information.[20]

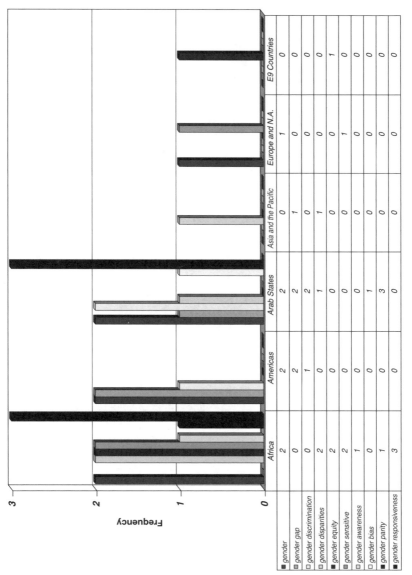

Fig. 5. Regional Frameworks' gender-related terms.

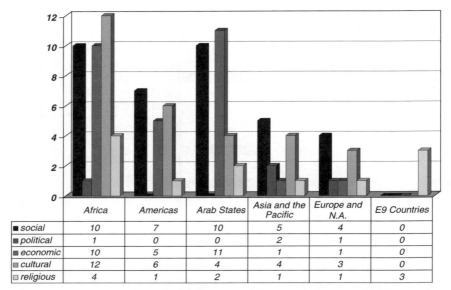

	Africa	Americas	Arab States	Asia and the Pacific	Europe and N.A.	E9 Countries
■ social	10	7	10	5	4	0
■ political	1	0	0	2	1	0
■ economic	10	5	11	1	1	0
▨ cultural	12	6	4	4	3	0
▢ religious	4	1	2	1	1	3

Fig. 6.   Regional Frameworks' structure-related terms.

EDUCATIONAL POLICIES AND THEIR LINKS WITH WID AND GAD

How may we situate and locate EFA policies in the development theories and rhetoric of WID and GAD? What is the extent to which the three conferences' documents align with the past and current trends in the educational development field? EFA policies indeed reflect the tenets of both WID and GAD but not necessarily in ways that we expect.

The *Preamble* documents from both the Jomtien conference and the Amman meeting emphasize the need for adult education, stressing education for women rather than men. This reference to women, an admittedly underserved population, supports the WID ideology in that it focuses on the individual, and not the gender relations that cause the inequity. It reaffirms the liberal feminist view that women do not have equal access to, nor do they participate in education at the same rate as men. Even though the documents were written during the GAD period, there are few references to gender in terms of the social structural elements that influence female education. In other words, even though the documents use the terms social, political, and economic, these terms refer to facets of a community.

While they are necessary and important in any examination of education, they are neither used in the context of gender, nor do they relate directly to ways we understand how the social structural elements influence educational opportunities for women. A content analysis does not provide the reasons for this omission. We may speculate, however, that the lack of awareness of existing development literature, or disagreement regarding the context in which women's education should be addressed, may have been a cause for its exclusion.

Jomtien's *Framework for Action* is a template for national governments, international aid organizations, non-governmental organizations (NGOs) to formulate plans of action for implementing the World Declaration on EFA (2000, p. 8). The *Framework* clearly outlines the "principles of action" that guide countries through the process of providing, engaging, and evaluating educational opportunities. For example, priority action at the national level includes assessing needs, developing policies, improving organizational capacities and information, and building partnerships in country. The regional level's priority action plan notes the need to exchange information, experience, and expertise. The priority action plan at the world level encourages cooperation among and between regions. Its wording resembles the GAD position that local, national, regional, and international cooperation is crucial to the fulfillment of stated educational goals and objectives.

The governing bodies recognize that cooperation amongst all levels is not guaranteed. Attempts to encourage countries to support the *Framework* when unconditional support is not forthcoming are addressed in the "Building Partnerships and Mobilizing Resources" part of the action plan. This section notes that

> women and girls especially may be deterred from taking full advantage of basic education opportunities because of reasons specific to individual cultures. Such barriers to participation may be overcome through the use of incentives and by programmes adapted to the local context and seen by the learners, their families and communities to be "productive activities" (pp. 9–10).

This statement targets females who have not enrolled in school, or those whose schooling has been interrupted. It suggests the use of inducement and enticement. Whereas the statement offers evidence of one of the GAD foci, i.e. integrated effort at local, state, and regional levels in education, it also seems to expose WID ideas. For example, in WID, recognizing that females have their inferior status in the community, plans are offered to elevate their status by launching initiatives and programs that would redress the inequity.

The language in this document suggests that females require special incentives to promote their participation. Alternate considerations, such as community discussions of social and cultural expectations of their lives as wives and mothers, which do not permit time to attend class, are not considered as a response to women's lack of participation. The ideological bent of the document is apparently built on the assumptions of liberal feminism, which regard the state as an essentially benevolent institution that will both design and implement initiatives to ensure women's equal access to education (Stromquist, 1998, 1999, 2001).

Similar findings are evident from the Mid-Decade Meeting in Amman 6 years later. The *Preamble* comprises six sections, each of which targets a different area. In the *Affirmation*, sections entitled "Gains Achieved," "Shortfalls," "The Road Ahead," "Emerging Challenges," and "Renewing the Pledge" refers to the selected key terms. The headings themselves provide a roadmap of sorts to understanding ideas associated with the terms in question. Children were the focus on the "Gains" section. Under "Shortfalls," gender gap is mentioned, even though the text did not consider the context in which inequity occurred. Instead, the document illustrates that children, adolescents, and adults failed to reach benchmarks, thus emphasizing the sexual division of educational inclusion. In the "Road Ahead and Emerging Challenges" section, no reference to sex or gender is made. Instead, reference is made to the role that society plays in the education of citizens. Although the texts in these sections hint at the social organizational structure that influences educational choices and chances, no reference to gender is made. Given this exclusion, we can only speculate that the authors may have noted the relationships between social structures and education, but did not connect them to the education of females, or that they simply chose to exclude the connection from their consideration. In the "Continuing Challenges" section, women and girls are once again highlighted as problems, thus reaffirming WID's main argument that sex itself is a more important reference than the larger constructs in which the individual is located. In sum, even though the Mid-Decade Meeting fell squarely within the period when GAD predominated in academic discussions, policy does not reflect its main tenets.

The Dakar meeting's *Framework for Action* uses gender-related terms more frequently than the Jomtien document, but this observation requires careful interpretive qualification. Although the term gender appears in the Dakar documents, other common GAD terms such as gender gap, gender stereotyping, gender issues, gender awareness, gender bias, and gender responsiveness appear three times or fewer in the entire Dakar document.

Moreover, references to sex (males and females) appear more frequently than references to gender. Other terms that appeared more frequently, such as gender responsiveness and parity, neither appear in all the documents, nor provide a strong context for a focused discussion of female education.

There is no increase in reference to structure-related terms (social, political, economic, cultural, and religious) in the *Introduction* statements, comparing the two from Jomtien in 1990 and Dakar in 2000. In fact, the use of all structure-related terms decreased in frequency. This revealing finding suggests that less, if any, attention was paid to GAD literature when the Dakar document was produced. The terms social, political, culture(al), and religion(religious) occur more frequently in the earlier Jomtien documents. The only term that is used slightly fewer times in the Dakar documents than in the Jomtien documents is economy. This may tell us that not only is less emphasis put on the social, political, cultural, and religious facets of educational policy, but also that economics is still the most prevalent concern of policymakers.

Having said this, we should not assume that references to gender automatically mean paying proper attention to the social structural elements that define gender. If we look at the context in which those terms are used, we uncover an equally interesting scenario. The Comparison of Gender- and Structure-Related Terms chart shows the frequency of the structure-related terms used in reference to gender. To tally this number, I totaled the gender-related terms for each region (Africa, the Americas, the Arab States, Asia and the Pacific, Europe and North America, and the E9 countries). Then, I charted the frequency with which the structure-related terms appeared in each region's Framework. The findings appear in the chart below (Fig. 7).

This chart shows that Africa and the Arab States both used gender-related terms more frequently than any of the other regions. In fact, these areas of the world chose to use these words twice as often as the Americas, Asia and the Pacific, Europe and North America, and the E9 countries. They were used approximately 50 times in both the Africa and Arab States documents, half that number in the Americas document, and a fraction of that number in the remaining plans. The Comparison chart also shows the frequency with which the structure-related terms are used in the documents. Africa may lead the pack here, with at least ten references to social, economic, and cultural, but that number is far fewer than the number of gender-related terms in the same document. In other words, though gender-related issues are included in the documents, they are not necessarily related to the structural social, political, economic, cultural, and religious references emphasized in the GAD literature. In the cases of the Asia, Europe, and the

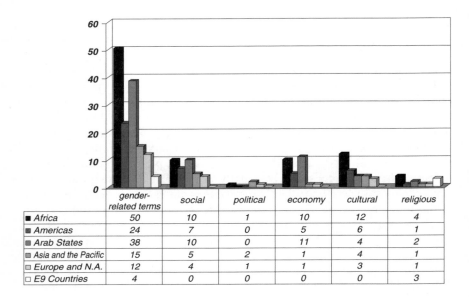

	gender-related terms	social	political	economy	cultural	religious
■ Africa	50	10	1	10	12	4
■ Americas	24	7	0	5	6	1
■ Arab States	38	10	0	11	4	2
▣ Asia and the Pacific	15	5	2	1	4	1
▢ Europe and N.A.	12	4	1	1	3	1
▢ E9 Countries	4	0	0	0	0	3

Fig. 7. Comparison of gender- and structure-related terms.

E9, not only are few references made to gender in the documents, but they are not couched in the social-structural terms of the GAD literature. Whereas the authors of the documents may be aware of the social, political, economic, cultural, and religious contexts within which females struggle for educational chances and opportunities, they make no direct linkage between those contexts and females' educational chances and choices in their texts.

The cases of Africa and the Americas yielded the same observation. Africa mentions gender-related terms over 50 times, but the combined use of the terms social, political, economic, cultural, and religious are tallied at barely half that rate. The Americas' document mentions gender-related terms over 20 times, but the terms social, economic, and cultural are referenced only a quarter as often. The terms political (not mentioned), and religious (noted several times), did not appear to play a role in the document's conceptualization of inferior female educational status. A greater discrepancy is noted in the Arab States report. Although gender-related terms appear almost 40 times, reference to the social, economic and cultural elements of the society are each mentioned at one-fourth the rate. This tells us that although social and economic forces may figure in the educational plans for the Arab States, they are not made explicitly in reference to female education, or even gender and education. The case is the same for the European report. Although we know that gender and education form a field that is squarely positioned in the social context in which it occurs, this report, like the others, fails to note the vital connection. The E9 is the most puzzling report. Documented evidence clearly shows that females lag behind and below their male counterparts at all levels of education, but this discrepancy is not noted. While we cannot explain why the E9 document largely excludes discussion of the existing social, cultural, and religious structures that are closely related to gender, we must begrudge the document's dereliction.

The foregoing content analysis demonstrates that the language in the EFA policy documents of 1990, 1996, and 2000 predominantly reflects the ideas commonly associated with the WID literature. Attention to the individual dominates the discourse. Numerous references to WID tenets are somewhat surprising, since its popularity in the development field has already diminished by 1990, and yet they figure prominently in the Jomtien conference proceedings. Indeed, the WID ideology continued to loom large in the Mid-Decade Meeting in Amman, as well as the 2000 meeting in Dakar, albeit to a lesser extent. Thus, the conclusion seems to be that the EFA documents have not aligned current scholarship with policy. While gender-related words appear in the documents, they claim neither ideological affinity nor policy commonality with GAD positions. In short, the use of gender-related terms on their own, without recognition in the social, cultural, political, and economic contexts in which they function, will do little to re-structure policy whose purpose is to redress gender inequity in education.

Yet another observation about EFA policy and its link to WID and GAD should be noted. I found that EFA policy addressed education for females by integrating, to varying degrees, fundamentals from the WID framework to explain women's oppression in terms of sexual identity, and the GAD framework to describe women's oppression in terms of the macro-social circumstances, situations, and conditions of their lives. However, the EFA policy allocates a substantial portion of its rhetoric to education of girls. Whereas the WID and GAD frameworks may be helpful to illuminate the connections between self, society, and education for women, we do not have a framework that explains girls' positions in the macro-social constructs that shape and influence their lives. Feminist thought has, to this point in time, applied the theories and ideas of both WID and GAD to the case of girls.

In sum, this content analysis revealed a disjunction between the current GAD research and EFA policies. It also illuminated the need to examine girls' lives, and the causes of the oppression they experience. We hope

findings of this nature illuminate the need to encourage future research that
hinges on the very integration of sound feminist development theory into
actual educational policies. Thus, the final section of this chapter suggests
several future directions in which the field may move to accomplish this goal.

FUTURE DIRECTIONS

Needless to say, educational policy – written by representatives from global,
regional, and national arenas – constitutes the fundamental underpinning
for the development, implementation, and evaluation of programs that seek
to achieve the goals of forging literacy among citizens. Sound policies are
the cumulative outcome of collaborative efforts among educational
specialists around the world to create comprehensive plans that truly
benefit the citizens they aim to serve. Therefore, future work in the field
must focus on three areas for both women and girls: the acknowledgement
of the macro-structural constructs of women's lives; the particular facets of
girls' lives that shape the chances for their educational participation; and the
successful attempts by females to gain an education that serves their needs in
the contemporary diaspora.

   This review shows that EFA policy may be peppered with the academic
jargon of the 1990s but it is largely based on inadequate ideology of the
1970s. Therefore, one future direction of the field must include the
construction of policies that recognize the educational needs of women in
terms of the traditional social, cultural, political, and economic situations. By
examining the education of women from a macroscopic perspective that
includes the real world in which they live and work, that is, by assimilating
the insights and findings of the academic theories such as GAD into
educational policy, we may realistically remove their obstacles of enrollment
in and completion of educational programs. This must include the study of
how gender influences educational choices for women. In so doing, we may
not regard gender as a problem, as Stromquist (1998, p. 98) puts it, but
rather as an act of life from which there is not escape.[21] It figures in any
rigorous and comprehensive examination of the lives of women in general
and their educational participation in particular. Until the powerful force of
gender is written into policy, we will fail to achieve the educational objectives
of strengthening female education. In other words, by appreciating gender,
situated as it is in the social structures that define opportunity, failure, and
achievement, we may finally free educational policy from an essentialist
framework that sees the female or the male, as a taken-for-granted, static

force or entity. In short, we must retool policy to reflect the social environment in which educational opportunities inhere. No individual has the ability to make decisions and complete tasks without the consideration and consent of others. Decisions are made within the social systems that allow them, and so, the social conditions that govern women's education chances must be explored and considered in future educational policy.

To be more specific, let us briefly consider how educational policy may fruitfully take into account the challenges to educational participation with reference to the social structures of the family, the community, and the state. Since families play a significant role in the education of women, we must then ask: What are the concerns of the family unit that promote and prohibit education for women? How do the economic needs of the family dictate education for women? How can we integrate these matters into educational policy for women?

The community, of which families are a part, may have needs and demands that affect education for women. Again, policy formulation requires the posing and answering of a series of questions: What are the community's needs? How are they brought to bear on women's chances for and completion of educational programs? How can the community promote the education of women, while meeting its needs and should the needs not be modified? In the community where a local school exists, how do the teaching staff and curriculum promote the retention of adolescent girls? To what extent does the staff encourage regular attendance in class? To what extent does it provide a safe and comfortable environment for female students? To what extent does it encourage secondary and higher education? How does the curriculum influence the retention of females? Is it appropriate? Is it comprehensive? In short, are the questions of leadership and curriculum, being fundamental elements of the schooling experience, fully addressed?

Existing educational policy is written at the national (and sometimes, regional) level. The policies' rhetoric may be based, in large part, on the agendas of the international agencies that devote considerable funding to countries that subscribe to their initiatives. But are the needs of the country carefully considered prior to the funding agency's offer of resources? To what extent do the goals of the local government align with the goals of the fund-granting multi-national organization? To what extent is there commitment to a collaborative process that honors the needs of both the funding agency and the local government? Yet another facet of the creation of policy is the voice of those who shape it. To what extent is equal representation of all groups accounted? In other words, does the dominant governing body project a louder, and more powerful voice than one of the minority ethnic groups? If so, what modifications can be made to address this inequity? Do women contribute to policy formulation at the same rate as men? Is there an attempt to recognize inequity and modify process to correct it?

A second future direction for the field must recognize the particular plight of girls. Girls, and young women, depending on their cultural, linguistic, economic, political, and national affiliations, confront different situations, reside in various conditions and are exposed to different circumstances as dictated by the unique social, religious, economic, and political environs of a community, and their roles as daughters and sisters. While WID and GAD offered general paradigms and theories that my have considerable cross-cultural resonance or even practical applicability, they do not always identify and consider local factors of girls. When educational policy is written, it must sensitively take into account those very native situations, conditions, circumstances that have direct bearing on girls' education in any one locale. In short, WID and GAD were no doubt written for and about women and their arguments and diagnoses of women's problems have much validity. But the lives of girls may be varied in multitudinous cultural settings, and they must be carefully and critically examined in order to complement any scholarship, including the WID and GAD models, that contribute to future educational policy.

Lastly, we need not question the need for a coordinated effort between the scholarly community that addresses gender-related issues, and practical design and implementation of policy (Stromquist, 1998). But as this study has shown, such coordination is not always achieved. In any event, academic theorizing must not take precedent over or ignore the actual effort to improve the lives of females. We must study the complicated amalgam of facets and layers of social life to complement our ameliorative effort to address the needs of females and their educational opportunities and pursuits. As Stromquist (2001) rightfully reminds us, sound educational policy that translates scholarly theories based on understanding social structural elements into functional, pragmatic programs that lead us toward equal education for all remains the ultimate goal of all who are involved in educational research.

NOTES

1. See Jaquette and Staudt (1988) and Young (1993).
2. See Upadhya (1996) and Young (1993) for discussion of the early WID framework.

3. Readers written or edited by authors such as Maggie Humm (1992), Josephine Donovan (1998), Linda Nicholson (1997), Bates et al. (1995) and Lynda Stone (1994) provide discussion of numerous categories of feminist thought, including, for example, Marxist feminism. It should also be noted, however, that since, the categorization of feminism that identifies a single cause for women's oppression has been criticized.

4. See Hartmann (1979), Eisenstein (1979), and Walby (1990).

5. See Hartmann (1979) and Walby (1990).

6. The absence of attention to the plight of girls will be made throughout this chapter.

7. For articles that examine the WID movement with regard to women's education in the governmental sector of nations, see Stromquist (1998).

8. Moser (1993). Also see Lather (1991).

9. Although women often earn an income, this role is usually not considered their primary responsibility.

10. Moser (1993).

11. Recognition of the overlapping similarities of feminist theories over the years has been noted in the edited collection of Bates et al. (1994).

12. The particular documents were selected from each of the three conferences because of their similarity in form that contributes to the validity of a content analysis.

13. The term childhood was not counted when used as an adjective with early, to suggest early childhood education, a topic related to but not directly included in this content analysis.

14. I recognize that these terms are not always evident in the GAD literature. They were selected for use in this review, and counted because of their inherent implication of a socially constructed, gender-related relationship between the sexes.

15. The terms "youth" and "adolescent" do not appear in all documents. I included the total number where applicable. "Structure-related" terms refer to macro-social maintenance systems of economics, politics, culture and religion.

16. The E9 countries, defined by the EFA conferences include Bangladesh, Brazil, China, Egypt, India, Indonesia, Mexico, Nigeria, and Pakistan.

17. It should be noted that the E9 Regional Framework was considerably shorter than all other region's frameworks. An explanation is not provided.

18. The series of documents neither define nor differentiate between adolescents and youth. It is not clear if these terms reference the same individuals.

19. Gender-related and structure-related terms were added to obtain this figure.

20. I identified only one incident where the gender-related term appeared in the same sentence as structure-related term. Content analysis can be conducted to show the few occurrences that these terms appear in the same sentence.

21. Stromquist (1998, p. 98), referencing WID units in emerging countries, states, "Through this approach, the state discourse successfully weakens the resolution of the problem of gender by failing to acknowledge the power asymmetry between women and men and concentrating instead on the problems of poor and destitute women."

REFERENCES

Bates, Ü. Ü., Denmark, F. L., Held, V., Helly, D. O., Hune, S., Lees, S. H., Pomeroy, S. B.,
    Somerville, C. M., & Rosenberg-Zalk, S. (1995). *Women's realities, women's choices: An
    introduction to women's studies.* New York: Oxford University Press.
Boserup, E. (1970; 1986). *Woman's role in economic development.* London: Allen & Unwin.
Buvinic, M. (1983). Women's issues in third world poverty: A policy analysis. In: M. Buninic,
    M. Lycette & W. P. McGreevey (Eds), *Women and poverty in the third world.* Baltimore:
    Johns Hopkins University Press.
Donovan, J. (1988). *Feminist theory: The intellectual traditions of American feminism.* New
    York: Continuum.
Eisenstein, Z. (1979). *Capitalist patriarchy and the case for socialist feminist.* New York:
    Monthly Review.
Hartmann, H. (1979). Capitalism, patriarchy and job segregation by sex. In: Z. R. Eisenstein
    (Ed.), *Capitalist patriarchy and the case for socialist feminism.* New York: Monthly
    Review Press.
Hartmann, H. (1981). The unhappy marriage of marxism and feminism: Towards a more
    progressive union. In: L. Sargent (Ed.), *Women and revolution.* Boston: South End Press.
Humm, M. (Ed.) (1992). *Modern feminisms: Political, literary, cultural.* New York: Columbia
    University Press.
Jagger, A. M., & Rothenberg, P. (Eds) (1984). *Feminist frameworks: Alternative theoretical
    accounts of the relations between women and men.* New York: McGraw-Hill.
Jaquette, J. S., & Staudt, K. A. (1988). Politics, population and gender: A feminist analysis of
    US population policy in the third world. In: K. B. Jones & A. G. Jónasdóttir (Eds), *The
    political interest of gender, developing theory and research with a feminist face.* London:
    Sage.
Lather, P. A. (1991). *Getting smart: Feminist research and pedagogy with/in the postmodern.*
    New York: Routledge.
MacKinnon, C. (1987). *Feminism unmodified: Discourses on life and law.* Cambridge: Harvard
    University Press.
Moser, C. O. N. (1993). *Gender planning and development: Theory, practice, and training.*
    London: Routledge.
Nicholson, L. J. (Ed.) (1997). *Feminism/postmodernism.* New York: Routledge.
Stone, L. (1994). *The education feminism reader.* New York: Routledge.
Stromquist, N. P. (1998). The institutionalization of gender and its impact on educational
    policy. *Comparative Education, 34*(1), 85–100.
Stromquist, N. P. (1999). Women's education in the twenty-first century: Balances and
    prospects. In: R. Arnove & C. A. Torres (Eds), *Comparative education: The dialectic of
    the global and the local* (pp. 179–205). Lanham: Rowman & Littlefield.
Stromquist, N. P. (2001). What poverty does to girls' education: The intersection of class,
    gender and policy in Latin America. *Compare, 31*(1), 39–56.
Upadhya, S. (1996). The status of women in Nepal – 15 years on. *Studies in Nepali History and
    Society, 1*(2), 423–453.
Walby, S. (1990). *Theorising patriarchy.* Oxford: Blackwell.
Young, K. (1993). Frameworks for analyses. *Planning development with women: Making a world
    of difference* (pp. 127–146). New York: St. Martin's Press.

World declaration on education for all. (1990). Preamble. New York: UNESCO Available: http://www.unesco.org/education/efa/ed_for_all/background/jomtien_declaration.shtml.
Framework for Action Framework for action: Meeting basic learning needs. (1990). New York: UNESCO Available: http://www.unesco.org/education/efa/ed_for_all/background/07Bpubl.shtml.
The Amman Affirmation. (1996). New York: UNESCO Available: http://www.unesco.org/education/efa/ed_for_all/background/amman_affirmation.shtml.
The Dakar affirmation. (2000). Paris: UNESCO Available: http://www.unesco.org/education/efa/ed_for_all/background/efinalrep96.pdf.
The Dakar framework for action. Education for all: Meeting our collective commitments. (2000). Paris: UNESCO Available: http://www.unesco.org/education/efa/wef_2000/index.shtml and http://unesdoc.unesco.org/images/0012/001211/121147e.pdf.

EDUCATION ON THE TRANSNATIONAL STAGE: A SHARED SPOTLIGHT, A POCKET OF HOPE ☆

Verónica R. Martini

I've spent an hour talking to the children in this school in the south of Chile. I've carefully looked at their well-kept notebooks. I've heard them read from their books and asked them questions about what they have read. Later, I will discuss with the teacher what he tries to do when he teaches them reading. And then the children will be asked to demonstrate some of what they have learned in math and in science and to read some poetry in Mapudungun – the language of the Mapuche, the indigenous group that claims the identity of most of the children in this school. But I will focus on these things later, for now I'm listening to the children... Jerónimo, a 10-year old with bright eyes, is more engaged than the rest. He is curious about the purpose of my visit. Finally he asks me "De dónde vienes?" – Where do you come from? I tell him that I come from the United States. He pauses to think and then says, "De donde los aviones se estrellaron contra las dos torres?" – Do you come from the place where the airplanes blew up the two towers? I

☆ This chapter is an expanded and updated version of a paper originally written for the course "Globalization and Education: The Research Agenda" at the Harvard Graduate School of Education, later presented at the 2002 Comparative and International Education Society Annual Conference. The author is grateful to Professor Marcelo M. Suárez-Orozco, and Teaching Fellow Desiree Baolian Qin-Hilliard for their invaluable insights and comments on the earlier draft, and to educator Jonathan A. Alderson, and this volume's editors, Alex Wiseman and David Baker, and the anonymous reviewers for their invaluable suggestions.

Global Trends in Educational Policy
International Perspectives on Education and Society, Volume 6, 173–196
Copyright © 2005 by Elsevier Ltd.
All rights of reproduction in any form reserved
ISSN: 1479-3679/doi:10.1016/S1479-3679(04)06007-4

tell him that I do come from the place where hijackers crashed several airplanes against
very tall buildings almost two years ago. The other children listen attentively as I answer
Jerónimo's question. I ask him where he has learned about this; "I've heard it on TV,"
he replies. I ask whether he has talked about this in school and he replies that he hasn't.

(Reimers, 2004)

Globalization has reached the lives and cultures of millions of individuals in
one-way or another. The impact of social, political, and economic transformations ensuing from globalization on people and their social relations
worldwide also promotes change at a more abstract level. That is to say that
as subjects, such as students and schools, are transformed, the disciplines
concerned with their study undergo change as well. Globalization thus
reaches and challenges more abstract conceptual structures and disciplinary
fields. Comparative Education is one of such disciplines.

Due to the potential magnitude of those debates and impact of those
consequent decisions, it becomes imperative to explore and understand the
educational opportunities (both present and missed) that globalization
presents, while identifying how they, in turn, influence the discipline
concerned with their study.

Globalization, as this chapter aims to elucidate, continues to tender educational opportunities through transnationalism: a space for exposure to
and interaction between otherwise unconnected individuals and their cultures. This transnational space, or stage, knows no geographic borders.
Rather, it becomes available as teachers and children incorporate it as a
context that promotes meaningful educational exchanges. Transnationalism
is not an experience limited to the minority of the world's children who can
travel from one country to another. As this chapter will describe, Globalization allows the transnational stage to be experienced locally, or virtually,
either through the experience of immigration, access to technology, or
availability of mass information – all ubiquitous elements of the globalization process.

When understood as a space for meaningful learning and teaching,
the transnational stage holds great superfluous opportunities for children to
acquire the skills that globalization will demand of them during adulthood. The transnational context also becomes a new dimension or lens
through which to assess perspectives, generate new questions, and
address hypotheses in the field of Comparative Education. An informed
dialectic between the concrete and the abstract holds the promise of change
that is valid both for legitimate educational practice and sound theory
building.

THE IMPACT OF GLOBALIZATION ON EDUCATION

The study of Education, as it traverses the borders of national states, has predominantly been framed in the field of Comparative Education. That discipline, its role producing knowledge, and the policy designs and decision-making it informs, is not estranged from global forces that continue to shape it (Arnove & Torres, 1999).

In a comprehensible account of the breadth of objectives of Comparative Education, Robert Arnove suggests three main dimensions as pillars of the discipline. (1) The scientific dimension supplies the means for theory building, as it promotes the "formulation of generalizable propositions about the workings of school systems and their interactions with their surrounding economies, polities, cultures, and social orders (Arnove, 1999, p. 4). (2) The pragmatic dimension, in turn, is concerned with the study and potential re-applicability of best educational policies and practices in different settings. (3) Finally, the global dimension sets the fields in an international context "where the nation-state is no longer the basic unit of analysis" (Arnove, 1999, p. 4).

Arnove's identification of the three dimensions of Comparative Education is particularly useful to understand how globalization impacts the discipline. Because globalization is reaching children worldwide regardless of their school level, the formulation of theories about the functioning of school systems as well as educational practices and policies around the world, are inevitably being transformed.

By definition, the international context is inherently integrated in the field of Comparative Education. The knowledge gained through the comparison of structures, policies, and practices adopted by different nation-states feeds back and affects the production of more complex hypotheses, the renewal of concepts, and the introduction of innovating policy propositions that may affect educational practices of systems other than those originally studied. As is the case with all scientific disciplines, it is important that concepts in the field be valid. It is also crucial that ideas be relevant, to the degree that likely policy recommendations directly affect those studied by the discipline.

According to McGovern (1999) "it is imperative for those involved in international and comparative education to recognize how knowledge in the field is rooted in historical, experiences, cultural practices and power relations" (p. 4). In order to attain knowledge that is both valid and relevant, it is critical for those involved in the field of Comparative Education to explore how the international context has evolved, how its insertion into the field is being reshaped, and what new educational challenges and opportunities have emerged from those processes.

But how, exactly, is the international context incorporated? How are those international education models, and consequently the field of Comparative Education, being reshaped? What and where is the "transnational" stage? Who is on it? And how does globalization relate to it? To understand how globalization interacts with the abstraction of this science it is necessary to explore how the phenomenon reaches the lives of those experiencing education transnationally.

GLOBALIZATION AND EDUCATION: THE EMERGENCE OF A TRANSNATIONAL STAGE

Like Jerónimo in the opening story, many children in the south of Chile, or the south of China, can access television: a technology their parents most probably never experienced when they were children. Growing per-capita television ownership and viewing in developing countries (Watson, 2004) represents, in many cases, availability of information at the touch of a button – information that is live, and perhaps being broadcasted instantaneously to both Chile and China.

The current global configuration of technology, or "technoscape," as Appardurai (1996) defines it, "now moves at high speeds across various kinds of previously impervious boundaries (p. 19). Because of the pace and expanse of technology around the world, it would not be unreasonable to hypothesize about the teacher in the opening story as having access to a computer, the Internet, and the host of information it affords through a single click. Neither would it appear irrational to imagine Jerónimo playing Nintendo with his friends after school – after a stop by MacDonald's for a super-size glass of *Diet Coke*, and before telephoning his brother, who has recently immigrated to the United States, where he works for a Mexican company that imports software from India.

Globalization, as historian Coatsworth has succinctly defined it, "is what happens when the movement of people, goods, or ideas among countries and regions accelerates" (Coatsworth, 2004, p. 38). Globalization integrates markets, technologies and nation-states "to a degree never witnessed before" while it produces a "powerful backlash for those brutalized or left behind by this new system" (Friedman, 1999, p. 9)

"Staying behind" in the new globalized system may be argued to be a direct result of conditions such as an individual's geographic location, socio-economic status, or country-specific cultural attitudes and practices regarding gender roles, for example. The backlash may also be a byproduct of the marginal role of Education in the framework of globalization – in other words, the missed educational opportunities that technology, for example, may provide for meaningful learning about each other and the world. As Suárez-Orozco and Qin Hilliard (2004) suggest, within the globalization debate, education is "an uncharted continent (p. 2)."

To position Education as a central component of the globalization process, educators worldwide, including administrators, policy makers, and politicians, must take full advantage of the plethora of opportunities that global transformations present. In order to minimize the effects of a potential backlash, children and teenagers around the world should be equipped with the skills that will later be demanded of them for their success. This is particularly true if one advocates the premise that "the lives and experiences of youth growing up today will be linked to the economic realities, social processes, technological and media innovations, and cultural flows that traverse national boundaries with ever greater momentum" (Suárez-Orozco & Qin Hilliard, 2004, p. 2).

Yet how can educators most effectively and efficiently promote global learning – learning that is relevant and meaningful in the global era? How can the Jerónimos of this world, and their teachers, and the schools they populate be further supported in their quest for meaningful education? Certainly, propositions to address these questions are many. This chapter seeks to answer them within a more definite framework, identifying a concrete element of globalization: a transnational stage, and the educational opportunities that it brings about. Before turning our attention to the specific elements of the transnational stage and its educational offer, however, it is necessary to clarify two interrelated points.

The first is concerned with an identification of the skills increasingly demanded of children growing up today for their success responding to the exigencies of an increasingly globalized and globalizing world. Some scholars have stressed the importance that children be taught skills that will ease their integration into ever more multicultural settings (Suárez-Orozco, 2004). "Children growing up in these and other [multicultural] settings are more likely than any other generation in human history to face a life of working and networking, loving and living with others from different linguistic, religious, and racial backgrounds" (Suárez-Orozco & Qin Hilliard, 2004, p. 4). Other authors emphasize the pressing need for children to become "digitalese;" that is to say, that they master the digital skills needed to operate computers and other information technology (Battro, 2004). Expert psychologist and educator Howard Gardner, on the other hand, underscores the importance that youth be educated to master basic literacy, while taught other skills including understanding of the global system, critical and creative thinking within the disciplines, knowledge of other cultures and traditions, and fostering of tolerance and appreciation across racial, linguistic, national, and cultural boundaries (Gardner, 2004, pp. 253–255).[1] While these skills differ in their specific applicability they could be argued to share a common end: they promote tolerance, understanding, and peace across the planet.

Departing from that premise, and before exploring the transnational stage as an agency to promote the skills described above, it is sensible to identify other educational models that have fostered those abilities through their curricula or design. The following paragraphs attempt to concisely describe how the international education and study abroad models have incorporated Arnove's "international context" in their design, while identifying similarities and differences in terms of the elements, participants, and challenges of those models.

A description of the scope of international education, understood as the curriculum offered at international schools, is followed by a review of the literature on another form of international education, as it continues to be delivered through study abroad and educational exchange programs. Finally, I reflect on the new dimension that globalization, as a revolutionary force affecting social relationships worldwide, continues to advance on to the transnational reach of education.

INTERNATIONAL EDUCATION: WHAT IS IT?

As introduced earlier, Comparative Education is most widely understood as a scholarly discipline concerned with the comparative study of educational systems and practices. While Comparative Education is the *science*, I suggest international education to be understood as the *type of curriculum, course of study, or educational program* that, shaped as a rather exclusive type of commodity, has emerged mainly during the last four decades. Even regarded as a concrete practice, the definition of international education has been subject to much pondering.

As suggested by Hayden (1998), if one compares conceptual definitions of international education of the 1960s and 1990s, as Jonietz did in 1991 in the *Yearbook of Education*, one is readily introduced to rather opposing ideas. On the one hand, there still is uncertainty about what international education really is. On the other, increasing figures as to the numbers of schools offering this type of instruction are witnesses to the steadiness of its growth. According to Jonietz (1991) the 1964 issue of the *Yearbook of Education* proposed the "existence of a new concept – international schools founded with the specific purpose of furthering international education" (p. 2). This new idea had been conceptualized around the emergence of nearly 50 international schools and the creation of the International School Association (Hayden, 1998).

At that time, the concept was judged "not only short on means and not far-reaching enough in its spread, but also uncertain of its aims and fundamental premises," (Jonietz, 1991, p. 2). Understood in this sense, however, during the last four decades, international education has experienced the kind of growth necessary to preserve the validity and recognition that it has today. This growth has been brought about by different factors.

Hayden (1998) suggests those reasons to gather mainly around an increase in the number of international schools, which grew from 50 in 1964 to nearly 1,000 in the mid-1990s. Knight and Leach (1964) identified seven types of international schools, and classified them as belonging to either one of the following categories: (a) national schools overseas, (b) International Schools Association (ISA) member schools, and (c) profit making schools. In the 1990s, international schools do not appear to have been so easily classifiable. While Jonietz (1991) suggests that international schools are the type that educate expatriates abroad, for example, others contend that such a definition is narrow, and does not take into account the fact that while a student body might be mainly international, the educational component might not necessarily provide students with the international context that many view as essential of institutions deeming themselves as international (Cambridge & Thompson, 2000). However, much scholarly contention there has been regarding the defining characteristics of international schools, the fact that the number of institutions under discussion has grown at such a rate is, undeniable, an indication of the development of international education overall.

Another factor pointing to such development is the emergence and growth of the International School Association (ISA), which was founded under Swiss Law in 1951 and is "the most senior organization in the world of international education" (ISA, 2004). As Renaud (1991) so eloquently describes, ISA's aim was to develop "a genuine international system of education…to meet the needs of the increasing number of mobile families" (p. 6) which had significantly expanded after the Second World War. After developing pre-school and primary school curricula, ISA was charged with developing a common curriculum for secondary schools to facilitate transition and mobility of students into the higher education sector. ISA was supported in this endeavor by three consecutive grants from UNESCO. These efforts led to the creation of the International Schools Examination Syndicate (ISES), later renamed International Baccalaureate Office (IBO) as the entity to provide with the infrastructure for the project (Renaud, 1991; ISA, 2004). As the International Schools Association proudly describes its achievements,

> In the 1980's the ISA created an international program for middle schools (11 to 16 year old students), which with further development by the IBO became the IBMYP (International Baccalaureate Middle Years Program). The establishment of a curriculum framework for Peace Education and Sustainable Development, designed as an instrument for schools to become more internationally minded.
>
> (ISA 2004)

The increase in the number of United World Colleges (UWC) from one in 1967 to ten in 2003 is another factor indicative of the expansion of international education. First conceived by German educator Kurt Hahn in the late 1950s as a positive response to the antagonism generated by the Cold War, the educational mission of Atlantic College, as the institution was first named, was to bring together teenagers from different cultures to a common space where they could learn about each other. "In 2003, there are ten UWC Colleges and 114 UWC National Committees and Selection Contacts. In the 41 years since Atlantic College opened, more than 27,000 students from 176 countries have attended the United World Colleges" (UWC, 2004).

Finally, the growth of international education also becomes perceptible with the creation of the European Council of International Schools (ECIS) in 1965, and its expansion as a non-profit membership organization whose mission is to "provide services to support professional development, curriculum and instruction, leadership and good governance in international schools located in Europe and around the world" (ECIS, 2004). Today, ECIS governs over 436 primary and secondary international schools around the globe and "creates opportunities for education and dialogue, encourages alliances with other organizations, and acts as a catalyst for the advancement of international education" (ECIS, 2004). All the factors mentioned above, according to Hayden (1998) outline the beginning of an international school system.

While the factors listed above seem to have contributed to the growth of international education as it relates to the increasing number of international schools, its growth as a type of education offering with a distinct type of curriculum is not so easily measurable. This is mainly because of the prevalent lack of accord as to what the purpose of international education is, or what its practice entails.

A thorough review of the literature of the past four decades suffices to uncover the ambiguities. Cambridge and Thompson's (2000) meticulous examination of existing literature suggests that the propositions about the educational purpose of international schools have been many, and have suggested various elements to be the core of the international school principles and curriculums. Among these are bilingual education, non-profit administration status, multinational student body, teaching staff, and governing boards. While some of these elements might still be found at international schools today, the main purpose of these institutions all along seems to have centered on the provision of an education that fosters global peace and understanding: a goal that is aligned with the emergence of these schools immediately following World War II.

As this author proposes, these international-education-related institutions have become defining factors of the "practice" of international education. As mentioned earlier, however, when it comes to the principles that inform that practice, there seems to be a lack of consensus rooted, primarily, in the uncertainty as to what these schools really are and the varied educational philosophies that underlie different institutions.

Reflecting on the lack of clarity about the purpose of international schools and the philosophies that direct them, Hayden and Thompson (2000) clearly sum up that "an international school may offer an education that has no claim to be international, while an international education may be experienced by a student who has not attended a school that claims to be international" (p. 2). The "conglomeration" of international institutions baptized as international schools, and the absence of a concrete educational philosophy framing their mainstream practice, indeed broadens the potential of the field of international education. It leaves international education in a place "where it may be experienced world-wide in schools other than international schools." (Hayden, 1998).

An understanding of the unique features of these schools and the populations they usually educate, however, becomes useful in narrowing the potential all-encompassing scope of these international institutions, thus providing us with a better sense as to what they really are. Of central importance to this effect is an understanding of the type of student body these schools host.

Referring to the average international school student, Walker (1998) describes a "much traveled, multilingual, sophisticated exterior" covering "vulnerable young people." Furthermore, these students' parents, "*by definition*[2], are professional people, frequently absent and often too busy to integrate into a temporary new culture" (p. 25). According to Langford (1998) "it appears to have been the U.S. foreign service, military and missionaries who initially grappled with the issue of raising children internationally" (p. 30). Her assumption that these social groups were the first ones to seek an internationally tailored kind of education is based on these people's pioneering experiences "in the field of moving families overseas by virtue of their extensive experience of relocation long before the business sector launched itself into the international market-place after World War II" (p. 31).

Langford's hypothesis is confirmed by historical sources such as the 1957 International Schools around the World Report, prepared by the International Schools Foundation Inc. in the United States, in collaboration with the International Schools Association. Describing the creation of international schools as a "sudden need," the report explains how "Governments, cultural agencies, big corporations, and international agencies will never be able to secure and retain the best type of official or representative [staff] *unless* adequate education facilities are provided for the children of their staff" (p. 5). As an example of families other than those headed by American parents, Langford (1998) offers the case of the traditional British boarding-school system, which served a similar need.

While the "elite" student body appears as a central feature of international schools, Allen (1998) on the other hand, offers his own anecdotal experience to illustrate other prevailing characteristics of international schools besides their constituting student bodies. Indeed, while working at an international school in Latin America, he found his work place situated "in a walled paradise of leafy luxury with armed security guards separating it from the economically impoverished *pueblo* outside. Students were bussed in from affluent suburbs" (p. 124).

Whether instructed through U.K. or U.S. curricula, whether expatriate, foreign-born or of mixed-nationalities, the literature suggests that, for the greatest part, the populations being educated at international schools usually belong to rather exclusive elites. As Allen (1998) suggests, in contrast to national schools, in international schools, it is neither the curriculum, nor the pedagogy that is distinctive, but rather the student body. Allen (1998) vividly illustrates the context of international schools by reflecting on issues of the latter's operational philosophies in host countries (e.g. the role of the New International School in Thailand, or the Kennedy School in Buenos Aires) and the potential impact they may have on those countries' non-elite nationals. "Through attending the 'local American, British, French, or international school', children in less-developed countries may gain access either to the economies of more-developed countries or to the socio-economic elite of their nation" (p. 129). He convincingly claims, however, that "students from less-developed countries can find access to an international school impossible, unless they are *already* part of the socio-economic elite" (p. 129). Through a concrete example, I will refer and expand on this issue of access to international education from within the national education system later on in this paper.

To follow Allen's argument, the financially privileged elites making up the majority of the student body at international schools, thus provide us with a clear sense of the "distinctiveness" of these schools. They also validate, in a sense, the concept proposed earlier in this paper: that international education is a rather exclusive type of commodity. As such, their potential for fostering global peace and understanding – skills previously identified as necessary for the success of youth growing up in today's globalized world – becomes limited to just an affluent few, and unreachable to the majority of children in schools around the globe; a majority for whom being empowered with the skills to participate in and to activate peace in their lives, their communities and their countries vis-à-vis the global environment is arguably even more paramount than for the small elite living under political and economic stability.

STUDY ABROAD AND EDUCATIONAL EXCHANGE PROGRAMS

Although the type of education detailed above is perceived as exclusive to a well-defined constituency of students, the international mobility these students benefit from is readily available to yet another sub-group of students through a different kind of educational experience. Study abroad and educational exchange programs, which operate from a different angle of the transnational setting, extend the offer of transnational mobility to a somewhat different student population. It is worth noting, at this point, that unlike the population educated at international schools (which can serve students K through 12) study abroad and exchange programs serve, predominantly, adolescents 15 and older. While these groups are different in terms of their educational experiences and needs, both are exposed to globalization's reach, and both have a right and a need for the skills that will best prepare them to develop as citizens of the globalization era.

In the 2000 Open Doors Report on International Student Mobility at the Millennium, Koh (2001) indicates that for the first time in the 51-year-long life of the Institute of International Education "the number of international students studying at U.S. institutions of higher education has surpassed half a million." Commenting on these students' personal profiles and on their institutions, Koh reports on the predominance of undergraduate students who are male, single and holding a category F (student) type visa. 48% of these students are located in just 50 U.S. counties, "concentrated in large metropolitan areas and are at over 2500 institutions" (p. 3). The education level sought by these students engage – they are present at every type of institution – is as varied as their nationalities and backgrounds.

While students from Europe make up a large 15% of overall international enrollments, an unsurpassed 54% from Asia make up more than half of all international students. This last figure, however, represents a decrease in the percentage from previous years. Based on the pervasive discourse of globalization and its significant effect on individual mobility, one could easily conjecture the increase in the numbers of students from Asia studying in the U.S. to be associated with the upward insertion of Asian countries into regional and global markets (Jenkins, 2004). It is worth noting, that in 2003, the leading country of origin of the international student population in the U.S. was India – precisely at a time when less expensive soft-skills are much in demand around the globe, as exemplified by India's thriving software industry is thriving (Bloom, 2004).

On the other hand, the fact that "After 5 years of steady growth, the number of international students attending colleges and universities in the United States in 2002–2003 showed only a slight increase over the prior year, up less than 1%, bringing the 2002–2003 total to 586,323" (Open Doors, 2003) may be associated with the factually domestic, yet globally publicized tragic attacks of September 11, 2001, which resulted in much stricter management and control of both permanent and temporary immigration flows into the U.S.

Although most of the literature consulted refers to study abroad and educational exchange programs as they have developed and continue to expand in the United States, other countries seem to experience a similar kind of phenomena; such is the case in the United Kingdom. In *Managing International Students*, Humfrey (1999) admits that, in the U.K., the field of international education has faced stiff competition, hindered in many cases by issues of financing and quality or EU expansion, as observed by the British Council. She proposes, however, that, despite these obstacles, the U.K. should sustain its efforts to provide education for overseas students as well as develop strategic plans to provide country nationals with opportunities to study abroad:

> For many years, the undergraduate study abroad programme...has allowed and encouraged North American students to study in and gain credits from a host institution. This system is now extended to Japan, Korea, Taiwan, Latin America and Australia.

British students, other than those on language programmes, have not found it easy to join such exchange schemes and most of the international traffic is one-way and brings income to the UK. The position is changing... The opportunities for the future will be yet more exciting and challenging. Institutions of higher education have already begun to make world alliances with establishments of similar quality to create on each campus a node of global university.

(Humfrey, 1999, pp. 151–152)

An attempt to define the exact nature of study abroad or educational exchange programs exactly are, is as futile and invalid as generalizing on their nature altogether. Although generalizations are difficult and would surely not be representative of the study abroad phenomenon, certain general guidelines define the broader framework in which these programs most commonly operate.

One of the prevailing features of educational exchange and study abroad programs, for example, is that they are most commonly displayed and most accessible at the higher education level (Klineberg, 1976; Hawkins & Cummings, 2000; Speakman Jr., 1966; Goodwin & Natch, 1988; Danesy, 1994). Also, in general, exchanges can be fostered on a bilateral or an omnilateral basis. According to Klineberg (1976), the former consists of one nation seeking to "improve [its] image and relations with, another nation." In the case of omnilateral, or multilateral exchanges, such as the Fulbright or the UNESCO fellowships, programs are "designed to better international understanding in general" (p. 16). These programs involve the participation of what have been identified as either *sending* or *receiving* countries, depending on the way in which the country's educational offer is made.

Finally, and in contrast to the imprecise, but more common goals of the international schools described earlier – where overarching objectives gather mainly around individual mobility or parental satisfaction – the goals ascribed to study abroad and exchange programs are usually concerned with the interests of the individual, the university, the country, and the community (Klineberg, 1976). In many cases, exchange programs seek to foster world peace and understanding, as is the case with Rotary International, American Field Services, UPEACE Worldwide, and other programs.

A review of the literature also reveals a number of concerns associated with this type of educational offer. For example, the structures in place for the selection and admission of foreign students into institutions other than their home countries' are not standardized or equal across countries. Not all programs require the same levels of previous academic achievement, for example. The level of preparation for what has been referred to as the "foreign sojourn" (Klineberg, 1976), also understood as the level of emotional development of the student to fully engage in a foreign culture, may also vary from program to program. Arguably, emotional maturity may be closely linked, for example, to the student's ability to cope with potentially challenging situations in regard to language ability, when the student is in a country, or enrolled in a program where instruction is not delivered in their mother tongue. The lack of consistent and appropriate mechanisms to assess potential success or failure of a student's adaptation to the new environment, I would argue, becomes another rather problematic issue in the design and administration of study abroad and exchange programs. This is a particularly critical issue to address in the case of students from lower socio-economic status, who are less likely than developed country nationals to have access to second-language study.

Finally, a challenge of central importance to this kind of educational offer is that known, among education experts and practitioners, as the "brain-drain" phenomenon. Ironically perhaps, it is the very skills provided by international education opportunities – second language acquisition, multicultural perspective, mediation skills – that allow graduates access as candidates for foreign jobs.[3]

The centrality of "brain-drain" to educational transnational traffic poses it as a phenomenon worthy of close attention. As Rao (1979) argues, the discussion of brain drain usually refers to two different kinds of people. These are "(1) educated and trained persons who migrate from developing countries to join the workforce of the developed countries immediately and, (2) students who go from developing to developed countries initially for the purpose of education and training but later decide to live and work in developed countries" (p. 3). For the purpose of the current discussion, I refer to "brain-drain" as it manifests among students in Rao's second group.

Understood as the migration of intellectual potential from less developed to more developed countries, the concept of brain-drain comes about as a challenge to Klineberg's (1976) claim about the balance between sending and receiving countries. The balance is indeed disturbed when the sending country is suddenly transformed into what Rao has called "a losing country."

> Almost every receiving developed country regards its overseas student program as part of its aid to developing countries and expects, and in fact emphasizes, that the student should return home with qualifications and skills that could benefit their home countries. On their part the home countries expect their students to return to contribute to social and political development at home.
>
> (Rao, 1979, p. 3)

The factors prompting foreign students from developing countries to stay on to live and work in the more developed host countries have traditionally been related to the host country's better employment opportunities and conditions, as well as additional opportunities for professional growth (Rao, 1979; Jenkins, 2004). Another "push factor" encouraging students to stay longer (maybe even permanently) in the host country, is directly associated with the inappropriateness of educational policies and structures in their home countries. These policies can be related to the developing country's overproduction of highly trained manpower – more so than the country can possibly absorb in its "employment market" (Rao, 1979, p. 5).

Inappropriate educational policies can also be in the form of unequal educational opportunities that many students may find in their countries of origin, especially, at the higher education level. The current organization of the education system in Argentina, for example, illustrates this last point on unequal educational offer.

In Argentina, higher education-level opportunities are offered by both university and non-university institutions. University-level institutions, both private and public, can be compared to American state and public universities. Non-university institutions comprise "institutes of higher education formation," and "technical institutes."[4] The latter are subsidized publicly and privately. Of the 1900 higher education institutions, 100 are national universities, while 1000 are institutes of tertiary formation; the remaining 700 are technical institutes (Taquini, Chastiglioni, & Rampazzi, 1998).

Physically, higher education institutions are distributed evenly across the country – according to the density of the population creating the demand for them. The academic offer of these institutions, however, especially in the case of public national universities, is different in the various regions (Parrado, 1995). This creates one form of inequality. The high concentration of students in universities, versus technical institutes, could be attributed to the traditional perception of national institutions as offering a "better" education than tertiary-level institutes. Besides the overpopulation of certain institutions in different settings, policymakers are also facing issues of who accesses the system and who is left out (Gertel, 1991). The differences in programs and course offerings at universities across the country are compounded by inequality of access of the different groups of the society.

The example of the Argentinean higher education system with its unequal distribution of the academic offer also helps illustrate the concept of unequal opportunities of access to international schools introduced earlier in this paper. In their majority, recognized international schools in Argentina are, not only clustered in metropolitan cities geographically accessible to a few, but they are also *private* institutions limiting access to the privileged few.

It would not be surprising then, that students deprived of higher education opportunities in their home countries – either because of geographic
location or socio-economic means, would embrace opportunities to study
abroad, which in many cases are offered on a merely meritocratic basis.

The different issues challenging the growth and expansion of study
abroad and educational exchange programs from within national education systems, should not be perceived, however, as mechanisms voiding
the merit of the latter as agents promoting international-mobility, and the
acquisition of skills such as cultural sensitivity and tolerance inherent to
these programs. Indeed, the fact that these programs are not limited to
elites, but in many instances available on a more meritocratic basis, offers
both hope and models of the feasibility to extend the opportunity of international education and study abroad to the reach of a broader group of
students. This is particularly true of the efforts of administrators who continue to encourage international mobility and foster cross-cultural understanding and competence through the thoughtful design of such programs
(see, for example, Jenkins & Associates, 1983; Garrod, 1999; Hawkins &
Cummings, 2000).

INTERNATIONAL EDUCATION, STUDY ABROAD
AND GLOBALIZATION: THE NEW CHALLENGE

International education and study abroad programs are concrete mechanisms through which the international context introduced at the beginning
of this discussion is incorporated into the field of Comparative Education.
Student body, a key element in international schools, is constituted, mostly,
by an elite easily identifiable in terms of their families' professional backgrounds, for example. In the case of study abroad and educational exchange
programs, students come from backgrounds more diverse – both in terms of
their countries of origin, financial status, and social groups. Most of the
literature consulted placed great emphasis on these transnational students'
acquired or inherited international mobility, while not much was mentioned
about the experience of the student bodies in the host countries. Perhaps this
is not a research aspect that can be ignored for much longer. The number of
transnationals that continue to incorporate and struggle to integrate into
national systems, in the United States for example, is in the increase. So are
the possibilities of cooperation between these groups that, as will be presented later on, are many and hold great potential.

GLOBALIZATION AND IMMIGRATION: THE EDUCATIONAL CONTEXT

According to Suárez-Orozco (2001), globalization is remapping cities – indeed, entire countries and regions throughout the world are changing through globalization's three constituting pillars of "(1) new information and communication technologies; (2) the emergence of global markets and post-national knowledge intensive economies; and (3) unprecedented levels of immigration and displacement" (p. 1). In reference to the unprecedented wave of immigrant children entering U.S. schools, the author successfully captures the colossal surge of globalization in a vivid description of its defining migrant participants:

> Immigrant children are now present in substantial numbers in school districts throughout the country... They now make up over 20 percent of the California school population. While California leads the nation in terms of numbers of immigrant students, no area of the country is untouched by immigration. Nationwide, there are now over 3.5 million ELL [English-language learners] youth enrolled in U.S. schools.
>
> (Suárez-Orozco, 2001, p. 8)

The heterogeneity of the immigrant population in terms of ethnic, racial, class, and gender backgrounds is also a feature of this group's different education attainment levels. As Suárez-Orozco (2001) explains, immigrants include "highly educated, highly skilled workers" at the same time as it comprises "large numbers of poorly schooled, semi-skilled workers" (p. 6). In some sense mirroring the patterns of their parents, immigrant children's experiences in the school context are also varied and different:

> The preponderance of evidence suggests that some immigrant children, especially those originating in families from more education, resources, connections, and skills, will indeed thrive in the era of globalization... These highly educated and skilled youth are likely to move rapidly into the more desirable sectors of the global economy, generally bypassing the traditional transgenerational modes of immigrant status mobility.
>
> (Suárez-Orozco, 2001, p. 12)

While this is true for a portion of immigrant children, another portion of them is enrolled at schools where "The little teaching that goes on is neither culturally relevant to the immigrant students' backgrounds nor pertinent to the realities of the global culture and the global economy these youth will eventually have to face" (p. 13).

Suárez-Orozco's description of the great cultural patchwork pattern enriching American schools' social quilt testifies to Arnove's conceptualization of globalization as the "intensification of world-wide social relationships" presented at the beginning of this chapter (Arnove & Torres, 1999, p. 1). Unlike the case of international education and study abroad programs, the kind of transnational interconnectedness of cultures brought forth by globalization originates and is readily available inside the national educational system. Thus, in the context of international schools and study abroad programs, while transnationalism opens the doors for transnational student mobility by acknowledging the borders characteristic of internationalism, globalization moves those borders to the national, even the closest classroom's setting. (It will cost about £900 for a British junior student to fly to Chile to study among people from another culture for the academic year. In many classrooms in the nation, and the world, immigrant children experience a similar kind of cultural plurality without going further than their schools). In today's world, and predominantly in developed nations, many youth experience transnationalism locally.

COMMON GROUNDS

Hayden's (1998) globally mobile international schoolchildren can be found in different pockets of the same transnational stage. The experiences of global nomads or third-culture kids, as international school students and foreigners studying abroad have been named (Langford, 1998), share a key commonality with the experiences of the children of immigration that make up an increasing majority in the schools of developed countries.

This commonality lies exactly in the students' perception of home, or displacement; in their perception of an identity that belongs neither here, nor there; in their sense of being at the crossroads of different social and cultural forces. Said (1999) beautifully captures this concept as he writes that "The exile, therefore, exists in a median state, neither completely at one with the new setting nor fully disencumbered of the old, beset with half-involvements and half-detachments, nostalgic and sentimental on one level, an adept mimic or a secret outcast on another" (p. 22).

In the case of international students abroad and at home, there is much literature testifying to this phenomenon (see, for example, Langford, 1998; Pearce, 1998; Drake, 1998). Suárez-Orozco and Suárez-Orozco (2001) on the other hand, refer to immigrants' dual frame of reference by describing this group as living "in the margins of two cultures," where they can paradoxically "never truly belong either 'here' or 'there'"(p. 92).

As explained above, in the field of education, transnationalism is experienced differently by different student bodies, depending on the kind of educational offer their global mobility experience assigns them. For students at international schools mobility appears to be easy to acquire, if not to inherit, from professional parents well acquainted with the international setting. The success of country-nationals studying abroad to incorporate into the transnational setting appears to depend greatly on the way through which they were able to access that setting – i.e. whether it was through individual efforts or university or governmental contracts. Zhou (1998) imaginatively designated "the highly select group foreign students" coming to the United States to seek a better education as "parachute kids" (p. 682).

In the case of children of immigration who have come to the United States following their parents, and have been immersed in a culture where dual references prevail, "bungee jumpers" would be a good descriptive term – the difference lying in the rather smoother ride that parachutists might experience compared to the continuous back-and-forth cultural pulls that bungee jumpers may, in many cases be subjected to.

Finally, youth like Jerónimo in the introduction to this chapter, emerge as active protagonists on the transnational stage, albeit from home. Through globalization, children and teenagers around the world are more exposed than ever before to national environments rich with a persistent influx of other cultures. Mostly in urban settings, youth are coming into contact with technology, and through it, information from all over the world that renders them intellectually and transnationally mobile. The advent of globalization creates educational opportunities in the sense that it provides us with alternatives to acquire the skills for success in a globalized world.

CONCLUSIONS: IS THE CURRICULUM THE WAY FORWARD?

The unequal opportunities that many immigrant children experience in the U.S. school context, for example, the common marginal characteristics that international students share, and the everyday experience of technology and multiculturalism, hold both the challenge and the promise for advancing educational equality, promoting meaningful learning for both success and global citizenship. The most resourceful mechanism for promoting the development of skills necessary for global mobility is the school curriculum.

Cooperation between transnationals presents an opportunity to position transnationalism as a space for meaningful learning about the world. Examples of programs in which these collaborative interactions happen are not few and far between. At Harvard University's Rockefeller Center for Latin

American Studies, a program was created through which Harvard under-
graduate Latino students were recruited to visit schools in the greater
Boston and Cambridge area, as resources for students who, sometimes
Latinos too, needed to learn more about their or their parents' superfluous
Latin American countries of origin. At a different Boston school, SAMTA
(South Asian Mentoring and Tutoring Association), a group of professional
volunteers (themselves immigrant from Asia), act as the first and most
valuable resource to contribute to the educational attainment of minority
Indian high schoolers. Community-oriented tutoring and mentoring training programs, such as the education program of Cambridge Community
Services for example, train "more successful Latino/a students already in
college to help and encourage Latino students who are afraid they are not
good enough to [pursue higher education]."[5] Academically oriented presentations on issues of immigration among diverse high-school populations
also hold the promise of promoting awareness while positively "un-teach-
ing" misconceptions on such a sensitive and media- and ideology-abused
topic.

Within the national context, global education, "an established body of
work and practice in the field of education [which] is absent from the curriculum of most schools in the American hemisphere" (Reimers, 2004, p. 6)
should be fully embraced by policy makers and educators worldwide.
Through a curriculum that encourages discussion on world events, as well as
critical thinking and debate on tolerance, peace, and understanding, youth
can develop the much needed skills for participatory world citizenship.

All of these initiatives can concretely be adopted as a vital part of today's
modern curriculum. Granted well-defined methodological frameworks,
these practices can only but enrich the lives of more disadvantaged transnationals, while supplying the means to acquire intellectual and social mobility through education.

CLOSING REMARKS: IMPLICATIONS AND
PROPOSALS FOR FURTHER RESEARCH

The most convincing proposed explanation for why students, especially American, decide to engage in study abroad programs is their eagerness to understand the world and the different peoples that inhabit it (Goodwin & Natch,
1998). The decreasing costs of foreign study as the dollar holds relatively strong
compared to the relatively higher costs of American higher education, have
also sent students to "hunt for bargains abroad" (Goodwin & Natch, 1988).

Globalization brings forth an option and opportunity to understand the world and the peoples that inhabit it, minus the added component of having to make a flight reservation. In the case of the United States, plurality of people and the cultures they represent are available in the neighborhood. In the educational context, that plurality is available in different degrees, at the nearest school. Globalization and the plethora of technological resources with which it equips many, creates an opportunity to experience transnationalism virtually, as well as physically.

The common grounds that international and foreign students share with country-nationals, for example, hold the promise of enriching and equality-promoting collaborations between the two. So does the incorporation of global education into curricula around the world. In essence, Willie's (1994) principle of marginality grants more mobile transnationals with a unique alternative to the traditional social roles of integrating or separating, and "falling between the cracks." International and foreign students are enabled, by virtue of their position "in, between, and beyond" two worlds (p. 1) to help other third culture youth become the integral global nomads that our rapidly globalized and globalizing world demands its citizens to be. "We have to recognize that part of the role of the third-cultured people of today is to be the culture bridge and culture brokers for the whole generation. The global nomad of today is the prototype of the citizen of the 21st century" (Langford, 1998, p. 30).

"Simple-minded solutions to improve the efficiency of educational institutions have prevented reflection on the purposes of our schools" (Reimers, 2004, p. 7). As argued in the introduction, and described in the preceding paragraphs of this chapter, through its impact on youth and their education worldwide, globalization affects broader theoretical paradigms. Reflection on the direction of Comparative Education as discipline of study is then as imperative a task. Besides providing us with answers to the feasibility of concrete educational practices globally, endeavors such as those described above, can continue to nurture the field of Comparative Education with updated perspectives and debates. The production of new knowledge is, no doubt, the desired means through which to create new theories and inform innovative policies that will ultimately affect the educational experiences and well-being of millions of citizens in today's globalized world.

As Giddens (2000) suggests, ours is a "runaway world" in need to be brought to heel. The efforts to promote that halt are greater than any educator or policymaker can undertake. The answer may then rest not in bringing it to heel, but in equipping as many students as possible with the skills to catch and keep up with it.

NOTES

1. For a complete catalog and full description of the skills suggested by Howard Gardner in this context, see Gardner, H. (2004).
2. Italics (mine) added for emphasis.
3. Although not the focus of this paper, a crucial question for study is how governments can support greater access to global education while promoting employment mobility in the national context. In depth analysis of this seeming paradox is of paramount importance in refining theories of national development.
4. Spanish: Institutos de Formación Superior and Tecnicaturas, respectively.
5. Personal interview with Sandra Canas, Director of Cambridge Community Services. November, 2001.

REFERENCES

Allen, K. (2000). The international school and its community: Think globally, interact locally. In: M. Hayden & J. Thompson (Eds), *International schools and international education: Improving teaching, management, and quality* (pp. 124–139). London, UK: Kogan Page Limited.

American Field Services. (2004). Available: http://www.afs.org/AFSI. Accessed June, 2004.

Appardurai, A. (1996). *Modernity at large: Cultural dimensions of globalization.* Minneapolis: University of Minnesota Press.

Arnove, R. F., & Torres, C. A. (1999). *Comparative education. The dialectic of the global and the local.* U.S.A.: Rowman & Littlefield Publishers, Inc.

Battro, A. (2004). Digital skills, globalization, and education. In: M. Suarez-Orozco & D. Baolian Qin-Hilliard (Eds), *Globalization: Culture and education in the new millennium* (pp. 78–96). The Ross Institute. Berkeley: University of California Press.

Bloom, D. (2004). Globalization and education: An economic perspective. In: M. Suarez-Orozco & D. Baolian Qin-Hilliard (Eds), *Globalization: Culture and education in the new millennium* (pp. 56–77). The Ross Institute. Berkeley: University of California Press.

Cambridge, J. C., & Thompson, J. J. (2002). *Towards the construction of a framework for the description and classification of international schools and other schools in an international context. Center for the study of education in an international context.* University of Bath. First Published in Collected Original Resources in Education, 24, 1.

Coatsworth, J. (2004). Globalization, growth, and welfare in history. In: M. Suarez-Orozco & D. Baolian Qin-Hilliard (Eds), *Globalization: Culture and education in the new millennium* (pp. 38–55). The Ross Institute. Berkeley: University of California Press.

Danesy, F. (1994). *Higher education credentials: A guide to educational systems in Europe and North America.* Chichester, England: John Wiley & Sons Ltd.

Drake, B. (1998). Pastoral care: The challenge for international schools. In: M. Hayden & J. Thompson (Eds), *International education: Principles and practice* (pp. 146–170). London, UK: Kogan Page Limited.

European Council of International Schools (2004). Available: http://www.ecis.org/Stats/stats.htm. Accessed April, 2004.

Friedman, T. (1999). *The Lexus and the Olive Tree.* New York: Anchor Books.

Gardner, H. (2004). How education changes: Considerations of history, science, and values. In: M. Suárez-Orozco & D. Baolian Qin-Hilliard (Eds), *Globalization: Culture and education in the new millennium* (pp. 235–258). The Ross Institute. Berkeley: University of California Press.

Garrod, A. (1999). Preface. In: A. Garrod & J. Davis (Eds), *Crossing customs: International students write on U.S. college life and culture.* Chestnut Hill, MA: Garland Studies in Higher Education.

Gertel, H. (1991). Issues and perspectives for higher education in Argentina in the 1990s. *Higher Education, 21,* 63–81.

Giddens, A. (2000). *Runaway World: How globalization is reshaping our lives.* New York, NY: Routledge.

Goodwin, C., & Natch, M. (1988). *Abroad and beyond: Patterns in American overseas education.* Cambridge, MA: Cambridge University Press.

Hawkins, J., & Cummings, W. (Eds) (2000). *Transnational competence: Rethinking the US–Japan educational relationship.* Albany, NY: State University of New York Press.

Hayden, M. (1998). International education in practice. In: M. Hayden & J. Thompson (Eds), *International Education: Principles and Practice* (pp. 1–8). London, UK: Kogan Page Limited.

Hayden, M., & Thompson, J. (2000). Preface. In: M. Hayden & J. Thompson (Eds), *International schools and international education: Improving teaching, management and quality* (pp. 1–11). London, UK: Kogan Page Limited.

Humfrey, C. (1999). *Managing international students: Recruitment to Graduation.* Buckingham; Philadelphia: Open University Press.

International Schools Association (2004). Available: http://www.isaschools.org/organisation.htm. Accessed May, 2004.

Jenkins, H. (2004). Pop cosmopolitanism: mapping cultural flows in an age of media convergence. In: M. Suarez-Orozco & D. Baolian Qin-Hilliard (Eds), *Globalization: Culture and education in the new millennium* (pp. 114–140). The Ross Institute. Berkeley: University of California Press.

Jenkins, H., & Associates (1983). *Educating students from other nations.* San Francisco, CA: Jossey-Bass Inc., Publishers.

Jonietz, P. (1991). Preface. In: P. Jonietz & D. Harris (Eds), *Yearbook of education.* London, UK: Kogan Page Limited.

Klineberg, O. (1976). *International educational exchange: An assessment of its nature and its prospects.* Paris: Mouton and Ecole des Hautes Etudes en Sciences Sociales.

Knight, M., & Leach, R. (1964). *International schools and their role in the field of international education.* Oxford: Pergamon Press.

Koh, H. (2001). Open Doors 2000: International student mobility at the new millennium. *International Education Newsletter, Office of International Education, Harvard Graduate School of Education,* Summer, 2001, 3.

Langford, M. (1998). Global nomads, third culture kids and international school. In: M. Hayden & J. Thompson (Eds), *International education: Principles and practice* (pp. 28–43). London, UK: Kogan Page Limited.

Ley Superior de Educación N. 24.521. Government of Argentina. Updated June, 3, 2001. Available: http://www.me.gov.ar/leysuper.htm. Accessed January, 2004.

McGovern, S. (1999). The field of international and comparative education: A history of ideas and methods in the United States. In: J. Kincheloe & L. Semali (Series Eds), *Indigenous knowledge and schooling* (p. 4). New York and London: Garland Publishing, Inc.

Open Doors (2003). Open Doors Report. Available: http://opendoors.iienetwork.org/. Accessed April, 2004.

Parrado, E. (1995). Expansion of schooling, economic growth and regional inequalities in Argentina. *Comparative Education Review, 43*(3), 338–364.

Pearce, R. (1998). Developing cultural identity in an international school environment. In: M. Hayden & J. Thompson (Eds), *International education: Principles and practice* (pp. 44–62). London, UK: Kogan Page Limited.

Rao, L. (1979). *Brain drain and foreign students*. Saint Lucia, Queensland: University of Queensland Press.

Reimers, F. (2004). Children and globalization: Schools, children and trust in the Americas. *ReVista: Harvard Review of Latin America*, Winter 2004, 4–8.

Renaud, G. (1991). The International Schools Association (ISA): historical and philosophical background. In: P. Jonietz & D. Harris (Eds), *World yearbook of education 1991: International schools and international education* (pp. 6–14). London: Kogan Page Limited.

Rotary International (2004). Available: http://www.rotary.org. Accessed May, 2004.

Said, E. (1999). Introduction. In: A. Garrod & J. Davis (Eds), *Crossing customs: International students write on U.S. college life and culture*. Chestnut Hill, MA: Garland Studies in Higher Education.

Speakman, C., Jr. (1966). *International exchange in education*. New York, NY: The Center for Applied Research in Education, Inc.

Suárez-Orozco, C., & Suárez-Orozco, M. (2001). *Children of immigration*. Cambridge, MA: Harvard University Press.

Suárez-Orozco, M. (2001). Globalization, immigrant children, and education. *Harvard Educational Review, 71*, 1–21.

Suárez-Orozco, M., & Qin-Hilliard, B. D. (Eds). (2004). *Globalization: Culture and education in the new millennium*. The Ross Institute, Berkeley: University of California Press.

United World Colleges (2004). Available: http://www.uwc.org/about_history.html. Accessed May, 2004.

UPEACE Worldwide. University of Peace, Costa Rica (2004). Available: http://www.upeace.org/regional. Accessed May, 2004.

Walker, G. (1998). Home sweet home: A study, through fictional literature, of disoriented children and the significance of home. In: M. Hayden & J. Thompson (Eds), *International education: Principles and practice* (pp. 11–27). London, UK: Kogan Page Limited.

Watson, J. (2004). Globalization in Asia. In: M. Suarez-Orozco & D. Baolian Qin-Hilliard (Eds), *Globalization: Culture and education in the new millennium* (pp. 141–172). The Ross Institute. Berkeley: University of California Press.

Willie, C. (1994). *Theories of human social action*. New York, NY: General Hall, Inc.

Zhou, M. (1998). "Parachute Kids" in Southern California: The educational experience of Chinese children in transnational families. *Education Policy, 12*(6), 682–704.

GLOBALIZATION OF EDUCATION AND STIGMA: A SENEGALESE CASE STUDY

Holger Daun

INTRODUCTION

The global expansion of primary and secondary education is accompanied by globalization of stigma of a type that did not exist before in the areas reached by the modern, rational, and secular education during the past decades. International organizations and national governments have established the number of years, age, grade conditions, and the level of knowledge that should be acquired for each stage. Often, children are classified in dichotomous categories such as enrolled–non-enrolled, completed–not completed, successful–not successful, wastage–not wastage, and so forth. As a result of this, children who leave primary school before they have finished the stipulated grades/number of years run the risk to be defined as "not fully competent" culturally and economically, not only from the "modern" perspective but from the "traditional" perspective and to be labeled and stigmatized. With the massive expansion of primary and secondary education, the number of "failing" students is increasing, especially in very academically oriented and selective education systems such as that in Senegal.

The findings from a longitudinal research study conducted by the author of more than 800 individuals in two Senegalese villages serves as an

Global Trends in Educational Policy
International Perspectives on Education and Society, Volume 6, 197–219
Copyright © 2005 by Elsevier Ltd.
ISSN: 1479-3679/doi:10.1016/S1479-3679(04)06008-6

empirical basis for this argument. The initial purpose of the study starting in the end of the 1970s was to investigate parent choice among different agents of socialization in an Islamized environment, where different learning systems existed; secular Western-type education as well as Islamic educational arrangements. The findings from a follow up study in 1989/1990 indicate that those who did not complete the primary level in many respects have worse life conditions than those experienced by others, although their knowledge and skills (as measured on simple tests) do not differ significantly from those of others. It seems that it is worse to have been enrolled at all and dropped out than to be not enrolled at all.

This paper compares the life situation (income, subjective health, participation in associational life, etc.) in 1999/2000 of those with incomplete primary education with that of the other individuals (with other types and stages of learning) in the same cohorts and the same villages. Some of the relationships between learning background, knowledge (as measured on tests) and life situation are presented. Finally, interpretations of the findings are hinted in terms labeling and stigmatization.

BACKGROUND

Senegal, at one time a French colony in West Africa, is to a large extent incorporated into the global economy but it has neither "strategic" natural resources or goods nor human capital with which to compete in the global market. Eighty percent of the population makes a living in the agriculture sector. A larger portion of the population is employed in service, administration, etc., than in the industrial sector. The industrial sector is of importance only in the Dakar region, where most industrial jobs are situated (Kassé, 1990). The number of employees outside the primary sector was at its maximum in 1985 and then decreased. Since then, the public sector has been shrinking.

The majority of the population is Muslim. With the emergence of the Murid brotherhood in Senegal during the 19th century, a hierarchical of system of *Marabuts* (Muslim leaders) and their respective followers (*talibé*) emerged. All Muslims are integrated into a network in which there are mutual rights and obligations between the *Marabut* and the *talibé*. At least since the 1980s, the Murid network also includes Senegalese migrants in Europe, East Asia, the Middle East, and North America (Ebin, 1993; Grégoire & Labazée, 1993).

One of the two villages in this study is situated in the region of Diourbel on the savanna in central Senegal and the other in the region of Casamance in the southern part of the country. The former village is inhabited mainly by Wolofs, who form the predominating ethnic group in Senegal. In this village, the soil has never been fertile. Agriculture is the principal activity and peanut production is dominant. Through their dependence on groundnut production for export, the farmers in the village are greatly influenced by international conditions. Due to the lack of land and other circumstances, migration from the village has been extensive. Men and women both work in agriculture but in addition, women also cultivate vegetables and are in charge of household activities. Apart from the majority of peasants there are also a few businessmen and artisans. Of all regions, Diourbel has always had the lowest rate of enrolment in the Western-type school, and this was still so in 1999. The rate of literacy (in French) in the adult population was 17% (9% for female adults) in 1989 (MINEC, 1989).

In Casamance, the Diola ethnic group constitutes one-fifth of the population, and the majority in the village concerned belongs to this ethnic group. They converted to Islam later than any other groups. Cultivation of rice, mainly for local consumption, is the principal production activity, and most of the activities related to this production are performed by women. The soil is fertile, and only rarely has it been difficult to produce a surplus in agriculture because of climatic conditions. The Diola are also known for their extensive seasonal migrations (even to other countries) for employment. Another Diola characteristic feature is the intensive network of organizations and associations; the village has a large number of organizations for different purposes. Those who once migrated to Dakar established an association there a long time ago. Migrants from the village can get support from this association when they settle in the capital. As in other African societies, associations, and organizations tend to be multi-functional and holistic (Anheier, 1989, p. 425; Hoerner, 1995) and a great deal of learning takes place in these contexts (Ndione, 1994).

RESEARCH DESIGN AND KEY CONCEPTS

In the study initiated in the 1970s, it was assumed that a broad socialization approach would give more fruitful insights into the matter of education than a study focussed solely on the Western type of schooling. Instead of taking the Western/modern system and the perception that there is enrollment and non-enrollment as the point of departure for the study, parental choice of "learning systems"[1] for their children formed the basis for the study. There were four different types of learning systems: the Western school (primary or secondary), the Quranic school, the Arabic school, and the Indigenous arrangements of socialization. Altogether there were some 840 children 6–13 years old in the two villages. Less than one-fourth of all children were enrolled in primary education, while the majority attended Arabic or Quranic schools or were socialized in indigenous learning systems (at home, in initiation rites, in apprenticeship schemes, and so on).

Since research funds were available for a continuation of the study, these individuals (school age children in the beginning of the 1980s) were followed-up in 1989/1990 and 1999/2000. At the time of the second follow up, they were somewhere between 25 and 35 years old. Approximately half of all household heads of the two village cohorts were sampled and this sample included 548 of the individuals participating in the study in the beginning of the 1980s. Out of these, 346 were found and interviewed and presented items intended to test knowledge and skills in different areas. Questions were also posed concerning information about income, housing conditions, participation, health, etc. Among those not encountered, the majority were abroad: in other African countries, Europe, Asia, and North America.

Generally, as Fig. 1 shows, the design assumes that there are certain relationships between learning background, level of knowledge on the test, and life situation. Two principal assumptions made were that: (1) each type of learning system is assumed to result in a certain level and type of knowledge; and (2) higher levels of knowledge contribute to a life situation.

Socialization is "a continuing, lifelong process that takes place in the context of the family, school, peer group, occupational setting, and radical resocialization settings" (Sturman, 1994, 5588). Thus, socialization is learning of all types: school education of the Western type is but one aspect of socialization and a great deal of learning takes place in other arrangements and situations.

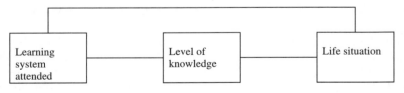

Fig. 1.   Design of Study.

Indigenous learning systems: These arrangements consist of the home compound/household, work, apprenticeship schemes, and rites of transition. The latter play an important role in the Diola village because males as well as females have to participate. Ceremonies are centrally organized for the whole village when the male *rites de passage* into adulthood are completed. The last ceremony took place in the mid-1990s. The interviewees refer to this event as the "circumcision". The girls are circumcised in the dry season every second year or more seldom, separately from the rights of initiation. These rites are less complex and are shorter than those for the boys, mainly because the girls are not seen to need the same competence as boys.

Many values and types of knowledge are differentiated according to gender; there is a female and a male "world". This implies that the content of socialization in the family and in productive activities is differentiated according to the gender division of labor. Boys learn things concerning the kinship relations, village affairs, communal activities, politics in the village and nature, while girls learn things related to household, child rearing, and sickness and health. This applies even in areas where women work in the fields (Ly Kane, 1985; Traoré, n.d.). All communities have arrangements for the transmission of practical, technical, vocational, intellectual, and moral knowledge (Nduka, 1974; Ocitti, 1971). An acceptable level of intellectual knowledge seems to be a pre-condition for being perceived as a potential adult. Ocitti (1971) summarizes the characteristics of African education in the following terms: *communalism, preparationism, functionalism, utilitarianism, perennalism,* and *wholitism.*

Islamic education can be classified into three levels: elementary (Quranic), post-elementary (post-Quranic), and higher education. In Quranic schools, children primarily learn the basics of Islam and memorize Quranic verses but learning manual work is also one important ingredient. Only a few pupils ever learn to read and write. They learn at their own pace and enter and leave the courses according to their (or their parents') preferences. When they feel that they have learnt a certain amount, they are examined by the Quranic teacher or older students in the study group. In reality most of the pupils memorize Quranic verses by heart but initially without knowing the meaning of the content, and only a minority of Quranic pupils ever learn the whole Quran.

Islamic education beyond the Quran stage increasingly takes place in Arabic schools that started to expand south of the Sahara in the 1970s with support from some Muslim countries. These schools are organized and structured in the same way as primary or secondary schools in that they have four or six grades (school years) and a similar time table. The pupils learn the "theory" of Islam, the Arabic language, mathematics, and some natural science and history in addition to the religious subjects. The curriculum of the Arabic school can, broadly speaking, be divided into religious subjects: the Arabic language, Muslim law, reading and writing, and purely secular subjects. In some schools, Arabic is not only a subject but also the language of instruction from the first day of school. Case studies have shown that both types of Islamic schools might be instrumental for jobs in the informal sector (artisan, small businessmen, tradesmen, etc.) (Daun, 1992, 1995; Oni, 1988; William & Armer, 1988).

Although Quranic and Arabic schools are different, they have a common denominator in the goal to create "good Muslims" and in that they give entrance to fields related to Islam and to the "traditional" sphere and the informal sector of society. Islam has to a large extent replaced the traditional religions but some pre-Islamic elements continue to exist – especially when socialization of children is concerned. Apart from this, they differ in structure and organization, knowledge distribution and "formalization". The Arabic schools include more de-contextualized and theoretical elements than the Quranic schools, and some Arabic schools deliver certificates, recognized as such at Islamic educational institutions in North Africa and the Middle East. However, certificates from an Arabic school do not automatically make an individual eligible for entrance into the formal and modern sector of society.

As Table 1 shows, the Western type of education system delivers certificates, which are nationally (and sometimes internationally) valid and make the holder eligible for entrance into fields (professionally and otherwise) of the "modern" and formal sector. Then the certificate makes the holder eligible for entrance into other fields related to the labor market, social networks, and so on. The Senegalese education system has continued to be as elitist and selective as it had been during the colonial period (Rideout & Bagayoko, 1994). The rate of repetition is comparatively high. The pupils who do not fulfill the requirements (mainly failing in the end of year examination) may not move to the next grade.

Two assumptions made here are that: (i) competence may be seen as a concept broader than possession of knowledge that is certified; and (ii) knowledge tested and certified is decontextual and overlaps only to some extent with the broader and practical skills and knowledge (e.g. life skills). These assumptions have several implications. First, a student may be able to pass the school tests but still be failed by the teacher due to lack of cultural and social competence; segment of the processes of schooling can be seen as

Table 1. Some Characteristics of the Learning Systems.

	Western Type of Education	Long Arabic or Quranic Education	Short Arabic or Quranic Education	"Indigenous" Education
Requirements	Dichotomization. Stipulated quantity of time and of knowledge	Not strictly dichotomized. Stipulated quantity of time and knowledge (but negotiatable)	Not strictly dichotomized. Formally, stipulated quantity of Quranic verses (but negotiatable)	Acquisition of local knowledge. Passing the rites (in practice: everybody does)
Competence	Western values. Reading and writing abilities in French. Decontextualized knowledge	Islamic values. Reading and writing abilities in Arabic. Muslim way of life. Some decontextualized knowledge Training for artisan-ship, farming, and religious tasks	Local and Muslim way of life. Training mainly for manual work	A large portion of "tacit" knowledge. Training mainly for manual work
Certificate	Nationally valid for modern and formal sectors	Sometimes delivered. Sometimes accepted at Islamic educational institutions	Oral or none. Symbolic	Oral. Symbolic

ritual for approval in the modern sector; to have acquired the behavioral pattern expected in this sector (Fuller, 1991). Second, a student may have acquired knowledge and skills useful in the local and national setting without being able to pass the school tests. Third, those certified do not necessarily have higher levels of knowledge than some those who are not certified.

Analytically, education may be seen to imply different types and degrees of learning: acquisition of cognitive knowledge (which is tested); acquisition of knowledge not tested; acquisition of "appropriate" behavioral patterns (and life styles) and internalization of world view. Each learning system produces a certain competence. Some individuals are able to acquire both the modern-secular competence and the more traditional variety of Islamic competence, while others do not succeed to acquire any of them.

LIFE SITUATION

"Life situation" is used here to cover some of the factors included in UNDP's Human Development Index (UNDP, 1990, 2001). Since one study cannot cover or measure all the areas of the life situation, a few indicators have been used to indicate the level within four domains:

(i) *material standard of living* (occupation, monetary income, and housing quality) – three items;
(ii) *well-being* (subjective health, social network, and pleasant experiences or events) – three items;
(iii) *participation* in associations (position) and decision-making – two items; and
(iv) *knowledge and skills* (within the areas of health – 14 items; agriculture – three items; politics – two items; and mathematics – three items).

Items for the tests were partially borrowed from UNESCO and other studies (Baldo & Furniss, 1998; Chinapah, 1992; Doyal & Gough, 1991; Miller, 1989; Pawar, Daun, Shangwu, & Xiaoda, 1992; UNDP, 1990) and partially invented especially for this study. The borrowed items were made for literate individuals and had to be adapted based on the fact that only a minority had attended primary school and were able to read and write in French (which is the official language and the educational language). The response alternates on most items of the knowledge test had the form of multiple choice except for mathematics items. Interviews were conducted in the mother tongue (Wolof or Diola) of the interviewees or French for those who so preferred, and the interviewees were allowed to use the time they needed in order to come up with an answer.

Interrelationships in high income countries but not necessarily in low income countries. For instance, some Muslims live a puritan way of life even if they could afford do otherwise, and some with a comparatively low monetary income could have high values on the other life situation items. However, those with IPE accumulate low positions in the life situation. The study was purely empirical, but when a number of unanticipated findings emerged it was judged as necessary to turn to some theoretical approaches.

Therefore, the concepts of labeling, and stigmatization were introduced to assist in the interpretation of the findings. Those having become stigmatized because they are seen not to have acquired the competence. Goffman (1963, pp. 2–3) describes stigma in the following way: "While a stranger is present before us, evidence can arise of his possessing an attribute that makes him different from others in the category of persons available for him to be, and of a less desirable kind – in the extreme, a person who is quite thoroughly bad, or dangerous, or weak. He is thus reduced in our mind from a whole and usual person to a tainted, discounted one. Such attribute is stigma". According to Cuzzort and King (1976, 251), stigmas – in Goffman's view – fall in three broad classes: gross physical defects, defects in character, and membership in a social class or group, which is not acceptable. It seems that the third type of stigma is relevant here.

Stigmatization starts with labeling by teachers and parents, among others, which becomes self-fulfilling prophecy (Blease, 1986; Griffiths, 1993; Harris, Rosenthal, & Snodgrass, 1985). The labeled individual starts to feel, think and behave according to the overt and covert messages from others (Black-ledge & Hunt, 1985; Weinstein, Marshall, Sharp, & Botkin, 1987). Those being labeled are, however, not pure victims, but following resistance theories, they are co-producers of their own situation (Bullivant, 1987; Giroux, 1988). For instance, in the southern village, teachers often complained in 1980–1981 that Diola children were too free and anarchistic.

FINDINGS

Since it was found that both men and women with incomplete primary education (IPE), differed from those with other learning backgrounds in unanticipated ways, this group of individuals will be focussed here.

Knowledge and Skills

What is the level of knowledge and skills among those with incomplete primary education – as compared to that of others? Those with incomplete primary education (IPE) are compared to those with another type of learning background in four aspects: health, agriculture, politics, and mathematics. Pair-wise *t*-testing of the means on the test in relation to learning background was conducted and this was made separately for men and women. (Examples of items used are presented in the Appendix A (Tables A1–A2).)

- *Health knowledge:* Generally, women have more correct answers then men in all learning categories except Islamic education.[2] The only statistically significant differences are that among men, those with secondary education have higher levels of knowledge than those with primary education or those with a long Islamic education but not than those with incomplete primary education (IPE). Among women, those with IPE or a long Islamic education score lower than those with incomplete or complete secondary education.
- *Agricultural knowledge:* Also in the domain of agriculture, women have a higher frequency of correct answers than men. Among men, there is only one significant difference; those with IPE score higher than those with full primary education. Among women the situation is almost the opposite; those with primary education have higher level of knowledge than those with incomplete primary, incomplete or complete secondary or long Islamic education.
- *Political knowledge:* Type of learning makes most difference in the political domain. Both indicators in this domain deal with national political items (the national motto and the title of the country's leader) that are taught in primary and secondary education and, as a result, those with this type of education have larger percentages of correct answers. Apart from this, those with IPE do not differ from others.
  In *mathematics*, when not taking learning background into account, women score significantly higher then men. Among men, those with some or full secondary education score higher than those with IPE or long Islamic education. Among women, those with IPE score lower than those with primary education or indigenous learning background.
- *All items together:* There are more health items than other items. Therefore, such items play an important role in the overall sums and means. Among men, those with incomplete or complete secondary education score significantly higher than those with primary education; that is, men with IPE do not differ from anybody else. On the other hand, among women those with incomplete/complete secondary education score higher than those with a long Islamic education or with IPE.

Table 2 presents the significant differences (pairwise *t*-testing) in relation to learning background. It is evident that the level of knowledge among those

Table 2. Significant Differences in Knowledge and Skills – Incomplete
Primary Education as Compared to Other Learning Backgrounds.

	Men	Women	Men/Women
Health Items	Sec > Pr, Ar/Kor	Sec > IPE, Ar/Kor	Women in most learning categories
Agricultural Items	IPE > Pr	Pr > IPE, Sec, Ar/Kor	Women in most learning categories
Political Items	Sec > Sec- > All others (incl. IPE)	Sec > Pr > Others (incl. IPE)	Men in all learning categories
Mathematical Items	Sec- = Sec > IPE, Ar/Kor	Pr, Ind > IPE	Women in all learning categories
All Items	Sec = Sec- > Pr	Sec > Ar/Kor, IPE	Women in most learning categories

Note: > = the category is significantly higher/has significantly more than most or all other learning categories (at least at 0.1 level); < = the opposite. Pair-wise *t*-testing has been applied; Ind. = Indigenous, (neither Western nor Islamic); Kor- = 2 years or less of Quranic education; Kor = 3 years or more of Quranic education; Ar- = 2 years or less of Arabic education; Ar = 3 years or more of Arabic education; Pr- = incomplete primary; Pr = complete (6 years) of primary; Sec- = incomplete secondary; Sec = 8 years of secondary. Less than 10 females had secondary education and in all tables they are merged with those having incomplete secondary education.

with IPE does not differ significantly from that among those with complete primary education or some type of Islamic education.

As can be seen from Table 2, those with IPE do not differ very much from those with other learning backgrounds. We shall now look at the relationships between learning background, level of knowledge, and life situation items.

Knowledge and Life Situation

Appendix A presents the cases in which life situation items of those with IPE differ significantly from those with other learning backgrounds.

Material standard of living

• *Income* ("during last year"): First, men earn considerably more than women, also within each category of learning background. For both men and women, the longer the education, the larger the variation in income. The large variations within each category of learning suggest that factors other than education alone determine the level of monetary income. Both among men and women, those with IPE have a significantly lower income than most others.

- *Occupation* (open-ended): It is evident that only complete secondary education has power enough to "channel" people to a certain life situation completely different from those of other learners. Men in most learning categories (except complete secondary education) have become farmers, and this tendency is four times stronger among those with IPE or some Islamic education than among those with complete primary education. Men with IPE have become Islamic teachers or medicine-men more than those with other levels of Western education! Among women, the occupations differ greatly within and between learning categories but those with IPE had more than other women a source of income apart from being housewives.
- *Quality of residence* (appropriate bedroom, drinking water, electricity, land, radio, TV – the interviewees could chose one or several of these alternates): Both men and women with IPE have lower quality of residence than many others, especially those with complete primary education. However, the majority of women are married and their quality of residence is that of their husband.

Well-being
For well-being, four indicators were used: health, network, pleasant events, and civil status.

- *Health* (as reported by the respondents themselves – fixed alternates): Among men, those with IPE are ill more often than those with incomplete secondary education. Among women, those with IPE do not belong to any of the extreme categories. That is, they report less than many others that they never are ill but also less that they are often ill. The respondents were also asked to mention with types of symptoms they had when ill and whom they consulted (not reported in Appendix B). Men with IPE mentioned problems with belly and head more than men with primary or secondary education, and they consulted modern institutions more than men with indigenous or any type of Islamic education. Among women, more types of symptoms were mentioned: belly, head, corporal pain in general, and others symptoms are mentioned more by those with IPE than those with some type of Islamic education and those with secondary education. They consulted modern institutions more and traditional institutions less than women with Islamic education.

- *Pleasant events* (open-ended): The respondents were asked to tell about pleasant, the question was open-ended. The answers were then classified into 12 categories. Men with IPE more than those with secondary education reported family events (such as own wedding and the birth of the first child) and religious events or work related issues. Among women, the pattern is similar although they mentioned work, trade, and harvest less than many others.

- *Network* (If you have problems, from whom or what can you get support — What type of problems and what support?): another indicator of well-being used here was frequency and types of problems and if the respondents could get support and from whom. Both questions were open-ended so the answers were spontaneous but have been classified into different categories — for the problems: (a) all types or many; (b) financial problems; (c) health; (d) other problems. The total percentages exceed 100, since several problems could be mentioned. The reported support has been classified to come from: (a) relatives; (b) friends; (c) marabut/village elders; (d) public authority or NGO; and (e) other. Sometimes, several "supporters" were mentioned by the respondents. Men with IPE reported more problems than many others, while both men and women with IPE reported less problems than those with a long Islamic education.
Men as well as women with IPE mentioned financial problems significantly more than other categories. Paradoxically, health problems were mentioned less than among respondents who had stated that they had been ill. Those with IPE more than others received help from relatives, and both men and women with this learning background had more than others the combination of "financial problems/support from relatives".

- *Married:* In high income countries, well-being — as defined by some researchers — correlates with civil status; the level of well-being is lower among those who live alone. It has not been possible to verify whether this is the case or not in developing countries. Studies have shown that Western education contributes to the postponement of marriage (Velkoff, 1998). On the other hand, enforced marriage is not uncommon in low income countries. Since women marry at an earlier age than men, the frequency of being married is significantly higher among the former than among the latter. Men with IPE or a long Islamic education are married to a larger extent than others, whereas among women only, those with secondary education deviate from the general pattern in that they are less likely to be married. As far as age has been possible to keep under control, the differences mentioned do not seem to be due to age differences.

Participation

- *Position:* The respondents were presented some ten types of associations (both informal and formal and traditional and modern) and one open option and were asked whether they were members or had specific functions in any of these associations. Those with IPE were less involved than many others.
- *Making own decisions:* The interviewees were asked in what contexts or situations they could make decisions on their own. Most of them mentioned their own household, own compound, own job or own agricultural fields. Men (and especially those with IPE) felt that they could decide in their jobs or on their farm, while women feel limited to the household, house or compound. Among women, there was a tendency among those with IPE to say that they could decide in matters related to work, trade, and farm. Also, a group of women with IPE insisted that they were never able to make decisions on their own!

  The answers to some other questions give additional information.
- *Number of children:* Other studies (some of them conducted in Senegal) have shown that primary and in particular secondary education result in people having fewer children (Hannum & Buchmann, 2003; Lewin, 1994; Lockheed, Fuller, & Nyirongo, 1989; UNICEF, 1985). This is not very evident among male respondents[3] but it is among female respondents. Men with IPE have more children than those with other levels of Western education. Among women, those with IPE have fewer children than those with long Islamic education but more than those with other levels of Western education.

The interviewees were asked to take a position in relation to an item concerning advantages and disadvantages of having many children. The principal difference existed between those having some secondary education and others; the former were more negative than the latter. Men with IPE mentioned negative things less and positive things more than men with incomplete or complete secondary education. Among women, non-completers of primary education mention negative things less than those with long Islamic education or secondary education and positive things less than those short Islamic education. It is worth mentioning that women with a long Islamic education frequently took a negative stand although, culturally and economically, they are expected to give birth to many children!

In summary, among women, those with IPE have lower monetary income than others and they combine being housewife with income-generating activities such as agriculture or trade; and have lower quality of residence. The pleasant events they mention are related to the family, work or religion.

According to themselves, they face many problems, mostly of economic nature, and they state – more than others – that they can get support from (extended) family members or relatives. They tend not to be involved in associational or organizational life, but to have more children than many other women.

Among men, those with IPE have lower monetary income, are farmers, have lower quality of residence, have more problems (especially financial problems), participate less in different associations, and feel that they can make decisions within a smaller "space" than others. All this despite the fact that their level of tested knowledge is not very different from that of others.

DISCUSSION

Several of the findings were un-anticipated; and, consequently, we have to ask (a) why learning background does not make more difference in the level of knowledge on tests than it does; and (b) why these small differences in knowledge make so much difference in life situation. As to the first question, we can start by assuming that something is wrong with the design of the test items; that is, the test items were too easy and/or too few and/or the grading of the correct answers has favored those who relied upon guessing and not solid knowledge. However, if this were the case, we would still have to explain why those with complete primary education or even full secondary education did not attain more than 70–80% of the maximum levels on the tests. The reason for this unanticipated level could be differences in test motivation. It has been shown that pupils participating in the international tests, for instance, have different levels of motivation for solving the tasks on the tests (O'Neil, 2003). It might be the case, that those with complete primary or some or complete secondary education had lower motivation than others to succeed on the tests. However, interviewers' accounts for the interview situation do not support this assumption; all interviewees seemed to make efforts to answer to the questions and solutions to the mathematical problems.

Therefore, we take as our point of departure that the test results accurately indicate important aspects of the respondents' knowledge and skills. The group never reached because living abroad, might be the "brightest" ones with the result that those encountered did not attain higher levels. However, there are still variations among them, and it is these variations that need interpretation.

Despite the small differences in tested knowledge and skills, there are substantial differences in life situations – related to learning background. For instance, those with IPE have significantly lower material standard of living, less well-being and less participation than many others although their level of knowledge on the tests does not differ very much from the others. How and why is it so? There are no simple answers to this question. In lack of in-depth knowledge about the respondents generated through qualitative research methods, we were looking for theories that could improve our understanding of the findings. However, first, some distinctions should be made. The acquisition and possession of knowledge and skills are embedded in an interrelated group of factors, which are partly complementary, partly contradictory. Three principal factors seem to be (i) *gender*; (ii) *certification* (whether the knowledge is certified or not by the state); and (iii) *individual and collective learning needs* (whether the acquisition and use of knowledge is an individual or collective affair).

Gender is the most important factor of screening and selection. It was shown in another study of the present population that girls married according to traditional patterns and criteria. Women with less than complete secondary education often married a partner and at an age that had been established by tradition, regardless of their learning background (Daun, 1992). In the 1999–2000 study, women displayed higher levels of knowledge than men in several domains and within the same category of learning background, but had, at the time of the study, a less favorable life situation. It is evident that gender influences the opportunity to convert knowledge and skills into life situation items such as quality of residence, income, pleasant events, decision-making power, and so on. Women are constrained by the prevailing culture and power structures.

As to the second factor, Western schooling itself is in some way to experience and learn a culture other than the local, rural culture. The experience itself of having attended the Western type of school and at least partially acquired the life style it represents seems to imply something of a break with the local culture. This was shown in Grindahl's (1972) study almost 40 years ago. With the expansion of primary education to new areas and new groups of people, this feature has been disseminated and more frequent. Fuller (1991), for example, argues that a great deal of the processes in schools are just *rites de passage* from the traditional world to the modern world. Only a completed level (primary or secondary) is accepted and certified by the state. Incomplete primary education is not perceived by authorities and formal sector employers as valid for jobs. "Drop-out" from the Western type of school before completion, is seen by the government and international agencies as wastage (UNESCO, 1998). This category of individuals is considered to represent non-knowledge and was, therefore, prevented from entering certain fields that would improve their life situation. Such an educational background does not signal the "appropriate" competence. Correlations between tested level of knowledge and life situation items (per gender) were studied, and significant correlations appeared almost exclusively among those with a long Islamic education or an incomplete primary education. This indicates that for these groups, actual knowledge has to be applied and proved in order to get access to certain fields and, consequently, to life situation items. For instance, there are many self-employed among men with IPE. For those who have complete primary education, there are few significant correlations between test scores and life situation items. This fact indicates that the "certified" platform has made it possible for them to enter fields that generate life situation items, sometimes regardless of their level of knowledge/skills (as measured on the test). They were able to do this without having to prove or negotiate their knowledge and skills, as they have entered the fields by the sheer influence or power of the certificate. Thus, to possess knowledge and skills without being able to manifest or articulate them in reading and writing in a European language seems to be a feature among those with IPE, an Indigenous or Islamic learning background.

With the structural adjustment programs (and the subsequent privatization and shrinking of the public sector), the number of jobs in the formal sector decreased while those in the informal increased. For many of the jobs in the latter, a complete primary education was and is not a precondition (Daun, 1998; Pritchett, 2001). Employees or self-employed in this sector have found their jobs through own efforts, demonstrated level of knowledge and/or traditional networks (Anheier, 1987; Hoerner, 1995; Kent & Mushi, 1995; McGrath & King, 1994; Ndione, 1994). Paradoxically, structural adjustment programs and liberalization thus have to some extent stimulated non-participation or non-completion in Western education.

These findings cannot be understood unless we place them in (i) a holistic context, or (ii) see them as in the context of stigmatization. The life situation here has been presented in an "atomized" way but the analysis and the interpretations have to take a holistic perspective; "life is holistic" in a society of the Senegalese type (Hoerner, 1995; Ndione, 1994; Zaoul, 1997). In Morocco, possession of knowledge was often not only or even primarily a private or individual matter, when Wagner (1993) conducted his study there; individuals were integrated into networks, and everybody in the network did not have to be literate. Senegal is similar to Morocco in this regard; there is in Senegalese society, a large number of networks (clans, associations, *Marabut–talibé* relationships, work groups, etc.) for mutual support. Everybody in such networks does not have to be literate but can rely upon his or her group.

Personal or individual life items should thus be seen in the context of those of the network. On the other hand, following the assumptions made previously, we may argue that those with IPE tend to be perceived as having incomplete competence both in the "modern" sphere of local and national community and the "traditional Muslim" sphere. They are unconsciously or consciously defined as having incomplete competence in the local community, and finally interiorize in their self-perception.

From the official and system perspective, those with incomplete primary education are not only considered wastage, but they also seem to be stigmatized in one-way or another. Another study conducted on the same individuals showed that those who had ended up with incomplete primary education in 1989–1990, had already during the schooling (in 1980–1981) been absent from school due to illness more often than other students, and teacher prediction of their school career in 1980 had to a large extent become a self-fulfilling prophecy some years later; those predicted to fail (especially girls), finally also did (Daun, 1995). Similar processes may be assumed to take place in Arabic schools and in relation to the Muslim community. (Quranic schools are different in this case, since they are not "dichotomized" – Table 1).

TENTATIVE CONCLUSIONS

The global discourse on education is silent about the fact that a large portion of studies reviewed by different researchers are uncertain about the effect of education on various features, both at individual level and at societal level (Hannum & Buchmann, 2003; Lewin, 1994). Processes of economic globalization are making local and national labor markets uncertain, particularly in low income countries, and impede education from being realized as human capital (Pritchett, 2001). The global spread of primary and secondary education is the positive side of the coin; the negative side is the globalization of the instrumental and rational view of knowledge and the increasing risk of failure in and of the education systems. To enter a very selective education system and not to complete seems to result in marginalization – at least in some aspects of the life situation – both from the "modern" (formal) sector and the "traditional" (informal) sector.

This marginalization is accompanied by labeling and some degree of stigmatization as "not complete" members of community.

NOTES

1. The term has been borrowed from King (1975). A learning system is a relatively permanent arrangement in which learning is one of the most important aspects of the processes taking place.
2. "Islamic education" is used when both Quranic and Arabic education are referred to.
3. The male respondents have not yet reached the age at which they have more than one wife.

REFERENCES

Anheier, H. K. (1987). Indigenous voluntary associations, nonprofits, and development in Africa. In: W. W. Powell (Ed.), *The nonprofit sector. A research handbook* (pp. 416–433). London: Yale University Press.

Anheier, H. K. (1989). Private voluntary organizations and development in West Africa: Comparative perspectives. In: E. James (Ed.), *The nonprofit sector in international perspective* (pp. 339–357). New York: Oxford University Press.

Baldo, M., & Furniss, E. (1998). *Integrating life skills into the primary curriculum*. New York: UNICEF.

Blackledge, D., & Hunt, B. (1985). *Sociological interpretations of education*. London: Routledge.

Blease, D. (1986). Teachers personal constructs and their pupils self-images. *Educational Studies*, *12*(3), 255–264.

Bullivant, B. M. (1987). *The ethnic encounter in the secondary school, ethnocultural reproduction and resistance. Theory and case studies*. London: Falmer.

Chinapah, V. (1992). *Monitoring and surveying learning achievements – A status report. EFA report no 1*. Paris: UNESCO.

Cuzzort, R. P., & King, E. W. (1976). *Humanity and modern social thought* (2nd ed.). Hinsdale, Ill.: The Dyden Press.

Daun, H. (1992). *Childhood learning and adult life. The functions of indigenous, Islamic and Western education in an African context*. Stockholm: Institute of International Education, Stockholm University.

Daun, H. (1995). Teachers' predictions and pupils' destinies: A West African survey. *International Review of Education*, *41*(5), 405–425.

Daun, H. (1998). Educational development in Guinea-Bissau in the light of liberalization and Islamic revitalization. In: H. Daun & R. N. Forsberg (Eds), *Political-Economic shifts and educational restructuring. A comparative study of education in Guinea-Bissau and Nicaragua* (pp. 73–112). Stockholm: Institute of International Education.

Doyal, L., & Gough, I. (1991). *A theory of human need*. London: The MacMillan Press.

Ebin, V. (1993). Les commercants mourides à Marseille et à New York. In: E. Grégoire & P. Labazée (Eds), *Grands comercants d'Afrique de l'Ouest. Logiques et pratiques d'un group d'hommes d'affaires contemporains* (pp. 101–123). Paris: ORSTROM.

Fuller, B. (1991). *Growing up modern. The western states build third world schools*. London: Routledge.

Giroux, H. A. (1988). *Teachers as intellectuals. Toward a critical pedagogy*. Mass.: Bertin & Garvey.

Goffman, E. (1963). *Stigma: Notes on the management of spoiled identity*. Englewood Cliffs, NJ: Prentice-Hall.

Grégoire, E., & Labazée, P. (1993). Approche comparative des reseaux marchands oest-africains contemporains. In: E. Grégoire & P. Labazée (Eds), *Grands comercants d'Afrique de l'Ouest. Logiques et pratiques d'un group d'hommes d'affaires contemporains* (pp. 9–36). Paris: ORSTROM.

Griffiths, M. (1993). Self-identity and self-esteem: achieving equality in education. *Oxford Review of Education, 19*(3), 301–317.

Grindahl, B. (1972). *Growing up in two worlds: Education and transition among the Sisala of Northern Ghana*. New York: Holt, Rinehart & Winston.

Hannum, E., & Buchmann, C. (2003). *The consequences of global educational expansion. Social science perspectives*. Cambridge, MA: American Academy of Arts & Sciences.

Harris, M. J., Rosenthal, R., & Snodgrass, S. (1985). The effects of teacher expectations, gender and behavior on pupil academic performance and self-concept. *The Journal of Educational Research, 79*(1), 173–179.

Hoerner, J.-M. (1995). *Le tiers-monde. Entre la survie et l'informel*. Paris: Harmattan.

Kassé, M. (1990). *Sénégal: Crise économique et ajustement structurel*. Ivry-sur-Seine: Editions Nouvelles du Sud.

Kent, D. W., & Mushi, P. S. D. (1995). *The education and training of artisans for the informal sector in Tanzania. Serial no. 18*. London: Overseas Development Administration.

King, K. J. (1975). *Primary learning systems in the third world. Some policy implications for planners*. Edinburgh: Centre of African Studies.

Lewin, K. M. (1994). *Education and development. The issues and the evidence. Serial no. 6*. London: ODA.

Lockheed, M., Fuller, B., & Nyirongo, R. (1989). Family effects on students' achievement in Thailand and Malawi. *Sociology of Education, 62*(4), 239–256.

Ly Kane, O. (1985). Le développement psycho-affectif de l'enfant à travers les rites africains. *Liens-ens de l'École Normale Superieure, 19–20.*

McGrath, S., & King, K. (with F. Leach & R. Carr-Hill) (Eds.). (1994). *Education and training for the informal sector*. London: Department for International Development.

Miller, D. (1989). *Market, state and community*. Oxford: Clanderon Press.

MINEC. (1989). *Situation économique de la région de Diourbel 1989*. Dakar: Ministry of Economy and Finance.

Ndione, E. S. (1994). *Réinventer le présent. Quelques jalons pour l'action*. Dakar: ENDA.

Nduka, O. A. (1974). African traditional systems of thought and their implications for Nigerian education. *West African Journal of Education, XVIII*, 2.

Ocitti, J. P. (1971). *African indigenous education as practiced by the acholi of Uganda*. Nairobi: East African Literature Bureau.

O'Neil, H. (2003). The role of student motivation on tests: high stakes vs. low stakes. Paper presented at the conference organized by *Evangelische Akademie*, December 15–17, 2003, in Stuttgart, Germany.

Oni, B. (1988). Education and alternative avenues of mobility. A Nigerian study. *Comparative Education Review, 32*(1), 87–99.

Pawar, P., Daun, H., Shangwu, Z., & Xiaoda, C. (1992). *Drafts instruments for assessing learning achievements – Survery questionnaires and tests. EFA Report No. 2.* Paris: UNESCO.

Pritchett, L. (2001). Where has all the education gone. *The World Bank Economic Review, 15*(3), 367–391.

Rideout, W. M., & Bagayoko, M. (1994). Education policy formation in Senegal. Evolutionary not revolutionary. In: USAID: *Education policy formation in Africa. A comparative study of five countries. Technical paper no. 12* (pp. 205–235). New York: USAID.

Sturman, A. (1994). Socialization. In: T. Husén & N. Postlethwaite (Eds), *International encyclopedia of education.* Oxford: Pergamon Press.

Traoré, A. (n.d.). *Étude de cas sur la participation de la famille aux activités scolaires dans une zone rurale en Afrique.* Paris: UNESCO.

UNDP. (1990). *Human development report 1990.* New York: Oxford University Press.

UNDP. (2001). *Human development report 2001.* New York: Oxford University Press.

UNESCO. (1998). *Wasted opportunities: When schools fail. Repetition and drop-out in primary schools.* Paris: UNESCO.

UNICEF. (1985). *Un sénégalais sur deux. Analyse de situation de l'enfance 1985.* Dakar: UNICEF.

Velkoff, V. A. (1998). *Women of the world. Women's education in India.* Washington, DC: U.S. Department of Commerce.

Wagner, D. (1993). *Literacy, culture and development: Becoming literate in Morocco.* New York: Cambridge University Press.

Weinstein, R. S., Marshall, H. M., Sharp, P. L., & Botkin, M. (1987). Pygmalion and the student. Differences in children's awareness of teacher expectations. *Child Development, 58*, 1079–1093.

William, R. M., & Amer, J. M. (1988). Islamic and western educational accomodation in a West African society: A cohort-comparison analysis. *American Sociological Review, 53*, 834–839.

Zaoul, H. (1997). The economy and symbolic sites of Africa. In: M. Rahnema (with V. Bawtree) (Ed.), *The post-development reader* (pp. 30–39). London: Zed Books.

APPENDIX A

Table A1. Examples of Items in the Knowledge and Skills Test.

Health items

If you have been bitten by a snake, you should try   True False I don't know
to cure yourself by making the blood circulate
A child who has measles can transmit it to other   True False I don't know
children playing with him?

Agriculture items

Fire is a big problem for the forests. Many forests   Three alternatives and ( ) I don't know
disappear every year due to people's imprudence.
Which two ways are the most effective one for
avoiding fire in the bush and the forests?

Political items

The chief of state in your country is   Five alternatives and ( ) I don't know

Mathematical items

Karim has bought 8 breads for 200 francs each. How
much does he have to pay?

Table A2. Life Situation of those with Incomplete Primary Education Compared with Others.

	Men		Women
Income	IPE < all others		IPE < Ar/Kor education, Pr, secondary.
Occupation	Farmer:	IPE > Pr, Sec-, Sec	IPE < Pr, Sec
	Artisan, tradesman:	IPE < Pr, Ar/Kor	IPE < Ind., Ar-/Kor, Pr
	Worker:	IPE < Sec-	Housewife: IPE < Ar/Kor; IPE > Pr, Sec
	Islamic teacher, medicine man:	IPE > Pr, Sec-, Sec	Housewife *and* other: IPE > Sec
Residence	Everything:	IPE < Pr, Sec	IPE < Pr
	Electricity:	IPE < Pr, Sec	IPE < Pr, Ar/Kor
	TV:	IPE < Pr, Sec	IPE < Ind., Ar/Kor, Sec.

Table A2. (Continued)

	Men		Women
Health	Not ill not during past five years or never:	IPE < Ar/Kor, Sec.	IPE < Ar/Kor, Sec.
	Often ill:	IPE > Sec-	IPE < Ar/Kor, Pr
Pleasant events	Marriage, child birth:	IPE > Sec-, Sec	IPE > Ind., Sec
	Religious, circumcision:	IPE > Pr, Sec-, Sec	IPE > all others except Ind.
	Work, trade, harvest:	IPE > Sec-, Sec	IPE < Ind. and all Islamic
Network	Number of problems:	IPE > Sec, Ind./Ar-/Kor-. IPE < Ar/Kor	IPE < Ar/Kor
	Type - "-: Financial	IPE > Ind/Ar-/Kor-, Pr, Sec.	IPE > all others
	Health	IPE < Ar/Kor, Pr	IPE < all others except Ind., Sec
	Help from: Relatives	IPE > Ind., Pr, Sec-, Sec	IPE > all others except Ind., Pr
	Marabut	IPE > all others except Sec.	IPE < Ar/Kor
	Public body	IPE < Pr	IPE > Ind., Ar-/Kor-
	Most frequent combination: Finance/relatives	IPE > all others	IPE > all others
Married		IPE > all others except Ar/Kor	IPE > Sec-, SecWork, trade, harvest:
Position	Modern:	IPE < all others except	IPE < Sec-/Sec
	Traditional:	Pr	IPE < Ind.
	None:	IPE < Sec	IPE > Ar-/Kor-
		IPE > Ar/Kor	
Decide	Never:	-	IPE > Islamic, Sec
	Work, trade, farm:	IPE > all others except	IPE > Ind., Pr
		Pr	Household: IPE < Ind.
No. of children		IPE > Pr, Sec-, Sec	IPE < Ind., Ar/Kor; IPE > Pr, Sec

MAPPING PARADIGMS AND THEORIES IN COMPARATIVE, INTERNATIONAL, AND DEVELOPMENT EDUCATION (CIDE) RESEARCH

W. James Jacob and Sheng Yao Cheng

INTRODUCTION

A number of theoretical paradigms provide a networking space for the trio and complementary fields of comparative, international, and development educational (CIDE) research. Critics periodically attribute the field's lack of a sound theoretical base or commitment to one area of scientific research or another as a primary weakness in the field.[1] Espoused theoretical paradigms often provide the knowledge debate arena in which academic fields interact and build together. In an alternative perspective from this criticism, we argue that the strength of the CIDE field resides in its ability to combine multiple theoretical perspectives that offer researchers a variety of potentially fruitful metatheoretical analyses. Thus, we do not view this lack of theoretical specification as a weakness; it is the very fabric that enables CIDE educationists to study and represent increasingly complex global and local education systems.

Global Trends in Educational Policy
International Perspectives on Education and Society, Volume 6, 221–258
Copyright © 2005 by Elsevier Ltd.
All rights of reproduction in any form reserved
ISSN: 1479-3679/doi:10.1016/S1479-3679(04)06009-8

In this chapter, we provide a typology of the most frequently chosen theories and metatheories of the CIDE field. The chapter begins with an examination of the so called "foundation" theorists generally associate with the field. Next, drawing from the literature, we define several key concepts of the metatheoretical aspects of this field, including scientific theories, paradigms, models, and metatheories. We then draw from the works of several contemporary CIDE theorists: Val D. Rust, Raymond A. Morrows and Carlos A. Torres, and Rolland G. Paulston, who have mapped the CIDE landscape over the past decade. We conclude this chapter with a model to help in selecting theoretical frameworks and research methodologies called the *Tai-Ji* Model of CIDE research.

BACKGROUND AND FOUNDATION THEORISTS OF CIDE

This chapter is not an attempt to refute or rewrite existing CIDE theories. Rather it is an attempt to map existing paradigms. According to Rust (2000b, p. 1) and Epstein (1994), *comparative* is generally the more academic or scientific aspect of the field; *international* education is usually related to cooperation, understanding, and exchange elements of the field. *Development* education, an increasingly important third category in our field, emphasizes action research, sustainability, cultural sensitivity, and localized educational needs.

Thomas (1998) defines comparative education as the study of educational likenesses and differences among regions of the world or between two or more nations. Fraser and Brickman (1968) would agree with Thomas in their definition of comparative education (they also provide a definition of international education):

- *Comparative education:* analysis of educational systems and problems in two or more national environments in terms of socio-political, economic, cultural, ideological, and other contexts. Comparative education discourages ethnocentric perspectives and supports understanding the factors, underlying similarities and differences in education in the various nations. Comparative education is not just a transplantation by one country of a schools system prevailing in another.
- *International education:* various kinds of relationships – intellectual, cultural, and educational – among individuals and groups from two or more nations. A dynamic concept which involves a movement across frontiers,

whether by a person, book or idea. It refers to the various methods of international cooperation, understanding, and exchange (i.e. exchange of teachers and students, aid to underdeveloped countries, and teaching about foreign educational systems). International education also accounts for international misunderstanding, ill will, hatred, and even war. International education experts are interested in the propaganda and dissemination of different types of political ideas abroad (p. 1).

Although comparative education and international education are generally considered the core categories[2] of the field, we have noted another increasingly important category of international education termed *development education*. This category encompasses a broad definition of international education programs at the local, national, and international levels. Key stakeholders in development education include local and national governments, nongovernmental organizations, bi-lateral organizations (e.g. CIDA, GTZ, and NORAD), and multi-lateral education organizations (e.g. World Bank, Asian Development Bank, and UNESCO).[3] Development education goals target sustainable, relevant, and culturally sensitive education programs. An underlying theme of development education is to create a synergistic atmosphere of cooperation and sharing of knowledge, skills, and technology among countries. This mutual participation increases the ability of nations to compete in a global-based economy, while maintaining cultural elements that are essential for their respective beliefs, traditions, and customs.

Comparative, international, and development education (CIDE) theory as we know it builds largely on the works of Kandel (1933, 1955), Hans (1961), and Brickman and Fraser (1968). Their perspectives of effective CIDE research encompassed a holistic approach by examining the historical, traditional, social, political, religious, economic, and cultural relationships associated with education in two or more countries. This perspective went unchallenged for several decades as CIDE researchers produced a number of cross-country case studies built on juxtapositions of the categories already mentioned.

Many scholars felt that the CIDE field lacked the analytical backbone necessary to perpetuate and weld the field together. Thus, since as early as the late 1950s, scholars like Holmes (1958, 1984), Bereday (1964), and Noah and Eckstein (1969) blazed inroads to make the field more rigorous. This attempt led to a train of scientific paradigm shifts as new social science theories were created, borrowed, and implemented on a broader scale by CIDE researchers. It is this foundation of comparative education that brings us to the scope of this chapter: to provide an analysis of existing CIDE theories and metatheories.

THEORIES, PARADIGMS, MODELS, AND METATHEORIES

The conventions of social science counsel us to use the term *theory* loosely in a variety of different contexts. Three reasons generally justify the use of research theory: interpretation, explanation, and predication. Thus, theory can be defined as an organized and systematic way of collecting, analyzing, and presenting data. It is a means for answering specific hypothetical problems. Popper (1959) argues that no theory or law can ever be entirely verified or proven by observations. Yet observations are fundamental in refuting theories that make incorrect predictions. Thus, a theory can be considered defensible if its implications have been repeatedly tested by experiments, without being refuted. Theories or models are, therefore, recursive generators of predictions (Heylighen, 1999).

But it should be emphasized that the object of our inquiry is not the reconstructed formal theories of interest to traditional philosophers of science. Instead, in analyzing theories of social reproduction in education, we will be studying what could be best described as *paradigms of research* and hence *research programs*, a combination of metatheoretical, theoretical, and methodological assumptions about how to develop a cumulative tradition of research.

The concept of *paradigm* is also associated with a historical community of researchers, specific exemplars of such research, and the normalization or institutionalization of research strategies following "revolutionary" breakthroughs. In his book the *Structure of Scientific Revolutions*, Kuhn (1996) defined paradigm as a set of beliefs that are widely accepted within a respective scientific community. Thus a paradigm allows scientific fields to establish avenues of inquiry, formulate questions, select methods with which to examine questions, define areas of relevance, and establish meaning within a given field. Adding to this definition, Kuhn emphasizes that a paradigm is essential to scientific inquiry in that "no natural history can be interpreted in the absence of at least some implicit body of intertwined theoretical and methodological belief that permits selection, evaluation, and criticism" (pp. 16–17). In order to be considered a scientific paradigm, "a theory must seem better than its competitors', but it need not, and in fact never does, explain all the facts with which it can be confronted" (pp. 17–18). Yet Kuhn also recognized the tendency of scholars within respective disciplines to challenge existing paradigms, thus creating an avenue for innovative research. Thus, an overarching theme of Kuhn's argument is that scholars have continuously demonstrated that more than one theoretical construction can always be placed on a given collection of data (see p. 76). While the application of different theoretical paradigms to the same hypotheses may lead to the same findings, Kuhn argues that this is not always the case.

Somewhat redefining Kuhn's thesis on reigning scientific paradigms and the emergence of new and competing paradigms, Small (2003) argues that revolutionary and normal science should be viewed as extremes on a time line spectrum of change. This contrasts with Kuhn's an all-or-nothing perspective on scientific paradigms and has been supported by Toulmin (1972) and Hull (1988). "Revolutionary change may only be an artifact of time scale," Small points out; "the longer a field persists, the more likely it is that a total morphing of its [perspectives] will occur, as new ideas edge out old ones" (Small, 2003, p. 399; Meyer, Kamens, & Benavot, 1992; Valverde, 2004). The fact that individuals tend to recognize only sudden or abrupt changes as "revolutionary" is not accurate, according to this perspective. Rather, evolutionary and gradual changes are rendered natural simply by the obsolescence and renewal of certain paradigms over time.

The traditional Newtonian paradigm of scientific research, focused on linearity, simplicity, and certainty, has been challenged of late by non-linear paradigms. Our definition of research linearity follows this traditional Neutonian paradigm, following the scientific method, sequence, and eventual results. An alternative research paradigm, composed of several theories, is often recognized by such labels as "nonlinearity," "postmodernism," "chaos theory," or the "sciences of complexity" (Gleick, 1988; Harding, 1998; Kellner, 1995; Kiel, 1991; Pagels, 1988; Southgate, 1996). The core of this alternative research paradigm is the study of non-linear systems. The advent of globalization, the Internet, and the trend toward a knowledge-based world economy opens CIDE research to a wide array of existing and potential linear and non-linear paradigms. It allows for what Nicholas C. Burbules (2003) has purported for a number of years: how globalization, media, and communication technology are increasingly changing the world of education. Burbules and Torres (2000) recognize the opportunities and the dangers of these irreversible educational shifts that have arisen from dialects associated with globalization and technological change. In a persuasive discourse on how globalization impacts national education systems,

Astiz, Wiseman, and Baker (2002) identify two interrelated dynamic process of globalization: *economic globalization* and *institutional globalization*. We would like to add a third factor to this relationship that is imperative to comparative education research, *cultural globalization*, mainly because of the rapid dispersive and assimilative impact of the media, values, and in many cases language on education.

Within these paradigms or theory programs, specific *models* guide research. The concept of model has been defined in a variety of ways (Morrow & Torres, 1995). Raymond Morrow and Carlos A. Torres borrow from Loic Wacquant's (1985) definition: "A *heuristic model* is a figurative representation of a perceived object used to guide one in pursuit of its knowledge. Its functions are twofold: it provides a notional ensemble, a perspective that permits an ordered perception of the empirical world; it is a directing scheme for theory construction and further investigations" (p. 19). The definition of the goal of scientific models is to address the question – in the context of specific theoretical, social, comparative, biologic, and physical systems – of what can be claimed for a model that has been constructed to describe that system. As a form of argument, Lehrer (1998, p. 121) notes, "Model-based explanations are typically judged by their explanatory coherence, by comparing the relative fit of models to data, and by the relative parsimony of description." John K. Gilbert and Susan Stocklmayer (as cited in Stocklmayer & Gilbert, 2002, p. 838) define a scientific model as "a representation of an idea, object, event, system, or process. A model is formed by considering that which is to be represented (the target) analogically in the light of the entities and structures of something which it is thought to be like (the source)." Along a similar vein, André Giordan (1989) notes,

> Generally speaking, modeling is a procedure that consists of producing a hypothetical representation, which takes the place of reality in order to describe reality and make it understandable. . . . The result of the process is a model, that is a transitive construct that has the properties of autonomy, coherence and relevance in relation to the problem under consideration (p. 326).

Coleman (2002, p. 135) identifies six general properties of conventional scientific models:

1. Models reflect a reality.
2. They are small representations of a reality.
3. They are simpler than the process/phenomenon they portray.
4. They are closed, not open, systems.
5. Any real situation can be analyzed if it can be described in terms of mathematical equations, and

6. The most important features of reality are correctly incorporated; less important features are initially ignored.

Yet not all scholars agree with Coleman that models must be "closed systems," as she indicates. Peter M. Senge (Senge, 1990; Senge, Cambron–McCabe, Lucas, Smith, Dutton et al., 2000) argues that many models are actually better understood as opened systems that are impacted by external forces. When asked whether educators can establish models of education in a closed system, Senge responded that he does not believe education leaders can establish an effective learning environment in a vacuum (O'Neil, 1995).

We define *metatheory* as an overarching theory devised to analyze entire theoretical systems. Thus, any set or group of theories would fall within the realm of a metatheory. *Metatheory* differs from *microtheory* in that a metatheory is an overarching theoretical paradigm that incorporates several theoretical perspectives. Microtheory, on the other hand, constitutes a set of assertions based on a shared set of assumptions (hypotheses), topics (i.e. curriculum reform, higher education, or educational access), and sources. Where theoretical perspectives may differ within a given metatheory, the assertions within a microtheory must be mutually consistent. Several microtheories may make up one or more theories that in turn constitute a metatheory. Both micro- and metatheories exist within local and global contexts or environments that encompass all education systems at all levels and are nested in nature. Thus, where microtheories may be used to explain various assertions of a specific educational topic, metatheories have the ability to examine entire educational and institutional systems.

The crux of our metatheoretical argument resides on two points. First, CIDE theories are increasing in number and evolving. Second, although these theories have been grouped and mapped in the past, we build on this categorization of previous scholarship by proposing that the strength of the CIDE field lies in its multi-theoretical reservoir. This depth allows researchers to draw from a broad theoretical base, necessary to analyze a number of complex and evolving contemporary issues.

The argument that metatheories and metanarratives are now redundant should be contested, in that this perspective neglects a fundamental element in the ultimate goal of scientific research – the right to seek after truth. Thus, our argument supports the perspective of Rust (2004), who argues that comparative, international – and we would add development – educational research hinges on the need for inclusion of a variety of research methods, approaches, and theories. No single research paradigm reigns in the CIDE research literature. Misinterpreting this perspective ostracizes viewpoints from all over the world that could shed insights on effective educational approaches in both research and practice. It places the qualitative and quantitative research divide on an equilibrium plateau and in many cases as complementary. It values indigenous knowledge at the same level as knowledge acquired from formal institutions of learning. However, several metatheoretical paradigms have emerged and evolved over the past half century that can generally be characterized within the CIDE research nexus. These are outlined in the following section.

THE EVOLVING CIDE FIELD

Early theorists had a clear idea of how to go about successful CIDE research. But this paradigmatic perspective did not hold its framework entirely; new theories and methodologies soon evolved to provide a more complete description and means of analysis to explain education systems throughout the world. Thus it is important to understand that the conventional theories of sociology have evolved and continue to evolve. In a recent chapter detailing the difficulty of viewing theoretical paradigms, Rust (2000a) graphically supports Rossiter (1982) position of two ways of seeing a political continuum model, as portrayed in Figs. 1 and 2.

It is clear from these figures that there may be one, two, or potentially several ways to view theoretical perspectives in politics, educational reform, and, we would add, CIDE theory. In an attempt to chart multiple theories used in CIDE, Paulston (1977, 1980, 1990, 1992, 1993a, b, 1994, 1996, 1999, 2000) produced a series of texts that map contemporary comparative education theories. Paulston (1992) mapped many CIDE theories used by researchers and practitioners at that time (Fig. 3). This map is similar to a later framework used by Morrow and Torres (1995, p. 26) and depicted in Fig. 4. We recognize that these scholars have not identified all theoretical paradigms incorporated by CIDE scholars worldwide. Rather, we have attempted to outline major metatheoretical paradigms, adding some theories that fit within these paradigms that are specifically relevant to CIDE research. No doubt the list relating to these figures is incomplete. Given the dynamic world of CIDE research and changing contexts that surround local

Left ◄——————————————► Right

Fig. 1. A Linear Model of Social Science Theory. Reprinted from Rust (2000; p. 64), with permission from Rowman & Littlefield Publishers, Inc.

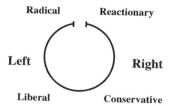

Fig. 2. Circular Model of Social Science Theory. Reprinted from Rust (2000; p. 64), with permission from Rowman & Littlefield Publishers, Inc.

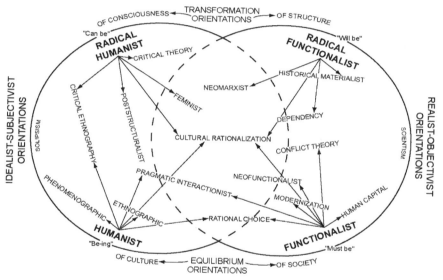

Fig. 3. A Macromapping of Paradigms and Theories in the Comparative, International, and Development Education Field. Reprinted from Paulston (1994; p. 931), with permission from Elsevier.

and global educational systems, new theories will need to be developed to help meet these dynamic needs. Such development will help obviate paradigmatic stalemates and provide an avenue toward paradigmatic shift through innovative, relative, and sustainable research.

Though the names of the metatheory quadrants may be labeled somewhat differently in Figs. 3 and 4, the quadrants and axis of both Paulston and

THE SOCIOLOGY OF RADICAL CHANGE

"Radical Humanist "   "Radical Structuralist"

SUBJECTIVE   OBJECTIVE

"Interpretive"   "Functionalist"

THE SOCIOLOGY OF REGULATION

Fig. 4. Four Paradigms for the Analysis of Social Theory. Reprinted from Morrow and Torres (1995; p. 26), with permission from the State University of New York Press.

Morrow and Torres' models bear striking similarities. Both allude to the subjective/objective divide; both have polarizations along the spectrum between change and regulation/equilibrium. Yet this subjective/objective and change/regulation divide suggests polarity amid the field. Although neither Paulston nor Morrow and Torres reference the other in defining these similar educational theory frameworks, they do attribute their framework as an adaptation of Burrell and Morgan (1979). The roots of both models have derivations from Burrell and Morgan's original framework. While it is true that comparative, international, and development educationists often "choose" between one theoretical framework or another, our position in this chapter is that this dynamic variety of theoretical possibilities is the essence of the field's comparative and theoretical strength. Rather than allowing that one theoretical perspective supersedes another, our position recognizes that comparative education research draws from a buffet of theories, metatheories, and paradigms. This allows for more diverse research choices and possible synergy than might exist if the field was wed to any singular paradigmatic perspective. While some scholars may argue that such an eclectic stance weakens the theoretical foundation of the CIDE field – leading to either widely differing interpretations of the same paradigm or redundant interpretations among researchers using different theoretical paradigms – we argue that this is not necessarily the case. Unless we establish a theoretical foundation that can adapt to the dynamic needs of local and global education systems, the field will defusably be handicapped because of its inability to adapt. The following sections relate directly to Paulston's and Morrow and Torres' frameworks outlined in Figs. 3 and 4, which we relate to a wide array of CIDE metatheoretical research.

THE SUBJECTIVE–OBJECTIVE DIMENSION

The subjective and objective duality has been a historical debate among theorists for many eras. It has been expressed in a number of different ways, including solipsism vs. scientism, idealism vs. materialism, and phenomenology vs. behaviorism. Morrow and Torres differ from Paulston in a few terms, such as using the word "humanism" rather than Paulston's "solipsism." "However, this duality," Morrow and Torres write,

> always refers back to an ontological distinction between the two different forms of 'being' which constitute social life: consciousness or subjectivity, on the one hand, through which individual and group intentions and beliefs are expressed through symbolic meaning; and, on the other, phenomena (i.e. structures) external to, and outside of consciousness, which, like the material causes in nature, have the effect of causing or determining individual and group behavior in a measurable and predictable way (pp. 26–27).

In our field, scholars tend to claim affinity for one or the other pole, given the potential methological problems associated with a more synergistic approach. Of the subject–object axis of metatheory, Morrows and Torres note that the respective theories tend to lean either toward an empirical-analytical knowledge or toward a historical hermeneutic knowledge. "Roughly speaking," they add, "this was the basis of the nineteenth-century German debate between the *Naturwissenschaften* (natural sciences) and the *Geisteswissenschaften* (cultural sciences)" (p. 27). Paulston argues that the subjective–objective dimension spans a spectrum from idealist to realist orientations (Fig. 5).

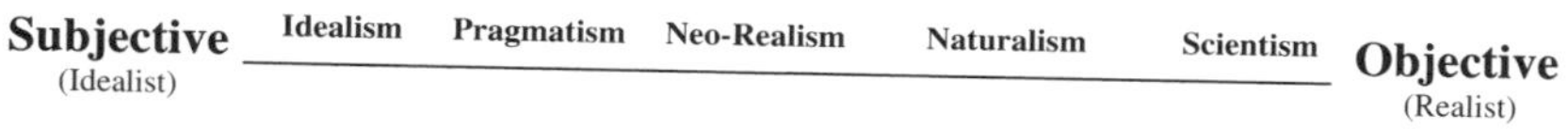

Subjective Idealism   Pragmatism   Neo-Realism   Naturalism   Scientism   **Objective**
(Idealist) —— (Realist)

Fig. 5. Subjective-Objective Spectrum of Social Theory. Reprinted from Paulston (1993), permission pending from the author's unpublished paper.

THE RADICAL CHANGE–REGULATION DIMENSION

A second dimension in which CIDE paradigms and theories can be classified is their conception of society. Morrow and Torres argue that the primary argument between the paradigmatic poles revolves around whether society is fundamentally good, organized in the interest of the whole, or "as advancing the interests of some groups at the expense of others and concealing this through cultural legitimations" (p. 29). This polarized dichotomy between radical change and regulation resembles an earlier debate between conflict theories and order. Emerging in the 1960s, the debate centered on Ralf Dahrendorf's critique of the consensus theory. The debate posited conflict factors of "confrontation, societal change, conflict, disintegration, and coercion against the theory of society based on the principle of social order stresses stability, integration, functional coordination, and consensus" (p. 29).

These two approaches constitute a fundamental break in CIDE theory, as well as a helpful foundation for classification. Where Morrow and Torres label the consensus theory paradigm regulation, Paulston calls it an "equilibrium orientation"; similarly, the conflict theory-based radical change paradigm of Morrow and Torres is called "transformation orientation" by Paulston. Though the paradigmatic names may differ, the polar theoretical tendencies remain constant in both frameworks.

FUNCTIONALIST PERSPECTIVE

Functionalist theory, as Parsons (1937) presents it, compared society to a biological organism, the different parts corresponding to the different institutions that make up a society. According to this theory, each institution performs a specific function for the good of the whole. Four essential functions became essential to maintain the social fabric: *adaptation to the environment*, whereby capitalism was deemed the economic system most suitable to the environment; *goal attainment*, generally performed by the government (it pursued liberal aims as defined by Western philosophers and theorists); *integration*, performed by religious and legal institutions that linked disaggregated portions of society together; and *latency*, which patterned the maintenance of societal values, especially viewing the family as an a historical basic human organization. Once modernized, the state generally took over several traditional functions of the family, including education.

According to Morrow and Torres (1995, p. 20), functionalist theory "was pioneered by the classical sociologist Emile Durkheim. The most famous version of this approach is the structural-functional theory of Talcott Parsons in the United States." There is wide agreement that the functionalist perspective dominated the field during the first three decades following World War II (Ninnes & Burnett, 2003; Paulston, 1994; Welch & Burns, 1992).

Rational Choice Theory

Grounded in the works of many sociologists who purport that people act rationally,[4] Rational Choice Theory asserts that social systems are organized in ways that structure the alternatives and consequences facing individuals so that they behave rationally. David Scott's (2000) definition of Rational Choice Theory explains that

> individuals are seen as motivated by the wants or goals that express their "preferences". They act within specific, given constraints and on the basis of the information that they have about the conditions under which they are acting. At its simplest, the relationship between preferences and constraints can be seen in the purely *technical* terms of the relationship of a means to an end. As it is not possible for individuals to achieve all of the various things that they want, they must also make choices in relation to both their goals and the means for attaining these goals (pp. 127–128).

According to Rational Choice Theory, individuals must weigh the outcomes of alternative courses of action and determine which will be best for them. Truly rational individuals will choose that which is likely to give them the greatest reward (Carling, 1992; Coleman, 1973). Some types of rational choice theories include decision theory, game theory, and prisoner's dilemma.

Modernization Theory

Modernization theory, which emerged in the 1950s, holds that the forces associated with industrialization will eventually transform all societies into modern industrial states. Modernization theory developed when it did primarily in a post-World War II era between the competing ideologies of capitalism and communism. Theorists in support of Modernization generally endorsed two theories that gained credence in the 1950s: evolutionary theory and functionalist theory (So, 1990). Modernizationists divided the world into three categories based on a cold war rational: *First World* nations, those that have reached an advanced stage of "modernization" or capitalism (i.e. United States, Canada, Western Europe, Australia, etc.); *Second World*, generally the communist bloc of nations who were aligned with a communist economic system; and *Third World* or all "developing" countries, usually the newly independent states that have sometimes endured hundreds of years of colonization by Western powers. Modernization provided the framework for Western powers to convince "Third World" countries that economic development and social justice were possible under capitalism. It purported that economic, social, and political change was interdependent within a society undergoing development.

It should also be noted that several different types of modernization theory have developed. Theorists subscribing to this framework include Alex Inkeles, Daniel Lerner, Neil J. Smelser, and Walter W. Rostow. One of the most famous modernization theories was developed by Rostow in his stages of economic growth theory. Rostow argues that "stimulus is needed in order to propel Third World countries" from one of the five stages to another. He mentions that a stimulus to the precondition stage would be a political revolution or a technological innovation. The five stages of development are:

1. Traditional
2. Precondition for Takeoff
3. Takeoff
4. Drive to Maturity
5. High Mass Consumption

According to Rostow's well accepted method, all that is needed is a mass amount of financial capital to invest in developing countries. This capital will act as a stimulus to propel less developed countries along to higher stages in his five-stage model.

Human Capital Theory

According to Baptiste (2001, p. 185), the term *human capital* refers to "knowledge, attitudes, and skills that are developed and valued primarily for their economically productive potential." The more you invest in a nation's human resources, the more prepared the nation's citizens will be economically. It views society from an economic standpoint, primarily looking at the inputs (i.e. education) and outputs (economic activity) of a nation's human capital (Little, 2003). Organizations, communities, and nations enjoy a certain amount of human capital in the various abilities of their people (Baker & Holsinger, 1996; Benavot, 1989). Theodore W. Shultz and Gary S. Becker were instrumental in popularizing human capital theory in the 1960s. Shultz (1961) and Becker (1964) conducted the first attempts to measure economic costs and benefits of education by incorporating rate or return analysis.

While human capital research has not been limited to education, it usually includes empirical measures of education and produces results that affect educators and education policy (Sweetland, 1996). Adam Smith, in his 18th century classic the *An Inquiry into the Nature and Causes of the Wealth of Nations*, is generally recognized for first recognizing human learning and skills as a form of human capital (Smith, 1776). Baptiste (2001) identifies three fundamental perspectives of Human Capital Theory. The first distinguishes between the knowledge and skills of individuals and human beings themselves. This perspective, supported by Mill (1859/1869) and Marshall (1890/1930), is rooted in the morals and values of universal human rights. Second, usually associated with Adam Smith, Irving Fisher, and the Chicago School, argues that individuals are indeed a form of capital. According to its proponents, this viewpoint does not demean individuals for considering themselves and others as capital. Rather, it views education and skills development as a source of autonomy and freedom. Finally, Karl Marx (Marx, 1887), who represents the third perspective of Human Capital Theory, argues that only when coupled with production is labor actually realized as capital. Marx felt that workers' innate labor power, and not the individual herself, is what equates to capital, when it is linked to a process of production.

Neofunctionalist Theories

In the basic synopsis of the Neofunctionalist argument, two or more nations agree to work for integration in a given governmental sector (i.e. economics, education, or health). In order to accomplish this task more effectively, an international bureaucracy may be established. The only way the respective governmental sectors can realize the full benefits of the integration is through a unified integration process. Neofunctionalist theories portray integration as a self-reinforcing process characterized by a succession of challenge-response cycles. The process of integration follows a series of challenges that interact with the participating group of nations. Metcalfe

(1997) notes, "The optimistic assumption of neofunctionalist theory is that the momentum of integration will stimulate the development of the additional capacities needed to ensure effectiveness" If the integrating parties are managed effectively, a new level of integration can be achieved, usually higher than individual countries could reach on their own. Paulston (1993a) asserts that Neofunctionalists are grounded in

> Parsons' logocentrism (i.e. a belief in reason as the controlling principle in the universe) and general social system perspective while opening their texts somewhat to rational actor approaches and interpretive perspectives; to conflicting social and cultural factors in educational planning and reform projects (but only at the project level); and to recognition of the centrality of structured inequality and interest group conflict in explanations of failed educational reform (pp. 12–13).

Sweet and Sandholtz (1998) view the primary causal force in the neofunctional school as "increasing levels of cross-border transactions and communications by societal actors" (p. 11). Examples of neofunctionalist supranational groups include the European Commission, the former Communist Bloc of nations in Eastern Europe, and OPEC. Neofunctional theory is based on transnational exchange activities, including educational exchanges, multinational corporation regulations, and other exchange policies (Fligstein & Mara-Drita, 1996; Moravcsik, 1995; Nylander, 2001).

RADICAL STRUCTURALIST (RADICAL FUNCTIONALIST) PERSPECTIVE

This approach shares much with the functionalist paradigm yet is directed at fundamentally different ends. Radical structuralism is committed to radical change, emancipation, and potentiality, in an analysis that emphasizes structural conflict, modes of domination, contradiction, and deprivation. Radical structuralism concentrates on structural relationships within a realist social world. Recognizing that the traditional Marxist structural determinism has for the most part disappeared from the CIDE theoretical landscape, Paulston notes how various forms of neo-Marxist theory have continued. Yet all forms of Marxism were significantly challenged during the late 1980s and early 1990s when the world witnessed the collapse of socialist theory and practice in Eastern Europe, the former U.S.S.R., and in many developing countries. Built almost entirely on the works of Marx, the radical structuralist perspective maintains an underlying tapestry of conflict, which is common to all of the quadrant's theories. This orientation argues that only through conflict can social change be initiated and sustained.

Historical Materialist

Materialism views production and reproduction as fundamental social processes that significantly influence, and in many ways determine, the nature of social systems, the patterns of social life associated with them, and patterns of historical change and development. The basis of historical development, according to Karl Marx and Alex Engels is the development of material production. This is an emphatic rejection of idealism, a materialist philosophy of history. Marx and Engels divided history into various periods or stages, on the basis of changing methods of production. Each period has an internal coherence and some stability. The transition from one period to another requires a rationale development or change process to the next level. Under this definition, history is not a succession of small cumulative changes; the transition from one stage to the next is in some sense a rapid change or revolution. Historical-materialist scholars argue that the culturalization of politics, has had detrimental effects on left theory and practice (Scatamburlo–D'Annibale & McLaren, 2004). Johnson (2000) notes, "From a materialist perspective, nonmaterial aspects of social life – including language, beliefs, and the structure of relationships and institutions such as the family, religion, and the state – are build upon an inevitably reflect how a society is organized around the basic tasks of production and reproduction" (pp. 185–186). The materialist approach is one of the most well-known aspects of Marx's theory of social change.

Dependency

Developing in a Latin American context, dependency theory posits that the root of the low levels of development in less economically developed countries is primarily their reliance, or *dependence*, on more economically advanced nations. It emerged in the 1960s and 1970s and was used to explain why many developing countries failed to develop economically, even with continual loans and investments from the industrial powers (Wiarda, 1999). The theory was a direct response to proponents of modernization and human capital theories of economic development. The crux of the dependency theory resided in the fact that in a capitalist-based world economy, many nations are placed on an unequal plane among economic powers (Velasco, 2002). Rather than narrowing and eventually eliminating the gap between developed and underdeveloped countries, the theory asserts that a perpetual dependency was established with a flaxen cord on the developing world until the nations were slowly dragged down to economic exploitation and potential ruin. This dependency limited development in Third World countries to a continual reliance on the technologies and investments that perpetuated a continued hegemonic relationship between developing and developed countries. Even some developing countries that had traditionally stable societies were forced into the wiles of the dynamic global market economy. An example of the dependency theory includes multinational corporations that build factories and hire laborers in developing countries, but exports are primarily removed rather than reinvested into the host country (So, 1990). Individuals primarily associated with the dependency theory include André G. Frank, Amin Samir, and Fernando Henrique Cardoso, former President of Brazil.

Neo-Marxist Theories

This perspective represents "the most well-known type of conflict theory," write Morrow and Torres (1995), "one for which the contradiction in the capitalist mode of production, especially those between labor and capital, are taken to be decisive" (p. 20). Neo-Marxist theories have particularly challenged the functionalist perspective address above. The theories reside in crises that inevitably follow capitalist-based societies. Neo-Marxist scholars argue that capitalist-based societies are not capable of overcoming these crises, requiring instead a revolution or form of sudden social change. Morrow and Torres (1995) note that Neo-Marxist theories differ from the traditional philosophy of Marx and Engels,

> because it has attempted to take into account subsequent changes in capitalism, especially the increased importance of massive cultural institutions (such as education and the mass media), as well as the strategic role of the liberal democratic state. For this reason, some neo-Marxists refer to their approach as an analysis of state monopoly capitalism (pp. 20–21).

Neo-Marxist theories were well developed by at least the 1970s and early 1980s. Although they have received less attention in recent decades, "there have been continued developments in neo-Marxist theory connected with the work of world-systems theorists and dependent development theorists" (Glassman, 2003, p. 33).

Conflict Theory

Conflict theories trace their roots to Karl Marx and his critique of capitalism, a theoretical perspective that has since developed along a number of lines that encompass everything from interpersonal relations to class struggle, religious conflict to terrorism, and familial education to the development of regional and national education policies. Harris (2004) contends that two general theories are useful in studying inequalities: functionalism and conflict theory. Analytical conflict theories can be considered neo-Weberian in some regards, because of Max Weber's influence on this set of theories (Morrow & Torres, 1995). Whereas Marx's conflict perspective was based on economics and relied on the unequal ownership and control of property, Weber argued for a broader view that encompassed such issues as religion, ethnicity, and race, as well as socio-economic relations. Some of key conflict theories include sexism, racism, and neocolonialism.

RADICAL HUMANIST PERSPECTIVE

Both Morrow and Torres and Paulston agree on the name of this paradigmatic quadrant. The radical humanist perspective emerged in the early 1980s as a more humanistic Marxism. This orientation drew on the earlier critical theoretical works of the Frankfort School, currently led by Jürgen Habermas in Germany. Henry Giroux is the primary figure of this paradigm in North America, and neo-Freirian scholars are the leading proponents of radical humanism in developing countries. Theoretical perspectives in the radical humanist quadrant include critical social theory; feminism; poststructuralism, along with postmodernism, postcolonialism, and media literacy; and critical ethnography.

Critical Theory

This perspective represents a type of theorizing that has been influenced by both neo-Marxist and conflict theory traditions. Unlike neo-Marxist theory, they reject the "theory of the dictatorship of the proletariat, and the primacy of class and economic determinants in the last instance, and in stressing the multidimensionality of power relations and the role of agency and social movements in social change" (Morrow & Torres, 1995, p. 21). Critical theories relate to various aspects of social struggle, including gender, race, religious, sustainable development, and sexual orientation. Paulston (1994) considers critical theory as the primary theoretical arm branching out of the radical humanist paradigm in Fig. 3. Some of the most influential education philosophers to include aspects of critical theories include Paulo Freire, Herbert Marcuse, and Karl Marx. For instance, Freire (1970) argued for a critical social theory framework, which deals with the topic of oppressive pedagogy. This framework sensitized the researcher to look for evidence of oppressive themes in the narratives. Freire's framework is appropriate to the topic because a number of scholarly works have identified education as an indicator of characteristics of an oppressed group.

Feminism

Feminism is a theory that men and women should be treated equally in political, economic, social, and educational contexts. Few feminist scholars would proclaim a single feminist methodology. Rather, most feminists attest that the feminist theory is wide-ranging and broadly defined. Harding (1986, 1998) has identified several alternative feminist epistemologies: empiricism, standpoint theory, and postmodernism, and postcolonialism. In her definition of strong objectivity in feminist theory, Harding (1991) writes,

> If the goal is to make available for critical scrutiny all the evidence marshaled for or against a scientific hypothesis, then this evidence too requires critical examination *within* scientific research processes. In other words, we can think of strong objectivity as extending the notion of scientific research to include systematic examination of such powerful background beliefs (p. 149).

Radical feminism, which arose in the 1960s and 1970s, views the subordination of women as the most basic form of oppression. Radical feminism considers socioeconomic class, race, and culture as various forms of oppression. This form of feminism focuses on revolutionary social change. "In a broader and deeper sense," adds Johnson (2000), "feminism is a variety of interrelated frameworks used to observe, analyze, and interpret the complex ways in which the social reality of gender and gender inequality is constructed, enforced, and manifested, from the largest institutional settings to the details of people's daily lives. These frameworks generate theories about psychological, spiritual, and social life and their consequences" (p. 120).

PostStructuralist Theory

Much like postmodernism, poststructuralist theory is difficult to define and place on a theoretical map (Hassan, 2003). Still, poststructuralism is generally thought to contain three primary features: the primacy of theory, the decentering of the subject, and the fundamental importance of the reader. de la Campa (1999) recognizes that the importance poststructuralist thought adds to the theoretical literature but also cautions that a predominantly European-based poststructuralist theory may not apply to all international contexts, at the risk of neglect of local perspectives. Hassan (2001) has identified four categories that have arisen from postmodernist theory: first, postmodern architecture, which departs from traditional architectural methods and combine aesthetic and historical elements; second, postmodernism, attributed by Pope John Paul II to condemn extreme relativism in values and beliefs; third, in cultural studies the term *postcolonialism*, adopted as the most relevant term of choice; and fourth, in pop culture, postmodernism as an underlying theme among star musicians, artists, and the media. Kellner adds that media culture is a rising field in the postmodernist theoretical branch of CIDE and is fundamental in shaping contemporary politics, economics, and cultures (Kellner, 1995; Kellner & Durham, 2001).

Positioned in the humanist and radical humanist paradigms, poststructuralist, and postmodernist theories highlight the use of language and the rejection of scientism and traditional rationalism. "Instead," Paulston (1994) adds, "the [postmodernist] social world is usually portrayed as a collage of multiple narratives or traces tied to specific forms of empowerment" (p. 930). In the early 1990s, Ninnes and Burnett (2003) argued in support of two comparative education scholars' calls to include alternative modes of examining the CIDE landscape, including the adoption of postmodernist theory. Whereas Masemann (1990) called for the field to examine additional methods of knowing, Rust (1991) argued for the inclusion of postmodernist theory in CIDE research, because it might provide additional perspectives to the existing CIDE theoretical framework.

Cultural Rationalization

This theory draws on a number of what were earlier viewed as ideological multifarious. This theory is largely attributed to Jürgen Habermas, the leading theorist in this ideology, who built on Marx's emancipatory narrative. The crux of Habermas's theory is that the free and open communication of the life-world is being impinged on by the formal rationality of the system. The cultural colonization of the life-world supports Weber's perspective that formal rationality is triumphing over substantive rationality (Ritzer & Goodman, 2004). Notable is that cultural rationalization is located within the pragmatic center of Paulston's framework in Fig. 3. Habermas has established a neo-normative "foundation for reconstructing Marxism in critical theory, in the intersubjective theory of communicative democracy of G. H. Meed, in Weber's theories of bureaucracy and progressive cultural rationalization, and in the action theory of Talcott Parsons" (Paulston, 1994, p. 929).

Critical Ethnography

A vital and growing variation of critical theory is known as *critical ethnography*. Critical ethnographies offer "thick descriptions of cultural and economic domination and examine prospects for resistance supposedly from the actor's viewpoint" (Paulston, 1994, p. 930). Critical ethnography combines theory and practice. Thus, followers of this form of ethnography argue that there must be a link between research practice and some issue of social change (Ogbu, Sato, & Kim, 1994).

INTERPRETATIVE (HUMANIST) PERSPECTIVE

The interpretive perspective is a theoretical paradigm founded on the idea that a "sociological understanding of behavior must include the meaning that social actors give to what they and others do," notes Johnson (2000, p. 161). Mutual interaction among participants in any setting produces interpretations, both by individuals and the group/s. Interpretive perspectives include symbolic interactionism, ethnography, and phenomenography. Contrasting with the notion that social life is solely based on objective and scientific orientations, the interpretive perspective falls within the subjective or "humanist" side of the CIDE framework.

Pragmatic Interactionist

Located at the in the intersubjective center of Paulston's CIDE framework, pragmatic interactionist theory differs from Marx's view regarding the function of how knowledge is used in terms of production and societal change. The pragmatic interactionist orientation argues that it is not just the function, but the very nature of knowledge itself, that is determined by our agenda for change. The best way to understand the world in which we live is in relation to our actions and interactions within it. From this perspective, actors seek to adapt their environment to their individual needs and desires (Radford, 2003). This theoretical perspective draws from the pragmatic works of John Dewey, G. H. Mead, Paulo Freire, Jürgen Habermas, and Richard Rorty. Pragmatic interactionist theory is particularly relevant to reflective research and action research models based on the unique educational contexts of the participants.

Ethnography

Ethnographic research incorporates a variety of research methods. Grounded in participant observations and interviews, ethnographic research is often "supplemented by other qualitative and quantitative techniques such as mapping, charting, questionnaires, document and artifact analysis, life histories, narratives, and experiments" (Ogbu et al., 1994, p. 2046). Geertz (1975) argues that ethnographers test theories in the very process of using them. He later adds that "ethnographers need to convince us . . . not merely that they themselves have truly 'been there,' but . . . that had we been there we should have seen what they saw, felt what they felt, concluded what they concluded" (Geertz, 1988, p. 16).

In CIDE, this perspective has been used to study HIV/AIDS education programs, literacy efforts, and political perspectives of students. Educational ethnography commonly comprises a triangulation of observations, interviews, and questionnaires (McNamee, 2001). While the ethnographic perspective claims to provide description of how ethnic groups and others view and interpret educational practices, ethnographic data as "thick description" are significantly strengthened by the imposition of an ethnological or ideological comparative overlay (Paulston, 1993a, p. 17).

Ethnography, ethnology, and ethnomethodology all fit into the ethnographic perspective. Ethnographies are detailed descriptions of social life and culture in a particular social system based on detailed observations of what people actually do. Ethnology is the branch of anthropology that studies how cultures develop historically and compare with other cultures. Ethnomethodology, meaning people's methods, is the branch of sociology that deals with the codes and conventions that underlie everyday social interactions and activities (Garfinkel, 1967).

Phenomenographic

Phenomenology offers CIDE scholars and practitioners an approach to understanding unique aspects of individuals and their meanings and interactions with others and the environment. Since education is dependent on the realities associated with individuals in numerous locations and contexts, specialized educational research should similarly reflect the contextual realities and concerns of the stakeholders (students, parents of students, teachers, administrators, policy makers, and fellow researchers) for whom scholars provide research. "In comparative education," Paulston (1994) adds, "phenomenographic studies have sought ...to characterize how researchers see, apprehend, and think about knowledge constructs such as 'paradigms and theories' at different times and in different knowledge cultures and subcultures" (pp. 930–932). Phenomenographic studies are subjective , interpretive, and often build on the alternative perspectives of other scholars and analyses. Husserl (1970) philosophical ideas about how science should be conducted gave rise to the descriptive phenomenological approach to inquiry. Akin to Freire's (2001) notion of *conscientisation* (Dyer & Choksi, 1998; Torres, 1998), Husserl felt that each individual's experience as perceived by human consciousness has value and should be an object of study.

NEOINSTITUTIONALIST PERSPECTIVE

Though not mentioned by Morrow and Torres, the neoinstitutional theoretical framework is an essential element of CIDE research. We would place the neoinstitutionalist perspective within the Paulston's idealist–subjectivist (Fig. 3) and Morrow and Torres' subjectivist end (Fig. 4) of the subjectivist–objectivist theoretical spectrum (Hirsch, 1997; Scott, 1995). John W. Meyer is largely responsible for its conception and popularization (Meyer, 1994; Meyer, Boli, Thomas, & Ramirez, 1997; Meyer & Hannan, 1979; Meyer et al., 1992; Meyer & Rowan, 1977). Simply defined, neoinstitutionalism focuses on the relationship among institutions, ideas, and processes. Rules, models, and norms that shape entire institutions, organizations, and networks are underpinnings of the neoinstitutionalist metatheory perspective. Eliasoph and Lichterman (2003) and DiMaggio and Powell (1991) assert that many organizational elements and forms recur in many organizations; these elements and forms exist in fields or institutional sectors of society, not only in singular organizations. From a neoinstitutional perspective, CIDE researchers examine organizational fields within an educational system to determine external forces, organizational environment, organizational culture, and local contextual needs (Arun, 2000). The neoinstitutional metatheory encompasses several theories, including systems theory, network theory, discourse theory, and the culturalist approach.

THE POWER OF THEORETICAL SYNERGY

Determining which theoretical framework to incorporate in CIDE research is often linked to the methods used to implement these espoused theories. This chapter, therefore, supports Hanson's (1981) emphasis on combining quantitative and qualitative methods in social science research, which he portrays in an article titled "Field Work Methodology for the Study of Latin American Ministries of Education." By combining qualitative and quantitative methods in social research, the researcher is better able to maximize his or her ability to substantiate an issue through the synergy of both approaches. Without a combined approach, the research is often open to criticism.

In his book *What's Wrong with Ethnography*, Hammersley (1992) argues that the distinction between qualitative and quantitative is of limited use and carries some danger:

> It is striking how prone we are to the use of dichotomies, and how these often come to represent distillations of all that is good and bad. "Qualitative" and "quantitative" are sometimes used to represent fundamentally opposed approaches to the study of the social world, one representing the true way, the other the work of the devil (p. 159).

One reason the distinction between the two is so misleading is that it obscures the breadth of issues and arguments involved in the methodology of social research. Hanson would agree with Hammersley that the scope of social research is so vast that it requires an eclectic researcher trained with a broad range of research skills.

Drawing again from Hammersley, we provide a brief outline on the history of the quantitative–qualitative debate below.

Mid-19th century:	Argument about the scientific status of history and the social sciences, quantification often being seen as one of the key features of natural science.
1920s and 1930s:	Dispute between advocates of case study and statistical method.
1940s and 1950s:	Quantitative method (survey and experimental research) becoming the dominant approach.
1960s-present:	A revival in qualitative types of research. This has led to detente in some cases, and to increased combination or integration of the methods.

Like Hanson, Hammersley leaves little doubt of his proclamation for qualitative research in the social sciences. Yet both authors also emphasize that a combined approach strengthens an overall argument that creates a synergy effect which provides additional support to an individual or organization's research. And so it is with CIDE theories. What is involved in social science research is not a simple contrast between two opposed standpoints (i.e. quantitative vs. qualitative, subjective vs. objective, or the transformation vs. equilibrium), but a range of positions sometimes located in more than one dimension. There is generally no necessary relationship between adopting a particular position on one issue and another position on the others. Many theoretical combinations are often quite appropriate.

One might say that CIDE scholars are attuned to Freire (2001) notion of concientization, by which scholars, educators, practitioners, and policy makers are encouraged to find new ways to spread and develop learning. Arnove, Cook, Epstein, Lisovskaya, and Rust (2002) discussed what the coursework for a comparative and international education university program should entail. After comparing several models that are currently in place at the participants' respective institutions, Epstein (2002) concluded that a model that focuses on geographic regions as well as theoretical and practical courses is the one others should adopt, because it offers the most comprehensive approach for students interested in the comparative and international education field.[5] Later, Rust (2003) expanded on his comparative and international education methodology definition. Rust delineated between the often misunderstood and entangled definitions of method, methodology, and epistemology in the field. Where method deals primarily with data collection and analysis, methodology refers to the theoretical analysis of the methods appropriate to the field or to the body of methods and principles particular to this branch of social science knowledge. We view the eclectic nature of the methodologies of CIDE as a unique strength. Thus our definition of methodology echoes Rust's assertion that it should be separate from and broader than the methods applied to our field. Research methodologies also generally have "theoretical implications in that they provide theories of how research does or should proceed" (Rust, 2003, p. 7). Discussing comparative education epistemology, Rust (2003) adds,

> I like to think of one's epistemological perspective to be the assumptions one holds. It isn't something one deliberates long and hard about, but something a person immediately and directly responds to. Those taking different philosophical positions will have different answers to epistemological questions. Those who believe in naturalism claim knowledge is gained by identifying natural causes and effects, and testing given explanations to see if they hold true, while the neo-realist sees a dualistic reality and truth exists when what is in the mind is identical to what is out there (p. 10).

In the midst of critics who often proclaim that sociologists should focus on a single theoretical framework or a specific metatheory, we argue that an eclectic theoretical approach to CIDE research should be maintained.

The selection of which research theory to use ought to depend on the purpose and circumstances of the research. There will be times when a radical humanist perspective is mandatory. Other circumstances will validate the need for a radical functionalist perspective, to show a differing point of view and analysis. We propose a new framework, or model, for viewing the theoretical systems or metatheories in CIDE research. We call this the Tai-Ji Model (Fig. 6).

The Tai-Ji Model is built on the dyad of "sameness" and "difference," which are "philosophical opposites, but they are not necessarily antagonistic or mutually exclusive, either in logic or in the real world" (Marginson & Mollis, 2001, p. 585). Approximately 4000 years ago, the Chinese ruler Fu Xi contributed a model to interpret the evolution of the universe, which he called *Tai-Ji*. The origin of the framework came during a time of chaos in Chinese history, when people were looking forward to realizing social stability and regulation. The practice of Tai-Ji emphasizes the theory of universal balance. Ancient Chinese philosophy attained the idea of a dynamic and constantly changing universe in which the five basic elements naturally existed. Although these elements have opposing characteristics, they simultaneously complement each other (Morton, 1995).

The Tai-Ji symbol depicts a circle that represents the universe; within it is a rotating image of two water drop-like shapes. The black (*Yin*) and white (*Yang*) seem to feed off each other. As one gets larger the other gets smaller, and as one gets smaller the other increases in size, always maintaining a

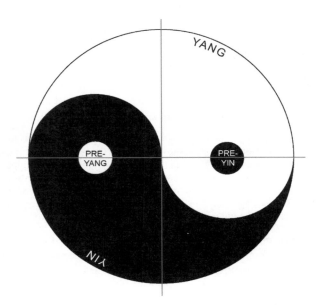

Fig. 6. Tai-Ji Model for framing Comparative, International, and Development education Research Paradigms.

balance. In essence, the Tai-Ji orientation asserts that the only certainty within this framework is change and the need to adapt, or counterbalance, those changes (Kong, 2000; Liu, 2000; Yang, 2002).

The Tai-Ji Model can be disaggregated into four essential parts, including *Yin, Yang, pre-Yin,* and *pre-Yang.*[6] After Fu Xi observed the movement of the sun, the moon, and stars for more than 40 years, he interpreted the regulation of life and nature as two extreme characters: Yin and Yang. Yin and Yang highlight two traditional dichotomy in the West – right and left. Yin has several meanings, including dark, moon, female, and negative; Yang refers to light, sun, male, and positive.

In contrast to the Western dichotomy of either left or right, Chinese philosophy adds other continuous categories: pre-Yin and pre-Yang. Pre-Yin is located within the area of Yang but represents the possibility of the coming of Yin. Following the same vein, pre-Yang resides within the area of Yin but represents the appearance of Yang. It is by these additional continuous categories (pre-Yin and pre-Yang) that the Tai-Ji Model can achieve balance, transformation, interaction, and dependent opposition. Phenomena that can be understood within this framework include the movement of stars, physical anatomy, agricultural systems, music, ethical values, progress of time, operations of governments, and historical social change – specific to the focus of this chapter on CIDE. There are no obvious borders between Yin and Yang, and no absolute direction between them. For instance, when one sees the sun hanging in the sky, one could deduce that it is daytime and not nighttime. Put in a terrestrial context, if it is daytime in the Western hemisphere it will be nighttime in the Eastern hemisphere.[7]

Several unique aspects of the Tai-Ji framework include multiple ways of viewing the same situation (i.e. from a radical functionalist, functionalist, or a radical humanist perspective). It emphasizes the global nature and interconnectedness of nations, while maintaining the obvious differences that exist simultaneously. The Tai-Ji Model offers a non-linear framework that has the ability to span time, space, and theoretical paradigms. Its strength lies in its ability to adapt to the need of the research/study, depending on the context of a given situation or country.

The Tai-Ji Model supports an eclectic approach to CIDE studies in that one, two, or several theoretical approaches may be appropriate for a given study, depending on the context and nature of the research being conducted. Different or even multiple theoretical approaches may be appropriate. If you select a given theoretical perspective, it may be important to supplement this with additional points of view, thus maximizing the effect of synergistic perspectives.

The Tai-Ji Model does not, therefore, act as a single theoretical paradigm, but rather as a filter model for determining which metatheoretical framework is most appropriate for a given research situation. The model could similarly be used to determine which methodology should be adopted. For instance, if a CIDE scholar were researching higher educational reform in China, she could choose to look at one specific metatheoretical framework that would best meet the needs of her hypothesis. Perhaps she would like to examine social justice issues of educational equity and access. While a neomarxist perspective from the radical humanist quadrant could be selected for this hypothesis, this researcher feels that the combination of feminist and critical theories would be more appropriate for her study. Thus, although an element of the radical functionalist perspective may be a possibility for examining these issues, she instead bases her findings in the radical humanist quadrant.

Another scenario for using the Tai-Ji Model would be to determine which guiding theories and data collection methods should be adopted by a team of researchers, policy makers, and educators who were trying to determine the best way to create and implement an HIV/AIDS education curriculum program in Ugandan secondary schools. Not only would the team have to establish an open dialog among participants, they should also apply sound development education principles throughout each stage of the planning, implementation, and evaluation processes. The Tai-Ji Model could also be used to determine which theoretical framework to guide the program, while similarly helping select which methods should be used. Thus the Tai-Ji Model simply reminds CIDE scholars, policy makers, and practitioners that they must make a conscious and reflective effort to determine which metatheoretical framework and methodology to adopt in a given research project or study.

The Janusian theory of acting and thinking bears a striking affinity to the Tai-Ji Model. Named after the Roman god Janus, who looked four ways simultaneously, the Janusian paradigm allows for alternative and competing hypotheses to exist. Both the Tai-Ji theoretical framework and the Janusian paradigm provide an alternative approach to linear-thinking, or a strictly scientific method manner of thinking, and make way for alternative viewpoints. This is not to say that the scientific method does not fit within these alternative frameworks, because it does. But the Janusian and Tai-Ji frameworks call on researchers to embrace differences as naturally occurring phenomena.[8]

MULTIPLE DIMENSIONS WITHIN EACH RESEARCH METATHEORY

Two key issues essential for social researchers include, first, determining which metatheory to use in their research, and, second, determining when to use a specific metatheory rather than another. Hanson feels that quality research requires an eclectic and instinctual ability to draw from multiple research methodologies and theories. Likewise, selecting which type of qualitative method to use is not an easy task. To assist the researcher, "Numerous research theories are available to this end." Hanson (1981, p. 259) also notes that "the quality of the product is going to be no better than the quality of the researcher and the care taken with the work." Effective research often requires multiple dimensions of several theoretical perspectives.

CONCLUSION

The CIDE theoretical landscape has undergone significant changes and mapping its terrain is often problematic. CIDE theories, paradigms, models, and metatheories have evolved as the field has adapted to a constantly changing world. Many education scholars insist that researchers should advocate a single theoretical framework. In this chapter, we have discussed avenues that broaden this perspective. Under this viewpoint, scholars are able to consider multiple theoretical viewpoints and then choose their favorite. As times and contexts change, so might the theoretical framework for our research. While time-tested methods and theories may still be relevant in contemporary CIDE studies, we must be open to new ideas. Only then are we able to meet the dynamic forces that face an increasingly globalized world community.

In the midst of critics who often proclaim that sociologists should focus on a single theoretical framework˙ or a specific metatheory, we argue for an eclectic theoretical approach to CIDE research. Prepared CIDE researchers come to the field with a bag of tools that includes a number of theoretical paradigms. The most relevant theories to use are those that are most context-relevant to the respective study engaged in. The Tai-Ji Model allows for this amount of latitude and is an excellent tool for helping determine which type of theoretical framework and methodology to use in CIDE research. Yet it differs from an altogether postmodern perspective that provides no literal theoretical foundation. The Tai-Ji Model urges CIDE scholars to be aware and knowledgeable of the broad range of theories and metatheories at our disposal; yet we must also be able to ascertain which one or set of theories would be most appropriate for a given study. Rather than limiting a study to one theory or method, the eclectic approach, as portrayed in the Tai-Ji Model, leads to greater synergy thereby maximizing the empirical foundation and analysis potential of the CIDE field.

NOTES

1. This debate is included in Val D. Rust (2000), "The Meaning of Comparative in Comparative Education," paper presented at the CIES Western Regional Conference, Brigham Young University, Provo, Utah; William K. Cummings (1999), "The Institutions of Education: Compare, Compare, Compare!" *Comparative Education Review* 43(4), 413–437; Peter Ninnes and Gregory Burnett (2003), "Comparative Education Research: Poststructuralist Possibilities," *Comparative Education* 39(3), 279–298; Val D. Rust, Aminata Soumaré, Octavio Pescador, & Megumi Shibuya (1999), "Research Strategies in Comparative Education," *Comparative Education Review* 43(1), 86–109; and D. Adams & Joseph P. Farrell (1969), "Societal Differentiation and Educational Differentiation," *Comparative Education* 5(3), 249–262.

2. By *core categories* of the field, we mean that these terms are the best recognized and accepted by scholars, policy makers, and practitioners in the realm of international education. Along with development education, the metatheoretical paradigms detailed in this chapter are attributed to comparative and international education.

3. Although development education programs have great potential to strengthen bilateral and multi-lateral relationships among agencies, governments, and nations, far too often this has not been realized (see, for instance, Smith, 2004; Samoff, 1999). Realizing that development agencies have not always been recognized as culturally sensitive or locally oriented, our definition of development education incorporates aspects that are fundamental for successful development programs, including a strong sense of local ownership, participation, open dialog among stakeholders, cultural sensitivity, and sustainability. Samoff (1999) argues that many development programs have been plagued by "agendas and procedures of the funding and technical assistance agencies, with constrained national participation, limited national control, and very little sense of national ownership" (p. 249). Criticizing the scientific research shortcomings of British aid efforts worldwide, Giles (2004) outlines how the British government hopes to rectify this weakness by boosting its scientific rigor in all aspects of program planning, implementation, and evaluation. With over a trillion dollars spent on development aid since the 1960s, Easterly (2001) notes that in many aspects development programs and agencies have fallen short of their desired goals.

4. See for instance Immanuel Kant (1788), *Critique of Practical Reason*, translated by L. W. Beck (Upper Saddle River, NJ: Prentice-Hall); Max Weber (1968), "Conceptual exposition," In: G. Roth & C. Wittich (Eds), *Economy and Society* (pp. 212–254), Vol. 1 (New York: Bedminister Press); and Talcott Parsons (1937), *The structure of social action* (New York: McGraw Hill).

5. Leon Tilky and Michael Crossley (2001), "Teaching comparative and international education: A framework for analysis," *Comparative Education Review 45*(4), 561–580.

6. Renowned Chinese theorist Ji-Shan Liu wrote that the combination of Yin and Yang is *Tao*. And this combination is also known as *Tai-Ji*. Tao is a very complicated term, not easy to describe in words. Lao-Tzu said that if you could interpret Tao into words, it would not in fact equate to the true meaning of Tao.

7. Within yang there is an element of Yin; within Yin there is always an element of Yang. In the heart of the winter season, seeds await their time to grow (like Yang awaiting its chance within the realm of Yin for its turn to emerge). Similarly, during a hot summer season, occasional desert storms bring coolness as a reminder of the approaching winter.

8. For more information on the roots of Janusian thinking in organizational theory literature, see Robert E. Quinn and Michael R. McGrath (1985), "The transformation of organizational cultures: A competing values perspective," In P. J. Frost, L. F. Moore, M. L. Louis, C. C. Lundberg & J. Martin (Eds), *Organizational culture* (pp. 315–334) (Beverly Hills, CA: Sage); Kim S. Cameron and Richard E. Quinn (1999), *Diagnosing and changing organizational culture: Based on the competing values framework* (Reading, MA: Addison-Wesley); and Albert Rothenberg (1979), *The emerging goddess: The creative process in art, science, and other fields* (Chicago: University of Chicago Press).

REFERENCES

Adams, D., & Farrell, J. P. (1969). Societal differentiation and educational differentiation. *Comparative Education, 5*(3), 249–262.

Arnove, R. F., Cook, B. J., Epstein, E. H., Lisovskaya, E., & Rust, V. D. (2002). The introductory course in comparative education. Panel presentation at the *Comparative and international education society annual conference*, Orlando, Florida.

Arun, R. (2000). Schools and communities: Ecologial and institutional dimensions. *Annual Review of Sociology, 26*, 395–418.

Astiz, M. F., Wiseman, A. W., & Baker, D. P. (2002). Slouching towards decentralization: Consequences of globalization for curricular control in national education systems. *Comparative Education Review, 46*(1), 66–88.

Baker, D. P., & Holsinger, D. B. (1996). Human capital formation and school expansion in Asia: Does a unique regional model exist? *International Journal of Comparative Sociology, 38*(1–2), 159–173.

Baptiste, I. (2001). Educating lone wolves: Pedagogical implications of human capital theory. *Adult Education Quarterly, 51*(3), 184–202.

Becker, G. S. (1964). *Human capital.* Princeton, NJ: Princeton University Press.

Benavot, A. (1989). Education, gender, and economic development: A cross-national study. *Sociology of Education, 62*(January), 14–32.

Bereday, G. Z. F. (1964). Theory and method: A general discussion. In: *Comparative method in education.* New York: Holt, Rinehart and Winston, Inc.

Brickman, W. W., & Fraser, S. E. (1968). Historical introduction. In: *History of international and comparative education* (pp. 1–19). Glenview, Ill.: Scott Foresman.

Burbules, N. C. (Ed.). (2003). *Educational Theory, 53*(4), 365–366.

Burbules, N. C., & Torres, C. A. (Eds) (2000). *Globalization and education: Critical perspectives.* New York: Routledge.

Burrell, G., & Morgan, G. (1979). *Sociological paradigms and organizational analysis.* London: Heinemann.

Cameron, K. S., & Quinn, R. E. (1999). *Diagnosing and changing organizational culture: Based on the competing values framework.* Reading, MA: Addison-Wesley.

Carling, A. H. (1992). *Social divisions.* London: Verso.

Coleman, A. S. (2002). Scientific models as works. *Cataloging & Classification Quarterly, 33* (3–4), 129–159.

Coleman, J. S. (1973). *The mathematics of collective action.* London: Heinemann.

Cummings, W. K. (1999). The institutions of education: Compare, compare, compare!. *Comparative Education Review, 43*(4), 413–437.

de la Campa, R. (1999). *Latin Americanism.* Minneapolis: University of Minnesota Press.

DiMaggio, P., & Powell, W. (Eds) (1991). *The new institutionalism in organizational analysis.* Chicago: University of Chicago Press.

Dyer, C., & Choksi, A. (1998). Education is like wearing glasses: Nomads' views of literacy and empowerment. *Journal of International Educational Development, 18*(5), 405–413.

Easterly, W. (2001). The failure of development. *Financial Times,* July 4, p. 13.

Eliasoph, N., & Lichterman, P. (2003). Culture in interaction. *American Journal of Sociology, 108*(4), 735–794.

Epstein, E. H. (1994). Comparative and international education: Overview and historical development. In: T. N. Postlethwaite & T. Hus (Eds), *International encyclopedia of education* (pp. 918–923). New York: Pergamon.

Epstein, E. H. (2002). The introductory course in comparative education. Panel discussion at the *Annual conference of the comparative and international education society*, Orlando, FL, March 7, 2002.

Fligstein, N., & Mara-Drita, I. (1996). How to make a market: reflections on the attempt to create a single market in the European Union. *American Journal of Sociology, 102*(1), 1–33.

Fraser, S. E., & Brickman, W. W. (Eds) (1968). *A history of international and comparative education*. Boston: Scott, Foresman and Co.

Freire, P. (2001). *Pedagogy of the oppressed* (M. B. Ramos, Trans. 30th anniversary ed.). New York: Continuum.

Garfinkel, H. (1967). *Studies in ethnomethodology*. Englewood Cliffs, NJ: Prentice-Hall.

Geertz, C. (1975). Thick description. In: C. Geertz (Ed.), *The interpretation of cultures*. London: Hutchinson.

Geertz, C. (1988). *Works and lives: The anthropologist as author*. Stanford, California: Stanford University Press.

Giles, J. (2004). Overseas aid policy needs better science input, inquiry finds. *Nature, 429*(6991), 492.

Giordan, A. (1989). The importance of modelling in the teaching and popularization of science. *Impact of Science on Society, 164*, 321–338.

Glassman, J. (2003). The spaces of economic crisis: Asia and the reconfiguration of Neo-Marxist crisis theory. *Studies in Comparative International Development, 37*(4), 31–63.

Gleick, J. (1988). *Chaos: Making a new science*. New York: Penguin.

Hammersley, M. (1992). *What's wrong with ethnography?*. New York: Routledge.

Hans, N. A. (1961). *Comparative education: A study of educational factors and traditions* (3rd ed.). London: Routlidge & K. Paul.

Hanson, M. E. (1981). Field research methodology for the study of Latin American ministries of education. *International Review of Education, 27*(3), 247–270.

Harding, S. (1986). *The science question in feminism*. Ithaca, NY: Cornell University Press.

Harding, S. (1991). *Whose science? Whose knowledge? Thinking from women's lives*. Ithaca, NY: Cornell University Press.

Harding, S. (1998). *Is science multi-cultural? Postcolonialisms, feminisms, and epistemologies*. Bloomington, Indiana: Indiana University Press.

Harris, S. R. (2004). Challenging the conventional wisdom: Recent proposals for the interpretive study of inequality. *Human Studies, 27*(2), 113–136.

Hassan, I. (2001). From postmodernism to postmodernity. *Philosophy and Literature, 25*(1), 1925–1940.

Hassan, I. (2003). Beyond postmodernism: Toward an aestheic of trust. *Journal of the Theoretical Humanities, 8*(1), 3–11.

Heylighen, F. (1999). The necessity of theoretical constructs. *Journal of Memetics – Evolutionary models of information transmission, 3*(1), 40–46.

Hirsch, P. M. (1997). Sociology without social structure: Neoinstitutional theory meets brave new world. *American Journal of Sociology, 102*(6), 1702–1723.

Holmes, B. (1958). The problem approach in comparative education: Some methodological considerations. *Comparative Education Review, 2*, 3–8.

Holmes, B. (1984). Paradigm shifts in comparative education. *Comparative Education Review*, 28, 584–604.

Hull, D. L. (1988). *Science as a process: An evolutionary account of the social and conceptual development of science*. Chicago: University of Chicago Press.

Husserl, E. (1970). *The crisis of European sciences and transcendental phenomenology: An introduction to phenomenological philosophy* (D. Carr, Trans.). Evanston, IL: Northwestern University Press.

Johnson, A. G. (2000). *The Blackwell dictionary of sociology* (2nd ed.). Malden, Massachusetts: Blackwell Publishers Inc.

Kandel, I. L. (1933). *Comparative education*. Boston: Houghton Mifflin Company.

Kandel, I. L. (1955). The content and method of comparative education. In: *The new era in education: A comparative study* (pp. 3–17). Boston: The Riverside Press Cambridge.

Kant, I. (1788). *Critique of practical reason*. In: L. W. Beck (Trans.). Upper Saddle River, NJ: Prentice-Hall.

Kellner, D. (1995). *Media culture: Cultural studies, identity, and politics between the modern and the postmodern*. New York: Routledge.

Kellner, D., & Durham, M. G. (Eds) (2001). *Media and cultural studies key works*. Malden, Mass.: Blackwell Publishers.

Kiel, L. D. (1991). Lessons from the nonlinear paradigm: Applications of the theory of dissipative structures in the social sciences. *Social Science Quarterly*, 72(3), 431–442.

Kong, L. H. (2000). *The viewpoint of Zhu Xi philosophy under the relation of confucianism and taoism*. Taipei: Chinese Taoism Press.

Kuhn, T. S. (1996). *The structure of scientific revolutions* (3rd ed.). Chicago: University of Chicago Press.

Lehrer, R. (1998). Models as explanations. *Issues in Education*, 4(1), 121–123.

Little, A. W. (2003). Motivating learning and the development of human capital. *Compare*, 33(4), 437–452.

Liu, G. Y. (2000). *Zhuang–Tzu and Lao–Tzu: Two key philosophers of taoism*. Taipei: Xue Fu Culture Press.

Marginson, S., & Mollis, M. (2001). Theories and reflexivities of comparative education. *Comparative Education Review*, 45(4), 581–615.

Marshall, A. (1890/1930). *Principles of economics* (8th ed.). London: Macmillan.

Marx, K. (1887). *Capital* (S. Moore & E. Aveling, Trans. 1st ed. in English). London: Swan Sonnenschein, Lowrey, & Co.

Masemann, V. (1990). Ways of knowing: Implications for comparative education. *Comparative Education Review*, 34(4), 463–473.

McNamee, M. (2001). The guilt of whistle-blowing: Conflicts in action research and ethnography. *Journal of Philosophy of Education*, 35(3), 423–441.

Metcalfe, L. (April 1997). *Flexible federalism*. Paper presented at the *Civil service systems in comparative perspective conference*. Bloomington: Indiana University.

Meyer, J. W. (1994). Rationalized environments. In: W. R. Scott & J. W. Meyer (Eds), *Institutional environments and organizations* (pp. 55–80). Thousand Oaks, CA: Sage.

Meyer, J. W., Boli, J., Thomas, G., & Ramirez, F. O. (1997). World society and the nation state. *American Journal of Sociology*, 103(1), 144–181.

Meyer, J. W., & Hannan, M. T. (Eds) (1979). *National development and the world system: Educational, economic, and political change, 1950–1970*. Chicago: The University of Chicago Press.

Meyer, J. W., Kamens, D. H., & Benavot, A. (1992). *School knowledge for the masses: World models and national primary curricular categories in the 21st Century.* London: Falmer.

Meyer, J. W., & Rowan, B. (1977). Institutionalized organizations: Formal structure as myth and ceremony. *American Journal of Sociology, 83,* 340–363.

Mill, J. S. (1859/1869). *On liberty.* London: Longman, Roberts, & Green.

Moravcsik, A. (1995). Liberal intergovernmentalism and integration: A rejoinder. *Journal of Common Market Studies, 33*(4), 611–628.

Morrow, R. A., & Torres, C. A. (1995). *Social theory and education: A critique of theories of social and cultural reproduction.* Albany, New York: State University of New York Press, Albany.

Morton, W. S. (1995). *China: Its history and culture.* New York: McGraw–Hill.

Ninnes, P., & Burnett, G. (2003). Comparative education research: Poststructuralist possibilities. *Comparative Education, 39*(3), 279–298.

Noah, H. J., & Eckstein, M. A. (1969). *Towards a science of comparative education.* London: Macmillan.

Nylander, J. (2001). The construction of a market: A frame analysis of the liberalization of the electricity market in the European Union. *European Studies, 3*(3), 289–314.

Ogbu, J. U., Sato, N. E., & Kim, E.-Y. (1994). Ethnography of education: anthropological approach. In: T. N. Postlethwaite & T. Hus (Eds), *International encyclopedia of education* (pp. 2046–2053). Oxford: Pergamon.

O'Neil, J. (1995). On schools as learning organizations: A conversation with Peter Senge. *Educational Leadership, 52*(7), 20–23.

Pagels, H. (1988). *The dream of reason.* New York: Simon and Shuster.

Parsons, T. (1937). *The structure of social action.* New York: McGraw–Hill.

Paulston, R. G. (1977). Social and educational change: Conceptual frameworks. *Comparative Education Review, 21*(June/October), 370–395.

Paulston, R. G. (1980). Education as anti-structure: Nonformal education in social and ethnic movements. *Comparative Education, 16*(1), 55–66.

Paulston, R. G. (1990). From paradigm wars to disputatious community. *Comparative Education Review, 34*(3), 395–400.

Paulston, R. G. (1992). Comparative education as an intellectual field: mapping the theoretical landscape. Paper presented at the *VIIth world congress of comparative education,* Prague, Czechoslovakia: Charles University.

Paulston, R. G. (1993a). *Mapping knowledge perspectives in studies of social and educational change.* Pittsburgh, Pennsylvania: University of Pittsburgh.

Paulston, R. G. (1993b). Ways of seeing education and social change in Latin America: A phenomenographic perspective. *Latin American Research Review, 28*(1), 177–202.

Paulston, R. G. (1994). Comparative and international education: Paradigms and theories. In T. N. Postlethwaite & T. Hus (Eds), *International Encyclopedia of Education* (2nd ed. pp. 923–933). Oxford: Pergamon.

Paulston, R. G. (1999). Mapping comparative education after postmodernity. *Comparative Education Review, 43*(4), 438–463.

Paulston, R. G. (2000). Imagining comparative education: Past, present, and future. *Compare, 30*(3), 353–367.

Paulston, R. G. (Ed.) (1996). *Social cartography: Mapping ways of seeing social and educational change* (Vol. 1024). New York: Garland Publishing.

Popper, K. (1959). *The logic of scientific discovery.* London: Hutchinson.

Quinn, R. E., & McGrath, M. R. (1985). The transformation of organizational cultures: A competing values perspective. In: P. J. Frost, L. F. Moore, M. L. Louis, C. C. Lundberg & J. Martin (Eds), *Organizational culture* (pp. 315–334). Beverly Hills, CA: Sage.

Radford, M. (2003). Contemporary perspectives on educational research. *Canterbury Papers, 3*(1).

Ritzer, G., & Goodman, D. J. (2004). *Sociological theory* (6th ed.). Boston, Mass.: McGraw–Hill.

Rossiter, C. (1982). *Conservatism in America*. Cambridge, MA: Harvard University Press.

Rothenberg, A. (1979). *The emerging goddess: The creative process in art, science, and other fields*. Chicago: University of Chicago Press.

Rust, V. D. (1991). Postmodernism and its comparative education implications. *Comparative Education Review, 35*, 610–626.

Rust, V. D. (2000a). Educational reform: Who are the radicals? In: N. P. Stromquist & K. Monkman (Eds), *Globalization and education: Integration and contestation across cultures* (pp. 63–76). Lanham: Rowman & Littlefield Publishers, Inc.

Rust, V. D. (2000b). The meaning of comparative in comparative education. Paper presented at the *CIES western regional conference*, Brigham Young University, Provo, Utah.

Rust, V. D. (January 2003). Method, methodology, and epistemology in comparative education. Paper presented at the *Comparative and international education western regional conference*, University of Hawaii.

Rust, V. D. (March 2004). Postmodernism and globalization: The state of the debate. Paper presented at the *Comparative and international education society annual conference*, Salt Lake City, Utah.

Rust, V. D., Soumaré, A., Pescador, O., & Shibuya, M. (1999). Research strategies in comparative education. *Comparative Education Review, 43*(1), 86–109.

Samoff, J. (1999). Education sector analysis in Africa: Limited national control and even less national ownership. *International Journal of Educational Development, 19*(4–5), 249–272.

Scatamburlo-D'Annibale, V., & McLaren, P. (2004). Class dismissed? Historical materialism and the politics of 'Difference'. *Educational Philosophy & Theory, 36*(2), 183–199.

Scott, D. (2000). Rational choice theory. In: G. Browning, A. Halcli & F. Webster (Eds), *Understanding contemporary society: Theories of the present*. London: Sage Publications.

Scott, W. R. (1995). *Institutions and organizations: Theory and research*. Thousand Oaks, CA: Sage Publications.

Senge, P. M. (1990). *The fifth discipline: The art and practice of the learning organization*. New York: Currency Doubleday.

Senge, P. M., Cambron-McCabe, N., Lucas, T., Smith, B., Dutton, J., & Kleiner, A. (2000). *Schools that learn: A fifth discipline fieldbook for educators, parents, and everyone who cares about education*. New York: Currency Doubleday.

Shultz, T. W. (1961). Investment in human capital. *The American Economic Review, 51*(1), 1–17.

Small, H. (2003). Paradigms, citations and maps of science: A personal history. *Journal of the American Society for Information Science and Technology, 54*(5), 394–399.

Smith, A. (1776). *An inquiry into the nature and causes of the wealth of nations*. London: Printed for W. Strahan; & T. Cadell, in the Strand.

Smith, A. (2004). Education, conflict and international development. *Adults Learning, 15*(5), 7–9.

So, A. Y. (1990). *Social change and development: Modernization, dependency, and world-systems theories*, Vol. 178. London: Sage Publications.

Southgate, B. (1996). *History: What & why? Ancient, modern, and postmodern perspectives*. London: Routledge.

Stocklmayer, S., & Gilbert, J. K. (2002). New experiences and old knowledge: towards a model for the personal awareness of science and technology. *International Journal of Science Education, 24*(8), 835–858.

Stone Sweet, A., & Sandholtz, W. (1998). Integration, supranational governance, and the institutionalization of the European policy. In: A. Stone Sweet & W. Sandholtz (Eds), *European integration and supranational governance*. Oxford: Oxford University Press.

Sweetland, S. R. (1996). Human capital theory: Foundations of a field of inquiry. *Review of Educational Research, 66*(3), 341–360.

Thomas, R. M. (1998). *Conducting educational research: A comparative view*. Westport, CT: Bergin and Garvey.

Tilky, L., & Crossley, M. (2001). Teaching comparative and international education: A framework for analysis. *Comparative Education Review, 45*(4), 561–580.

Torres, C. A. (1998). *Democracy, education, and multiculturalism*. Lanham, Maryland: Rowman & Littlefield Publishers, Inc.

Toulmin, S. E. (1972). *Human understanding*. Oxford: Clarendon Press.

Valverde, G. A. (2004). Curriculum convergence in Chile: The global and local context of reforms in curriculum policy. *Comparative Education Review, 48*(2), 174–201.

Velasco, A. (2002). Dependency theory. *Foreign Policy, Nov–Oct 2002(133)*, 44–45.

Wacquant, L. J. D. (1985). Heuristic models in marxian theory. *Social Forces, 64*, 17–45.

Weber, M. (1968). Conceptual Exposition. In: G. Roth & C. Wittich (Eds), *Economy and Society*, Vol. 1 (pp. 212–254). New York: Bedminister Press.

Welch, A. & Burns, R. J. (1992). Introduction. In: R. J. Burns & A. Welch (Eds), *Contemporary perspectives in comparative education*. New York: Garland Publishing.

Wiarda, H. J. (1999). Toward consensus in interpreting Latin American politics: Developmentalism, dependency, and the Latin American tradition. *Studies in Comparative International Development, 34*(2), 50–69.

Yang, L. B. (2002). *Chinese classic interpretation: Taoism*. Taipei: Himalayan Publishers.

GLOBAL PERSPECTIVES FOR TEACHER EDUCATION

Diane G. Gal

Incorporating global perspectives into American teacher education programs has grown with some success over the past decades. (Banks, 2001b; Gutek, 1993; Merryfield, 1997; Spring, 1998) Generally, the goals of global education are to help students develop multiple perspectives, cultural consciousness, intercultural competencies, respect for human rights and dignity, and to combat prejudice and discrimination. However, there remain different conceptualizations of global education and alternate approaches to infusing it into teacher education programs (Merryfield, 1997; Tye & Tye, 1992). Despite "definitional ambiguities," global education is viewed as useful to teachers "in guiding [students] in their 21st century journey to shape a more peaceful world." (Kirkwood, 2001). Related, but less successfully incorporated into teacher preparation programs is consideration of how the process of globalization impacts our lives and our educational endeavors. Here, globalization is understood as a process of change in economic, political, and cultural arenas and is characterized by an increasing world-wide interconnection that is seen as alternately beneficial and harmful.

September 11, 2001 brought most Americans to a point of dramatic disorientation, not least of all about the role of teachers and the nature of their education. Prior to September 11, Americans were, like the townspeople in Goethe's Faust "talking at the front gate about war and murder far behind, far away..." Now, they wonder if they are ready and able to meet the

Global Trends in Educational Policy
International Perspectives on Education and Society, Volume 6, 259–287
Copyright © 2005 by Elsevier Ltd.
All rights of reproduction in any form reserved
ISSN: 1479-3679/doi:10.1016/S1479-3679(04)06010-4

challenges that have hastened through their front gate. Engaging prospective teachers in considering big picture issues and how they relate to their daily lives and teaching practices is imperative. Further, the field of comparative and international education is well positioned to meet these needs for teachers in both Western industrialized and developing countries. The focus of this chapter will be on the circumstances and opportunities for incorporating discussions and practical response to issues related to globalization in teacher education programs through the revitalization of college level teacher preparation courses. Coming to grips with this issue is no less timely for countries around the world, as they are all grappling, in their own ways, with the varied impacts of globalizing forces. For example, Brazil continues to search for ways of bridging the income and education gaps between areas like Bahia and Sao Paulo. India has turned to new forms of distance learning for teachers who are motivated to serve in remote, rural areas. Poland seeks to better align its teacher preparation with European standards and expectations for a democracy. Considering the current circumstances of the United States, Brazil, India, and Poland stimulates our thinking about how different landscapes of social and educational needs still reflect similar human aspirations. While teacher education continues to be narrowly defined, expectations of teachers are growing, and they should be offered avenues to consider broader issues that impact their lives and their work. These countries offer examples of different avenues through which teachers can develop global perspectives. The United States, Brazil, and India represent democratic countries from different world regions that have large and diverse populations in terms of race, ethnicity, economic levels, and religion. Poland is ethnically and religiously quite homogenous, yet offers an interesting experience of a society in transition to democracy. With their recent acceptance into the European Union, they are poised for a change in demographics as well.

The ongoing challenge of colleges of education and professional organizations has been to agree on what prospective teachers must need to know and do in order to teach in changing, diverse communities. Their overriding concern is of how best to prepare teachers for 21st century diverse and democratic societies. However, the accepted knowledge and skills set for prospective teachers is still narrowly defined in most countries, and leaves very little room to engage in reflective discussions on individual and collective engagement with an accelerating process of globalization. It is precisely at this time, when we have been dramatically reminded of our intimate, but not particularly romantic connectedness with the world that discussions are necessary on how to prepare motivated individuals both to teach, and to be activists in their communities.

Recent events, although tragic, represent an opportunity to find ways of coming to terms with the knowledge that is most important for school children to learn, an individual and collective identity, and the obligations to act in a democracy. More specifically, we are compelled to re-imagine our work as teachers. One important avenue to begin this process is through courses that should be offered in teacher education programs. Scholars with specializations in comparative and international education are especially well suited to bring a crucial element into the discussion: global perspectives on the nature of knowledge, different viewpoints on the nature and impact of globalization, and a critical lens on the current standards, accountability and performance model of education that dominates Western policy discourse, and is so prevalently exported to less developed societies via international aid organizations, including the IMF and World Bank.

This chapter begins by defining global education, the process of globalization and how they have been linked to the provision of teacher education. The discussion then turns to the various teacher education programs that are emerging in different countries. This is followed by consideration of the ways by which emerging theories and research in the field of comparative and international education can support and enrich these programs. Throughout, the interplay between larger processes of globalization and specific educational experiences of new teachers is discussed. This interplay takes on some urgency just now, as social and political calamities are no longer passively observed via media as they occur some place "far away." As a result, we have come to the uncomfortable point of revisiting our deepest convictions about ourselves, about living in democracies, and about taking action in the world, both individually and collectively.

GLOBAL EDUCATION AND GLOBALIZATION

"Global education involves (1) the study of problems and issues which cut across national boundaries and the interconnectedness of cultural, environmental, economic, political, and technological systems and (2) the cultivation of cross-cultural understanding, which includes development of the skill of "perspective-taking," that is, being able to see life from someone else's point of view. Global perspectives are important at every grade level, in every curricular subject area, and for all children and adults.

(Tye & Tye, 1992)

The literature generally suggests that the best way to infuse global perspectives into teacher education programs is by modeling pedagogy through the use of not just readings and lectures, but role plays, case studies, and collaborative investigation of useful resources among colleagues. Merryfield (1997) sets out methods for pedagogy for global perspectives that include exploration of self-knowledge, cross-cultural experiences and skills, perspective consciousness, values analysis, and authentic learning. Given the wide range and capacities for educating large numbers of new teachers in many countries, infusing global perspectives into otherwise technically oriented training programs is often poorly managed.

Nonetheless, the OECD characterizes teachers as "professionals, role models and community leaders," who are asked to "manage the far reaching changes that are taking place in and outside of schools." (OECD, 2001, p. 9). Professional organizations like the American Association of Colleges of Teacher Education have acknowledged the impact of globalization, and have commented on the need to attend to the increasing plurality of values, issues, and players in the world arena. It is hard to determine how many colleges of education are actively taking up this call to arms and incorporating global perspectives in any consistent way into their programs. However, American schools that seek accreditation with organizations like the National Council for the Accreditation of Teacher Education (NCATE, 1994) are bound to their guidelines which value and define global education as "the viewpoint that accepts the interdependency of nations and peoples and the interlinkage of political, economic, and ecological and social issues of a transnational and global nature." (N. C. f. A. o. T. Education, 1994). According to NCATE, accredited colleges of teacher education must adjust their programs and ensure to impart appropriate knowledge and to model effective teaching (especially to students of diverse backgrounds) in order to meet the needs of our new economy, and information society.

There are plenty of studies that show that student performance in learning basic skills increases when teachers complete accredited education programs and are fully licensed. (Darling-Hammond, 1992, 2002; N. C. f. A. o. T. Education, 2001; Wenglinsky, 2000) Few would argue against prospective teachers learning both content knowledge and specific methods that have proven to get students reading, writing, and computing. However, teachers' preparation should not preclude engagement in a dialogue about broader issues. Indeed, on the surface, it is hard to disagree with NCATE's statement that "student learning must mean not only basic skills but also the knowledge and skills necessary to succeed as a responsible citizen and contributor to the new economy." (N. C. f. A. o. T. Education, 2001). This, however, leaves open to interpretation what constitutes a responsible citizen and whether the new economy is viewed as viable or desirable from any number of different perspectives.

The underlying tensions of such rhetoric may never be explored by new teachers who face multiple challenges like failing urban schools in America, poor rural villages in Brazil and India, and ideologically different generations of students in Poland. Often valued more for their willingness to adopt and unquestioningly follow rigid curriculum guidelines, discipline procedures or teaching behaviors (like drilling and following scripted dialogues or timed curriculum blocks), teachers in these settings are pressed into the service of doing what is most often antithetical to engaging in practices that are true to their own reflective convictions and philosophies of education. What these new teachers identify, through their own experiences, are difficult social and economic problems that continue to thwart their best efforts and intentions even if they are well educated and certified.

We should engage future teachers in considering what connections can be made between global perspectives in education and the conceptualization and experience of globalization both at home and around the world. Globalization is understood as an emerging pattern of interconnectedness in not only the economic realm, but in social, cultural, technological, environmental, and health arenas. These new ways of connecting and interacting shape national and local public policy agendas, including education, since it influences how we generate meaning and concepts around schooling, and the role and education of teachers. For example, Smyth and Shacklock charge that one result of globalization is that our schools increasingly serve the needs of economic growth and are less concerned with improving society.

"The role and function of education are undergoing dramatic changes in response to these economic imperatives. The notion of a broad liberal education is struggling for its very survival in a context of instrumentalism and technocratic rationality where the catchwords are 'vocationalism,' 'skills formation,' 'privatization,' 'commodification,' and 'managerialism'." (Smyth & Shacklock, 1998).

Indeed, prevailing policies for teacher education in Brazil focus on raising the quality and quantity of teachers' knowledge and skills. In order to meet their immediate need for better qualified teachers, Brazil has created alternative routes to certify large numbers of teachers as quickly as possible. In addition to distance education providers and private teacher preparation institutions, broader based organizations like the Landless Workers' Movement have stepped into the role of teacher educator. (Diniz-Pereira, 2002)

The Landless Workers' Movement provides 2,800 rural school teachers with an education that encompasses not just technical skills, but professional preparation that is linked to political and cultural activism. While teaching knowledge, skills, behavior, and attitudes necessary for teaching subjects, they link discussion and action research with bigger picture issues in an effort to help teachers identify and change local social problems. Collaborative teacher research in schools and communities can lead to important social reform in some contexts (Diniz-Pereira, 2002).

Some see the underlying assumptions and overt consequences of globalization as full of opportunities for personal economic improvement, technological advancement, and a worldwide political coming together with all boats rising. The role of education in this case is to provide appropriately educated workers to support this vision. Others see globalization as a threatening phenomena that aggravates the economic and educational marginalization of the already disenfranchised. For them, education and teachers should resist what globalization represents and must act to change the tide that only buoys the boats of the already advantaged.

On the economic level, globalization impacts employment opportunities and the goal of education gets restricted to the changing needs of the workforce, and a new information economy that feeds off a consumer mentality. On the political level, we must contend with the unnerving sense that, in the face of terrorism, a democratic nation-state's government is limited in how it can respond without fundamentally challenging the values upon which it exists. In schools, teachers' roles in explaining this while assuaging fears goes far beyond the need to pump basic facts and skills into the future workforce.

On the cultural level, general populations in many countries are rapidly becoming more diverse, and this is reflected in schools. In these settings, education plays a crucial role in forming personal and community (or civic) identities. A major thrust of schooling must be to foster respect and tolerance of other cultures, races, ethnicities, and to live together peacefully by finding common ground within differences, by developing a sense of interdependence. (Banks, 2001a). Teachers, and teacher educators by extension, are simultaneously enmeshed in the processes of globalization, while they are positioned (and morally obligated) to think and act on its effects, such that all children are engaged in meaningful and nurturing educational experiences. This is particularly poignant at a time when teachers are called upon to suspend their race to test skills and to attend to the physical and psychological needs of children directly threatened by dramatic events like

September 11 as well as more subtle shifts in local circumstances as a result of globalization.

> "As experienced from below, the dominant form of globalization means a historical transformation: in the economy, of livelihoods and modes of existence; in politics, a loss in the degree of control exercised locally – for some, however, little to begin with – such that the locus of power gradually shifts in varying proportions above and below the territorial state; and in culture, a devaluation of a collectivity's achievements or perceptions of them. This structure, in turn, may engender either accommodation or resistance. Most agents acquiesce, but others attempt to write a script that embraces macroeconomic growth processes and new technologies while linking them to social equity and reform programs.
>
> (Mittelman, 2000)

As more people come forward to teach the most disadvantaged and disenfranchised in urban centers and remote rural villages around the world, we must ask whether they are guided to acquiesce to given circumstances, or encouraged to "write a script" based on considered, moral, and humane motivation.

ENGAGING THOSE MOTIVATED TO TEACH

Between 1990 and 1997, the total number of teachers working in formal education sites at all levels worldwide increased from 52 million to 59 million – 2/3 of them in the developing world.[1] Demand for qualified teachers in the next decades will continue to increase, and this will impact teacher recruitment and education around the globe. Brazil's major challenge will be to raise the level of qualifications among the teaching force. For example, fewer than 22% of primary teachers hold tertiary qualifications. (OECD, 2001) Similarly, in Poland, significant numbers of teachers are already working without necessary qualifications. As a result, in the last decade, Poland's education policies have focused on in service preparation of teachers. Polish educators continue to struggle with establishing coherent content and methods for pre service and in service teacher education programs, and finding ways to coordinate the work of higher education institutions and schools (Nagy, 2000). The National Center for Education Statistics estimates that American public schools will need between 1.7 and 2.4 million new teachers by 2008–2009, mostly in poor inner cities (Hussar, 2001). For the last two decades, India has experimented with various means of training millions of teachers so that they can meet their goal of universal primary education.

Despite their different contexts, each of these countries are presently faced with the challenge of educating those who are motivated to teach. Although policy documents often express high expectations of teachers while lamenting the poor quality of teacher education programs, there has been a broad trend toward setting standards for the required knowledge, skills, and dispositions that teachers must possess in order to best serve students' needs for the 21st century. Each country offers examples of how large numbers of teachers can be both trained with technical skills, and educated to become engaged actors in their own contexts.

For more than two decades, India has been experimenting with various means of educating teachers in order to meet its goal of universal primary education. Their challenge has been to ensure their more than 4.3 million teachers are qualified to teach, especially the many disadvantaged children in remote rural areas. India anticipates significant growth in the near future with particular need for qualified elementary school teachers willing to work in these areas (Gulati, 1999). Recent national education policy has emphasized pre service and in service education and the solidification of infrastructure for education and research at national, state, and local levels. The National Council for Teacher Education was established in 1995 and is responsible for planning and assessment, and setting standards for teacher education programs and institutions. However, some autonomy and discretion for planning and managing educational services at local levels have been given to District Institutes of Education and Training.

Some of the most innovative possibilities for improving the quality and quantity of teacher education have been via distance education in India. The Indira Ghandhi National Open University has collaborated to offer a comprehensive program granting a Diploma in Primary Education through distance format, incorporating "self-study print materials, audio and video programs, theoretical and activity-oriented assignment, tutorials and academic counseling, contact sessions and internships, radio and TV broadcasts and teleconferencing." (Gulati, 1999).

Since 1998, other pilot programs for in service primary teacher training using interactive technology have been underway in collaboration with the Government of India, UNESCO, and the International Telecommunication Union, providing content knowledge and models of pedagogical skills to teachers in remote areas. Although at present there is less focus on professional development in terms of engaging in discussion about the role education plays in building a sense of community among diverse cultures, languages, and traditions (Rajput & Walia, 2001) there is room for expanding the experience now that the infrastructure is in place.

There are other hopeful signs in smaller projects that involve teachers in broader discussions and in potentially planning new programs or policies relevant to their contexts in India. For example, the Global Initial Teacher Education project links teacher education institutes in India, Kenya, and England to discuss the interrelationship of "local and global social issues," and how they are connected to their school curriculum and teaching practices (Inbaraj, Kumar, Sambili, & Scott-Bauman, 2003). Although focused on gender issues, and without practical influence on the policy level, it is a good example of how growing distance education infrastructure can serve the purpose of expanding teachers' global perspectives. Other recent initiatives to engage teachers in collaborative research as part of their in service teacher education have been introduced through several District Institutes of Education and Training in recent years. Teachers' response has been positive as the process involved working "with" rather than "on" or "about" them, and asked them to "probe and illuminate the complex social realities in which teaching and learning are embedded." (Dyer & Choksi, 2002).

Brazil's recent educational policies have been aimed at improving enrollment and retention of students, and raising the level of qualifications among the teaching force. The OECD estimates that between 58% and 78% of currently employed primary school teachers have not completed college level education (OECD, 2001). This may partly be a result of previous policy that gave elementary school teachers the option of earning degrees either at the college level, or at the secondary level with added teacher training coursework. However, this option will be phased out in the next few years.

Despite recent shifts in devolving authority over educational decision making from central to state and local levels, there is an increasing government influence over defining the standards and assessments for teachers' knowledge and competencies. In the late 1990s, the Brazilian government confirmed the need to educate primary school teachers at higher levels and established that their education can and should continue in higher education institutions outside the regular university system. This was partially in response to the growing concern that the university programs were overly theoretical and did not meet the practical needs of teachers. In addition, the government was pressed to quickly and efficiently solve the problem of school dropouts which ultimately affected social and economic productivity. As a result, alternative routes for teacher certification were created, such as distance education options, a variety of in service certification programs, and private teacher preparation institutes.

Most of these alternatives meet the need to develop technical, or practical classroom teaching skills, but only some routes have emerged that educate more broadly, like the program developed as part of the Landless Workers' Movement. Almost 3000 teachers working in more than 1000 schools, grades 1–8 participated in the past few years. This teacher education program covered technical preparation while at the same time engaged teachers in political and cultural issues that impact their work and daily lives. While learning the skills and knowledge necessary for their daily work, teachers considered bigger picture issues in order to identify problems and avenues for change. Specifically, they learned to conduct collaborative research and create action plans for their schools and their communities (Diniz-Pereira & Emilio, 2002).

Freire's work in Sao Paulo with 33,000 teachers during the early 1990s is another promising example of creating spaces for teachers to consider global issues and how they relate to their specific contexts. As head of the Municipal Department of Education in Sao Paulo during the tenure of the Workers' Party, Friere expected teachers to actively participate in curriculum development and to collaborate with peers, students, and families – all activities that were contrary to their previous experience with directives and set curricular materials. The program activities required teachers to critically examine their own lives and work in relation to the disadvantaged families and children they served. It was a comprehensive teacher education based on experiencing, reflection, dialogue, reading, research, and curriculum development in order to "reorient teachers' attitudes and behaviors and developing new pedagogy and understanding." (Wong, 1995). There have been reports of mixed results, largely because teachers were unaccustomed to the new expectations and lacked the required skills and dispositions to participate effectively. However, the Interdisciplinary Project and Continuing Professional Education Groups serve as promising examples of re-envisioning teachers' work.

In a similar way, the more recent initiative called the Citizen School Project in the city of Porto Alegre has been established and developed by a broad range of constituents, including educators, community members, parents, and students. Based on principles of social justice, respect, and interpersonal relationships, the work focuses on serving the underprivileged children who are most often excluded from educational opportunities due to poverty and failure. Through various activities and seminars, teachers are supported in developing new roles, responsibilities and skills in examining problems of the community within the curriculum (Gandin & Apple, 2004).

Globalization has influenced education policy in many countries with the result that schools are pressed to produce students who will be useful in the changing economic climate. As such, renewed national standards, curricula, and evaluation schemes have impacted the preparation and education of teachers in every global region. Yet, especially in large, diverse countries, national curricula and standards do not guarantee improved teaching and learning. Some argue that in Brazil, as a result of globalization and new policy initiatives, an "excluding educational project" is emerging which supports "teachers who should be creative without being critical and who are able to work in teams as long as they do not participate in collective bargaining nor promote union organization...they should be technically competent and politically less active." (Flores & Shiroma, 2003). Yet, clearly, there are examples of teacher education programs that do not constrain prospective and in service teachers in this way.

Poland's experience is useful to explore as an example of a post-communist transition society whose educational reforms have focused on developing democratic citizens. Poland's challenge has been to build democratic institutions while embracing new ideologies and habits of behavior in all aspects of social and political life. Schools, universities, and colleges of education have been among the most critical institutions Poland has had to reform in the last 15 years. Although the Ministry of National Education has changed teacher certification standards, the most difficult task has been changing the characteristic, didactic ways of thinking and teaching among teachers at all levels. Most Polish teachers are solid subject specialists, but few have the knowledge or skill to incorporate content with innovative pedagogy. Complicating matters, the OECD has characterized teacher training in Poland as "very fragmented" and, although diverse in content, limited in offerings that cover curriculum development, assessment, or innovative pedagogical styles (Nagy, 1998).

Cooperation between institutions of higher education and schools remains disjointed, leading to government efforts to provide finances and support for in service training to a variety of outside organizations that are less resistant to change and oversight of government initiatives. These alternative avenues for in service training offer services more quickly, and demonstrate benefits in schools more quickly as well. One result has been an increase in foreign interest and involvement in providing assistance in creating avenues through which teacher education can incorporate discussions of broader global issues and how they relate to teachers' work. This has been especially helpful for Poles who have had to overcome "mistrust in participation, and passivity toward conditions and events." (Putkiewicz, 1996).

One such collaborative effort between the Polish Ministry of National Education and the Ohio State University was "The School in a Democratic Society." This project addressed new ways of training pre service teachers as well as for training personnel on school organizational and operational issues relevant for a democracy (Hamot, 1998). A cohort of Polish educators trained with peers in the United States, and developed a draft syllabus for a sequence of college courses that would focus on the needs of their own changing context. Unit topics included consideration of teachers' roles, the school's connection with local communities, and the role of schools in democratic society. (Hamot, 1998) Other courses in university settings have begun to involve student teachers in educational research which can also become an avenue to "help candidates to teach as well as teachers to think independently about education." (Putkiewicz, 1996).

New York City is a leading example of how quickly teacher shortages impact the neediest urban schools in America. Those intrepid individuals who choose to pursue teaching as a profession in a city like New York can enter the profession via traditional or alternative routes. The more traditional routes include 4-year BA programs, MA programs, and fifth year certification. Among the growing alternative routes are Teach for America and the New York City Teaching Fellows Program. In fact, there has been a recent upsurge in applicants to teach in NYC schools. For example, in a 2001 New York Times article, Abby Goodnough reported that in September of that year, 5000 mid career changers applied for teaching jobs in NYC compared with 1250 the previous year (Goodnough, 2002). By 2003, the Teaching Fellows Program would accept 2400 prospective teachers from 20,000 applicants. In general, this would seem to be good news, but what remains troubling is not just Goodnough's reminder that economic refugees from technology and finance industries are now applying for teaching jobs in record numbers. Interest in teaching was reportedly driven by both the economic recession (and job losses) and the terrorist attacks which, according to many applicants' essays, gave many prospective teachers pause about their lives and what they were doing. While it was clear that most of these applicants for teaching positions would meet their bottom line need for a job, and so meet their economic motivation for pursuing a teaching job, it remains unclear what they could anticipate regarding their desire to re-examine their lives and their newly adopted profession.

Teach for America's (TFA) mission is to build a cadre of individuals who are motivated to make fundamental changes in schools and outside schools. TFA attracts bright, motivated college graduates who are willing to commit 2 years to working in a poorly performing urban school. In exchange, they remain connected with the TFA network and engage in periodic professional development activities. The thrust is to nurture these individuals' leadership so that they can address immediate educational challenges as well as the socio-economic circumstances in which so many urban children live. A recent evaluative study indicates that 96% of 317 principals polled feel that TFA teachers were advantageous to their schools and their students. (Raymond, Fletcher, & Luque, 2001) TFA's approach to carefully choosing college graduates to move through their alternative program is unique in that they explicitly look for and nurture individuals who approach the challenges of teaching in failing urban school holistically. In other words, they work with each TFA fellow in their tasks in the classroom but also nurture each fellow's capacity to take a leadership role in addressing the broader, socio-economic circumstances of the community. Much is expected of the fellows, and their work is worth watching.

The New York City Teaching Fellows Program attracts mid-career changers who are willing to work in the city's worst performing schools, and offers them support networks and financial assistance. After an intensive pre-service program, these fellows begin teaching and studying for their Masters degree from a college of education. This 4-year-old program has attracted much interest in New York, but has not yet been closely studied. However, each fellow does become part of a cohort that pass through a traditional teacher education program at a local college (Stein, 2002). Once in such a program, they most certainly will engage in a required educational foundations course.

The thrust of foundations courses is to grapple with big picture questions about education, and relate them to the daily realities of schools. The point is to contextualize teaching and learning, and study schools as institutions. Most often, the courses take a multidisciplinary approach and explore questions of educational provision, inequality, and change. Students begin working out their own educational philosophy, and consider the ways that social context influences the form and function of education in formal school settings, and in informal settings outside schools. Optimally, it serves as a framework for understanding schools, schooling, teachers' roles, and the relationship of school to society. Students gain an understanding of how problems in education are related to larger social, economic, and political issues. The Council of Learned Societies in Education (CLSE) states that the aim of foundations courses is to engage prospective teachers in "understand[ing] and respond[ing] to the social contexts that give meaning to education itself – both in and out of schools." (Education, C. o. L. S. i 1996). They go on to explain that teachers should demonstrate a "concern for cultural and educational consequences of present circumstances, events and conditions to respond to social issues and crises of the times." (Education, C. o. L. S. i. 1996). This could be an open invitation to comparative and international education researchers, poised to meet the needs of teachers who work in a most dramatically, changing, global environment, regardless of whether they are in New York City, Bombay or Bahia.

In the past decades, foundations courses in America have taken on multicultural and global perspectives with variable commitment. To illustrate, a brief review of three popular texts for foundations courses shows the different approaches to including global perspectives, or utilizing comparative and international education research. While each text has its own strength and unique approach, there is no consistency in how they incorporate or relate global issues, much less discussions of broad processes related to globalization in the economic, political, and cultural arenas. The point is that teachers should analyze violent events like September 11, as well as the numbing problems of urban neglect or rural isolation, and situate them in a global context. In this way, they are given a space to explore the problems of schooling in context, and to reflect on how it is related to the effects globalization has not just in the economy, but in politics, culture, and other arenas. As Britzman queries, "How does teacher education come to notice that the world matters?" (Britzman, 2000).

Exploring Education: An Introduction to Foundations of Education, by Sadovnik, Cookson, and Semel (2001) establishes that the study of foundations of education offers students the theories and empirical insights they need to incorporate their own experiences and perspectives to enhance critical literacy. Critical literacy is understood as the "ability to connect knowledge, theory, and research evidence to the everyday experiences of teaching," and thus, produce "reflective practitioners." (Sadovnik et al., 2001). The editors illustrate these theories and empirical studies by using primary sources from various books and journals, in addition to their own supplementary narrative. Incorporating global perspectives is clearly not a priority. They add a reprint of Stigler and Hiebert's (1999) TIMSS Videotape Study of 231 8th grade German, Japanese, and American math classes. This was tucked into their chapter on the structure of U.S. education, which focused on issues of governance and teacher professionalism. The point of the overall chapter is "to create a broad frame of reference that grounds the perceptions of education in their organizational and social realities." The structure of education for the United States is reviewed and compared to structures of education in Great Britain, France, the former Soviet Union, Japan, and Germany. Their narrative justifies the inclusion of these brief overviews as a means of comparing the relative "openness" of different school systems (are they educating mainly the elite or a broader population) and a means of glimpsing the way different countries express values through education.

McNergney and Herbert's (2001) *Foundations of Education: The Challenge of Professional Practice* offers brief comparisons between education in the United States and education in Canada, Mexico, Japan, India, U.K., Denmark, Singapore, and South Africa. Their treatment of these brief overviews goes beyond just comparing the school systems organizationally, and tries to add insights into "how others think", and the values and issues that are pertinent to other countries. Their justification for adding a chapter entitled Global and Comparative Education is to "enhance understanding of global interdependence," and to gain knowledge of diversity to enhance our teaching and professionalism. The authors add a review of the 1995 TIMSS study and indicate that they feel it represents a restrictive comparison, one that we must somehow move beyond to consider "activities in which we all engage that make us more alike than we are different from one another." However, they seem to restrict their own vision by going on to say "the real challenge for American public education is to educate workers today for careers and jobs they will fill tomorrow" (McNergney & Herbert, 2001). Multicultural understanding is important, it seems, as a means of educating students to participate more effectively with such multinational pacts as NAFTA, GATT, and the EU expansion.

Kincheloe, Slattery, and Steinberg (2000) take a completely different approach to foundations of education. Rather than stating or illustrating what already is, or even providing alternative primary sources that explore the details of various contemporary educational issues, this text is rooted in philosophy. The purpose of this text is to engage students in a "metaconversation about the nature of educational theory and practice. This process involves an exciting search for a new and better way of living in our complex and often confusing global society."(Kincheloe et al., 2000). The authors prod the student to consider how our postmodern condition is linked to elements of globalization in an adverse way, by "exaggerat[ing] the power of dominant elites."(Kincheloe et al., 2000) The historical, political, economic, and curricular considerations of American education are reviewed in such a way that student teachers engage in a "new way of making sense of and producing knowledge" and nurturing a sense of social justice. To understand the way events are shaped and the way history flows, we must first understand the "influence of information formats." (Kincheloe et al., 2000).

Incorporating global perspectives in foundations courses should include grappling with how the processes of globalization affect every facet of teachers' lives, and the lives of those less fortunate. Teachers should be engaged in sorting out educational policy and how it is enmeshed in social, political, and cultural environment. As envisioned in most scholarship on global perspectives, teachers must be prepared to respect and understand diverse perspectives, to teach diverse populations, and to recognize that the ways in which other countries organize their educational systems to reflect their values. But teacher education programs also need to help prospective teachers see how globalization's impact on the way we structure our lives potentially constrains the life chances and educational experiences of the disenfranchised.

It can certainly seem daunting to ask pre-service teachers to rethink the ways we organize our lives and the education of our children from a global perspective or to explore what globalization does and what we do in conjunction with this overarching process. Until recently, most prospective teachers might have thought that this is a rather useless mental exercise. Yet, since, September 11, it is, perhaps, the central and defining activity of our time, and teacher educators must find ways of incorporating such discussion into our programs.

This can be accomplished in a variety of ways. For example, TFA's alternative route to teaching may be limited to 8000 teachers nationwide. Yet, this organization is an example of redefining what a teacher is and what a teacher should be expected to do over a period of time both in schools and in communities. They expect that their college educated, alternately trained teachers explore their practice in such a way that it moves them from meeting the students' basic educational needs to meeting the broader social and economic challenges facing the children within their own communities. This approach is an example of tackling the complex problems of education starting with a vision of "writing a script" that resists the urge to conform.

At Teachers College's "Teach-In" hundreds of participants discussed not only how teachers can better help students deal with the immediate effects of September 11, but how Americans think about war, violence, and the effects of living in a "new global environment." Participants grappled over questions of how to balance civil and human rights, and how Americans envision a sense of community at this time of crisis. Appropriately, new teachers were given professional development credit for attending the workshop. Such workshops, whether considered professional development or informal discussions, provide crucial forums for self-exploration, and for building a sense of a community.

Yet, the far majority of America's future 2.4 million new teachers will first earn degrees at colleges of education. Therefore, incorporating discussion about globalization, its effects on our lives and our vision of education (among other considerations), should be a minimum requirement for foundations courses. Indeed, these courses typically explore the historical events that have shaped our education system, and the political, social, and philosophical arguments around the purpose of education. Optimally, these classes should allow for some critical examination of the conflicting viewpoints and outcomes of schooling in America. However, teacher educators must make room in such courses for the consideration of not only what is, or what has already transpired, but what might be.

On the political level, if globalization contributes to the ease with which terrorist acts are justified and carried out, teachers must grapple with this knowledge. They should be given forums to discuss their positive or negative feelings about schools' commitments and focus in times of crisis. Teachers should be asked to link the reality of the limits of democratic governments to protect its citizens, and the fears that children may still harbor for their safety. Related to this uneasy realization is the concern over giving up some civil rights for a sense of more security. Does this compromise our values as a democracy or change the way we interact in our society? These questions are not just for academics, philosophers, or social studies teachers to ponder – they are important questions for all of us.

The economic impact of globalization is most often linked to analyses of educational reform efforts. Spring (1998, 2004) argues that our educational system is set up to support and feed a market economy, while at the same time it is viewed as a way of solving problems like poverty that is exacerbated by an increasingly global market economy. On a more local level, teachers should be encouraged to explore how the official, seemingly common sense rhetoric for higher standards and a return to basics still translates to very different classroom and life experiences for children across the country. Some teachers in urban cities may find a position in a progressive school like Central Park East in New York City, or the Citizen School in Porto Alegre, where teachers' input and discretion on all school matters is expected. Some will find their schools rigidly enforcing drill, repetition, and scripted dialogues. The majority will work in schools that officials and the general public have deemed inadequate or failing to perform, based on national and international standardized test results. Prospective teachers must know this. They must be given an opportunity to engage in deliberating over what actions they can take to mitigate the effects of marginalizing the less fortunate even further.

McLaren and Farahmandpur (2001) suggest that prospective teachers might be asked to consider what a "working class revolutionary pedagogy" might look like in their own contexts. The aim of such pedagogy is to resist the economic effects of globalization by helping teachers and students develop critical consciousness and find strength to act in solidarity. It would "help students and workers recognize how their subjectivities and social identities are configured in ways that are structurally advantageous to the status quo." (McLaren & Farahmandpur, 2001). Prospective teachers are asked to interpret the dynamics of our society, and to suspend belief that our capitalist society is successful due to individual input. Rather, they are asked to consider the ways in which one person is successful by virtue of privilege while another person is constrained for lack of such privilege, which is often defined by race, class, and gender. McLaren and Farahmandpur (2001) see teachers as potential activists, who should teach in ways that raise student consciousness, get them politically active, and empower them to contribute to improving social conditions.

Public perception of teacher incompetence has historically beleaguered the profession that is in the habit of unconvincingly defending itself in the face of these charges. Yet the importance of giving prospective teachers space for being reflective of their personal, cultural, national, and global identities has been recognized. It is an important part of coming to an understanding of how knowledge is constructed and contextualized. It is also an important part of thinking about how and why we do things in schools, and how it might look different. Equally important is thinking about how and why we might collectively work toward different goals that do not necessarily meet the workforce needs of a globalized market economy that leaves unexamined the circumstances in which so many poor and minority children struggle to keep up, much less excel to higher standards.

In many countries, there is evidence of programs that attempt to address the knowledge and attitudes necessary for preparing to teach in multicultural school environments, especially in under-served areas. However, they are often not part of higher education institutions whose members are slow to change expectations and practices if they differ from prevailing policy prescriptions, or the cultural expectations of the general society, or the "communities with cultural authority to impose standards on their members." (Pickert, 2001). In today's policy climate, education policies and professional communities like the OECD, UNESCO, NCATE, and AACTE drive teacher education programs with only a cursory nod to the value that the field of comparative and international education could offer.

"New teachers need to be ready to learn and to act on what they learn, and they need to develop a professional ethos rooted in caring about children as well as in critical perspectives on education." (Lytle, 2000). The last is the crux of what teacher educators must animate for future teachers. Teachers should nurture students' visions of their future and understanding of their present context, as much as their abilities in internalizing the basics.

While current education policy trends acknowledge the increasing importance of "internationalizing" higher education, they offer few specific statements on how teacher preparation programs can engage its students to this end aside from ensuring they meet rigorous new standards.

As democracies in all world regions continue to become more diverse, fostering understanding and tolerance becomes imperative. Known for his scholarship on multiculturalism, Banks (2001a) continues to call on teachers to become global citizens, and to help students find ways to make meaningful change in the world. He expects teachers to understand how knowledge is constructed and is related to their social, political, and economic contexts. In addition, he charges teachers with the task of helping students produce and use knowledge to take action. He re-envisions citizenship education as multicultural citizenship education. Banks argues that in the face of growing diversity in democracies around the world, we should be helping teachers and students develop a balance of cultural, national, and global identifications. The aim is "to understand the ways in which knowledge is constructed; to become knowledge producers; and to participate in civic action to create a more humane nation and world." (Banks, 2001a). Reflecting on one's own sense of identity benefits Banks' American white, middle class female teacher education students, as much as the diverse teacher education students in Porto Alegre, Sao Paulo, Warsaw, or New York City. The task of teacher education should be to assist prospective teachers to think and act in social practice.

A ROLE FOR COMPARATIVE AND INTERNATIONAL EDUCATION

The field of comparative and international education has traditionally explored the theories, policies, and practices related to the interplay between schools and society in local, national, regional, and global contexts. Recent education policy initiatives in many countries, including the United States, Poland, Brazil, and India, have been influenced by research like the IEA's

TIMSS study comparing student performance on high stakes tests. Certainly, international studies based on assessments like TIMSS has been, and should continue to be discussed and critiqued as they ultimately impact policy decisions on the form and function or our own educational system. However, other work by comparative and international education researchers should be part of this discussion as well, and it could be incorporated into the programs that prepare teachers, including: studies of alternative teaching approaches or curricular choices; studies demonstrating different perspectives on the nature of knowledge; studies presenting different viewpoints on the nature and impact of globalization; studies offering a critical lens on the current standards, assessment, and accountability model of education policy.

ALTERNATIVE TEACHING APPROACHES OR CURRICULAR CHOICES

Explorations of alternative teaching approaches or curricular choices constitute an area of work by comparative and international education researchers that has long gained mainstream visibility. For example, the appeal of Montessori methods in early childhood education continues in many countries, and more recently, there has been an increase in interest in the Reggio Emilia approach (New, 2003; Stegelin, 2003). Both are based on theories of how children learn and how classroom interactions should reflect this knowledge. Americans have long embraced several Japanese teaching techniques, like Suzuki music, Shotokan martial arts, and Kuman math. Japanese lesson study has also captured attention as a way to improve teachers' professional development. (Curcio, 2002; Fernandez, 2002; Fernandez, Cannon, & Chokshi, 2003) Interestingly, these latter adoptions are based on a growing fascination with high achieving nations, most often as evidenced on high stakes national tests. This is clearly in evidence as we troll the globe for science and math teaching approaches and curricula choices from Singapore and China, both high achievers according to the TIMSS assessment. Work by Gregory and Clarke (2003) and Ma (1999) on, respectively, Singapore and China's mathematics curricula and teaching methods have begun to influence the way math is taught, and the way teachers of math are prepared.

The literature offers a variety of examples of how the preparation of teachers might best meet the needs of the populations they teach, in the contexts they live and work. For example, Stigler and Hiebert (1999) work suggests that along with standards and assessments, Americans must focus on changing teaching itself while recognizing that it is an activity influenced by culture. Certainly, Paolo Freire's work has held out an alternative view of how education can be used as an emancipatory vehicle for the most dispossessed, in the least developed societies. However, other recent work demonstrates how teacher professional development can be enhanced through action research (Diniz-Pereira, 1997). The common view of teachers running through all this work is one of engaged intellectuals. Moreover, across different settings, there is evidence that teachers as researchers are sensitive to the importance of context and culture in planning and carrying out their work (Maseman & Welch, 1997).

GLOBAL PERSPECTIVES ON THE NATURE OF KNOWLEDGE

Cross-cultural dialogue helps teachers develop an international understanding of contemporary world events, specifically by demonstrating how culture and context impact educational values, decisions, public policies, and practice (Crossley & Watson, 2003). Work by comparative and international educators like Hayhoe and Pan (2001); Hayhoe (1988); and Watkins and Biggs (1996, 2001) focus on how conceptions of knowledge itself are intimately connected to cultural and contextual influences. These studies help temper the rush to adopt methods and curricula uncritically, just as it cautions to temper the willingness to make recommendations for other countries to do the same. Research such as Alexander (2001) demonstrates this by comparing various aspects of primary education in English, French, Indian, Russian, and American contexts, and the descriptions vividly suggest that differing conceptions of knowledge get communicated via classroom interactions and curricular choices in a variety of ways.

Local knowledge and a commitment to culturally traditional ways of interacting and communicating values can enhance, rather than detract from academic achievement and developing global perspectives. While preparing students for standardized tests, two schools in Colombia show us how, via projects aimed at integrating knowledge and skills on sustainable community and economic development, they can also be vehicles of locally valued knowledge (Arenas, 1999). In a similar way, traditions and ways of knowing valued in the Inuit community in Canada have been integrated into mathematics curriculum with success (Yamamura, Netser, & Qanatsiaq, 2003). Whether they work in urban or rural settings, teachers should have the opportunity to reflect on these examples, as a way of making sense of their own circumstances, and the choices they make in their schools and classrooms.

VIEWPOINTS ON THE NATURE AND IMPACT OF GLOBALIZATION

Focusing too closely on education's role in meeting economic, human capital needs over other social needs is shortsighted. It is shortsighted to make use of TIMSS type studies exclusively to inform policy and practice, or to haphazardly adopt different curricula or teaching methods without concurrently giving due consideration to the many interpretative analyses available in comparative and educational research. Decisions about education policy and practice are optimally made by considering not only the economic environment, but the social, cultural, and religious environment unique to a particular context, and how all of these are responding to the process of globalization. This dynamic, occurring across the globe, presses us to raise the question of the role of public education and how, as a social institution and conduit for ideology, schools may either exacerbate or mitigate the tensions that arise between ethnic, cultural, and religious cleavages in different contexts.

For more than a decade, the countries of East and Central Europe have been sorting out these types of tensions, as they reoriented themselves to new social, political, and economic commitments. The former Yugoslavia stood out as the most painful transition experience. However, a study of teachers in Croatia revealed that educators, in the mid 1990s, were going through a self-evaluative process and making meaning about their work and aspirations for democracy in new ways, by considering new paradigms (Gal, 2001). Recent work by Milligan (2003) explores tensions between Muslims and Christians in the Southern Philippines, and the contradictory role of schools in both transmitting and transforming cultural values. The Philippines, just as Bosnia, India, and Israel, face challenges in providing education to diverse populations who are in open conflict over political, cultural, ethnic, and especially, religious values and loyalties. As Milligan points out, the United States has a history of grappling with this issue, most recently with conservative fundamentalist and evangelical Christians as well as with growing numbers of immigrants representing diverse religious beliefs (Milligan, 2003).

The Caribbean's historical experience with diverse population helps them appreciate the value of being aware of "elements that differentiate" them, which helps them "read" the global and better appreciate the increasingly interdependent global community (Louisy, 2001). Yet, the impact of technology on how we define and participate in public spaces, both locally and globally, highlights the changing nature of education and global interdependence. As pointed out by Burbules (2000), schools are often referred to as "communities," yet with the broad increase in technology use, we see the concept of educational communities in a problematic way. Burbules posits that the Internet is becoming a "global community" in as much as it transmits "communication, information, culture, and goods and services around the world." However, the nature of this activity is more akin to a "metacommunity" where individuals congregate and coexist, but often lack the type of cohesiveness of the traditional understanding of a community. Further, the Internet holds out the chance to be part of many different kinds of communities, and different types of interactions at varied levels of commitment. These emerging patterns of connection and interaction change the nature of engagement in community, and pushes us to consider "who is seeking to foster a sense of community, among which groups and for what purposes?" (Burbules, 2000). As educators, we must respond to this trend in a considered way, and ensure that it becomes part of the intellectual preparation of teachers who are rushing to integrate technology, as resources allow, into their classrooms.

CRITICAL LENS ON THE CURRENT STANDARDS, ASSESSMENT AND ACCOUNTABILITY POLICY MODELS

It is quite clear that the United States is not alone in rapidly adopting high stakes standardized testing as a means of measuring achievement for all grades. Recent studies confirm that this trend is growing around the world (Phelps, 2000). One of the major concerns over this trend is that many countries use the tests to assess, sort, and validate future work prospects for their citizens. Noah and Eckstein (1998) compared results on national achievement tests in eight countries and showed how they can have both benefits and drawbacks. For example, in several of the countries examined in their book, they documented differences in educational and career opportunities that result from over reliance on these measures (Noah & Eckstein, 1998).

There is a rising, if not robust trend of cautionary research on measuring achievement, and attempting to close achievement gaps between racial, ethnic, and economic groups, solely on the basis of standardized tests. Comprehensive approaches to closing these gaps are urged, including extensive support for minority and low performing schools, and parent and community support (Kober, 2001). In addition, the impact of focusing on good results on high stakes tests can have a negative impact on the diversity, creativity and freedom within the curriculum (Berlak, 2001). Comparative and international education research can offer examples of successful use of alternative assessments in determining learning outcomes of students from Israel (Dori, 2003) to Canada (Marinez-Brawley, 2000). Further, it can provide lessons from countries like England and Singapore, which have relied heavily on high stakes testing of students and teachers, and remain highly ranked on international achievement comparisons. National curricula and assessments in England and Singapore are depicted as "limited" in value, not least because they classify people and schools "according to specific, often narrow, criteria," and convey via the curriculum a "value-laden message regarding what should be taught and assessed" (Gregory & Clarke, 2003).

Wrapped up with the discourse on achievement is the need for accountability. Recent efforts to move education from the public to the private sector hold out the promise that offering families a choice to exit an underperforming school will exert pressure on those schools to improve, while satisfying discriminating families who will let their feet do the talking. Yet, the experience with privatization of education in countries around the world has been variable. In addition to the growing research being generated on charter schools and experiments with voucher programs in the United States, many comparative and international education researchers have been reporting on the range of effects of privatization from various countries around the world, including Chile, New Zealand, South Africa, and China. (Plank & Sykes, 2003) Although privatizing education implies leaving educational access and provision open to the market and individual initiative, many countries' private schools rely on public subsidies, like France, Argentina, and Zimbabwe. Nonetheless, moving education from the public to private realm inevitably involves reorganizing the roles and responsibilities of the state, the economy and society. Moreover, the influence of external aid organizations like the World Bank have been criticized for inappropriately advising privatization, deregulation, and decentralization policies in environments like Latin America, where such policies clashed with local control and needs, often exacerbating inequities (Rhoten, 2000; Torres, 2002) Historically, one of the major roles of public schools has been to support social cohesion. Arguably, privatizing education would provide more choice, perhaps more efficiency or equity, but what of social cohesion?

Taken together, research in these four areas offers prospective teachers an education that values them as intellectuals, as well as skilled practitioners. Infusing work by comparative and international educators into pre service and in service courses for teachers helps them better grapple with pressing contemporary issues that impact the work they do as much as the lives they choose to lead in society.

CONCLUDING REMARKS

Re imagining our work as teachers requires us to give consideration to the dynamics of global change and how it connects to what we do in our own backyards. Educators must engage in a dialogue that includes not only multiple perspectives, but alternative visions for action. In our current policy climate, teacher education programs may feel compelled to follow prevailing standards and expectations, but would benefit greatly if they broadened their field of vision.

Global education incorporated into alternative in service programs, schools, or foundations courses for teachers can be enhanced by work from the field of comparative and international education. Used in this way, global education can foster an understanding of what other cultures' contributions have been to improving not just a global economic environment, but a global human environment. These may be animated by different landscapes of social needs, differing in terms of what combinations of requirements their context present, but they are similar in terms of what human requirements arise across cultural, religious, ethnic, or political demarcations.

The pedagogical task ahead of teacher educators is to engage prospective teachers in thinking about how the very big picture, and their very specific smaller picture intersect. Educating teachers is ultimately a process of making meanings in this way, not just about collecting snippets of best practices or classroom management techniques. Yes, it matters that teachers can teach students reading and writing skills, but on September 11, it mattered more that teachers were able to be humane, thoughtful, and caring. What matters more after September 11, is that we acknowledge and engage in the disorientation of our changing circumstances. Teacher education may not be able to prepare future teachers for all unforeseen events, but it can give them time and space to delve into larger existential and political questions. We need to reorient ourselves by digging deeper into the forces and events that shape our lives and the way we come to see ourselves as individual "I's" and a collective "we," as our world increasingly engages in processes of globalization.

NOTES

1. See www.ilo.org

REFERENCES

Alexander, R. J. (2001). *Culture and pedagogy: International comparisons in primary education.* Malden, MA: Blackwell.
Arenas, A. (1999). If we all go global, what happens to the local? In defense of a pedagogy of place. *Annual meeting of the comparative and international education society,* Toronto, Canada.
Banks, J. A. (2001a). Citizenship education and diversity: Implications for teacher education. *Journal of Teacher Education, 52*(1), 5–16.
Banks, J. A. (2001b). *Cultural diversity and education: Foundations, curriculum and teaching.* Boston: Allyn and Bacon.
Berlak, H. (2001). *Academic achievement, race and reform: Six essays on understanding assessment policy, standardized achievement tests, and anti-racist alternatives.* California: EDRS.
Britzman, D. P. (2000). Teacher education in the confusion of our times. *Journal of Teacher Education, 51*(3), 200–205.
Burbules, N. C. (2000). Does the internet constitute a global educational community? In: N. C. Burbules & C. A. Torres (Eds), *Globalization and education: Critical perspectives.* London: Routledge.
Crossley, M., & Watson, K. (2003). *Comparative and international research in education.* London: RoutledgeFalmer.
Curcio, F. R. (2002). *A user's guide to Japanese lesson study: Ideas for improving mathematics teaching.* Reston, VA: National Council of Teachers of Mathematics, 39.
Darling-Hammond, L. (1992). Teaching and knowledge: Policy issues posed by alternative certification for teachers. In: W. D. Hawley (Ed.), *The alternatives for teachers.* Washington, DC: ERIC Clearinghouse on Teacher Education.
Darling-Hammond, L. (2002). Variation in teacher preparation: How well do different pathways prepare teachers to teach. *Journal of Teacher Education, 53*(4), 286–302.
Diniz-Pereira, J. E. (2002). Teacher identity construction in different contexts of teacher education in Brazil. *Annual Meeting of the American Educational Research Association,* New Orleans, LA.

Dori, Y. J. (2003). From nationwide standardized testing to school-based alternative embedded assessment in Israel: Students' performance in the matriculation 2000 project. *Journal of Research in Science Teaching, 40*(1), 34–52.

Dyer, C., & Choksi, A. (2002). Democratising teacher education research in India. *Comparative Education, 38*(3), 337–351.

Education, C. o. L. S. i. (1996). Standards for academic and professional instruction in foundations of education, educational studies, and educational policy studies, San Francisco: Caddo Gap Press for American Educational Studies Association.

Education, N. C. f. A. o. T. (1994). NCATE standards. Washington, DC: National Council for Accreditation of Teacher Education.

Education, N. C. f. A. o. T. (2001). Professional standards for the accreditation of schools, colleges and departments of education. Washington, DC: National Council for Accreditation of Teacher Education.

Fernandez, C. (2002). Learning from Japanese approaches to professional development: The case of lesson study. *Journal of Teacher Education, 53*(5), 393–405.

Fernandez, C., Cannon, J., & Chokshi, S. (2003). A U.S.-Japan lesson study collaboration reveals critical lenses for examining practice. *Teaching and Teacher Education, 19*(2), 171–185.

Flores, M. A., & Shiroma, E. (2003). Teacher professionalisation and professionalism in Portugal and Brazil: What do the policy documents tell? *Journal of Education for Teaching, 29*(1), 5–18.

Gal, D. G. (2001). Making meaning in a changing society: A study of teachers and democracy in Croatia. *Comparative and International Education.* New York: Teachers College, Columbia University.

Gandin, L. A., & Apple, M. W. (2004). New schools, new knowledge, new teachers: Creating the citizen school in Porto Alegre, Brazil. *Teacher Education Quarterly, 31*(1), 173–198.

Goodnough, A. (2002). *More applicants answer the call for teaching.* New York: New York Times.

Gregory, K., & Clarke, M. (2003). High-stakes assessment in England and Singapore. *Theory into Practice, 42*(1), 66–74.

Gulati, A. K. (1999). Country Report – India. Ensuring opportunities for the professional development of teachers. Innovation and reform in teacher education for the 21st century In Y. Tabata & L. Griek. *The Asia-Pacific Region.* Hiroshima, Japan: United Nations Educational, Scientific and Cultural Organization. 56–65.

Gutek, G. (1993). *American education in a global society: Internationalizing teacher education.* Prospect Heights, IL: Waveland Press.

Hamot, G. E. (1998). A case of teacher education reform in Poland's transitional democracy: The school in a democratic society. *European Education, 30*(2), 5–24.

Hayhoe, R. (1988). Knowledge categories and Chinese educational reform. *Interchange, 19* (3–4), 92–111.

Hayhoe, R., & Pan, J. (Eds) (2001). *Knowledge across cultures: A contribution to dialogue among civilization.* Hong Kong: University of Hong Kong, Comparative Education Research Centre.

Hussar, W. J. (2001). *Predicting the need for newly hired teachers in the U.S. to 2008–09.* Washington, DC: National Center for Education Statistics.

Inbaraj, J., Kumar, S., Sambili, H., & Scott-Bauman, A. (2003). Women and citizenship in global teacher education: The global-ITE project. *Gender and Development, 11*(3), 83–93.

Kincheloe, J. L., Slattery, P., & Steinberg, S. R. (2000). *Contextualizing teaching: introduction to education and educational foundations.* New York: Longman Press.

Kirkwood, K. F. (2001). Our global age requires global education: Clarifying definitional ambiguities. *The Social Studies, 10–15.*

Kober, N. (2001). It takes more than testing: Closing the achievement gap. *A report of the center on education policy.* Washington, DC: Center on Education Policy Achievement.

Louisy, P. (2001). Globalisation and comparative education: A Caribbean perspective. *Comparative Education, 37*(4), 425–438.

Lytle, J. H. (2000). Teacher education at the millennium: A view from the cafeteria. *Journal of Teacher Education, 51*(3), 174–179.

Ma, L. (1999). *Knowing and teaching elementary mathematics: Teacher's understanding of fundamental mathematics in China and the United States.* Mahwah, NJ: Lawrence Erlbaum Associates.

Marinez-Brawley, E. (2000). Seizing alternatives: Ways of knowing, rural research and practice the helping arts. Issues affecting rural communities: *Proceedings of the international conference on rural communities and identities in the global millenium,* Nanaimo, BC Canada.

Maseman, V., & Welch, A. (Eds) (1997). *Tradition, modernity and post modernity in comparative education.* Boston: Kluwer.

McLaren, P., & Farahmandpur, R. (2001). Teaching against globalization and the new imperialism: Toward a revolutionary pedagogy. *Journal of Teacher Education, 52*(2), 136–150.

McNergney, R. F., & Herbert, J. M. (2001). *Foundations of education: The challenge of professional practice.* Boston: Allyn & Bacon.

Merryfield, M. (1997). A framework for teacher education. In: M. Merryfield, E. Jarchow & S. Pickert (Eds), *Preparing teachers to teach global perspectives: A handbook for teacher educators.* Thousand Oakes, CA: Corwin PRess.

Milligan, J. A. (2003). Teaching between the cross and the crescent moon: Islamic identity, postcoloniality and public education in the Southern Philippines. *Comparative Education Review, 47*(4), 468–492.

Mittelman, J. H. (2000). *The globalization syndrome: Transformation and resistance.* Princeton, NJ: Princeton University Press.

Nagy, M. (1998). Teacher training in Central Europe: Recent developments. *European Journal of Education, 33*(4), 393–407.

National Council for Accreditation of Teacher Education. (1994). *NCATE Standards.* Washington, DC: NCATE.

New, R. S. (2003). Reggio Emilia: New ways to think about schooling. *Educational Leadership, 60*(7), 34–38.

Noah, H. J., & Eckstein, M. A. (1998). The two faces of examinations. In: H. J. Noah & M. A. Eckstein (Eds), *Doing comparative education: Three decades of collaboration* (pp. 211–229). Hong Kong: University of Hong Kong.

OECD. (2001). *Teachers for tomorrow's schools: Analysis of world education indicators.* Paris: UNESCO.

Pereira, R. D. (1997). Teachers' in-service education: A proposal for turning teachers into teacher-researchers. In: V. Masemann & A. Welch (Eds), *Tradition, modernity and postmodernity in comparative education.* Boston: Kluwer.

Phelps, R. P. (2000). Trends in large-scale testing outside the United States. *Educational Measurement: Issues and Practice, 19*(1), 11–21 31 countries clear trend to add not drop testing programs.

Pickert, S. (2001). Changing views about international activities in American teacher education programs. *Annual meeting of the comparative and international education society*, Washington, DC.

Plank, D. N., & Sykes, G. (Eds) (2003). *Choosing choice: School choice in international perspective.* New York: Teachers College Press.

Putkiewicz, E. (1996). Educational research and teacher education in Europe. *European Education, 28*(1), 45–54.

Rajput, J. S., & Walia, K. (2001). Teacher education for social cohesion: The Indian context. *Prospects, 31*(3), 325–332.

Raymond, M., Fletcher, S. H., & Luque, J. (2001). *Teach For America: An evaluation of teacher differences and student outcomes in Houston, Texas.* Stanford University: Center for Research on Education Outcomes at the Hoover Institute.

Rhoten, D. (2000). Education decentralization in Argentina: A "global-local conditions of possibility" approach to state, market, and society change. *Journal of Education Policy, 15*(6), 593–619.

Sadovnik, A. R., Cookson, P. W., & Semel, S. (Eds) (2001). *Exploring education: An introduction to foundations of education.* Boston: Allyn & Bacon.

Smyth, J., & Shacklock, G. (1998). *Re-making teaching: Ideology, policy and practice.* New York: Routledge.

Spring, J. (1998). *Education and the rise of the global economy.* Mahwah, NJ: Lawrence Erlbaum Associates.

Spring, J. (2004). *How educational ideologies are shaping global society.* Mahwah, NJ: Lawrence Erlbaum.

Stegelin, D. A. (2003). Application of the Reggio Emilia approach to early childhood science curriculum. *Early Childhood Education, 30*(3), 163–169.

Stein, J. (2002). *Evaluation of the NYCTF program as an alternative certification program.* New York.

Stigler, J. W., & Hiebert, J. (1999). *The teaching gap: Best ideas from the world's teachers for improving education in the classroom.* New York: Simon & Schuster.

Torres, C. A. (2002). The State, privatisation and educational policy: A critique of neo-liberalism in Latin America and some ethical and political considerations. *Comparative Education, 38*(4), 365–385.

Tye, B. B., & Tye, K. A. (1992). *Global education: A study of school change.* Albany: SUNY Press.

Watkins, D. A., & Biggs, J. B. (Eds) (1996). *The chinese learner: Cultural psychology and contextual influences.* Hong Kong: University of Hong Kong: Comparative Education Research Centre.

Watkins, D. A., & Biggs, J. B. (Eds) (2001). *Teaching and the Chinese learner: psychological and pedagogical perspectives.* Hong Kong: University of Hong Kong, Comparative Education Research Centre.

Wenglinsky, H. (2000). *How teaching matters.* Princeton, NJ: Educational Testing Service.

Wong, P. L. (1995). Constructing a public popular education in Sao Paulo, Brazil. *Comparative Education Review, 39*(1), 120–141.

Yamamura, B., Netser, S., & Qanatsiaq, N. (2003). Community elders, traditional knowledge, and a mathematics curriculum framework. *Education Canada, 43*(1), 44–46.

THE WORLD COUNCIL OF COMPARATIVE EDUCATION SOCIETIES: A PRELIMINARY HISTORY

David N. Wilson

INTRODUCTION

This chapter reports on a project undertaken during the author's two-term tenure as President of The World Council of Comparative Education Societies (WCCES) to document the history of this organization. The WCCES was founded at the First World Congress of Comparative Education, held in Ottawa, Canada in 1970. The author attended that First World Congress as a young academic and has subsequently attended five of the eleven World Congresses held to date. The two-volume *Proceedings of the First World Congress of Comparative Education Societies* was helpful in commencing this project.

Unfortunately, the WCCES archives for the first 14 years of its existence were destroyed in a flood at the Palais des Nations in Geneva, Switzerland, where the UNESCO International Bureau of Education, which housed the WCCES Secretariat, was located. Therefore, existing archival materials only fully cover the period when Raymond Ryba was Secretary-General of the WCCES, although his archives contain some material from this period.

Global Trends in Educational Policy
International Perspectives on Education and Society, Volume 6, 289–307
ISSN: 1479-3679/doi:10.1016/S1479-3679(04)06011-6

Following the death of Raymond Ryba, access to his archival materials has made it possible to commence a history of the WCCES. Initially, the origins of the field of Comparative and International Education were documented in the author's Comparative and International Education Society (CIES) Presidential Address in 1993 and two WCCES Presidential addresses, prior to this chapter on the history of the WCCES (Wilson, 1998).

This chapter presents an overview of the field and the WCCES from its creation in 1970 to the present and serve as the *point d'appuis* for an in-depth history of the WCCES. The chapter will conclude with an examination of the scope of the field of Comparative and International Education. The relationships between national CIE societies and the WCCES is important because the larger global society gives members of small national societies access to colleagues and publications worldwide.

Why Compare Educational Systems?

Harold Noah (1984) wrote 20 years ago:

> Comparative Education can deepen understanding of our own education and socie-ty"and"can help us understand better our own past; locate ourselves more exactly in the present; and discern a little more clearly what our educational future may be.

These assertions remain valid today and constitute the *raison d'être* for the activities of Comparative and International educators. In its broadest sense the field can be defined as:

> The cross-cultural comparison of the structure, operations, aims, methods, and achieve-ments of various educational systems and the societal correlates of these educational systems and their elements.

(Wilson, 2003)

One of the foremost tasks of Comparative Education is to identify what education contributes – after factoring out other factors – to various traits of societies. Comparative and International educators make use of these findings to reform, improve, modernize educational systems worldwide (Wilson, 2004). Having presented a very brief introduction to the field, the chapter will now examine the historical origins of the WCCES.

Antecedents of the World Council of Comparative Education Societies

The field of Comparative Education dates from the work of Marc-Antoine Jullien,

Esquisse et vues préliminaires d'un ouvrage sur l'éducation comparée [Outline and preliminary views of a work on comparative education] (Jullien, 1817), which was the first use of the term. However, Jullien's work was lost until re-discovered by Pedro Rosselló in the 1920s at a Quayside bookstall in Paris. Other developments led to the beginnings of the field and the creation of organizations of Comparative Educators.

The grand tradition of expositions and conferences prominent from the latter part of the 19th century also influenced the emergent field of comparative education. Van Daele (1993, p. 78) wrote that the birth of collaboration was traceable to numerous conferences held between 1885 and 1920, which led to the establishment of The International Bureau of Education (IBE) in 1926.

The IBE was the first international organization in the education sector and, under the direction of Pedro Rosselló, continued the development and dissemination of information about educational systems and practices. The IBE realized the dream of Marc-Antoine Jullien, the first known author on Comparative Education (Brickman, 1960), for such an international organization. IBE became affiliated with UNESCO in 1948.

Brickman (1973, p. 10) wrote that annual meetings of those interested in comparative education began in the United States in 1935. These meetings were convened by an Advisory Committee on Comparative Education of the U.S. Office of Education.

PROFESSIONAL SOCIETIES

The growth of professional societies of comparative and international educators dates from the establishment in the U.S.A. of the Comparative Education Society (CES) in 1956. The parallel motivation for the formation of the CES, according to Brickman (1966, p. 7) was Gerald Read's "discovery" that "travel expenses for an organization were substantially lower than for an unorganized group."

As a graduate student in the mid-1960s, the author attended several CES conferences at The University of Chicago, where the participants usually numbered about 60 persons. Several heated debates took place between Joe Katz, founder of the Comparative and International Education Society of Canada, and C. Arnold Anderson of the University of Chicago over the proposed world council of comparative education. Katz favored an organization of national comparative education societies while Anderson asserted that the CES already played such a role.

The Comparative Education Society in Europe (CESE) was established in 1963 as the first regional society. Several national bodies in Europe evolved from CESE after it changed its constitutional provisions concerning constituent groups. These include the Sezione Italiana della CESE (SICHESE), established in 1986, and L'Association Francophone d'Éducation Comparée (AFEC), which was founded in 1973 as the first language-based society. The second language-based society is the Kommision für Vergleichende Erziehungswissenschaft in der Deutschen Gesellschaft für Erziehungswissenschaft (KVEDGE), which is a commission of the German Pedagogical Society. The British section of CESE was founded in 1966 and in due course became the British Comparative and International Education Society (BCES) that later merged with another organization (BATROE) to become the British Association of International and Comparative Education (BAICE) in 1997.

Other comparative and international education societies were formed in the 1960s and 1970s. The Japan Comparative Education Society (JCES) [*Nihon Hikaku Kyoiku Gakkai*] began in 1964; and the Comparative and International Education Society of Canada/Sociète canadienne d'éducation comparée et internationale (CIESC/SCECI) was founded in 1967 as the first bilingual society, as well as the first to combine the terms "comparative" and "international." The Korean Comparative Education Society (KCES) was established in 1968.

These were the comparative and international education societies that were in existence at the time the World Council of Comparative Education Societies was established in 1970 at the First World Congress of Comparative Education, held at The University of Ottawa.

POST-1970 SOCIETIES

Societies formed after the establishment of the WCCES, and with the encouragement of the WCCES include:

1973   The Australia and New Zealand Comparative and International Education Society (ANZCIES).
1974   The Chinese Comparative Education Society – Taipei (CCES-T), the Sociedad Española de Educación Comparada (SEEC) and the Dutch-Speaking Society of Comparative Education (NGVO) *Nederlandstalig Genootschap voor Vergelijkende Studie van*

> *Opvoeding en Onderwijs* as another European language-based
> society.

1979   The China Comparative Education Society (CCES) and the
       Comparative Education Society of India (CESI).
1983   Sociedade Brasiliera de Educação Comparada (SBEC).
1988   Czech Pedagogical Society (Comparative Education Section).
1989   The Comparative Education Society of Hong Kong (CESHK) and
       the Hungarian Pedagogical Society (HPS).
1991   Greek Comparative Education Society (GCES) and the Southern
       African Comparative and History of Education Society (SACHES),
       became the second regional and second bilingual society.
1992   The Bulgarian Comparative Education Society (BCES).
1995   The Comparative Education Society of Asia (CESA) became the
       third regional society.

Other national societies for which founding dates are unavailable include:

The Israel Comparative Education Society (ICES), which is a section of the
Israeli Educational Research Association founded in 1975.
The Russian Council for Comparative Education (RCCE).
The Polish Comparative Education Society (PCES).
The Ukrainian Comparative Education Society (UCES).
The Nordic Comparative and International Education Society (NOCIES).

Societies, which previously existed but are now dormant or defunct include:

The Egyptian Comparative Education Society (ECES), founded in 1983.
   London Association of Comparative Education (LACE), founded in 1979
   by Brian Holmes.
The Nigerian Comparative Education Society (NCES).
Sociedad Argentina de Educación Comparada (SAEC).
Sociedad Colombiana de Educación Comparada (SCEC), founded in 1984.
Sociedade Portuguêsa de Educação Comparada (PCES), established in
   1990.

In 2001, a new Argentinean society was being established. Nascent societies have been established in the Philippines, Cuba, and Francophone
Africa and the Cuban and Philippine Societies were admitted to the WCCES
in 2004.

THE WORLD COUNCIL OF COMPARATIVE
EDUCATION SOCIETIES

Following the proliferation of national, regional and language-based comparative and international education societies in the 1960s, Leo Fernig, Director of the IBE in Switzerland, Gerald Read of the CES, Joe Katz, founder of the CIESC, Matsunori Hiratsuka, founder of the JCES, Sun-Ho Kim from the KCES, and others founded The WCCES in 1970 "on the occasion of the first International Education Year". (*Proceedings,* p. 1) Michel Debeauvais noted that "Gerald Read was "one of the five comparativists who created the World Council" (Debeauvais, 1987, p. 39).

Brian Holmes described these antecedents in 1977, noting that:

> Many years ago when Gerald Read talked to me about the creation of a non-governmental world Academy of Comparative Educationists, we had in mind that such an organization would help international organizations by providing working papers, offering technical advice, and preparing research projects based upon international collaboration. Leo Fernig welcomed the idea and ... encouraged comparative educationists to act in this advisory capacity.
>
> (Holmes, 1977, p. 2)

The International Committee of Comparative Education Societies comprised Joe Katz, Gerald Read and Brian Holmes. This Committee set up the International Planning Committee for the First World Congress, chaired by Joe Katz. Committee members included Matsunori Hiratsuka from Japan, Sun-Ho Kim from Korea, Gerald Read and Stuart Fraser from the U.S.A., Joseph Lauwerys from the U.K., Philip Idenburg from the Netherlands, and Lionel Desjarlais, Andrew Skinner, Fred Whitworth, Anthony Paplauskas-Ramunas, and Robert Lawson from Canada. At the conclusion of the First World Congress, the mandate of the International Planning Committee was extended "until the next World Congress with power to co-opt additional members as a World Council for Comparative Education." A Secretariat was established at The University of Ottawa (*Proceedings*, p. 172).

The "Final Statement of Resolution" set out the program for the establishment of the "World Council of Comparative Educational (sic) Societies," as follows:

- The World Council, having regard to the recommendations of the First World Congress, and in consultation with the participating societies prepare a constitution for approval by the Second World Congress
- The World Council be charged with issuing a newsletter and with responsibility for convening a second World Congress in 1973

- The World Council seek consultative status with UNESCO
- The World Council seek funds designed to help achieve the objectives of the council and the Congress (*ibid.*)

The list of participants comprised 147 registrants and 48 students, of whom 65 registrants and 31 students were from Canada, 40 registrants and 15 students from the U.S.A., 6 from the U.K., 5 each from Germany and Japan, 3 from Cuba, 2 each from France, Korea, Nigeria, Sweden, and the U.S.S.R., one each from Argentina, Australia, Ethiopia, Cameroon, Ceylon, Colombia, India, Jamaica, South Africa, Tanzania, Turkey, Uganda, and Venezuela, and one student each from France and Greece. The list of participants is a veritable "Who's Who" of Comparative and International Educators and is included in Appendix I.

The Table of Contents for the First World Congress *Proceedings* lists several other prominent comparative and other educators, and international agency personnel as authors of published papers, who were not listed as registrants. These include Kazim Bacchus from The University of Alberta, Shmuel Eisenstadt of Hebrew University in Jerusalem, Israel, Margaret Gillett from McGill University, Robert Lawson from The University of Calgary, Douglas Ray from The University of Western Ontario, Hermann Röhrs from Heidelberg University in Germany, Avigdor Farine from l'Université de Montréal, Sun Ho Kim from Kyung Hee University in Korea, and Robert Gardiner of the United Nations Economic Commission for Africa.

WCCES FOUNDERS

What do we know about some of the principal founders of the WCCES? Joe Katz (1910–1988) obtained his Ph.D. from The University of Chicago in 1940, taught Comparative and International Education at The University of British Colombia, served as President of the CES and then as founder of The Comparative and International Education Society of Canada (CIESC). He became the founding President of the WCCES. Masunori Hiratsuka (1907–1981) was the first Director of the Institute of Comparative Education and Culture at Kyushu University from its founding in 1954–1964 when became the Director of the National Institute of Educational Research. Following that appointment, he apparently joined The University of Tokyo. Hiratsuka was President of JCES in 1970 and served as President of the WCCES between 1977 and 1980. Sun-Ho Kim (b. 1926),

Professor at Kyung Hee University, was the founding President of the Korea Comparative Education Society (KCES) in 1968. The KCES President in 1970 was Hyung-Jin Yoo from Kon-kuk University. The KCES hosted a Pre-Congress meeting prior to the World Congress held in Japan. The IX World Congress of Comparative Education was hosted by the KCES at The Korea National University of Education in 2001. Gerald Read, Professor at Kent State University, was a former President of the CES. Andrew Skinner (1902–1995) of The University of Toronto served as President of the CIESC.

Although Arnold Anderson (1907–1990) of The University of Chicago was bitterly opposed to the creation of the WCCES, it is noteworthy that Steward Fraser, Professor at George Peabody College of Education and a former CES President, and Philip Foster of The University of Chicago the CES President at that time, were in attendance. In his published address, William H. E. Johnson, one of the founders and a former President of the CIES, notes that he was one of the "official delegates" to the World Congress (*Proceedings*, 1970, p. 56).

Although neither present at the First World Congress, nor listed as a member of the International Planning Committee, Leo Fernig (d. 1999), Director of the IBE moved the WCCES Secretariat from Ottawa to Geneva. The author has long understood that Fernig was one of the WCCES founders, but no archival evidence is available to prove or disprove that understanding. Bob Lawson, then Professor at The University of Calgary, who was not present at the First World Congress, was included on the International Planning Committee. Lawson later became President of the CIESC and, following his move to Ohio State University in 1991, President of the CIES. Philip Idenberg, Professor at The University of Amsterdam, and Joseph Lauwerys (1902–1981), Professor at The University of London, were also not listed as registrants at the First World Congress, but were identified as members of the International Planning Committee.

The WCCES Statutes and By-Laws were approved at the Second World Congress in Geneva in 1973. The WCCES was incorporated under Swiss law in 1973 and "has the status of an International Society." (Ryba, 1984, p. 8) The WCCES also attained "consultative status as a non-governmental organization (Category C) with UNESCO," according to Raymond Ryba (*ibid.*). Vandra Masemann negotiated "Category B" status for the WCCES in 1980. In 1999, David Wilson negotiated the revised WCCES status as an NGO in Operational Relations with UNESCO (Wilson, 2002).

WCCES SECRETARIAT

In 1972, the Secretariat of the WCCES was moved from the University of Ottawa to the Palais Wilson in Geneva. The Secretariat was affiliated with the International Bureau of Education of UNESCO (IBE) and began publishing a WCCES Newsletter in 1973. Leo Fernig served as the first WCCES Secretary-General until his resignation in 1982. Mme. Anne Hamori of the IBE served as the Assistant Secretary-General and Newsletter Editor until 1982. A branch Secretariat was established in London with two Assistant Secretaries-General between 1981 and 1984. These were initially Martin McLean, who was replaced by Leo Boucher and David Turner of BCIES. Raymond Ryba of the BCIES was elected Secretary-General in 1984 and served until 1995. The Secretariat was relocated to The University of Manchester. Vandra Masemann served as Secretary-General from 1995 until 1999. Mark Bray of the HKCIES served as Assistant Secretary-General from 1997 to 1999 and is the current WCCES Secretary-General. The Secretariat was relocated to The Comparative Education Center of The University of Hong Kong. Unfortunately, the archival documents for the first decade of the World Council were lost in a flood at Palais Wilson, the IBE Headquarters in Geneva, in 1984. The WCCES history project is based largely upon archival documents collected by Raymond Ryba during his tenure as Secretary-General from 1983 to 1995.

WCCES MEMBERSHIP

The WCCES then took the lead in encouraging and nurturing the establishment of additional member societies. This encouragement and nurturance of new member societies was deemed to be the best means for the development of the field. The dates when societies were established were provided above, but the dates when new member societies joined the WCCES have been difficult to ascertain. AFEC and ANZCIES were admitted to WCCES membership at the Second World Congress in Geneva in 1974. Tetsuya Kobayashi, JCES President and Chair of the WCCES Admissions Commission developed criteria for the admission of new societies in 1983. The need for such a policy arose from the controversy surrounding the request for membership by two societies representing Italy and the

London Association of Comparative Education (LACE), founded by Brian Holmes, which was considered to be a second British society. LACE was admitted when it was decided that it was an international society, rather than a second British society. At the V World Congress both SICHESE and the second Italian society, CESI applied for WCCES membership, but were encouraged to cooperate and re-apply. Unfortunately, the requested cooperation failed to materialize and SICHESE was admitted in 1987 while CESI was not admitted.

China, Brazil, Colombia, Egypt, and LACE were admitted to WCCES membership at the V World Congress in Paris in 1984. The Nigerian Association for Comparative Education was admitted into the WCCES in 1988. Israel and the U.S.S.R. were admitted to membership at the VII World Congress in Montréal in 1989. The Chinese Comparative Education Society – Taipei (CCES-T) was founded in 1974 and joined the WCCES in 1992. CCES-T had 36 members at the time it was established and 350 at the time it was accepted as a WCCES member society in 1988 at the CESE Conference in Madrid.

The Comparative Education Society of Asia, CESA became the second regional Comparative and International Education Society upon its establishment in 1995 and has held previous conferences in Tokyo in 1996 and Beijing in 1998. Professor Yoshio Gondo was the President and CESA had 223 members in 1996, with the largest number of members from Japan, followed by Hong Kong, Taiwan, and Korea. (Bray & Gui, 1999; *CERCular*, 1997, No. 1, p. 7) At the Third CESA Conference, held in Taiwan in 2001, Byung-jin Lee of the KCES was elected President. The fourth CESA Conference was held in Bandung, Indonesia in 2002.

WORLD CONGRESSES

The theme of the First World Congress, held in Ottawa, Canada in 1970, was *Education and the Training of Teachers* and *Educational Aid for Developing Countries*. The Second World Congress was held in Geneva in 1974 with 300 participants and the theme was *Efficiencies and Inefficiencies in Secondary Education*. The Third World Congress was held in London in 1977 with the theme *Cultural Diversity and Political Unity in Education*. The Fourth World Congress was held in Tokyo in 1980 with the theme *Tradition and Innovation in Education*. A Pre-Congress meeting was held in Seoul, Korea with the theme *Education in Developing Nations*.

The Fifth World Congress was held in Paris in 1984 with the theme *Dependence and Interdependence in Education.* Over 600 participants from 80 countries were in attendance. The Fifth World Congress was originally to have taken place in Monterrey, Mexico in 1983, but the Universidad de Monterrey withdrew its support in 1981 as a result of the Mexican fiscal crisis and the CIES was unable to re-schedule the Congress in the U.S.A.

The Sixth World Congress was held in Rio de Janeiro, Brazil in 1987 with the theme *Education, Crisis and Change.* The Congress was attended by 538 participants, 238 from abroad and 300 from Brazil. Due to competing applications from CCES and CIESC, a compromise planned for the VII World Congress to be held in Canada and the VIII to be held in China.

The Seventh World Congress was held in Montréal, Canada in 1989 with the theme *Language, Literacy and Development.* The Eighth and Ninth World Congresses were to have taken place in Beijing, China, but were cancelled due to political and economic difficulties. The Eighth World Congress was held in Prague in 1992 with the theme *Education, Democracy and Development.* The Ninth World Congress was held in Sydney, Australia in 1996 with the theme *Tradition, Modernity, and Post-Modernity in Education.* The Tenth World Congress was held in Capetown, South Africa in 1998 with the theme *Equity and Transformation in Education.* The Eleventh World Congress was held in Chung'buk, Korea in 2001 with the theme *New Paradigms and New Challenges: Moving into the 21st Century.*

World Congress themes were chosen by the host national society and approved by the WCCES Executive Committee. While these various themes were intended to set the agenda for the World Congresses, there were no constraints for participants to relate their papers to the themes. The publications containing selected World Congress papers have conformed to the Congress themes, at least in their book titles.

WCCES PRESIDENTS

The founding President of the World Council of Comparative Education Societies was Joe Katz of the CIESC and served from 1970 to 1973. Brian Holmes was elected the second President of the WCCES at the Second World Congress in Geneva in 1973 and served until 1977. Matsunori Hiratsuka of the JCES served as President between 1977 and 1980. Erwin Epstein of CIES served as WCCES President from 1980 until his resignation in 1983. Michel Debeauvais of AFEC became the Acting WCCES President in 1983, was confirmed in office in 1984 at the Fifth World Congress, and served until 1987. Vandra Masemann of the CIESC became President in 1987 with her term to run until 1989. However, her term was extended at the VII World Congress, due to the postponement of the World Congress in Beijing. In 1991, Vandra Masemann and Wolfgang Mitter became Co-Presidents and Wolfgang Mitter became WCCES President in 1992 at the VIII World Congress. David Wilson of the CIESC became WCCES President in 1996 at the IX World Congress in Sydney and served for two terms. Joe Katz, Vandra Masemann and David Wilson also have the distinction of previously serving as Presidents of both the CIESC and CIES. Ann Hickling-Hudson of ANZIES became WCCES President in 2001.

WCCES VICE-PRESIDENTS

The 'tradition' of WCCES Vice-Presidents appears to have begun after the Vth World Congress. One Vice-President was appointed by the Member Society hosting the current World Congress, while the other Vice-President was appointed by the Member Society designated to host the next World Congress. Since the VIII and IX World Congresses in Beijing were postponed, and later cancelled, Vandra Masemann and Wolfgang Mitter were appointed Co-Presidents in 1991, while Jirzi Kotasek of the Czech and Slovak Pedagogical Society, the host for the VIII World Congress, was appointed Vice-President while Gu Minguyan of CCES remained as Vice-President. Anthony Welch of ANZCIES became Vice-President in 1992, at the VII World Congress and was succeeded by Harold Herman of SACHES in 1996. In turn, Harold Herman was succeeded by Namgi Park of KCES in 1998 and in 2001 Kiok Yoon was nominated by KCES to serve as Vice-President until the XII World Congress.

WCCES EXECUTIVE COMMITTEE MEETINGS

The WCCES Executive Committee comprises the representatives – normally the Presidents – of the Member Societies. The Executive Committee holds *formal* meetings annually and tri-annually at World Congresses. In addition, the 'tradition' of holding *informal* WCCES Executive Committee meetings arose, due to the alternation of formal meetings between the annual conferences of the CIES and the bi-annual conferences of CESE. Before 1982, the WCCES Executive Committee met infrequently and irregularly at various conferences. As far as is known, this 'tradition' dates from meetings in conjunction with the 1982 CIES Conference in New York and the 1985 CESE Conference in Antwerp. Binding WCCES decisions can only be taken at formal WCCES Executive Committee meetings.

WCCES NEWSLETTERS

While the IBE in Geneva was able to provide administrative and financial support to the WCCES, a *WCCES Newsletter* was published and distributed to both WCCES Member Societies and individuals. The archival materials contained a list of countries receiving the newsletter in 1977. A total of 890 newsletters were sent with 308 distributed to Western Europe, 53 to Eastern Europe, 309 to the Western Hemisphere, 24 to the Middle East, 55 to Africa, and 141 to Asia-Oceania. The country breakdown for some of these data is presented in Appendix II. These newsletter distribution data indicate the number of Comparative and International educators who may have been actively involved in the field in 1977 (Holmes, 1990).

THE SCOPE OF COMPARATIVE AND INTERNATIONAL EDUCATION

A decade ago Altbach examined "trends in Comparative Education" and noted that the field "looks in many directions at once, and this has helped to shape a field that is left without a clearly defined center." (Altbach, 1991, p. 491) In the author's 1993 CIES Presidential Address Heyneman's 1992 Presidential Address assertion that the field was "alive and well at the periphery but that it is dead in the center where attention is devoted to academic issues with no obvious product" (Heyneman, 1993, p. 386; Wilson, 1994, p. 449) was disputed. Wilson countered that Heyneman overlooked one important "product," graduates of our academic programs and quoted Adams that "in addition to perpetuating the field, our students also redefine it." (*ibid.*). This rejoinder also applies to Altbach's assertions.

Altbach also examined the field in terms of the "interplay between societal and academic developments as they affect the field." (Altbach, 1998). The author's prosopographic studies have also examined aspects of the interplay between societal and academic developments. By focusing upon the mobility of our students, these studies also examine the mobility of the field itself – a mobility that is global in scope, and as such, constitutes another dimension of globalization. Altbach recognized such pursuits by noting that the field "by its nature is international and is influenced by worldwide trends in research and scholarship." (Altbach, 1991, p. 494). The author proposes to include other worldwide trends in forthcoming examinations of influences on the field.

THE NEWER COMPARATIVE EDUCATION
COMMUNITIES

A decade back, Altbach also examined what he termed to be "the smaller comparative education communities" in Korea, Brazil, Taiwan, Japan, and China. He noted that they "look toward the main centers of comparative education activity for orientations to research trends and methodology." Fortunately, he acknowledged, "as these communities grow in size and self-confidence, they develop a greater degree of independence." He also asserted that this "show(s) an impressive worldwide spread of the study of comparative education."(Altbach, 1991, p. 494) Indeed, that is exactly what has transpired during the past decade. This author's earlier prosopographic studies have commented upon the viability of the field in these (and other) nations. It is also interesting that Altbach commented upon the "highly unequal" "knowledge base and communication network" (*ibid.*).

The author's second WCCES Presidential Address updated this assertion by noting that this situation had improved during that past decade. While the "main 'gatekeepers' of knowledge" still reside in "major English-speaking countries" (*ibid.*). It was indicated that the publication of journals in China and Taiwan, texts in Hong Kong and elsewhere and electronic communications had begun to redress this imbalance (Ryba, 1984; Wilson, 2001).

Bray and Gui recently examined comparative education communities in "Greater China," which they defined as comprising China, Taiwan, Hong Kong, and Macao. The prosopographic elements in their article inform us that the Chinese Comparative Education Society (CCES) membership has grown from "fewer than 100 members" at its founding in 1979 to an estimated 500 in 2001 (Bray & Gui, 2001, p. 455). Similarly, the Chinese Comparative Education Society – Taipei (CCES-T), which was established in 1974, has 320 members in 2001. (*ibid.*, p. 458) The Comparative Education Society of Hong Kong (CESHK), founded in 1989, had 80 members in 2001 (*ibid.*, p. 461).

Hayhoe notes that "in 1979 the China Comparative Education Society was established at ...[a] meeting convened by Zhu Bo at South China Normal University in Guangzhou." She further noted "Zhu Bo of Shaanxi Normal University and South China Normal University ... had returned from study in the United States in 1949." (Hayhoe, 2001, p. 7) "published under the title B*ijiao Jiaoyu [Cc nparative Education]"* in 1982 (*ibid.*). Professor Liu Fonian of the Normal University of East China was the founding CCES President and Professor Gu Mingyuan (2001) served as President of the CCES from 1984 until 2001.

Huang Shiqui (1984) wrote in 1984 that the first Chairman of the CCES was "Professor Liu Fuonian, then President of East China Normal University" and "Zhang Tian-en, then Deputy Director of the Central Institute of Educational Research" was elected as Vice-Chairman. He further noted that the "journal published by the Central Institute of Educational Research ... *Wai Guo Jiaou* (Foreign Education)" became the "organ of the Society" (1984, p. 1)

With respect to international mobility, Huang Shiqi wrote "three delegates from China attended the IV World Congress of Comparative Education held in Tokyo in 1980; and they were Professor Ku Mingyuan (sic) of Beijing Normal University, Mr. Jin Shibai of the Central Institute of Educational Research." The third attendee was not mentioned (*ibid.*, p. 3).

GLOBALIZATION OF COMPARATIVE AND INTERNATIONAL EDUCATION

Bray and Gui (2001) assert that "the forces of globalization and the work of...[the] WCCES, which acts as a forum for Comparative Education scholars in different parts of the world...does...form a global field." (2001, p. 452). They cite Halls (1990) and Zhang and Wang (1997) to counter "the perception that Comparative Education originated in the West" by showing the "multiple origins of the field in different parts of the world." (*ibid.*, p. 466). Finally, they assert that "CCES-T and CESHK are, in per capita terms, the largest societies of their type in the world," although they also acknowledge that "in absolute numbers, the largest society among the 28 WCCES members is the U.S.-based CIES, which at the turn of the millennium had 2300 individual and institutional members," also noting that "one third of the CIES membership was international" (*ibid.*, p. 468).

In an article published in *Korean Universities Weekly*, prior to the XI World Congress of Comparative Education, this author noted that "evidence of the prominent role played by Comparative and International Educators in the globalization of national educational systems arises from their research and consulting impact upon those systems." It was concluded that, "the field of Comparative and International Education, which studies all aspects of education throughout our ever-shrinking globe and facilitates the borrowing of aspects of education and adaptation to other nations' educational systems, has itself become *globalised*" (Wilson, 2001).

While some critics assert that globalization has only negative and destructive effects, and may be destroying indigenous cultures, societies and institutions, these negatives should not obscure positive outcomes of international interchange, borrowing and cooperation. These activities are part of the *melioristic* trend in Comparative Education for improvement of national educational systems by the addition of models, practices, innovations, etc., borrowed or transferred from other national educational systems' (Wilson, 1994). These positive outcomes also include the education of Comparative and International educators from many nations, who may study and promote knowledge of their own cultures, societies and institutions, and in doing so, may prevent their destruction.

REFERENCES

Altbach, P. G. (1991). Trends in comparative education. *Comparative Education Review, 35*(3), 491–507.

Altbach, P. G. (1998). Issues in the development of education for teaching: Hong Kong in international perspective. *Comparative education bulletin (No. 1) CERC.*, pp. 2–5.

Bray, M., & Gui, Qin (1999). From the director. *CERCular – CERC newsletter, No. 1*, p. 1.

Bray, M., & Gui, Qin (2001). Comparative education in greater China: Contexts, characteristics, contrasts and contributions. *Comparative Education, 37*(4), 451–473.

Brickman, W. W. (1960). A historical introduction to comparative education. *Comparative Education Review, 3*(3), 6–13.

Brickman, W. W. (1966). Ten years of the comparative education society. *Comparative Education Review, 10*(1), 7.

Brickman, W. W. (1973). *Comparative education: Concept, research and application.* Norwood (Pennsylvania): Norwood Editions.

Debeauvais, M. (1987). Tribute to gerald read. *WCCES newsletter* p. 39.

Halls, W. D. (Ed.) (1990). *Comparative education: Contemporary issues and trends.* Paris: UNESCO and Jessica Kingsley Publishers.

Hayhoe, R. (2001). Introduction. In: Gu Mingyuan (Ed.), *Education in China and abroad: Perspectives from a lifetime in comparative education.* Hong Kong: Comparative Education Research Centre, University of Hong Kong.

Heyneman, S. P. (1993). Quantity, quality and source. *Comparative Education Review, 37*(4), 918–923.

Holmes, B. (1977). News from the world council of comparative education societies. *WCCES newsletter: Vol. 5*, Number 1, March, 1977, p. 2.

Holmes, B. (1990). Western Europe. In: W. D. Halls (Ed.), *Comparative education: Contemporary issues and trends* (pp. 69–108). Paris: UNESCO and London: Jessica Kingsley.

Huang Shiqui (1984). A brief account of the Chinese society of comparative education. *Archives of the World Council of comparative education societies*. Paris, 3 July, 1984.

Jullien, M.-A. (1817). *Esquisse et vues préliminaires d'un ouvrage sur l'éducation comparée*. Paris: Publisher Unknown.

Proceedings of the First World Congress of Comparative Education Societies. (1970). 2 volumes. Ottawa: WCCES Secretariat.

Ryba, R. (1984). Note on the world council of comparative education societies. *WCCES Newsletter: 10*. p. 8.

Van Daele, H. (1993). *Que sais je? L'éducation comparee*. Paris: Presses Universitaires de France.

Wilson, D. N. (1994). Comparative and international education: Fraternal or siamese twins? A preliminary genealogy of our twin fields. *Comparative Education Review, 34*(4), 449–486.

Wilson, D. N. (1998). On being international: Confessions of an academic-practitioner. Presidential Address at the *X World Congress of comparative education*, Cape Town, South Africa.

Wilson, D. N. (2001). The prospects for comparative education in a globalised world. Published in *Korean Universities Weekly*, May 2001 (in Korean).

Wilson, D.N. (2002). A prosopographic and institutional history of comparative education. Manuscript prepared for: Jürgen Schriewer (Ed.), *Discourse formation in comparative education* (Vol. 2) (publication cancelled). Frankfurt: Peter Lang, Comparative Studies Series.

Wilson, D. N. (2003). The future of comparative and international education in a globalised world. In: M. Bray (Ed.), *Comparative education: Continuing traditions, new challenges and new paradigms* (pp. 14–33). Dordrecht: Kluewer Academic Publishers.

Wilson, D. N. (2004). To compare is human: Comparison as a research methodology. *World Studies in Education, 4*, 1–2.

APPENDIX I

The list of participants is a veritable "Who's Who" of Comparative and International Educators, including:

Oskar Anweiler from Ruhr-Universität in Germany
Robert Belding from the University of Iowa
William Brickman from The University of Pennsylvania
Gustavo Cirigliano from Universidad de Buenos Aires, Argentina
Victor Couch from The University of Sydney, Australia
Daniel Dorotich from The University of Saskatchewan, Canada

Appendix I. (*Continued*)

Max Eckstein from Queen's College, City University of New York
Reginald Edwards from McGill University, Canada
Harold Entwistle from Sir George Williams University, Canada
Philip Foster from The University of Chicago (CIES President in 1970)
William Halls from Oxford University, U.K.
Richard Heyman from The University of Calgary, Canada
Brian Holmes from The University of London, U.K.
Torsten Husén from The University of Stockholm, Sweden
William H.E. Johnston from The University of Pittsburgh
Wendell P. Jones from U.C.L.A.
W. Senteza Kajubi from Makerere University in Uganda
Joe Katz, University of British Columbia, President of the CIESC, Canada
Denis Kallen from the OECD, Paris
Edmund King from The University of London, U.K.
Tetsuya Kobayashi, Director of the UNESCO Institute of Education,
    Hamburg
Nathan Kravetz from the UNESCO IIEP, Paris
Roger Magnuson from McGill University, Canada
Zoya Malkova, Academy of Pedagogical Sciences, U.S.S.R.
James Maraj of The Commonwealth Secretariat Education Division
Byron Massialas, University of Michigan
Ralph Miller, University of Calgary, Canada
Reg Murray, University of The West Indies, Jamaica
Augustine Mwingira, University of Dar-es-Salaam, Tanzania
Harold Noah, Columbia University
Franklin Parker, University of West Virginia
Gerald Read, Kent State University
Saul Robinsohn, Vice-President of CESE, Germany
Suzanne Shafer, Arizona State University
Andrew Skinner, University of Toronto, Canada
Ernest Stabler, University of Western Ontario, Canada
Margaret Sutherland, Queen's University, U.K. Chair of BCES/CESE
Alexandre Vexiliard, University of Ankara, Turkey
David Wilson, OISE, Canada
Mathew Zachariah, University of Calgary, Canada

APPENDIX II

WCCES Newsletter Distribution – 1977.

France	78	Australia/NZ	58
Germany	29	U.K.	77
Switzerland	25	Spain	25
Netherlands	14	Italy	14
Sweden	11	Belgium	13
Denmark	6	Portugal	7
Finland	2	Austria	4
Norway	1	Greece	2
U.S.A.	194	Canada	63
Argentina	13	Other	39
India	20	Korea	18
Japan	2	Other Asia	43

NOTES ON CONTRIBUTORS

David P. Baker is Professor of Education and Sociology at The Pennsylvania State University. He studies the role of education in the social construction of modern society. He publishes widely on the comparative and historical analysis of schooling and higher education. He frequently assists in the planning of large cross-national studies of academic achievement for multi-national agencies and individual national governments.

Sheng Yao Cheng is Assistant Professor at the National Chung Cheng University in Taiwan. He received his Ph.D. in Comparative and International Education at the University of California, Los Angeles (UCLA). He is also a Research Coordinator at the Center for International and Development Education (CIDE) at UCLA. His dissertation and current research center on educational policy analysis with an emphasis on minority education and social justice. Additional research interests include comparative and international education, sociology of education, policy analysis, and the politics of identity among minority and marginalized groups. His MA thesis was later published into a book on education in Hong Kong during its transition from the United Kingdom to China. He also conducted extensive research on higher education in China, Singapore, the United States, Taiwan, Hong Kong, and the Netherlands.

Holger Daun holds a Ph.D. in Political Science and in Comparative and International Education. He is a Professor of Comparative and International Education and Director of the Institute of International Education at Stockholm University. He has been involved in different evaluation studies for SIDA (Swedish International Development Cooperation Authority), UNESCO and UNDP. He is a leading researcher on globalization and education reform. He has published several books and a large number of articles, particularly on education reform and globalization.

Diane G. Gal received her doctorate from Teachers College, Columbia University in Comparative and International Education. Her dissertation research on teachers, democracy, and educational reform in an East Central European transition country was supported by Fulbright and American Council of Learned Societies grants. Her current research interests include: democratic education theory and practice; comparative perspectives of international education reform; teacher education and professional development; and the impact of globalization on learning and educational organization. She teaches social foundations and educational research courses at Queens College, City University of New York and serves as a faculty liaison for the New York City Teaching Fellows program.

Stephen P. Heyneman served the World Bank for 22 years. Between 1976 and 1984 he helped research education quality and design policies to support educational effectiveness. Between 1984 and 1989 he was in charge of external training for senior officials worldwide in education policy. And between 1989 and 1998, he was responsible for the Bank's education policy and lending strategy; first for the Middle East and North Africa and later for the 27 countries of Europe and Central Asia. In 1998 he was appointed as Vice President in charge of international operations of an education consultant firm in Alexandria, Virginia. In September, 2000 he was appointed as Professor of International Education Policy at Vanderbilt University in Nashville, Tennessee. He received his BA in Political Science from the University of California at Berkeley, his MA in African Area Studies from UCLA in 1965, and his Ph.D. in Comparative Education from the University of Chicago in 1976.

W. James Jacob is Assistant Director at the Center for International and Development Education (CIDE) at the University of California, Los Angeles where he also received his Ph.D. in Comparative and International Education. His work focuses on HIV/AIDS education curriculum development, program evaluation, social change and development, and higher education organizational analysis in developing countries with a geographic emphasis on East Africa and China. He has worked as a Policy Analyst and Evaluator of HIV/AIDS education programs in Uganda from 2001 to 2004, where he was simultaneously the Principal Investigator of a sub-Saharan African HIV/AIDS literacy education research program. He is currently conducting a study on the influences of the market economy on Chinese higher education.

Nancy O'Gara Kendall received her Ph.D. from Stanford University's International and Comparative Education program with a minor in African studies in 2004. She received the Gail P. Kelly Award for Outstanding Dissertation from the Comparative and International Education Society. She recently joined Florida State University's Educational Leadership and Policy Studies department. Her research examines the intersections and effects of political, social, and economic forces in education policy practices, primarily in Southern and Eastern Africa. Recent work has examined the intersections of political democratization, economic liberalization, HIV/AIDS, and gender relations in school practices in Malawi; the effects of Education for All (EFA) on the policymaking arena in Malawi; and the effects of EFA on the education of orphans and vulnerable children in Southern Africa. She is currently conducting research on the effects of increased U.S. federal funding of abstinence-only education efforts on policy practices in U.S. and Southern African schools.

Verónica R. Martini holds a Master's degree in International Education Policy from the Harvard Graduate School of Education, and a Master's degree in Secondary English Education from Armstrong Atlantic State University in Savannah, Georgia. In her native Argentina, she trained and worked as Professor of English as a Foreign Language for several years. In 2002, she interned in the Outreach Department of the David Rockefeller Center for Latin American Studies at Harvard University, where she runs the Speakers Bureau series in Cambridge and Boston schools, and created a Mentor/Tutor Program for Latino students at a local high school. She currently serves both as a Research Associate for Corporate Partners, Development and External Relations at that Center, and in the staff of the New England–Latin America Business Council, where she leads special development activities.

Mary Ann Maslak is an Assistant Professor of Education at St. John's University in New York. Her research focuses on comparative and international educational development, with a particular emphasis on girls' and women's education. She served as chair of the Gender and Education Committee of the Comparative and International Education Society from 2001 to 2004.

Jordan Naidoo the Basic Education Specialist at Save the Children has extensive experience in policy analysis, monitoring and evaluation, community mobilization, decentralization, and governance and democratization in education. He received his Masters in Education (M.Ed.) from the University of Natal, South Africa and Doctorate in Education (Ed.D.) from Harvard University Graduate School of Education. He has taught for a number of years in South Africa, and in the 1990s worked at the Education Policy Unit at the University of Natal and at the Center for Education Policy Development (CEPD) as a Policy Analyst and researcher focusing on school integration and educational transformation. He was the Coordinator of the Decentralization and Education Management theme in the Association for Development of Education in Africa (ADEA) study, *Improving the Quality of Education,* and has recently worked at the International Institute for Education Planning (UNESCO, Paris) on issues related to decentralization and school evaluation.

Diane Brook Napier was born and raised in South Africa where she received her undergraduate education. She is a naturalized American citizen, residing in the United States. Her research interests focus on post-colonial educational reform policies, democratic transformation policies, and implementation issues in sub-Saharan Africa (especially South Africa) and in other developing countries; issues of race, ideology, language, and justice/injustice; human resources development (education, health, housing, labor); and environmental issues. She has conducted ethnographic and action research in South Africa and surrounding countries since 1990, and has participated in research and training partnership activities in several South African schools, teachers training colleges, and universities.

David N. Wilson is Professor Emeritus of Comparative and International Education, Educational Planning, TVET, Policy Analysis, Higher Education, ICT, and Development Education at the Ontario Institute for Studies in Education, University of Toronto, Canada. He has served with UNESCO, ILO and Asian Development Bank while on leave from OISE. His international experience has been in Africa, Asia, Caribbean, Eastern Europe and Latin America. He has also served as President of Comparative and International Education Society of Canada, Comparative and International Education Society (USA), World Council of Comparative Education Societies and International Society for Educational Planning. His publications include Comparative and International Education, Educational Planning, Non-Formal Education, ICT, Open and Distance Universities, Community and Technical Colleges, TVET, and Knowledge Management. Currently, Senior Research Specialist at UNESCO-UNEVOC International

Centre and Co-editor of *International Handbook on Technical and Vocational Education and Training.*

Alexander W. Wiseman is Assistant Professor of Education at The University of Tulsa. He writes, teaches, and presents regularly on internationally comparative analyses of national education systems, youths' transitions from school to work, and the managerial activity of school principals. He received his BA in Letters from the University of Oklahoma, his MA in International Comparative Education from Stanford University, and a dual-degree Ph.D. in both Educational Theory and Policy and Comparative and International Education from the Pennsylvania State University.

AUTHOR INDEX

Abdel Halim, A.E. 65, 89
Abu-Duhou, I. 110, 114, 122
Achola, P.P.W. 64, 97
Adams, D. 69, 95, 251, 253
Adams, D.W. 118, 122
Adams, R.S. 67, 86, 89
Aguerrondo, I. 77, 89
Akiba, M. 2, 10, 20, 129, 142
Albrecht, D. 70, 89
Alexander, N. 41, 52
Alexander, R.J. 279, 284
Allen, K. 182, 194
Altbach, P.G. 61, 63, 67–68, 73, 89, 91, 94, 301–302, 304
Alvarez, B. 77, 89
Alvarez de Testa, L. 66, 92
Amer, J.M. 202, 217
Anderson, B. 8, 18
Anderson, C.A. 24, 26, 52–53
Anheier, H.K. 199, 213, 215
Appardurai, A. 176, 194
Apple, M.W. 268, 285
Arenas, A. 279, 284
Ariasingam, D.L. 37, 56
Arnove, R.F. 61, 67–68, 89, 175, 190, 194, 246, 253
Arriaghi, G. 125, 142
Arun, R. 245, 253
Ascher, W. 37, 52
Ashton, D. 9, 18
Astiz, M.F. 11, 18, 64, 69, 90, 107, 122, 226, 253
Atkin, J.M. 12, 18
Attah-Safoh, A. 66–69, 71, 77, 90
Ayee, J.R.A. 108, 122

Aypay, A. 8, 19
Azfar, O. 108, 122

Bagayoko, M. 202, 217
Bailey, T.R. 9, 19
Baker, D.P. 1–2, 4–5, 10–11, 15–18, 20–21, 64, 69, 90, 107, 122, 129, 142, 226, 235, 253
Baldo, M. 204, 215
Ball, S.J. 1, 9, 11, 18–19
Balogh, T. 32, 52
Banda, K. 126, 132, 136, 141–142
Bane, L. 61, 97
Banks, J.A. 259, 264, 277, 284
Baptiste, I. 234–235, 253
Barnett, M. 37, 52
Basabas-Ikegucchi, C. 70, 90
Bates, Ü.Ü. 169–170
Battro, A. 177, 194
Becker, G.S. 24, 52, 235, 253
Benavot, A. 8, 19, 225, 235, 244, 253, 256
Bennell, P. 38, 41, 52
Bereday, G.Z.F. 223, 253
Bergsen, H. 51–52
Berlak, H. 282, 284
Berman, E. 38, 52
Bhola, H.S. 77, 90
Biersteker, T. 37, 52
Bigelow, W. 80, 90
Bjork, C. 69, 90
Black, P. 12, 18
Blackledge, D. 205, 215
Blaug, M. 24, 52, 66, 90
Blease, D. 205, 215
Bloom, D. 184, 194

Boakari, F.M. 64, 97
Boli, J. 6, 8, 17, 20, 244, 255
Boli-Bennett, J. 4, 8, 20, 63, 96
Boserup, E. 148, 170
Botkin, M. 205, 217
Bowman, M.J. 24, 26, 52–53
Boyd, W.L. 16, 19
Bracey, G.W. 11–12, 19
Bray, M. 66, 74, 90, 302–304
Brickman, W.W. 223, 253, 291, 304
Britzman, D.P. 272, 284
Brook, D.L. 59, 65–66, 70, 73, 74,
    80–82, 87, 90
Brook, G.A. 70, 74, 90
Brook Napier, D. 67, 69–70, 74, 80–81,
    83–84, 86, 90
Brosio, G. 102, 108, 122
Brown, D. 37, 53
Brown, L.D. 37, 54
Bryson, J.C. 68, 90
Buchmann, C. 8, 19, 210, 214, 216
Bullivant, B.M. 205, 215
Burbules, N.C. 225, 253, 281, 284
Burnett, G. 233, 241, 256
Burnett, N. 40, 53
Burns, R.J. 233, 258
Burrell, G. 230, 253
Buvinic, M. 148, 170

Cambridge, J.C. 179, 181, 194
Cambron-McCabe, N. 227, 257
Cameron, K.S. 253
Canales, J. 66, 91
Cannon, J. 278, 285
Capper, J. 78, 91
Caracelli, V. 14, 19
Carling, A.H. 233, 253
Carnoy, M. 8, 13, 19, 37, 41, 53,
    72, 75, 91
Carter, D.S.G. 9, 19
Castro, C. 51, 53
Chabbott, C. 8, 19, 61, 67, 91
Chalker, D.M. 64, 91

Chantharaskul, A. 77, 95
Chapman, D.W. 68, 70, 91, 118, 122
Chasin, B.H. 67, 75, 92
Cheema, G.S. 121–122
Chen, D. 67, 86, 89
Chen, H.S. 78, 91
Cheng, Y.C. 67, 91
Chinapah, V. 204, 215
Chisholm, L. 82, 91
Chokshi, S. 278, 285
Choksi, A. 244, 253, 267, 285
Chowdhury, K.P. 61, 67, 91
Christie, P. 80, 91
Chung, F.C. 38, 53
Chung, J. 78, 91
Chunsakorn, P. 77, 95
Cisneros-Cohernour, E.J. 77, 91
Clark, W.H. 68, 94
Clarke, M. 278, 282, 285
Clarke, R. 68, 73, 94
Coatsworth, J. 176, 194
Colclough, C. 37–38, 41, 53
Coleman, A.S. 226, 253
Coleman, J.S. 233, 253
Collier, P. 51, 53
Cook, B.J. 246, 253
Cooper, S. 63, 92
Cornia, G. 50, 53
Craig, H. 76, 93
Craig, J. 38, 53
Crook, R.C. 101, 122
Crossley, M. 258, 279, 284
Crowson, R. 8, 19
Crump, S. 9, 20
Cummings, W.K. 63, 67–69, 75, 78, 91,
    95, 253
Curcio, F.R. 278, 284
Curtin, T.R.C. 41, 53
Cuzzort, R.P. 205, 215

Danesy, F. 185, 194
Darling-Hammond, L. 262, 284
Daun, H. 197, 202, 204, 212–215, 217

de la Campa, R. 241, 253
De Sigueira, A.C. 43, 53
Deacon, B. 4, 19
Debeauvais, M. 24, 52, 294, 304
Deboer, G.E. 8, 19
Denmark, F.L. 169–170
Denning, S. 42, 53
Dharmadasa, K.H. 75, 92
Diniz-Pereira, J.E. 263–264, 268, 284
Donovan, J. 147, 170
Dori, Y.J. 282, 285
Doronila, M.L.C. 68, 92
Dorsey, B.J. 61, 78, 92
Doyal, L. 204, 215
Drake, B. 190, 194
Dutton, J. 227, 257
Dyer, C. 244, 253, 267, 285
Dzvimbo, K.P. 68, 92

Easterly, W. 253
Ebin, V. 198, 216
Eckstein, M.A. 17, 20, 223, 256, 281–282, 286
Eisenstein, Z. 169–170
El Tawila, S. 68, 94
Eliason, L.C. 6, 19
Eliasoph, N. 245, 253
Elizalde, A. 6, 20
Elizandro Y Carr, S. 68, 77, 92
Epstein, E.H. 17, 19, 222, 246, 253, 254
Escobar, A. 131, 142
Evans, D. 67, 92

Fagerlind, I. 6, 19
Farahmandpur, R. 276, 286
Farrell, J.P. 33, 55, 251, 253
Feonova, M. 51, 53
Fergus, H.A. 66, 92
Ferguson, J. 130–131, 141–142
Fernandez, C. 278, 285
Finnemore, M. 37, 52
Fiske, E.B. 104, 122
Fletcher, S.H. 271, 287

Fletcher, T.V. 12, 19
Fligstein, N. 236, 254
Flores, M.A. 269, 285
Foster, P.J. 26, 31, 48, 54
Fox, J. 37, 54
Franke, R.W. 67, 75, 92
Fraser, S.E. 223, 253
Freire, P. 246, 254
French, H. 51, 54
Friedman, T. 176, 194
Fuentes, B.O. 68, 77, 92
Fullan M.G. 100, 122
Fuller, B. 121–122, 203, 210, 212, 216
Furniss, E. 204, 215

Gal, D.G. 259, 280, 285
Gandin, L.A. 268, 285
Gardner, H. 178, 194–195
Garfinkel, H. 244, 254
Garrod, A. 188, 195
Gavin, M. 25, 54
Geertz, C. 243, 254
Geldt, J. 81, 92
George, S. 50, 54
Gershberg, A.I. 102–103, 106, 121, 124
Gertel, H. 187, 195
Giacchino-Baker, R. 77, 92
Gibbon, P. 51, 54
Giddens, A. 193, 195
Gilbert, C. 51, 54
Gilbert, J.K. 226, 258
Giles, J. 254
Gill, J.I. 66, 92
Gilliomee, H. 85, 92
Ginsburg, M.B. 63, 89, 92
Giordan, A. 254
Giroux, H.A. 205, 216
Glassman, J. 238, 254
Gleick, J. 225, 254
Goffman, E. 205, 216
Gomes, R. 65, 93
Gomez, 66, 91

Goodlad, J.I. 63, 93
Goodman, D.J. 242, 257
Goodnough, A. 270, 285
Goodwin, C. 185, 192, 195
Gore, C. 51, 54
Gorostioga, J.M. 89, 92
Gough, I. 204, 215
Graham, W. 14, 19
Green, F. 9, 18
Greene, J. 14, 19
Gregory, K. 278, 282, 285
Grégoire, E. 198, 216
Griffiths, M. 205, 216
Grindahl, B. 212, 216
Gui, Qin 302–304
Gulati, A.K. 266, 285
Gupta, A. 141–142
Gutek, G. 259, 285
Gutmann, A. 42, 54

Haas, E.B. 42, 54
Habte, A. 32, 54
Haddad, W.D. 61, 67, 93
Hammer, J. 41, 54
Hammersley, M. 245, 254
Hamot, G.E. 270, 285
Hannum, E. 8, 19, 66, 68, 71, 77, 87, 93, 210, 214, 216
Hans, N.A. 223, 254
Hansen, W.L. 24, 54
Hanson, E.M. 67, 73, 93
Hanson, M. 117, 122
Hanson, M.E. 250, 254
Hanushek, E.A. 13, 19
Harding, S. 225, 240, 254
Harris, M.J. 205, 216
Harris, S.R. 239, 254
Hartmann, H. 147, 149, 169–170
Hartshorne, K. 79, 93
Hassan, I. 241, 254
Hayden, M. 178–181, 190, 195
Hayhoe, R. 279, 285, 303–304
Haynes, R.M. 64, 91

Heath, J. 70, 93
Heilleiner, G. 37, 54
Held, V. 169–170
Helly, D.O. 169–170
Heneveld, W. 76, 93
Henry, M. 7, 9, 20
Herbert, J.M. 273, 286
Herman, H. 81, 93
Heylighen, F. 224, 254
Heyneman, S.P. 23, 26, 28–29, 32–33, 40–41, 43, 48, 54–55, 301, 305
Hickling-Hudson, A. 72, 76, 88, 93
Hiebert, J. 272, 279, 287
Hinchcliffe, K. 37, 55
Hirsch, P.M. 244, 254
Hobson, R.K. 83, 93
Hoerner, J.-M. 199, 213, 216
Holmes, B. 223, 254–255, 294, 301, 305
Holsinger, D.B. 235, 253
Hopenhayn, M. 6, 20
Houang, R.T. 11, 20
Howard, S. 81, 93
Hu, N.B. 71, 93
Huang, H.S. 78, 93
Hughes, K.L. 9, 19
Hull, D.L. 225, 255
Hulse, M. 4, 19
Humes, W. 120, 122
Humfrey, C. 184–185, 195
Hune, S. 169–170
Hunt, B. 205, 215
Hunter, W. 37, 53
Hussar, W.J. 265, 285
Husserl, E. 244, 255

Ilon, L. 37, 55
Inbaraj, J. 267, 285
Inkeles, A. 13, 19
Ishengoma, J.M. 74, 98

James, D. 9, 18
James Jacob, W. 221
Jansen, J. 66, 73, 93

Jaquette, J.S. 168, 170
Jenkins, H. 184, 187, 195
Johanson, R.K. 61, 66–67, 93
Johnson, A.G. 237, 240, 242, 255
Johnson, D. 66, 80, 93
Johnson, M. 62, 94
Johnson, S. 18–19
Jolly, R. 50, 53, 55
Jones, E. 40, 55
Jones, P. 26, 28, 33, 55
Jonietz, P. 179, 195
Jullien, M.-A. 291, 305
Jung, J.H. 8, 20

Kafula, H. 61, 67, 70, 94
Kahkonen, S. 108, 122
Kamens, D.H. 225, 244, 256
Kandel, I.L. 223, 255
Kane Berman, J. 85, 94
Kant, I. 255
Karagozoglu, G. 66, 94
Kardam, N. 37, 55
Karp, M.M. 9, 19
Kasanda, C.D. 89, 98
Kassé, M. 198, 216
Kazi, A.A. 67, 94
Kellner, D. 225, 241, 255
Kelly, G.P. 61, 63, 89, 94
Kendall, N. 125, 132, 141–143
Kent, D.W. 213, 216
Kent, R. 70, 94
Khanna, A. 42, 55
Kiel, L.D. 225, 255
Kim, E.-Y. 242–243, 256
Kim, H. 67, 69, 94
Kimko, D. 13, 19
Kimmelman, P. 17, 20
Kincheloe, J.L. 273, 286
King, E.W. 205, 215
King, K. 213, 215–216
Kirkwood, K.F. 259, 286
Kleiner, A. 227, 257
Klineberg, O. 185–186, 195

Knight, M. 179, 195
Kober, N. 282, 286
Koh, H. 183, 195
Komarov, V.E. 24, 52
Kondowe, S. 140, 142
Kong, L.H. 248, 255
Kuhn, T.S. 224, 255
Kumar, S. 267, 285
Kuster, S. 141–142

Labazée, P. 198, 216
Langford, M. 181–182, 190, 193, 195
Lanyi, A. 108, 122
Lather, P.A. 169–170
Lauglo, J. 40, 55
L.C. 66, 91
Leach, R. 179, 195
Lebeta, V. 67, 70, 74, 81, 86, 90
Lee, K. 127, 143
Lee, M. 67, 69, 94
Lees, S.H. 169–170
Lehmann, Oswald, H. 63, 97
Lehrer, R. 226, 255
LeTendre, G.K. 2, 4–5, 10, 17–18, 20,
    129, 142
Levin, H. 32, 55
Lewin, K.M. 210, 214, 216
Lewis, W.A. 24, 48, 55
Lichterman, P. 245, 253
Lillis, K.M. 74, 94
Lindahl, R.A. 63, 94
Lingard, B. 7, 9, 20
Lisovskaya, E. 246, 253
Litman, A. 51, 53
Little, A.W. 235, 255
Liu, G.Y. 248, 255
Lloyd, C.B. 68, 94
Lockheed, M. 50, 56, 210, 216
London, N.A. 66, 94
Louisy, P. 281, 286
Lovejoy, B. 9, 20
Loxley, W. 32, 56
Lucas, T. 227, 257

Lulat, Y.G.M. 68, 73, 94
Lunde, L. 51–52
Luneta, K. 84, 94
Lungu, G.F. 72, 94
Luque, J. 271, 287
Lutjens, S. 72, 75, 94
Ly Kane, O. 201, 216
Lynch, P.D. 69, 78, 94
Lytle, J.H. 277, 286

Ma, L. 278, 286
MacKinnon, C. 149, 170
Mandela, N. 79–80, 94
Manor, J. 37, 53, 101, 122
Mara-Drita, I. 236, 254
Marais, M.A. 66, 81, 94
March, J. 7, 20
Marginson, S. 2, 9, 20, 247, 255
Marinez-Brawley, E. 282, 286
Marshall, A. 235, 255
Marshall, H.M. 205, 217
Martin-Beltrans, M. 132, 143
Martini, V.R. 173
Marx, K. 235, 255
Maseko, J. 82, 95
Masemann, V. 241, 255
Matsaso, L.M. 83, 95
Max-Neef, M. 6, 20
Mazrui, A. 38, 56
Mbeki, T. 80, 86, 95
McGinn, N.F. 60, 63, 65, 73, 76, 86, 95–96, 107, 124
McGovern, S. 175, 196
McGrath, M.R. 257
McGrath, S. 213, 216
McGurk, N.J. 80, 95
McKnight, C.C. 11, 20
McLaren, P. 237, 257, 276, 286
McMahon, W. 42, 56
McMahon, W.W. 8, 20
McNamee, M. 243, 255
McNergney, R.F. 273, 286
Meagher, P. 108, 122

Mehran, G. 68, 95
Mensch, B.S. 68, 94
Merchant, B.M. 77, 91
Merritt, R.L. 6, 19
Merryfield, M. 70, 95, 259, 262, 286
Metcalfe, L. 236, 255
Meyer, J.W. 4–5, 8, 18, 20, 225, 244, 255–256
Mill, J.S. 235, 256
Miller, D. 204, 216
Miller, R.M. 66, 95
Miller-Grandvaux, Y. 112, 123
Milligan, J.A. 69, 95, 280–281, 286
Mingat, A. 127, 143
Mitchell, T. 129, 143
Mittelman, J.H. 265, 286
Mollis, M. 2, 9, 20, 247, 255
Moravcsik, A. 236, 256
Moreno, R.P. 77, 91
Morgan, G. 230, 253
Morrow, R.A. 226, 228, 230, 233, 238–239, 256
Morton, W.S. 247, 256
Moser, C.O.N. 148, 169–170
Moulton, J. 115, 123
Mtonga, H.L. 67, 95
Mundy, K. 28, 47, 56, 132, 143
Murphy, L. 132, 143
Mushi, P.S.D. 213, 216
Musonda, L.W. 74, 95
Muyebaa, K.C. 68, 73–74, 87, 95

Nagy, M. 269, 286
Naidoo, J. 99
Natch, M. 185, 192, 195
Ndandane, M. 84, 95
Nderitu, S. 78, 91
Ndione, E.S. 199, 213, 216
Nduka, O.A. 201, 216
Nelson, P. 37, 56
Netser, S. 259, 280, 287
New, R.S. 278, 286
Niane, B. 103, 111–112, 123

Nieuwenhuis, F.J. 82, 84, 95
Ninnes, P. 233, 241, 256
Noah, H.J. 17, 20, 223, 256, 281–282, 286
Nordtveit, B.H. 112, 123
Nyathi, F.S. 83, 93
Nyirongo, R. 210, 216
Nylander, J. 236, 256

Ocitti, J.P. 201, 216
Odav, K. 84, 95
OECD. 262, 265, 267, 286
Ogala, P. 78, 91
Ogbu, J.U. 242–243, 256
Olowu, D. 101–102, 123
Olsen, J. 7, 20
Olson, M. 51, 56
O'Neil, H. 211, 216
O'Neil, J. 227, 256
O'Neil, M.H. 9, 19
Oni, B. 202, 217

Pagels, H. 225, 256
Palmer, B.S. 66, 71, 95
Parkay, F.W. 77, 95
Parrado, E. 187, 196
Parsons, T. 232, 252, 256
Patrinos, H. 37, 40, 53, 56
Patrinos, J. 37, 56
Paulston, R.G. 61, 67, 73, 95, 228–229, 233, 236, 240–244, 256
Pawar, P. 204, 217
Pearce, R. 190, 196
Pereira, R.D. 279, 286
Pescador, O. 257
Phelps, R.P. 281, 287
Picciotto, R. 43, 56
Pickert, S. 276, 287
Pitsoe, V.J. 82, 84, 95
Plank, D.N. 69, 95
Pomeroy, S.B. 169–170
Pono, M.O. 66, 68–69, 96
Popper, K. 224, 256

Potenza, E. 82, 96
Potisook, P. 77, 95
Pritchett, L. 213–214, 217
Psacharopoulos, G. 32, 37, 54, 56
Putkiewicz, E. 269–270, 287

Qanatsiaq, N. 259, 280, 287
Quinn, R.E. 253, 257

Radford, M. 243, 257
Raghu, R. 63, 92
Rajput, J.S. 266, 287
Ramirez, F.O. 4, 6, 8, 17, 20, 61, 63, 67, 91, 96, 244, 255
Rao, L. 186–187, 196
Raymond, M. 271, 287
Reilly, D. 76, 96
Reimers, F. 38, 56, 60, 63, 65, 73, 76, 86, 96, 174, 192–193, 196
Renaud, G. 179–180, 196
Rhoten, D. 283, 287
Ribot, J. 101, 123
Riddell, A. 67, 96, 141, 143
Rideout, W.M. 202, 217
Ritzer, G. 242, 257
Rivarola, M. 121–122
Rizvi, F. 7, 9, 20
Rodrik, D. 25, 54
Rondinelli, D. 121–123
Rosenberg-Zalk, S. 169–170
Rosenthal, R. 205, 216
Rossiter, C. 228, 257
Rothenberg, A. 257
Rowan, B. 244, 256
Rubinson, R. 4, 8, 20
Rust, V.D. 222, 227–228, 241, 246–247, 253, 257
Rutherford, D. 108, 122
Ryba, R. 296, 302, 305
Sabelli, F. 50, 54
Sabers, D.L. 12, 19
Said, E. 190, 196
Saif, P.S. 67–68, 96

Saint, W.S. 71, 96
Salmi, J. 43, 56
Sambili, H. 267, 285
Samoff, J. 37–38, 40, 42, 56, 70, 80–81, 96, 257
Sandholtz, W. 236, 258
Sanford, J. 51, 57
Sato, N.E. 242–243, 256
Saunders, M. 67, 96
Scatamburlo-D'Annibale, V. 237, 257
Schlemmer, L. 85, 96
Schmidt, W.H. 11, 20
Schmitz, S. 66, 68–69, 96
Schultz, T. 24, 57
Schulz, W. 63, 97
Schwille, J. 87, 96
Scott, D. 233, 257
Scott, W.R. 244, 257
Scott-Bauman, A. 267, 285
Senge, P.M. 227, 257
Sepulveda–Stuardo, M. 33, 55
Shacklock, G. 263, 287
Shaker, P. 65, 89
Shangwu, Z. 204, 217
Sharma, M. 68, 71, 96
Sharp, P.L. 205, 217
Shaw, M. 61, 97
Shibuya, M. 257
Shiroma, E. 269, 285
Shultz, T.W. 235, 257
Slattery, P. 273, 286
Small, H. 225, 257
Smith, A. 235, 257
Smith, B. 227, 257
Smith, F. 81, 83, 96
Smith, W.L. 81, 96
Smyth, J. 263, 287
Snodgrass, S. 205, 216
So, A.Y. 233, 238, 258
Somerville, C.M. 169–170
Soudien, C. 84, 96
Soumaré, A. 257
Southgate, B. 225, 258

Spalding, S. 66, 72, 97
Speakman, C. 185, 196
Spring, J. 259, 275, 287
Staudt, K.A. 168, 170
Stegelin, D.A. 278, 287
Stein, J. 271, 287
Steinberg, S.R. 273, 286
Stewart, F. 37, 50, 53, 57
Stigler, J.W. 272, 279, 287
Stocklmayer, S. 226, 258
Stone, L. 169–170
Stone Sweet, A. 236, 258
Streeten, P. 32, 52
Stromquist, N.P. 42, 56, 146, 149, 162, 166, 168–170
Stubbs, P. 4, 19
Sturman, A. 200, 217
Sung, J. 9, 18
Suárez-Orozco, C. 190, 196
Suárez-Orozco, M. 189–190, 196
Sweetland, S.R. 235, 258

Tan, J. 127, 143
Tashakkori, A. 14, 20
Tavana, G.V. 66, 68, 97
Taylor, A. 9, 20
Taylor, N. 74, 97
Taylor, S. 7, 9, 20
Te Riele, K. 9, 20
Teddlie, C. 14, 20
Theissen, G.T. 64, 97
Thomas, G. 244, 255
Thomas, H. 69, 97
Thomas, R.M. 222, 258
Thompson, J. 61, 97, 181, 195
Thompson, J.J. 179, 181, 194
Thrupp, M. 11, 21
Tilak, J.B.G. 71, 97
Tilky, L. 258
Tlou, J. 70, 95
Todoric–Bebic, S. 43, 55
Tomasevski, K. 50, 57
Torney-Purta, J. 63, 97

Torres, C.A. 175, 190, 194, 226, 228, 230, 233, 238–239, 244, 256, 258, 283, 287
Torres, R.M. 100, 123
Toulmin, S.E. 225, 258
Traoré, A. 201, 217
Tsang, M.C. 77, 97
Tsodzo, T.K. 70, 97
Tye, B.B. 259, 261, 287
Tye, K.A. 259, 261, 287

Upadhya, S. 168, 170

Vaizey, J. 24, 52, 57
Valverde, G.A. 11, 20, 225, 258
Van Daele, H. 291, 305
Van Dam, A. 67, 97
Velasco, A. 238, 258
Velkoff, V.A. 209, 217
Vengroff, R. 104, 123
Verspoor, A. 50, 56, 75, 97
Vickers, M. 3, 5–6, 12, 21
Villenueva, N. 66, 91
Vines, D. 51, 54
Vlaardingerbroek, B. 74, 78, 97
Voigts, F.G.G. 115, 123
Vulliamy, G. 67, 96

Wacquant, L.J.D. 226, 258
Wagner, D. 213, 217
Walby, S. 169–170
Walia, K. 266, 287
Walker, G. 181, 196
Wapenhans, W. 29, 57
Watson, J. 176, 196
Watson, K. 13, 21, 40, 57, 279, 284
Watt, P. 111, 123
Weber, E. 85–86, 98
Weber, M. 258
Weick, K.E. 4, 21
Weiler, H. 6, 19, 108, 124
Weinstein, R.S. 205, 217

Weisbrod, B.A. 24, 54
Welch, A. 38, 57, 233, 258
Welsh, T. 107, 124
Wenglinsky, H. 262, 287
Wheeler, C.W. 78, 87, 96, 98
Wiarda, H.J. 237, 258
Wiley, D.E. 11, 20
William, R.M. 202, 217
Williams, D. 51, 57
Williams, P. 34, 57
Willie, C. 193, 196
Wilson, D.N. 289–290, 301, 304–305
Windham, D. 32, 57
Winkler, D.R. 102–103, 106, 121, 124
Wiseman, A.W. 1–2, 10–11, 15, 18, 20–21, 64, 69, 90, 107, 122, 129, 142, 226, 253
Wong, K. 8, 19
Wong, P.L. 268, 287
Wood, R. 37, 57
Woodhall, M. 32, 38, 56–57
Woods, N. 51, 57

Xiaoda, C. 204, 217

Yamamura, B. 280, 287
Yang, A. 77, 98
Yang, L.B. 248, 258
Yeboah, A. 78, 98
Yoder, K. 112, 123
Young, K. 168, 170
Young, T. 51, 57
Youngman, D.J. 74, 98

Zachariah, M. 75, 98
Zaoul, H. 213, 217
Zegarra, H. 63, 92
Zhou, M. 191, 196
Ziderman, A. 70, 89
Zimba, R.F. 89, 98
Zungu, B. 67, 70, 74, 81, 86, 90

SUBJECT INDEX

accountability 11
adapting school calendar 116
Africa 101
apartheid 80
Asian Development Bank (ADB) 46

Baker, James 36
Baker Plan 36
benchmarking 15
between-nation comparisons 14
brain-drain 186
Brazil 267

Central Eastern Africa 130
centralization 11
Chad 112
civil society 132
colonial legacy 69, 72
community participation 103
community schools 111
community-based initiatives 111
comparative education 175
comparative education research 59
comparative international and
    development education 221
comparative and international education
    277, 301, 303
conflict theory 239
context of schooling 13
critical ethnography 242
critical theory 239
cross-national comparisons 2, 63–64
cross-national studies 2
cultural globalization 226
cultural rationalization 241

decentralization 11, 100, 104, 117
deconcentrated teacher management 113
deconcentration 101, 104–105, 110
delegation 105, 110
democratization 69, 71, 86, 139
dependency 237
dependency feminism 147
developing countries 60–73, 75–76, 87–88
development education 223
devolution 105, 110

economic development 25–26, 49
economic globalization 226
economic productivity 12
economic purposes of schooling 9
economic rate of return 32
education and development 43
Education for All (EFA) 61, 67, 125,
    145, 160
education investments 26
education management 103
education ministries 114
education sector 29, 40, 42
educational exchange 183
educational outcomes 2
educational policies 6, 160
educational policy 6, 132, 167
educational policymaking 3
educational systems 1
EFA *see* Education for All
Ethiopia 115
ethnography 243

feminism 240
foundations of education 272–273

Free Primary Education 125
functionalist theory 232

Gambia 112
gender and development 145
Ghana 24, 78
global economic order 9
global education agenda 24
globalization 70, 174–176, 189, 197, 261,
    269, 303
Guinea 111

head teacher 103, 134–135
headmaster 119
historical colonial legacy 69
historical materialist 237
HIV/AIDS 84, 103
human capital 9, 24

IEA *see* International Association for
    the Evaluation of Educational
    Achievement
IMF *see* International Monetary Fund
immigration 189
in-service teacher training programs 117
income growth 24
incomplete primary education 205, 207
India 266
indigenous education 203
indigenous learning systems 201
infrastructure 25, 33
Institute of International Education
    183
institutional autonomy 104
institutional globalization 226
institutionalization of international
    comparative education policy 5
institutionalized organizations 4
International Association for the
    Evaluation of Educational
    Achievement (IEA) 2
international comparisons 1
international education 178, 188, 222

international education policy 3
international educational comparisons
    12
International Monetary Fund 2,
    36, 126
international organizations 24, 48
International School Association 179
internationalized education policy 17
internationalized policymaking 1, 10
interpretive perspective 242
involving school management
    committees 116
Islamic education 201
isomorphism in educational policy 7

Japan 13

Knowledge Management (KM) 42

labor market 9
Latin American 6, 36, 77
learning systems 203
legitimization 13
lending priorities 24, 28
life situation 204
loan covenants 44
local curriculum adaptation 116

Malawi 130
Mali 111
management of education 102, 114
managing school resources 116
manpower forecasting 26, 31
market competition 9
Marxist feminist theories 146
mass modern schooling 8
McNamara, Robert 30, 38, 44
Meltzer Commission 46
metatheory 227
methods of comparison 12
microtheory 227
mixed governance and policymaking
    model 11

modernization 12, 69
moral hazard 49
multinational organizations 5

Namibia 115
national development 8
national education research 15
neo-Marxist theories 238
neocolonialism 68
neofunctionalist Theories 235
neoinstitutionalist 244
New York City 270
Nigeria 115
non-governmental organizations
148

obstacles to reform 62, 65, 76
Organisation for Economic
Co-operation and Development
(OECD) 2, 5, 15
outcomes based education (OBE) 70
outsourcing 112

parental behavior 134
personnel management 116
phenomenographic 244
PISA *see* Programme for International
Student Assessment
policy 129
political agendas 7
political democratization 128
post-colonial states 68
poststructuralist theory 241
pragmatic interactionist 242
principal 119
priorities and strategies 42–43
private provision 112
program contracts 113
Programme for International Student
Assessment (PISA) 3, 5

quality improvement 115, 117
Quranic and Arabic schools 202

radical feminism 149
rate of return methodology 32
rational choice theory 233
recurrent expenditure 33
reform capacity 15
reform implementation 60–65, 71–73,
76–78, 85–86
reform results 60, 72, 74, 87
Russia 43

school-based management 110
secondary education 27
Senegal 110, 197, 198
September 11 272
socialist feminism 147, 149
Somalia 28
South Africa 64, 67, 69–70, 73–74, 76,
79, 81, 83–84
Soviet Union 43
stake holding 112
stigma 197
structural adjustment program 126
study abroad 183, 188
sub-Saharan Africa 99, 104
sustainability 33

Tai-Ji Model 248–249
Tanzania 74, 107, 115
teacher education 68, 82, 259
teacher education issues 68, 70, 74
Teach for America 270
technology 176
television 176
textbooks 33
Third International Mathematics and
Science Study (TIMSS) 3, 15, 63, 278,
280
third wave of political democratization
128
TIMSS *see* Third International
Mathematics and Science Study
transnational 173–174, 190

transnational space or stage
  174, 176
transnational mobility 183
typology of management
  decentralization 110
typology of education decentralization
  105

U.N. lending institution 24
U.S. AID 75
U.S. Department of Defense 30
Uganda 110, 114
United Nations Educational,
  Scientific, and Cultural
  Organization (UNESCO) 2, 41, 47, 50
United States 13
United World Colleges 180
Universal Declaration of Human Rights
  151
universal primary education (UPE) 61,
  71, 185

vocational education 51
vocational school fallacy 31

western education system 202–203
within-nation gains 14
women in development 145
World Bank 2, 5, 23–25, 27–28,
  30, 32–33, 36, 40, 44, 51, 127, 148
World Conference on Education For All
  126
World Council of Comparative
  Education Societies (WCCES) 289,
  294
world culture 5–6, 64
World Declaration on Education for All
  152
world system 5–6

Zambia 111

SET UP A CONTINUATION ORDER TODAY!

Did you know that you can set up a continuation order on all Elsevier-JAI series and have each new volume sent directly to you upon publication? For details on how to set up a **continuation order**, contact your nearest regional sales office listed below.

To view related Educational Research series, please visit:

www.elsevier.com/education

The Americas
Customer Service Department
11830 Westline Industrial Drive
St. Louis, MO 63146
USA
US customers:
Tel: +1 800 545 2522 (Toll-free number)
Fax: +1 800 535 9935
For Customers outside US:
Tel: +1 800 460 3110 (Toll-free number).
Fax: +1 314 453 7095
usbkinfo@elsevier.com

Europe, Middle East & Africa
Customer Service Department
Linacre House
Jordan Hill
Oxford OX2 8DP
UK
Tel: +44 (0) 1865 474140
Fax: +44 (0) 1865 474141
eurobkinfo@elsevier.com

Japan
Customer Service Department
2F Higashi Azabu, 1 Chome Bldg
1-9-15 Higashi Azabu, Minato-ku
Tokyo 106-0044
Japan
Tel: +81 3 3589 6370
Fax: +81 3 3589 6371
books@elsevierjapan.com

APAC
Customer Service Department
3 Killiney Road #08-01
Winsland House I
Singapore 239519
Tel: +65 6349 0222
Fax: +65 6733 1510
asiainfo@elsevier.com

Australia & New Zealand
Customer Service Department
30-52 Smidmore Street
Marrickville, New South Wales 2204
Australia
Tel: +61 (02) 9517 8999
Fax: +61 (02) 9517 2249
service@elsevier.com.au

30% Discount for Authors on All Books!

A 30% discount is available to Elsevier book and journal contributors on all books *(except multi-volume reference works)*.

To claim your discount, full payment is required with your order, which must be sent directly to the publisher at the nearest regional sales office above.